The Language of Wisdom and Folly

The Language of
Wisdom and Folly

BACKGROUND READINGS IN SEMANTICS

Edited and with an Introduction by

the late IRVING J. LEE

School of Speech
Northwestern University

INTERNATIONAL SOCIETY
FOR GENERAL SEMANTICS
540 POWELL STREET · SAN FRANCISCO

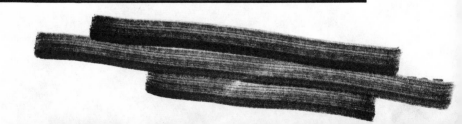

Reprinting this book has been made possible through a
grant from the Frances R. Dewing Foundation.

International Society for General Semantics

First Printing, 1967

L.C.C.C. No.—67-30831

To
ALFRED KORZYBSKI
who first put these issues into perspective for me

Contents

PART IV. QUESTIONS AND ANSWERS

PART V. THE AMBIGUOUS WORD

PART VI. THE RECOGNITION OF DIFFERENCES

PART VII. VERBAL FASCINATION

CONTENTS

PART VIII. THE STRUCTURAL PATTERNS AND IMPLICATIONS OF A LANGUAGE

PART IX. ESCAPE FROM VERBALISM

Preface

Just because a man can talk easily, it does not follow that he necessarily talks sensibly. Fluency is no guarantee of adequacy. The literate man may speak grammatically, coherently, persuasively—and still give voice to folly. For the expression of wisdom requires a doctrine and methodology which go beyond the rhetorical.

The discipline of the adequate statement is something more than the finding of "the right word" or the exercise of rules for simplicity or the achievement of "tone." It has rather to do with the avoidance of distortion, oversimplification and confusion and the discovery of means for accuracy, rigor, proper proportion and nonidentification.

This emphasis takes us from a concern with the language as such to *the language situation*, to a set of relationships involving (1) facts inside or outside human skins, (2) someone evaluating the facts in a certain sort of way, and (3) the use of a language which represents the evaluation and/or the facts in varying degrees of structural similarity. The explicit and systematic formulation of the characteristics of each of these along with their interrelations and effects has been made in the subject matter of general semantics. But long before and after that formulation students in widely separate fields have written on aspects of it. These readings are but a sampling from that vast literature on a few of the basic issues, e.g., the kinds of questions and statements, the modes of ambiguity and exactness, the recognition and obliteration of differences, the varieties of word magic, the onset and escape from verbalism.

Though these selections do not "cover" what is available, it is hoped that they will serve as starting points for further exploration.

I am pleased to acknowledge my debt to Alfred Korzybski, from whose systematizations I have borrowed freely, and to recognize here my obligation to my wife, Laura Louise Lee, for the hours she gave to the preparation of the manuscript.

I. J. L.

Evanston, Illinois
January, 1949

Introduction

A concern with human talking is nothing new. Rhetoric, logic and poetics are almost our oldest academic disciplines. The 20th century is being referred to as the Atomic Age, but those who live in it can hardly escape the stream of verbalization coming from the radio, movies, newspapers, magazines, books, pulpit and platform. It could with some, though not necessarily equal, relevance be called the Verbal Era, because never before has any people been so incessantly exposed to so much verbal output.

The silence of another age is now broken by public address systems and nation-wide hookups. Rarely before have so many people put in their day's work reading, writing, listening and talking. In front of every man handling tobacco leaves or herding sheep there are men billing, recording, accounting, selling, calculating—verbalizing endlessly. If the products of mill and factory are hidden in their handsome packaging, the advertising and public-relations agencies seek to counter that modesty by spot announcements and full-page ads. Rarely before have there been so many special-interest groups and sects promising salvation, planting stories, reaching for listeners and selling via third-class postage. The competition of dogmas goes on without seasonal variation. From anthropology to zoology, books and papers are produced with such restless zeal that librarians clamor evermore for space.

Apart from a certain weariness which the more sensitive recipients of this verbal barrage may experience, there seems little reason to quarrel with the fact of quantity. Some questions, however, might well be raised about the adequacy, the good sense, the significance of all this talk. By what means is some of it to be dismissed and a residue to be studied and preserved?

There have always been some answers to these questions. But it seems only recently that many of the questioners have sought to focus directly on the character of the talk situation itself. Since men talk to themselves and to each other for countless reasons and on countless

xiii

occasions, the opportunities for inadequacy are also countless. There are, of course, a very great number of occasions when it makes little difference whether people talk sense or whether they avoid it. The "tea-talk," the chitchat and banter of people at work or play, the ceremonial formulae, the obligatory social amenities, the "sweet nothings" —these are not usually studied for evidence of calculated and reflective analysis. In these moments we expect people to let down. But what shall be said of the well-publicized industrialist whose talking at his desk is a model of rigor and who at another time subsidizes the publication of racist myths? Is that kind of letdown equally permissible? What shall be said of the scientist whose precision and exploratory attitude in the laboratory have widened the horizons of our knowledge of materials but whose rigidity and ououtverbalization have made a shambles of his home life? Can that kind of letdown be considered inconsequential?

The exaggerated puffing, distortions and non sequiturs of certain kinds of campaign speaking, newspaper editorializing and national advertising have been sufficiently analyzed so that they are somewhat discounted in advance. But should the failure of people in crucial moments to recognize that they are speaking in patterns something less rigorous than they use in their specialties be as amiably disregarded? And is it not possible that in the lesser moments of living we may learn habits which intrude into the less frivolous moments of human deliberation? May not the time have come when we ought to think of extending the areas in which we talk sense?

Certain it is that the occasions when men are at odds with each other and with themselves are not fewer today. One hears a shrillness and an impatience in public discussions which do little to simplify the work of getting agreements. The evidences of public and private confusion are easy to find. The hostilities of the courtroom have their counterparts around the conference table and in the legislative assemblies.

What goes on here? What influences are at work? The answers take many forms, psychological, political, sociological, Freudian, Marxian— and a host of others. Each would establish the acts in a perspective, focusing on them some set of informing principles. The answers might not be equally significant. There would be differences in scope and immediacy, but whatever causes may be assigned, we know about these human disagreements because people talk and/or act.

What is proposed here is a way of looking at the talk situation in terms of the relationship of three of its most important aspects—the nonlanguage matters being talked about, the character of the evaluation involved in the talking, and the language itself.

Fundamentally, there is no "problem of the word" in the sense that the language is the cause of either our communication or our behavior difficulties in the way that a defective tube prevents reception on the radio. It is possible to analyze a language in isolation, but when it is to be found *in use,* it is in relationship with other aspects of the talk situation. It may be useful to outline these aspects.

A. A person comes into relationship with a transaction, situation, relationship, person, object, feeling, etc., in some way. There is, in other words, some *fact* outside or inside the skin with which a person is acquainted.

B. Following this acquaintance, reactions of the most complicated sort take place in the nervous system of the participant. The description of this *nervous registering* is the province of the neurologist, physiologist, anatomist, etc.

C. Following, or perhaps concurrently with the nervous registering of the fact, there is a taking account, a sizing-up, an estimating, a consideration, an assessment, an appraisal of it. This inner *evaluation* is a shorthand way of referring in overall fashion to whatever feelings, ideas, thoughts, conceptions, conclusions, judgments, analyses, etc. arise in the nervous mechanism of the person involved. This description, by emphasizing the response of the organism-as-a-whole, succeeds in avoiding the artificial splitting implied in the usual "sense," "intellect," "emotion" categories. This evaluation phase can be analyzed substantively, that is, with statements of the variety, depth and quality of what goes on, by means of the methods of introspection and electrical measurements of muscular, blood pressure, and other bodily changes, etc. Or analysis can be made of the character of the evaluation in terms of specified rules and postulates derived from logical, mathematical, physico-mathematical, psychiatric, or other analytical disciplines. The results of this study would be statements about the coherence, accuracy, oversimplification, distortion, confusion, identification, and any other aspects of adjustment, congruence or disturbance which may be involved. We should have, in short, something said about the *adequacy* of the evaluation. This sizing-up-evaluating may be in the range from the accurate to the inaccurate, from the superficial and partial to the thorough and relatively complete, from a full to a limited consciousness of what one is doing. It might, indeed, miss and misevaluate the situation. The analysis of what happens in the nervous system during this process need not concern us. It is enough if there is cognizance of the function in relation to the situation.

D. Following, or along with, the evaluation, the person verbalizes and/or acts overtly or covertly, "out-loud," or silently, explicitly or implicitly. He may smile, blush, perspire, get cold, grow tense or relaxed, etc. Gestures and other nonverbal signs can be used, but our interest is in the utterance, the expression in terms of a language. The talk may refer or point to the situation or the inner evaluation, to the situation in the light of the evaluation, to aspects of each or to both in every sort of combination.

Whatever the talk has reference to, it can be the focus of analysis. Questions like these can be raised: What is the character of the utterance which accompanies or on occasion creates or intensifies agreement or disagreement? May the pattern of the talk itself generate new occasions for misunderstanding and confusion? Are certain kinds of talk more likely to affect the individual or his listeners than other kinds? Do definable modes of talking go with definable modes of acting? Do any terms or propositions imply relationships among facts or happenings which are not to be found? Are there characteristic language patterns which impose certain ways of looking on evaluators? Are specific forms of misevaluation frozen into specific linguistic forms? What assumptions about the structure of facts are reflected in what ways of talking about those facts? Does the oversimplification of a person's evaluation of a situation show itself in any oversimplification in his utterance? Does an evaluation based on a certain kind of verbal description of a situation result in action different from that caused by an evaluation based on another?

One who looks at the talk situation is not committed to any ingenuous notion that the language is *the* cause of confusion, nor is he committed to the equally easy assignment of *the* cause of confusion to the language-user. The causes would rather be located in the interrelations of the evaluation-language-fact totality. There seems to be little point in wrangling about which comes first. A boy born in the circumscribed culture of, say, Athens in 400 B.C. has at hand words and characteristic patterns of utterance which may be presumed to influence what he sees and how he evaluates and how he talks about what he sees. That boy grown to manhood may, by accident or design, come to see and evaluate in ways which contradict the conventional. He may then put his new evaluations into terms which imply a different structuring of events. There is now another way of talking at hand. And with it others may be influenced to talk and evaluate anew.

This point of view is, then, a means of culling out of the talk situation the manifestations of what goes with what, what modes of talking with what modes of conflict or creativity, what patterns of evaluation with what patterns of talking, what assumptions about happenings with what kinds of utterances, what implications of structure in the language with what discoverable facts—and so on. When these cullings have been sorted and systematized, we will have available the materials from which to fashion both a discipline and a methodology with which to deal with the human adventure—and if not that, we will at least know what the participants ought to know.

As one takes this perspective, he may be moved to look upon the language as an instrument for use and study in very much the way an artist or technician considers his materials and tools. There is a feeling that the character of the instrument influences what is produced. One can get from an Amati what cannot be gotten from a mail-order violin. The electron microscope reveals what Leeuwenhoek's homemade fittings never could. We have come to expect few miracles of precision and sensitivity from crude, ill-formed devices.

Could not such reflections lead to a suspicion about our language? Might we not unwittingly be using an instrument whose very limitations would make confusion and conflict natural consequences? Why should anyone expect human affairs to run smoothly if the key ingredient in human functioning is itself defective? If healthy vegetables do not grow in impoverished soil, why should we look for productive relationships in a complicated civilization when human communication must be carried on in an antiquated medium? Maybe we're trying to operate a high-powered transmitter with a B-battery.

This is the devil theory of language. But the metaphor in these terms is too engaging. This view of the instrumental needs widening. A language is nothing fixed and created once and for all as was Leeuwenhoek's microscope. A language has within it the means of correction, hardly available to a 17th-century naturalist trying to cope with the recalcitrance of his materials. If a set of terms implies antiquated notions, it is perfectly possible to rephrase or recombine them to imply a new set of notions. Or, if that is not possible, one devises terms which embody the desired formulations. A fish net with big holes is not likely to hold minnows. But there are expedient foldings and shirrings which can reshape the holes. A language is subject to this kind of instrumental adaptability.

There is, however, something in the instrument-image. The fish net *at any moment* might be inadequate. One ten feet by six feet might not contain a whale. And even it must be set, hauled and handled. Ineptitude in these practices is not without its effects. The manipulation of a language can itself be the product of art and experience. There is a way of fouling a net, of tearing it, of letting it out and bringing it in without a catch. May not these things happen to the language when used by the clumsy and unwary?

This, then, is a surer notion. Where and when in the uses of the instrument are we moved to oversimplification, indefiniteness, verbalism detached from life, identification instead of differentiation, magical observances? Is it not wiser to prod the man unaware of the evaluations embedded in his way of talking than to bedevil the black marks he puts on paper and the swirling vibrations he produces in the air? If we seem thus to give up a most convenient devil, we shall at least keep an eye on the deviltry done in that name.

There is more to the fish-net analogy. There are many kinds of nets, for different purposes, for use in different places. The fisherman whose livelihood is bound up with them will learn what can be done with each. Words appear, too, designatively, expressively, analytically. Some merely give form to sentences. Whatever they do, they do differently in the service of prayer, consolation, exhortation, poetry, prediction, combat, advice, comedy, analysis and synthesis. How are these functions to be described? Wherein is the difference? If the fisherman would seem to use the equipment of a technological discipline for his purposes, should not the drama of the human enterprise be informed by a comparable discipline? This, it would seem, is an objective of the perspective urged here.

Suppose a student is persuaded that it is desirable to pursue this business of the language in use. Where is he to look? He will be embarrassed by the riches at hand. He will find discussions of the nature and role of language in its relation to fact and evaluation in the writings of mathematicians, logicians, physicists, anthropologists, lawyers, physicians, psychiatrists, philosophers, sociologists, educators, artists, rhetoricians, literary critics, grammarians. He will discover that those studies of nature and life which go beyond the immediacies to deal with the fundamental questions of method and principle sooner or later arrive at a consideration of language.

In this vast body of references to language one discerns some broad purposes. The one, let it be called the linguistic, is focused on the language as an artifact and deals with questions like these: What are the languages? How are they related, developed and differentiated? What are the constructions peculiar to each and to all? How are the elements of a language to be analyzed? What is the history of individual words? What modes of expression achieve and are denied status?

The second, let it be called the behavioral, is focused on the language as an adjunct to or as an aspect of behavior, and is concerned with such questions as these: How do people learn their own or a new language? How are words recognized, learned, remembered, forgotten? What are the neurological, physiological, anatomical, sociological, etc., components of the speaking, reading, writing, listening process? Where and how do people differ in the above processes? What is the relation of language to all the other symbolic forms?

The third, let it be called the general semantic, is focused on the language as it is involved in human evaluation and as it is related to the facts it is intended to represent.

These are not the only broad areas, nor are they necessarily the largest or most significant. The listing of these is but a convenient way of defining the general semantic orientation by contrast. These distinctions, it should be noted, are not as decisive as I may have suggested, for on occasion the linguistic and behavioral efforts reach into the general semantic, even though the reverse is not so readily found. It may be that the distinction cannot be applied to some specific cases; nevertheless, such a distinction is a way of sensitizing students to a difference, for the single-minded study of language, for example, as artifact may not and need not focus on the role of language in human evaluation.

Apart from any immediate value this emphasis may have in throwing light on what human beings do a great deal of the time, namely, talk, I should urge consideration of another issue: its connection with bridging the gap that now exists between workers in widely separate areas.

The extraordinary specialization in all disciplines makes commonplace the observation that specialists no longer "talk the same language."

Where is the meeting ground of physicist and poet, theologian and technician, philosopher and politician, psychiatrist and artist? Apart from the effort to reconcile any points of disagreement between such diverse interests, there is the question of discovering what each does when he is most and least efficient and productive. These specialists talk, theorize, make decisions and act. A perspective by which we were able to describe the character of the evaluation involved and the role of the talking in such evaluation might well be the meeting ground of the disciplines. On that ground it would be possible to learn whether, for example, the men of science and art are engaged in antithetical or merely different works; whether the artistic achievement can be understood by reference to any phase of the scientific effort or vice versa; whether the procedures which make for human achievement and inspiration in one are not paralleled in the other. On that ground, too, there might be occasion for cross-fertilization, the breeding of new insights. Might not the laboratory technician, looking at the human misevaluations classified by the psychiatrist, get a fresh view, perhaps, of his own rigidities and waste motion? Might not the philosopher, tangled in the nets of verbalism, find sources of strength in facing the surgeon's sometimes sure and sometimes fumbling probing of facts? Might not the rhetorician, bent on persuasion, find pause in the mathematical physicist's ruthless search for rigor in his inference-making?

There is reason to believe that mere exposure to the formalities of another discipline would do little to fertilize a specialist's mode of approach unless the exposure were accompanied by some general theory of evaluation. Thus, little might be accomplished if, say, a physicist and an editorial writer were to study each other's specific handling of apparatus and prose forms. But it is conceivable that each might learn much by observing how the other handles his pet postulates when faced with a new fact. Or suppose there were some means of sharply differentiating the talking about facts and the making of inferences about them, would there not be some point in comparing the way a psychiatrist and a religionist approach the task of sizing up the "problem" of an unhappy person?

In short, wherever it becomes possible to describe in any specialty patterns of approach and talk which have application beyond that specialty, we will be on the way to the making of an organon of knowledge which might pool some of the resources of scholarship now scattered in the far reaches of library lists and stacks.

These readings represent an attempt to bring together some samplings on a small number of the topics encompassed by a general semantic point of view. They make clear that the present interest emphasizes and seeks to integrate positions and conclusions which have long been attended to in less organized fashion. In a sense, there is little in these pages which is not the common property of specialists. But before that wisdom can be put to use there is need for codification.

There are weaknesses in a set of readings like this. First, it does not begin to convey a sense of the conflicts in point of view which are to be found. The conflicts range in intensity and scope from those who differ epistemologically to those who consider the language issues irrelevant. The full elaboration of these disagreements must await the coming of a latter-day encyclopedist or the intensive cooperation of specialists now moving their separate ways.

Second, this collection hardly suggests the extraordinary stores of data and theory which are now available on the nature and role of language. Thus, the literature on psychiatry and psychoanalysis, rhetoric and poetry, mathematical logic and historical writing, legal pleading and religious preaching—to list only some obvious areas—includes material enough for many harvests. There are, as well, the striking omissions of the writings of such men as Plato, Aristotle, Jeremy Bentham, Immanuel Kant, Benedetto Croce, G. H. Moore, A. N. Whitehead, Charles S. Peirce, Ludwig Wittgenstein, Sigmund Freud, Bertrand Russell—and a host of others. It will be unfortunate, indeed, if readers of what is in these pages are led to believe that they include more than they do.

The deficiency is not merely quantitative but is in the issues as well. Thus, for example, a theory of meaning as such is hardly hinted at. Whatever may be the strengths or shortcomings of existing doctrine, the approaches and classifications suggested by C. K. Ogden and I. A. Richards in *The Meaning of Meaning,* John Dewey in *Experience and Nature*, George H. Mead in *Mind, Self and Society*, Moritz Schlick in *Gesammelte Aufsätze,* C. I. Lewis in *An Analysis of Knowledge and Evaluation* provide both starting points and directions for either the synthesis or reconstruction of the theory.

I can offer in extenuation of these and other omissions only a statement of my purposes in preparing this collection. From the list of possible topics I have chosen those which seem to bear on some of the elementary, if not fundamental, aspects of the relations between language, fact and human evaluation. If students obtain a sufficient awareness of what is herein indicated, they should have a basis for further adventuring. This is by no means to imply that the selections exhaust even these issues. It will be enough if they suggest the enormity of what has been neglected in the traditional subject-matter categories which pass over rather than focus on the relationships which are here considered momentous. Furthermore, an effort was made to search for obiter dicta as well as sophisticated treatments on the assumption that if a specialist in an area not directly concerned with our problem found it necessary to say anything about any aspect of it, he might make a contribution to our understanding by his very avoidance of the formalist approaches. I have tried, too, to bring together materials which have not been readily available, but which, nonetheless, are directly relevant. Frequently the selections represent the collateral or incidental interests of the writers. Some tackle the language problem as a central matter. In other cases the writers might be amazed at this use of their work intended for objectives far different and for contexts far removed from this one.

Because I have aimed at little more than to provide some background materials for study, I have not thought it necessary to supply information about the writers or to give my opinions about the adequacy of their analyses or to attempt to assess their role in the historical development of this point of view. It is, perhaps, too soon to make the latter effort since there is reason to believe that in the coming years the language problem is to receive increased attention. If there is merit in the notion that there is *some* relation between language, fact and evaluation, and if this compilation serves only the modest function of moving readers to consideration of what is involved therein, and, perhaps, to further study of those who have made the general semantic perspective explicit, it will have accomplished its purpose.

PART I

The Recognition of Words as Such

"In the beginning was the word. . . ." But now there are words without end and so much with us that it is not easy to think of living without them. We take them so much for granted that it may be difficult to realize how a person comes to know about them—and to explain what they are like and why they are so useful and necessary. Nor at first glance is it obvious that they are of many sorts. Development, transference, pointing, representation, denotation, abstraction and approximation are but a few of the terms by which to describe what goes on when they are in use. And so verbally saturated have we become that it may be worth while to note in passing that even erudition must have its roots in what is not words.

Everything Has a Name [1]

HELEN KELLER

The most important day I remember in all my life is the one on which my teacher, Anne Mansfield Sullivan, came to me. I am filled with wonder when I consider the immeasurable contrast between the two lives which it connects. It was the third of March, 1887, three months before I was seven years old.

On the afternoon of that eventful day, I stood on the porch, dumb, expectant. I guessed vaguely from my mother's signs and from the hurrying to and fro in the house that something unusual was about to happen, so I went to the door and waited on the steps. The afternoon sun penetrated the mass of honeysuckle that covered the porch, and fell on my upturned face. My fingers lingered almost unconsciously on the familiar leaves and blossoms which had just come forth to greet the sweet southern spring. I did not know what the future held of marvel or surprise for me. Anger and bitterness had preyed upon me continually for weeks and a deep languor had succeeded this passionate struggle. . . .

The morning after my teacher came she led me into her room and gave me a doll. The little blind children at the Perkins Institution had sent it and Laura Bridgman had dressed it; but I did not know this until afterward. When I had played with it a little while, Miss Sullivan slowly spelled into my hand the word "d-o-l-l." I was at once interested in this finger play and tried to imitate it. When I finally succeeded in making the letters correctly I was flushed with childish pleasure and pride. Running downstairs to my mother I held up my hands and made the letters for doll. I did not know that I was spelling a word or even that words existed; I was simply making my fingers

[1] From *The Story of My Life* by Helen Keller, pp. 21–24, 29–30, copyright, 1903, 1931, by Helen Keller. Reprinted by permission of Doubleday & Company, Inc.

go in monkey-like imitation. In the days that followed I learned to spell in this uncomprehending way a great many words, among them pin, hat, cup and a few verbs like sit, stand and walk. But my teacher had been with me several weeks before I understood that everything has a name.

One day, while I was playing with my new doll, Miss Sullivan put my big rag doll into my lap also, spelled "d-o-l-l" and tried to make me understand that "d-o-l-l" applied to both. Earlier in the day we had had a tussle over the words "m-u-g" and "w-a-t-e-r." Miss Sullivan had tried to impress it upon me that "m-u-g" is *mug* and "w-a-t-e-r" is *water,* but I persisted in confounding the two. In despair she had dropped the subject for the time only to renew it at the first opportunity. I became impatient at her repeated attempts and, seizing the new doll, I dashed it upon the floor. . . .

We walked down the path to the well-house, attracted by the fragrance of the honeysuckle with which it was covered. Some one was drawing water and my teacher placed my hand under the spout. As the cool stream gushed over one hand she spelled into the other the word water, first slowly, then rapidly. I stood still, my whole attention fixed upon the motions of her fingers. Suddenly I felt a misty consciousness as of something forgotten—a thrill of returning thought; and somehow the mystery of language was revealed to me. I knew then that "w-a-t-e-r" meant the wonderful cool something that was flowing over my hand. That living word awakened my soul, gave it light, hope, joy, set it free! There were barriers still, it is true, but barriers that could in time be swept away.

I left the well-house eager to learn. Everything had a name, and each name gave birth to a new thought. As we returned to the house every object which I touched seemed to quiver with life. That was because I saw everything with the strange, new sight that had come to me. On entering the door I remembered the doll I had broken. I felt my way to the hearth and picked up the pieces. I tried vainly to put them together. Then my eyes filled with tears; for I realized what I had done, and for the first time I felt repentance and sorrow.

I learned a great many new words that day. I do not remember what they all were; but I do know that mother, father, sister, teacher were among them—words that were to make the world blossom for me, "like Aaron's rod, with flowers." It would have been difficult to find a happier child than I was as I lay in my crib at the close of that eventful day and lived over the joys it had brought me, and for the first time longed for a new day to come. . . .

I had now the key to all language, and I was eager to learn to use it. Children who hear acquire language without any particular effort; the words that fall from others' lips they catch on the wing, as it were, delightedly, while the little deaf child must trap them by a slow and often painful process. But whatever the process, the result is wonderful. Gradually from naming an object we advance step by step until we have traversed the vast distance between our first stammered syllable and the sweep of thought in a line of Shakespeare.

At first, when my teacher told me about a new thing I asked very few questions. My ideas were vague, and my vocabulary was inadequate; but as my knowledge of things grew, and I learned more and more words, my field of inquiry broadened, and I would return again and again to the same subject, eager for further information. Sometimes a new word revived an image that some earlier experience had engraved on my brain.

I remember the morning that I first asked the meaning of the word, "love." This was before I knew many words. I had found a few early violets in the garden and brought them to my teacher. She tried to kiss me; but at that time I did not like to have any one kiss me except my mother. Miss Sullivan put her arm gently around me and spelled into my hand, "I love Helen."

"What is love?" I asked.

She drew me closer to her and said, "It is here," pointing to my heart, whose beats I was conscious of for the first time. Her words puzzled me very much because I did not then understand anything unless I touched it.

I smelt the violets in her hand and asked, half in words, half in signs, a question which meant, "Is love the sweetness of flowers?"

"No," said my teacher.

Again I thought. The warm sun was shining on us.

"Is this not love?" I asked, pointing in the direction from which the heat came, "Is this not love?"

It seemed to me that there could be nothing more beautiful than the sun, whose warmth makes all things grow. But Miss Sullivan shook her head, and I was greatly puzzled and disappointed. I thought it strange that my teacher could not show me love.

A day or two afterward I was stringing beads of different sizes in symmetrical groups—two large beads, three small ones, and so on. I had made many mistakes, and Miss Sullivan had pointed them out again and again with gentle patience. Finally I noticed a very obvious error in the sequence and for an instant I concentrated my attention on the lesson and tried to think how I should have arranged the beads. Miss Sullivan touched my forehead and spelled with decided emphasis, "Think."

In a flash I knew that the word was the name of the process that was going on in my head. This was my first conscious perception of an abstract idea.

The Development of Vocabulary[1]

W. W. SAWYER

Try to imagine, if you can, a caveman (or whoever it was who first developed language) trying to say to a friend, "What this writer says about the square root of minus one does not agree with my philosophy at all." How would he manage to make his friend understand what he meant by such abstract words as "philosophy," "minus one," "agree," and so forth? Every child, in learning to speak, is faced by the same problem. How does it ever come to know the meaning of words, apart from the names of people and objects it can see?

It is instructive to take a dictionary, and to look up such words. Almost always, one finds that abstract words, the names of things which cannot be seen, come from words for actual objects or actions. Take, for instance, the word "understand." Both in German and English it is connected with the words "to stand under." In French, "do you understand?" is "comprenez-vous?" which means "Can you take hold of that?" rather like the English phrase, "Can you grasp that?"

[1] From *Mathematician's Delight*. New York: Penguin Books, Inc., 1946, pp. 22–23. Copyright, 1946, by Penguin Books, Inc. Reprinted by permission of Penguin Books, Ltd.

Still today, people make such remarks as "Try to get that into your head."

In learning to speak, a child follows much the same road. It learns the names of its parents and of household objects. It also learns words which describe its feelings: "Are you hungry?" "Are you tired?" "He looks happy." "Don't be frightened." "Can't you remember?" "Say you are sorry."

Every philosopher, every professor, every school teacher who ever lived began in this way—with words to describe things seen, or things felt. *And all the complicated ideas that have ever been thought of rest upon this foundation.* Every writer or speaker who ever invented a new word had to explain its meaning by means of other words which people already knew and understood. It would be possible to draw a huge figure representing the English language, in which each word was represented by a block, resting on other blocks—the words used to explain it. At the bottom we should have blocks which did not rest on anything. These would be the words which we can understand directly from our own experience—what we see, what we feel, what we do.

For example, *philosophy.* Philosophy is what a *philosopher* does. Philosopher means *"a lover of wisdom."* The meaning of *love,* and of being *wise,* we have to learn from everyday life.

The Phenomenon of Language [1]

SUSANNE K. LANGER

The process of transforming all direct experience into imagery or into that supreme mode of symbolic expression, language, has so completely taken possession of the human mind that it is not only a special talent but a dominant, organic need. All our sense impressions leave

[1] From "The Lord of Creation," *Fortune,* Vol. XXIX, No. 1, January, 1944, pp. 140–146. Copyright, 1944, by Time, Inc. Reprinted by permission.

their traces in our memory not only as signs disposing our practical reactions in the future but also as symbols, images representing our *ideas* of things; and the tendency to manipulate ideas, to combine and abstract, mix and extend them by playing with symbols, is man's outstanding characteristic. It seems to be what his brain most naturally and spontaneously does. Therefore his primitive mental function is not judging reality, but *dreaming his desires.*

Dreaming is apparently a basic function of human brains, for it is free and unexhausting like our metabolism, heartbeat, and breath. It is easier to dream than not to dream, as it is easier to breathe than to refrain from breathing. The symbolic character of dreams is fairly well established. Symbol mongering, on this ineffectual, uncritical level, seems to be instinctive, the fulfillment of an elementary need rather than the purposeful exercise of a high and difficult talent.

The special power of man's mind rests on the evolution of this special activity, not on any transcendently high development of animal intelligence. We are not immeasurably higher than other animals; we are different. We have a biological need and with it a biological gift that they do not share.

Because man has not only the ability but the constant need of *conceiving* what has happened to him, what surrounds him, what is demanded of him—in short, of symbolizing nature, himself, and his hopes and fears—he has a constant and crying need of *expression*. What he cannot express, he cannot conceive; what he cannot conceive is chaos, and fills him with terror.

If we bear in mind this all-important craving for expression we get a new picture of man's behavior; for from this trait spring his powers and his weaknesses. The process of symbolic transformation that all our experiences undergo is nothing more nor less than the process of *conception,* which underlies the human faculties of abstraction and imagination.

When we are faced with a strange or difficult situation, we cannot react directly, as other creatures do, with flight, aggression, or any such simple instinctive pattern. Our whole reaction depends on how we manage to conceive the situation—whether we cast it in a definite dramatic form, whether we see it as a disaster, a challenge, a fulfillment of doom, or a fiat of the Divine Will. In words or dreamlike images, in artistic or religious or even in cynical form, we must *construe* the events of life. There is great virtue in the figure of speech, "I can *make* nothing of it," to express a failure to understand something. Thought and memory are processes of *making* the thought content and the memory image; the pattern of our ideas is given by the symbols through which we express them. And in the course of manipulating those symbols we inevitably distort the original experience, as we abstract certain features of it, embroider and reinforce those features with other ideas, until the conception we project on the screen of memory is quite different from anything in our real history.

Conception is a necessary and elementary process; what we do with our conceptions is another story. That is the entire history of human culture—of intelligence and morality, folly and superstition, ritual, language, and the arts—all the phenomena that set man apart from, and above, the rest of the animal kingdom. As the religious mind has to make all human history a drama of sin and salvation in order to define its own moral attitudes, so a scientist wrestles with the mere presentation of "the facts" before he can reason about them. The process of *envisaging* facts, values, hopes, and fears underlies our whole behavior pattern; and this process is reflected in the evolution of an extraordinary phenomenon found always, and only, in human societies —the phenomenon of language.

Language is the highest and most amazing achievement of the symbolistic human mind. The power it bestows is almost inestimable, for without it anything properly called "thought" is impossible. The birth of language is the dawn of humanity. The line between man and beast —between the highest ape and the lowest savage—is the language line. Whether the primitive Neanderthal man was anthropoid or human depends less on his cranial capacity, his upright posture, or even his use of tools and fire, than on one issue we shall probably never be able to settle—whether or not he spoke.

In all physical traits and practical responses, such as skills and visual judgments, we can find a certain continuity between animal and human mentality. Sign using is an ever evolving, ever improving function throughout the whole animal kingdom, from the lowly worm that shrinks into his hole at the sound of an approaching foot, to the dog obeying his master's command, and even to the learned scientist who watches the movements of an index needle.

This continuity of the sign-using talent has led psychologists to the belief that language is evolved from the vocal expressions, grunts and coos and cries, whereby animals vent their feelings or signal their fellows; that man has elaborated this sort of communion to the point where it makes a perfect exchange of ideas possible.

I do not believe that this doctrine of the origin of language is correct. The essence of language is symbolic, not signific; we use it first and most vitally to formulate and hold ideas in our own minds. Conception, not social control, is its first and foremost benefit.

Watch a young child that is just learning to speak play with a toy; he says the name of the object, e.g.: "Horsey! horsey! horsey!" over and over again, looks at the object, moves it, always saying the name to himself or to the world at large. It is quite a time before he talks to anyone in particular; he talks first of all to himself. This is his way of forming and fixing the *conception* of the object in his mind, and around this conception all his knowledge of it grows. *Names* are the essence of language; for the *name* is what abstracts the conception of the horse from the horse itself, and lets the mere idea recur at the speaking of the name. This permits the conception gathered from one horse experience to be exemplified again by another instance of a horse, so that the notion embodied in the name is a general notion.

To this end, the baby uses a word long before he *asks for* the object; when he wants his horsey he is likely to cry and fret, because he is reacting to an actual environment, not forming ideas. He uses the animal language of *signs* for his wants; talking is still a purely symbolic process—its practical value has not really impressed him yet.

Language need not be vocal; it may be purely visual, like written language, or even tactual, like the deaf-mute system of speech; but it *must be denotative*. The sounds, intended or unintended, whereby animals communicate do not constitute a language, because they are signs, not names. They never fall into an organic pattern, a meaningful syntax of even the most rudimentary sort, as all language seems to do with a sort of driving necessity. That is because signs refer to actual situations, in which things have obvious relations to each other that require only to be noted; but symbols refer to ideas, which are not physically there for inspection, so their connections and features have to be represented. This gives all true language a natural tendency toward growth and development, which seems almost like a life of its own. Languages are not invented; they grow with our need for expression.

In contrast, animal "speech" never has a structure. It is merely an emotional response. Apes may greet their ration of yams with a shout of "Nga!" But they do not say "Nga" between meals. If they could *talk about* their yams instead of just saluting them, they would be the most primitive men instead of the most anthropoid of beasts. They would have ideas, and tell each other things true or false, rational or irrational; they would make plans and invent laws and sing their own praises, as men do.

Symbolic Pointing[1]

W. A. SINCLAIR

Speech is simply gesture made audible. Speech is simply gesture that can be listened to, instead of watched. Speech is an extremely complex system of more or less standardized and conventionalized noises, and writing is an even more highly standardized and conventionalized system of visible marks upon a surface, but, in principle, speech and writing are as much gesture as is pointing with the finger.

The origin of language appears to have been roughly as follows. Our remotest human ancestors, when they attempted to draw the attention of others of their kind to anything in particular (or when they behaved in a way which did in fact draw attention to it, intention or no intention) pointed and gesticulated in its direction. These movements were accompanied by various movements in the flexible tissues in other parts of the body, especially when any high degree of vigour was put into the action. Among these were movements in the tongue, lips, windpipe and associated parts. This was further accompanied in certain cases by contraction of the walls of the chest and movements of the diaphragm, which led to the expulsion of air from the lungs through the windpipe over the tongue and between the teeth and lips,

[1] From *An Introduction to Philosophy*. London: Oxford University Press, 1944, pp. 113–119. Reprinted by permission.

thereby creating noises. The gestures and the noises together resulted in drawing attention to the object or situation in question, and then in course of time the noises alone served to do so, i.e. the noises became significant speech. Later, after thousands upon thousands of years, conventionalized marks upon surfaces came to be employed to represent the conventionalized noises.

Consider an example. When a biologist writes, and you read, that the hind leg of a horse is homologous with your own leg (i.e. that it is similar in structure, though it may look different because the proportions are different), what is happening? What he does is to arrange the printer's black marks on paper so cunningly that you, sitting in your chair by the fire, have your attention drawn to certain matters to which he could otherwise have drawn your attention only by leading you up to a horse and pointing with his hands. If he had used his hands alone, he could by pointing have made you notice that your leg and the horse's hind leg appeared altogether different, because your leg is jointed in the middle, so that the lower part below the knee can bend backwards but not forwards, while the horse's hind leg is jointed in the middle so that the lower part can bend forwards but not backwards. The biologist could then by gesture make you bend your knee, raising your heel but keeping the ball of your foot on the ground, and he could point to the horse's middle joint and to your ankle (not your knee). It would then begin to dawn on you that these two did in some way correspond. He could next point to your knee and to the horse's large upper joint encased in the flesh of its haunch, and you would then see clearly that these corresponded also, and that your leg and the horse's hind leg were indeed homologous. Whether he points with his hands or uses black marks printed in a book is only a difference of technique. It is in practice a very important difference, because much more subtle matters can in many cases be pointed out by words and sentences than can be pointed out by the hands; but whichever technique he adopts, what he is doing is in principle the same. By pointing or by words he is making you select for attention the bone structure of the horse's leg and of your own, and is making you neglect the remainder of what your sense-organs are capable of detecting in the situation, and he is making you group together what you select in such a way that the horse's leg and your own no longer appear merely different, but are seen as essentially similar in structure, even though they differ in the relative proportions of their parts. . . .

If the biologist in our example were unskilful in pointing, you might have difficulty in understanding what he was driving at when he pointed. To be effective, he needs some natural aptitude and a good deal of acquired skill gained by long practice. If he were unskilful in handling the English language, you might similarly have difficulty in understanding what he was driving at when he wrote. Here also to be effective he needs both some natural aptitude and a good deal of acquired skill gained by long practice. . . .

The drawing of your attention to the homology between the horse's leg and your own leg would probably not be the only result of his pointing. You might well find that he had started you thinking not only of horse's legs, but of riding a horse at the gallop and hearing and feeling the wind past your ears and the beat of the hooves on the turf, which is what is happening to me as I write about it, or he might have started you thinking of some childhood holiday spent on a farm, or of some other "associations," as we commonly call them. Further, all sorts of feelings and emotions might be aroused in you according as you are interested or not in horses and their legs.

If you were reading the biologist's book, precisely the same would occur. The words and sentences would not only direct your attention to the homology, but would also direct your attention to these associated matters, and they would also arouse these emotions and feelings. This parallelism between pointing and the use of words is interestingly complete, if you work it out. The biologist could not have pointed out the horse's joints unless he had possessed hands. If he had not suitable and manageable hands and fingers with which to point, then we should either not understand him at all, or should misunderstand him. Similarly in his book, if he had not suitable and manageable words to write with we should either not understand him at all, or should misunderstand him. For some purposes there are suitable words available in our vocabularies. For others there are not. Since men through countless generations have conventionalized and developed this system of symbolic pointing which we call language, we can all generally find suitable words to direct other people's attention to what we wish, provided that it is the commonplace things of daily life that we wish to direct their attention to. On the other hand, when we wish to direct their attention, and our own, to less plain and obvious matters, we fall into difficulty, because we have to use for that purpose words which were originally developed and used for other and more matter-of-fact purposes, i.e. we have to use words as metaphors. The parallelism between having words to write with and fingers to point with is very close.

Again, if this biologist had singularly beautiful hands and moved them gracefully, you might find your attention concentrated on them, rather than on what they were pointing to. You might find greater interest and pleasure in the beauty of their form and the grace of their movement than in the homology between your leg and the horse's leg. In the same way, if he were to write singularly beautiful English prose, you might find enjoyment and interest rather in the ring and rhythm of his words and sentences than in the things he was using those words and sentences to point out.

In the case of a biological text-book, and in similar writings, the grace and rhythm of the word pattern are comparatively irrelevant, as are any emotions that might be aroused, or any associations that might be revivified. The writer on such subjects must of course write English that is not unduly disjointed or cacophonous, and he must avoid arousing ludicrous associations and unwelcome emotions, but beyond this, he is not greatly concerned with such points. On the other hand, in those writings commonly called "literary," the situation is different in some respects. Think of any familiar verse of poetry or passage of prose that gives you delight, and analyze your enjoyment of it. You will find that only a part of the enjoyment comes from the contemplation of the situation to which it draws your attention. Much comes from the beauty of the words, considered as a mere pattern of sound and rhythm; and from the emotions it arouses in you; and from the associated situations it happens also to make you think of.

The Mobile Word[1]

HENRI BERGSON

In reality, man is a being who lives in society. If it be true that the human intellect aims at fabrication, we must add that, for that as well as for other purposes, it is associated with other intellects. Now, it is difficult to imagine a society whose members do not communicate by signs. Insect societies probably have a language, and this language must be adapted, like that of man, to the necessities of life in common. By language community of action is made possible. But the requirements of joint action are not at all the same in a colony of ants and in a human society. In insect societies there is generally polymorphism, the subdivision of labor is natural, and each individual is riveted by its structure to the function it performs. In any case, these societies are based on instinct, and consequently on certain actions or fabrications that are more or less dependent on the form of the organs. So if the ants, for instance, have a language, the signs which compose it must be very limited in number, and each of them, once the species is formed, must remain invariably attached to a certain object or a certain operation: the sign is adherent to the thing signified. In human society, on the contrary, fabrication and action are of variable form, and, moreover, each individual must learn his part, because he is not preordained to it by his structure. So a language is required which makes it possible to be always passing from what is known to what is yet to be known. There must be a language whose signs—which cannot be infinite in number—are extensible to an infinity of things. This tendency of the sign to transfer itself from one object to another is characteristic of human language. It is observable in the little child as soon as he begins to speak. Immediately and naturally he extends the meaning of the words he learns, availing himself of the most accidental connection or the most distant analogy to detach and transfer else-

[1] From *Creative Evolution* by Henri Bergson, pp. 157–158. Copyright, 1911, by Henry Holt and Company. Copyright, 1938, by Arthur Mitchell. Reprinted by permission.

where the sign that had been associated in his hearing with a particular object. "Anything can designate anything"; such is the latent principle of infantine language. This tendency has been wrongly confused with the faculty of generalizing. The animals themselves generalize; and, moreover, a sign—even an instinctive sign—always to some degree represents a genus. But what characterizes the signs of human language is not so much their generality as their mobility. *The instinctive sign is* adherent, *the intelligent sign is* mobile.

Of the Twofold Meaning of Terms— In Extension and Intension[1]

W. STANLEY JEVONS

The meaning of a term in extension consists of *the objects to which the term may be applied;* its meaning in intension consists of *the qualities which are necessarily possessed by objects bearing that name.* A simple example will make this distinction most apparent. What is the meaning of the name "metal"? The first and most obvious answer is that metal means either gold, or silver, or iron, or copper, or aluminum, or some other of the 48 substances known to chemists, and considered to have a metallic nature. These substances then form the plain and common meaning of the name, which is the meaning in extension. But if it be asked why the name is applied to all these substances and these only, the answer must be—Because they possess certain qualities which belong to the nature of metal. We cannot, therefore, know to what substances we may apply the name, or to what we may not, unless we know the qualities which are indispensable to the character of a metal. Now chemists lay these down to be somewhat as follows: (1) A metal must be an element or simple substance incapable of

[1] From *Elementary Lessons in Logic: Deductive and Inductive,* Lesson V. London: Macmillan and Co., Limited, 1871.

decomposition or separation into simpler substances by any known means. (2) It must be a good conductor of heat and electricity. (3) It must possess a great and peculiar reflective power known as metallic lustre.[2]

These properties are common to all metals, or nearly all metals, and are what mark out and distinguish a metal from other substances. Hence they form in a certain way the meaning of the name metal, the meaning in intension, as it is called, to distinguish it from the former kind of meaning.

In a similar manner almost any other common name has a double meaning. "Steamship" denotes in extension the Great Eastern, the Persia, the Himalaya, or any one of the thousands of steamships existing or which have existed; in intension it means "a vessel propelled by steam-power." Monarch is the name of Queen Victoria, Victor Emmanuel, Louis Napoleon, or any one of a considerable number of persons who rule singly over countries; the persons themselves form the meaning in extension; the quality of *ruling alone* forms the intensive meaning of the name. Animal is the name in extension of any one of billions of existing creatures and of indefinitely greater numbers of other creatures that have existed or will exist; in intension it implies in all those creatures the existence of a certain animal life and sense, or at least the power of digesting food and exerting force, which are the marks of animal nature.

It is desirable to state here that this distinction of extension and intension has been explained by logicians under various forms of expression. It is the peculiar misfortune of the science of logic to have a superfluity of names or synonyms for the same idea. Thus the intension of a term is synonymous with its *comprehension,* or *connotation,* or *depth;* while the extension is synonymous with the *denotation* or *breadth.* This may be most clearly stated in the form of a scheme:

| The extension, extent, breadth, denotation, domain, sphere or application of a name consists of the individual things to which the name *applies*. | The intension, intent, depth, connotation, or implication of a name consists of the qualities the possession of which by those things is *implied*. |

---

[2] It is doubtfully true that all metals possess metallic lustre, and chemists would find it very difficult to give any consistent explanation of their use of the name; but the statements in the text are sufficiently true to furnish an example.

Of these words, *denotation* and *connotation* are employed chiefly by Mr. J. S. Mill among modern logical writers, and are very apt for the purpose. To denote is to *mark down,* and the name marks the things to which it may be applied or affixed; thus metal denotes gold, silver, copper, etc. To connote is *to mark along with* (Latin *con,* together; *notare,* to mark), and the connotation accordingly consists of the qualities before described, the possession of which is implied by the use of the name metal.

When we compare different but related terms we may observe that they differ in the quantity of their extension and intension. Thus the term *element* has a greater extension of meaning than *metal,* because it includes in its meaning all metals and other substances as well. But it has at the same time less intension of meaning; for among the qualities of a metallic substance must be found the qualities of an element, besides the other qualities peculiar to a metal. If again we compare the terms *metal* and *malleable metal,* it is apparent that the latter term does not include the metals antimony, arsenic, and bismuth, which are brittle substances. Hence *malleable metal* is a term of narrower meaning in extension than metal; but it has also deeper meaning in intension, because it connotes or implies the quality of malleability in addition to the general qualities of a metal. *White malleable metal* is again a narrower term in extension because it does not include gold and copper; and I can go on narrowing the meaning by the use of qualifying adjectives until only a single metal should be denoted by the term.

The reader will now see clearly that a general law of great importance connects the quantity of extension and the quantity of intension, viz.—*As the intension of a term is increased the extension is decreased.* It must not be supposed, indeed, that there is any exact proportion between the degree in which one meaning is increased and the other decreased. Thus if we join the adjective *red* to metal we narrow the meaning much more than if we join the adjective *white,* for there are at least twelve times as many white metals as red. Again, the term white man includes a considerable fraction of the meaning of the term man as regards extension, but the term blind man only a small fraction of the meaning. Thus it is obvious that in increasing the intension of a term we may decrease the extension in any degree.

Two Types of Names [1]

FLOYD HENRY ALLPORT

Our vocabulary of science contains two types of names. The first consists of words denoting objects which impinge, directly or through the surrounding media, upon our sense organs—objects which can be observed, described, manipulated, analyzed, experimented with, and generalized about. The objects which such names indicate do not appear to come to us through any reflection or theorizing of our own, but by our stumbling upon something which is outside ourselves. Words such as rock, tree, acid, water, fish, and man, are names denoting this type of experience. Objects of this sort can be singled out by pointing with our hand or by turning our eyes or our bodies; they can also be taken apart and experimentally studied through the use of our sense organs, our nerves, and our skeletal muscles, aided by the instruments and techniques of science. We can react to them in a manual and bodily manner, for they are capable of precise location in space. Such objects, we may say, are *capable of explicit denotation*. It is with objects of this sort that all experimental and descriptive investigations of the world about us begin. Things which are *not* of this sort, terms for example denoting natural laws, formulas, and hypotheses may or may not be present in our thinking at the beginning of an investigation; but some sort of outer, explicitly denotable object *must* be present. Otherwise no investigation of the world about us is possible.

The second type of names used in scientific work are those dealing not with objects capable of being explicitly treated, but with abstract things, such as relationships. These abstractions are phases of our experience with which we can deal only by *thinking* or *talking* about them. They cannot be heard, seen, handled, or pointed to with any part of our bodies. Such terms include properties (such as length,

[1] Reprinted from *Institutional Behavior* by Floyd H. Allport, pp. 15–20, by permission of The University of North Carolina Press. Copyright, 1933, by The University of North Carolina Press.

hardness, redness, etc.) which we "abstract" from explicitly denotable objects by the process of reflection. They also include the laws or hypotheses which we formulate about objects in order to describe their actions. We talk, for example, of such things as gravitation, electrical change, erosion, growth, reproduction, evolution, and personality. We do not respond directly *to* these concepts; we cannot take them apart or manipulate them. We can only make responses of thought or communication *about* them. We can speak, write, or make gestures to denote them; we can employ them as symbols of communication; but we cannot in treating of them bring our bodies into direct and explicit contact with the things about which we are talking. Such things, we may say, are capable only of *implicit denotation*.

In actual scientific research explicit and implicit forms of denotation are closely related. We react to objects which are explicitly denotable, and then, in order to standardize and record our reaction and to convey an understanding of it to others, we make other responses whose reference is *implicit*. An apple falls, according to our experience, always toward the earth. Now the realities denoted by the terms "apple" and "earth" are both capable of being reacted to by our bodies in an explicit manner, that is, of being explicitly denoted. We need, however, in addition to "apple" and "earth," some term to designate the relationship (tendency to move toward each other) which we have found to exist between them. We therefore employ a special term "gravitation." Now gravitation is not something we encounter in an explicit manner; it is something which we seem to discover by reflection. It derives its meaning not by pointing or by making responses directly *to* the apple and earth, but rather by thinking or talking *about* them. Gravitation, therefore, is capable of *implicit,* not of explicit, denotation. To take another illustration: we react with our bodies to pieces of wire and to plates in acid solutions. These are explicitly denoted objects. From the result of this experience we think and talk about currents, watts, ohms, conductance, resistance, and the "laws" of electrical phenomena in general. This second class of entities are capable only of implicit denotation. A biologist encounters organisms. As he manipulates, dissects, and experiments with them, he makes inferences also in the nature of biological laws and principles. These latter are implicitly denoted entities. To a psychologist, a man, as a physical organism, is explicitly denotable; but his habits or his traits of personality, like the principles of growth and conductance, are capable only of implicit denotation.

Now it is to our second class of terms, names for things which are *implicitly* denoted, that the notion of an institution belongs. Just as the concepts of conductance and resistance pertain to the action of the parts, or explicit materials, used in a particular combination known as an electric circuit, so the terms university, industry, church, or state, refer to activities, or habits, which individuals in certain relationships perform. This institutional arrangement of uniform and cooperating habits, like the actions of the parts of an electric circuit, gives us a formula, a means of generalization, and a basis of prediction. But useful as the notion of an institution may be for such ends, it is absolutely incapable, in itself, of being explicitly denoted, pointed to, or manipulated. In the case of the electric circuit we find that it is only when we turn from the concept of the circuit to the *materials operating* as a circuit that we can begin an investigation or learn anything new about electrical science. And similarly it is only when we abandon the institution for a time and fix our attention on the individuals that we discover a reality which can be encountered and which affords us a starting point in our investigation of the human world about us. We do not study institutions, but *individuals,* as tangible objects. Institutions are the things we say *about* the objects, that is, the individuals, we study.

Notwithstanding their convenience, a danger besets the use of names for things implicitly denoted against which we must be continually upon our guard. We are prone to forget that such things are known to us *only* in this implicit, or conceptual manner. Sometimes we delude ourselves into believing that they are subject to the same experimental study as objects capable of explicit denotation, or that the conclusions reached in talking about them have the same value and validity as those discovered in dealing with explicitly denoted things. This is a fatal error. It is a confusion of explicit objects with the formulations which we make *about* them. Tied up in our own definitions we travel in circles, postulating nature instead of discovering it. This error of confusing the implicit with the explicit in experience is accountable for the dilemma of scholars and laymen in their attempt to define an institution. Since institutions are experienced only in an implicit manner, it is impossible to define them, as entities distinct from individuals, by reference to any class of explicitly denoted, natural objects. Yet the unquenchable desire of some writers to endow them with an existence like that of rocks, trees, and men, and to subject them to the same methods of study, has led these authorities to attempt the impossible. As we have seen, they have succeeded only in producing empty collective abstractions; or else they have resorted to analogies, which, though explicit enough in their reference, are false if taken literally and irrelevant if taken otherwise.

A falling apple strikes us, and we take our cue from it (and from similar experiences) for phrasing a useful generalization concerning falling bodies. The law of gravitation, however, does not strike us. We can neither see it, handle it, nor make it the direct object of our investigation. A physicist who started by looking about him for a force or substance known as gravity which he might subject to experimental analysis would be like the man who set out to find the end of the rainbow. In order to experience gravitational phenomena at all one must deal with *falling or moving objects* which can be explicitly handled. Similarly, a student of social science who sought at the start to lay his hands upon an institution as such and subject it to direct analysis would soon find himself lost in a sea of words. If his investigation is to be profitable, he must search first for concrete, explicitly denoted materials which are behaving institutionally, and from whose behavior he may make his generalizations in terms of the institutional concept. Such materials he will find in the individual human beings about him. It is true that he must also have in mind a notion of what he means by "behaving institutionally" when he selects his objects for explicit study; just as the physicist must have a notion of what "falling" means in practical experience in order that he may find falling objects and study their action. But neither "institution" nor "falling" can be defined in explicit terms, and neither can be taken alone, in the absence of objects which are explicitly denotable, as the beginning of a scientific investigation.

Precision in Natural Language [1]

LEONARD BLOOMFIELD

REPORTING STATEMENTS

To discuss the meaning of all the varieties of utterances would be equivalent to outlining a complete sociology. We need deal only with a single type, the report, since it alone is required for science.

The welfare of a community depends, so far as the actions of people are concerned, most directly upon simple handling activities whose occasion and performance are plainly observable—activities such as the gathering of food, hunting, fishing, construction of dwellings, boats, and containers, manufacture of clothing and tools, etc. These are manipulations of non-human objects, satisfactory in their biophysical aspect. Even where human bodies figure as objects, as in surgery or conflict, these actions suffice in themselves, with a minimum of biosocial significance. The situation in which an act of this sort will succeed does not always present itself in full to the performer; another person may mediate by speech: "There are berries beyond the cliff"; "The fish are biting today"; "My moccasins need patching"; etc. Reports like these concern matters where behavior is uniform: in general, people will agree on the outcome of a test. This is the sphere of ordinary life out of which science grows forth. Natural science grows forth directly; the scientific study of man is hampered by the difficulty of subjecting biosocially conditioned behavior to such simple and testable reports.

If we try for a moment, and with full recognition of inadequacy, to ignore the forms of language, we may perhaps say that a report of this kind conveys, in the first place, the verbal substitute of a stimulus: "It's raining." Here the "it" is an empty and merely formal indication of a point of reference, for which there is in this case no practical need. In

[1] From "Linguistic Aspects of Science," *International Encyclopedia of Unified Science,* Vol. I, No. 4, pp. 33–35, 36–38. Chicago: The University of Chicago Press, 1939. Copyright, 1939, by the University of Chicago. Reprinted by permission.

most instances, however, some other stimulus, which has already affected the hearer or has been verbally represented to him, serves as a
point of reference for the placing of the new stimulus which the hearer
has not experienced: "There are some apples in the pantry"—the last
three words may represent nothing new, a familiar complex of stimuli
to which the apples are now added. This adherence of a new stimulus
to an old one is perhaps the practical background that is formalized in
the actor-and-action or subject-and-predicate constructions which ap-
pear in the favorite sentence types of many languages: "The fish | are
biting | today"; Russian *"Iván dóma,"* literally "John | at home." How-
ever, there is no rigid agreement between the structure of the practical
stimuli and the formal structure of the utterance.

The behavior of the speakers distinguishes very well between the
features of the report which convey the relevant handling stimulus and
the features of purely social and personal significance, such as especially
the formal structure. Two reports of different structure ("There are
berries beyond the cliff" and "Behind the steep cliff over there you
can find some berries") may mediate the same simple handling sequence; it is only the accompanying personal and social adjustments
which differ. It is a well-tried hypothesis of linguistics that formally
different utterances always differ in meaning; they may be *equivalent,*
however, as to some one partial phase of meaning. Of this, the best
example is the practical phase of the simple report; out of it there
grows forth the equivalence of variously worded statements in scientific
discourse. Here, as in the simple reporting of ordinary language, the
equivalence covers the phase of meaning which is observable indifferently by all persons.

ABSTRACTION AND APPROXIMATION

A report concerning a simple handling activity covers, in a rough
way, only so much of the situation as is useful. If the speaker is
prompted, say by an additional question ("What color are the
apples?"), he is usually able to extend his report. Moreover, he can
often subject himself, in the way of continued observation, to further
stimuli of the complex in question ("I'll look and see how many apples
there are"). Every apple has a color, and every set of apples a number,
but these features are not communicated in the report, "There are
some apples in the pantry." It is a trick of pseudo-philosophy to postulate a metaphysical "concept" of an apple to account for the imperfect

reporting function of the word "apple." The obvious fact is simply that a speech does not mention every feature of stimulus. Since the ranges of stimulation and of predisposition are to all practical purposes continuous, and language can provide only a discrete set of forms, this *abstract* character of language is inevitable: not all the features of a situation appear in the report. If we do not consider the extension of an object, we may speak of it as a "point"; if we speak of one dimension only, we may call it a "line"; if of two only, we call it a "surface"; terms like "straight line," "plane," "triangle," etc., add further characteristics, but still leave unmentioned certain simple features which are present in every object. This does not create a world of "concepts."

By lengthening his report, the speaker may tell more: we distinguish degrees of *approximation*. So far as the speaker has observed, or else perhaps only under reservation of irrelevant detail, the linear object if turned in a certain way would occupy the same position as before; hence the speaker says that the "line" is a "straight" one. It may be true that no object has been found to fulfill this condition to such an extent as to appear "straight" under our best observation with mechanical aids. This means merely that the speaker did not employ these aids or else that his report was incomplete in this respect.

Although the meanings of language are discrete, there is no limit to their cumulation. By extending his utterance, the speaker may come closer and closer to a full picture of the situation. This is familiar, for one thing, from the art of fiction. In the realm of handling operations one rarely approximates beyond the features that are useful. In the scientific expansion of this domain, however, one often dwells upon features which have no immediate use in practical life—such features, for instance, as appear in the botanist's systematic classification of families, genera, and species. Accordingly, scientists and specialists in practical operation invent *technical terms,* either by redefining everyday expressions or by borrowing or creating new words. A technical term, then, replaces long phrases, or even a complicated discourse, and its meaning is fixed by an agreement of definition, which, in science, receives explicit formulation and strict adherence.

The useful approximation, in a simple society, will be a rough one; as civilization progresses, usefulness is discovered in closer approximations. Utterances and responses become more variable. This *variability* of response in individuals, and, thanks to manifold specialization of individuals, in the community, may yield a basis for a scientific definition of what we mean in everyday life by such words as "welfare" or "happiness."

Thought and Its Instrument—Language

WILLIAM A. WHITE, M.D.

It does seem necessary to preface any consideration of the subject [the language of schizophrenia] by a few brief statements regarding language and thought in general for unless we do we run the risk of taking over to our subject fragments, at least, of the outworn metaphysical and static concepts with which psychology is even yet sadly hampered.

In attempting to do this we are immediately met by certain tacit assumptions that belong to the category that I have designated, because of their very dangerous implications for our thinking, the pitfalls of the obvious. Among these tacit assumptions are these: that the world corresponds to our ways of thinking about it, and that language expresses these ways of thinking, and therefore the qualities as they exist in the world, quite accurately. I cannot undertake an exhaustive discussion of these points but must rest with urging the dynamic point of view as I see it.

To put it tersely, the idea that the world is as we see it and that language conveys from one to another an accurate account of things is one of those absolutistic concepts of which man has always been so fond because he is always wanting to settle things for once and all: he is always seeking rest in final solutions. But final solutions, like so many things that seem desirable, are but wishes for they nowhere exist and if they did they would not be desirable after all for they would spell death, not life.

[1] From "The Language of Schizophrenia," *Archives of Neurology and Psychiatry,* Vol. 16, No. 4, October, 1926, pp. 396–398. Copyright by American Medical Association. Reprinted by permission.

For example, it seems obvious that there is no similarity between the redness of the rose that we perceive and a certain rapidity of vibrations in a hypothetic medium—the ether. One set of occurrences are physical phenomena, the others are mental, two separate categories which are incommensurable one in terms of the other. Similarly the world is full of individual men but there is no such thing as man in the abstract and yet language is replete with such abstract terms. To put these matters in a few words I will quote Hobson [2] who says: "It must, however, be observed that the experience of an individual is, in its fullness of detail, unique and incommunicable; it is only incompletely made intelligible to other individuals by means of language or other forms of symbolism. Thus language, in its very nature, involves abstraction in which the elements of actual individual experience are replaced by symbols which fail to represent with absolute completeness what they are designed to describe."

It is manifestly impossible to discuss language quite separately and distinctly without considering, by implication at least, thought, of which language might be said to be the instrument. In the most primitive animals there is nothing that corresponds to thought. These animals are truly systems of reflexes. In them action follows immediately on the heels of stimulus. There is no hesitation, no intervening delay. The translation from stimulus to reaction is immediate, smooth and effective.

As we advance in the course of evolution to more complex, higher types this immediate translation of stimulus into action is ever more and more interrupted until, not only the interval between the two is or may be considerable but the resulting reaction becomes less and less predictable. It is in this interval between stimulus and action that thought occurs, that ideas and concepts are formed, and formulated into symbols.[3]

Presumably this occurrence of thought, this prolongation of the time between stimulus and action, this increase in indeterminateness of the action, are due to increasing complexity of the problems of adaptation and the introduction of more than one possible reaction to any

[2] Hobson, E. W.: *The Domain of Natural Science,* New York, The Macmillan Company, 1923.
[3] "Now it is, psychologists tell us, just in this interval, this space between perception and reaction, this momentary halt, that all our mental life, our images, our ideas, our consciousness, and assuredly our religion and our art, is built up." Harrison, J. E.: *Ancient Art and Ritual,* New York, Henry Holt & Co., 1913.

given situation. As a result the several possibilities are weighed, there is doubt, examination of the advantages of the several possibilities, and decision, all of which corresponds, in physiologic terms, to the choice of the final common path.

In the primitive reflex organism the nervous pathway from receptor to effector is a single uninterrupted nerve fiber. The conditions that are going to make thought possible probably made their first appearance on the stage with the advent of the synaptic type of nervous system.[4] With the possibility of the nerve current being shunted in any one of several directions at the synapse the conditions were introduced that made for hesitation, increase in time interval, delay due to closely balanced forces that do not make for one path much more strongly than another, indetermination, in short for qualities which are associated with thought.

Now if, as we have seen, our thoughts and our symbols are not replicas in any sense of reality—what does take place in this region? The object of thought is action and it is only when the circumstances are highly complex and the forces many and working in different directions that there occurs that delay that permits of thought. Thought and its instrument language do not portray reality; they are rather ingenious dexterities that enable us to find our way about.[5] So long as they serve this purpose they are useful and true; but to the extent that they fail, they lose both their usefulness and their truth. A study of language shows the constant discarding of symbols, the acquisition of new symbols and the changing meaning of symbols that continue to be used for a considerable period.[6] The responsiveness of the symbol to changing conditions, its capacity to take on new meanings under different circumstances, is of the utmost importance for our inquiry, for we find that schizophrenic thought, which is quite different from ours, makes use largely of the same words that we do in its expression.

[4] Herrick, C. J.: *Neurological Foundations of Animal Behavior*, New York, Henry Holt & Co., 1924.

[5] Vaihinger, H.: *The Philosophy of "As If,"* New York, Harcourt, Brace & Co., 1925.

[6] The value of the symbol in the course of development may be found discussed in White, W. A.: *Mechanisms of Character Formation*, New York, The Macmillan Company, 1920.

PART II

The Functions and Purposes of Language in Use

Why talk or write? The purposes are many. Sometimes to describe things and happenings. Sometimes to express a mood. Often to enjoin, cajole, bemuse or exhort others. Occasionally, to indicate why things are valued and appreciated. Frequently to make small talk, "the sounds of sociability." Now and then to give names to things and feelings. And sometimes even to play a role.

It is no mere academic exercise, this recognition of the ways men make the language function. For there are times when human decisions are at stake, when the scientific should be distinguished from the artistic, the cognitive from the expressive. This is not to give a preferential status to either, but to make sure that the one will not be used as if it were the other. The kinds of talking which stir men may, perhaps, be of little use when there is need for a different kind of wisdom.

The Three Primary Forms of Discourse[1]

CHARLES W. MORRIS

A form of discourse is a specialization of language for the better accomplishment of some specific purpose. The everyday language of a people is an amazingly complex sign structure performing a multitude of individual and social functions. Its very protean character is its strength, for it provides the matrix in which and through which all human activities are interlocked in symbolic expression as they are interlocked in practice. This strength, however, involves a fundamental weakness: the very multiplicity of functions performed prevents the adequate performance of any one specialized function. So it is that men have gradually devised certain specializations of their common language for the more adequate performance of various specific tasks. Such specializations are here referred to as forms of discourse.

Forms of discourse can be analyzed in terms of the functions they have been elaborated to perform, and light can be thrown on the characteristic human activities and their interrelations by a study of the nature of the forms of discourse which are the products and the instruments of these activities. In practice each approach aids the other, and both will be used in the account which follows.

It seems unlikely that all the characteristic forms of discourse are equally basic. A distinction can be made—analogous to that in the theory of colors—between primary and secondary forms of discourse. Secondary forms of discourse are those built up out of other forms of discourse; primary forms of discourse are those which are not a function of other forms of discourse. The present position is that there are three primary forms of discourse (the scientific, the aesthetic, and the technological), and that all other forms are secondary, that is, are a

---

[1] From "Science, Art and Technology," *The Kenyon Review*, Vol. I, No. 4, Autumn, 1939, pp. 410–420. Reprinted by permission of author and editor.

function of these primary forms.[2] A brief characterization of the three primary forms of discourse will provide an opportunity to show something of the interrelation of science, art, and technology, and to emphasize some of the cultural implications of these interrelations.

The scientific form of discourse has received the most careful and elaborate analysis of any of the forms of discourse. Logicians have for the most part restricted their attention to the language of science; such a work as the *International Encyclopedia of Unified Science* is mainly devoted to such analysis.

It seems a fruitful hypothesis that the language of science is controlled primarily, and perhaps exclusively, by a single aim: to make possible accurate predictions. Beings living in a spatio-temporal structure of objects are dependent upon what happens at regions in this structure. It is important for such beings to be able to take account of what will occur in certain space-time regions on the basis of what is already found to occur in these or other space-time regions. For only if a being can predict with accuracy can it prepare itself for what it will encounter in its continued existence.

It is believed that detailed examination of scientific discourse would confirm this directive hypothesis; here only a point or two can be made. First, scientific discourse is rich in devices (such as coordinate systems) for accurate references to space-time regions and for elaborate descriptions as to what exists in those regions. It accordingly stresses the relation between signs and what they denote, and it controls its statement in terms of that relation. Thus the question whether a certain sign combination is true is the question whether it denotes something with the properties specified, and in the control of this question everything is rigorously excluded which is not evidence for the existence of the object in question. This means, as a second characteristic of scientific discourse, that it rests upon, and issues in, statements which are confirmable, i.e., statements upon whose truth or falsity empirical evidence can be brought to bear. Such statements (the scientific substructure) are not, however, the only statements within scientific dis-

[2] The number of the primary forms of discourse corresponds to the three dimensions of sign functioning: scientific discourse brings into prominence the relation of signs to objects denoted (the semantical dimension), aesthetic discourse accents in a distinctive way the sign structure itself (the syntactical dimension), technological discourse emphasizes the efficacy of the signs in the practice of the users (the pragmatical dimension). The theory of discourse is thus one development of the general theory of signs (technically called semiotic).

course: the deriving of predictions from statements about the properties of certain space-time regions requires (in the third place) an apparatus for derivation (logic and mathematics) and statements from which the derived statements follow (scientific theories). Logico-mathematical statements and scientific theories may together be regarded as constituting the superstructure of the language of science; both are controlled by their relation to the essential task of science—to make possible accurate predictions. It is demanded of the tools of deduction that from true statements only true statements are obtained; even the demand that a scientific system be non-contradictory is related to the fact that from a contradictory system any statement whatever can be deduced, so that no specific prediction can be made. And it seems to coincide with scientific practice (though not all positivists have seen this) to admit any hypothesis such that from statements about the properties of specified space-time regions confirmable statements can be obtained about further properties of these regions or about the properties of other regions.

Scientific discourse is, in summary, statemental or predictive in character, and the statements are either confirmable (or disconfirmable) in terms of empirical evidence, or are statements used in obtaining confirmable statements upon the basis of other confirmable statements.[8] Scientific discourse provides man with a map such that he can determine his expectations with increasing accuracy on the basis of what he encounters in direct experience. Science as an institution involves all the procedures by which such discourse is obtained; science as a habit of mind involves a preference for the scientific form of discourse and the procedures utilized in the control of such discourse. Science as a whole ministers to man's need to be able to determine correctly his expectations, and hence his activity, in terms of the evidence which lies at hand. It is in the realization of this purpose that scientific discourse has been evolved and is being progressively controlled.

Men have, however, other needs than that of accurate prediction. As beings with needs, and so values, they are concerned with the vivid portrayal of what they value, and in devices by which their needs can be satisfied. Aesthetic discourse ministers to the first interest;

[8] For the detailed development of such a view of scientific discourse—without however the emphasis on the control of predictions—see the writings of R. Carnap, especially "Foundations of Logic and Mathematics," in the *International Encyclopedia of Unified Science*, Vol. I, No. 3 (University of Chicago Press, 1939).

technological discourse to the second. By "aesthetic discourse" is meant that specialized type of language which is the actual work of art (the poem, the painting, the music); the term does not refer to discourse about art, unless, indeed, this discourse is itself aesthetic rather than scientific or technological.

That art is a language, that the work of art is in some sense a sign, is the basic doctrine of aestheticians from Plato to Dewey. It is an intelligible interpretation of the doctrine of "imitation" to regard it as a theory of the sign-character of the work of art. For "imitation" was never originally limited to literal reproduction of existing objects (thus Aristotle speaks of the imitation of what is or what men think to be or what ought to be); to affirm that the work of art was an imitation was to affirm that it was a sign, and, indeed, a sign of a specific character: an image or icon "imitating" what is designated by embodying in itself the characters of any object the sign could be said to denote. From this point of view it is possible to regard Aristotle's *Poetics* as a treatise in aesthetics written from the standpoint of the theory of signs. Thus the approach to art as a form of discourse is an ancient and common heritage in aesthetics; the modern theory of signs, in proportion as it is more precise and elaborate, should be able to make clear the foundational material which was hardly more than implicit in ancient formulations, should be able to make more specific the nature of aesthetic discourse, and should be able to free the sign theory of art from the Platonic metaphysics of universals which has enshrouded the doctrine from Plato to Schopenhauer and Santayana and which itself arose out of inadequacies in the existing theories of signs.[4]

If the work of art can be regarded as a sign, the central question is as to the nature of the designating sign and the nature of what is designated (in technical terms, the nature of the sign vehicle and the designatum). The view proposed is that the aesthetic sign designates the value properties of actual or possible situations and that it is an iconic sign (an "image") in that it embodies these values in some medium where they may be directly inspected (in short, the aesthetic sign is an iconic sign whose designatum is a value). To give content to this statement it would be necessary to analyze in detail the notion

[4] An article, "Aesthetics and the Theory of Signs," published in *The Journal of Unified Science* (formerly *Erkenntnis*), 1939, attempts to sketch an aesthetics based on the general theory of signs. I shall not in the present remarks on art attempt to cover the same ground or make use of the more precise terminology there developed. This theory had in genesis no connection with the classical doctrine of imitation.

of value and the characteristics of iconic signs, but this is neither practical nor advisable in the present context. For whatever theory of value be maintained, it must be recognized that objects have value properties among their total set of properties (an object can be insipid, sublime, menacing, oppressive, or gay in some contexts just as it may have a certain mass or length or velocity in other contexts), and that aesthetic media, since they themselves are objects, can embody certain value properties (a small piece of cork could hardly be sublime, but it could be insipid or even gay).

From this point of view the artist is one who molds some medium so that it takes on the value of some significant experience (an experience which may of course arise in the process of molding the medium and need not antedate this process). The work of art is a sign which designates the value or value structure in question, but has the peculiarity, as an iconic sign, that in spite of its generality of reference, the value it designates is embodied in the work itself, so that in perceiving a work of art one perceives directly a value structure and need not be concerned with other objects which the aesthetic sign might denote (technically, other denotata than the sign vehicle itself).[5] In works of art men and women have embodied their experience of value, and these experiences are communicable to those who perceive the molded medium. Art is the language for the communication of values.

If such is the function of art, detailed examination should show that aesthetic discourse is language specialized for the adequate accomplishment of this purpose. Since the work of art is an icon and not a statement, aesthetic discourse is not restricted to signs whose truth is confirmable, and it needs no elaborate set of indexical signs for accuracy in space-time references. Since the aim is not prediction, the requirements of consistency or non-contradictoriness take on a special form: it is only necessary that the component signs in the total sign structure be such as to build up the total icon with the value in question, and such consistency in the presentation of a value may even involve sign combinations which the logician of scientific discourse would class as contradictory. Since the aesthetic sign itself embodies the values it designates, in aesthetic discourse the perceptual properties of the sign vehicles themselves become of great importance, and the artist constantly ex-

---

[5] "Abstract" art (perhaps automorphic or metamorphic art would be a more exact name) might seem an exception to a sign theory of art. That this is not so is argued in the previously mentioned article, "Aesthetics and the Theory of Signs."

periments with special syntactical combinations of these signs to obtain desired value effects. Since the work of art does designate, and in many cases denotes the value properties of actual situations, aesthetic discourse is by no means a mere "expression of the emotions": value properties are objectively relative properties of objects and in dealing with them aesthetic discourse is concerned with the same world with which science and technology are concerned. It is for this reason that aesthetic discourse can often be given a paraphrase in scientific discourse, as in the prose restatement of the content of a poem. Nevertheless, the type of concern is different, for the presentation of value is not to be confused with making statements about value: science itself may make statements about values as about anything else. Art does not, except incidentally, make statements about values, but presents values for direct experience; it is not a language about values, but the language of value.

The third form of primary discourse may be called technological discourse. It is distinguished by such signs as "ought," "should," "do," "do not." A sentence in technological discourse has in function, if not in fact, the form of a command; its purpose is not to report a situation or present a value but to induce a mode of action. Such a sentence ("Paint of this kind ought to be applied in this way") implies an accepted value, whether stated or not (the permanency of the painting, etc.); it may suggest a scientific statement ("This mode of application best realizes the value in question"); it has an irreducible rhetorical or imperative component ("Apply the paint in the way described!"). Various subdivisions of technological discourse are defined in terms of the ends for which techniques are indicated—medical discourse, engineering discourse, agricultural discourse, and the like. Each profession has its own imperatives, its own *oughts,* relative to the values it seeks to control.

The question as to the relation of morality to technology may be put in terms of the relation of moral discourse to technological discourse. The simplest possibility would be to equate the two forms of discourse, so that any action is moral in so far as it aims to utilize techniques adequate to realize some value. While there is much to be said for such a position, it does not seem to correspond to general usage as well as a view which would make moral discourse a subspecies of technological discourse (and so morality a form of technology).

The question then arises as to the basis of differentiation. The moral attitude may be held to arise when the endeavor is made to maximize the positive value of a situation in which values are in conflict. Morality would then become a technology of technologies, consisting of those techniques for the maximum integration and utilization of the various techniques which a community has available for the satisfaction of its interests. The community may of course be wrong in its belief as to which techniques do in fact perform this function, and it is here that the moral individual may feel forced to deviate from the moral techniques recognized by the community. Since morality is a technology, it will, when alive and vigorous, vary with changes in the component techniques of which it is a function. Yet, since it is a function of all techniques, it is not surprising that its changes should be slow, disappointingly slow, when measured in terms of the changes within specific technologies. Perhaps the technological conception of morality would aid in taking as seriously the problems set by the interaction of techniques upon one another as are now taken the problems which arise in special technological fields.[6]

The three primary forms of discourse are simply the development of three basic functions found in the everyday language, which permits making statements, presenting values, and controlling behavior. The primary forms of discourse are related as these three basic human concerns are related. The purposes to be realized are distinct and the corresponding forms of discourse are irreducible. Proficiency in the use of one form of discourse by no means involves proficiency in the use of the others; indeed, in the life of the individual the forms of discourse are often in competition, both because of the differences in human abilities and because of the shortness of human life. But while the individual may have to make a choice, society as a whole need not, for the adequate accomplishment of each of the three basic purposes requires the fulfilment of the others.

If interests are to be satisfied and values realized it is helpful to present vividly what has been attained and what is being sought, and aesthetic discourse provides such presentation. It is also desirable to know the consequences of proposed courses of action under the conditions which

[6] Though the present terminology is not used, important material bearing on what we have called technological discourse, and on its relation to scientific discourse, is found in the monograph by John Dewey, "Theory of Valuation," *International Encyclopedia of Unified Science*, Vol. II, No. 4, University of Chicago Press, 1939.

have to be met, and scientific discourse favors such accuracy in prediction. Technological discourse gives the stimulation to act upon the techniques deemed effective in the realization of the values sought.

Scientific discourse does not entice by the presentation of value nor seduce to action by the advocacy of a technique; it represents the subordination of interest to the mapping of the structure of the existential. Yet it is clear that the direction of science is in a general sense determined by what values men at the time hold, and that science provides the basis for the control of all techniques, since the determination of whether a given procedure does or does not reach a certain goal is a scientific question. Further, the scientist may be helped in the scientific study of values by the vivid portrayal of the value whose conditions he endeavors to trace. He may obtain stimulation through the aesthetic presentation of the value of scientific activity and results. And as a scientist aiming to realize the ends of science, he is a technologist since he must develop and control the techniques adequate to his purposes. If science provides the basis for the control of technological discourse, it is also true that the development of science is inseparable from the development of technology.

Aesthetic discourse has as its field the presentation for direct inspection of the whole realm of values, negative as well as positive. Since men's values are a function of their interests and the world in which such interests arise and operate, the presentation of value will, by and large, require reference to persons and the world, so that aesthetic discourse may incorporate within itself and for its own purpose the statemental character of scientific discourse. It may, further, concern itself with the value of scientific and technological activity and their results. Its presentation of negative value might seem to endanger the work of the moralist, and indeed it does endanger encrusted moral customs. But if morality means the active endeavor to maximize positive values, the moralist needs to have before him for consideration all that interests, so that in the larger sense the free development of art is a vital aid in the development of a vigorous and progressive morality. Finally, the artist is himself technologist in that he must work his will upon some material or other. As technologist he can utilize whatever scientific knowledge can be obtained about his media and about the adequacy of his techniques to attain their ends.

The technologist in turn can only be grateful for the vivid presentation of the values whose status in nature he attempts to control, and for what scientific material he can draw upon to control the efficacy of his techniques. The same is true of the moral technologist. A vital morality can only be helped by a vigorous art and a courageous science which stop before no value or fact. For a morality which is not alert to all that men need and find good or evil is blind and fossilized, while a morality whose injunctions are not constantly corrected by scientific knowledge of the situations with which the injunctions deal, and of the adequacy of the commanded techniques in such situations, is dogmatic and superstitious.

The activities of the scientist, the artist, and the technologist are mutually supporting activities, and their differences and interrelations may be discerned in the differences and interrelations of scientific, aesthetic, and technological discourse.

Two Functions of Speech [1]

KENNETH BURKE

===========

We might distinguish two functions in the communicativeness of speech. Speech is communicative in the sense that it provides a common basis of feeling—or it is communicative in the sense that it serves as the common implement of action. In primitive societies these two functions are nearly identical: the emotional overtones of the tribal idiom stimulate the kinds of behavior by which the tribe works and survives. The word for the tribal enemies will contain the overtones of evil that re-enforce the organization for combating the enemy. Or the words for the tribal purposes will contain favorable overtones which perpetuate these same purposes. By such an identity between the *communion* and *action* aspects of speech, the vocabulary of doing, thinking, and feeling is made an integer.

But the great variety of new matter and new relationships which science and commerce had brought into the modern world had broken

[1] From *Permanence and Change.* New York: New Republic, Inc., 1935, pp. 223–226. Copyright, 1935, by New Republic, Inc. Reprinted by permission.

this integral relationship between thought and feeling in the communicative medium. Hence a paradox: scientists attempted to make a *neutral* vocabulary in the interests of more effective *action*. They learned that by "suspending judgment," by inventing a non-moral vocabulary for the study of cosmic and human processes, they could get a much clearer idea as to how these processes work, and could establish a more efficient system of control over them. In a strictly moral approach, where one's attitude towards the object is formed in advance, the range and quality of one's observations are restricted by the attitude. If one studied criminals, for instance, on the moral assumption that they are wilfully bad, one might automatically vow himself to purely vindictive kinds of treatment; but if one studied them by *suspended judgment,* simply as *social phenomena,* one might learn important new facts about the genesis of crime, and from these facts a whole new program for the treatment and prevention of crime might follow. In such ways, it was held, *neutrality* of approach might eventually further the ends of *action.*

But speech in its essence is not neutral. Far from aiming at suspended judgment, the spontaneous speech of a people is loaded with judgments. It is intensely moral—its names for objects contain the emotional overtones which give us the cues as to how we should act towards these objects. Even a word like "automobile" will usually contain a concealed choice (it designates not merely an *object,* but a *desirable object*). Spontaneous speech is not a *naming* at all, but a system of attitudes, of implicit exhortations. To call a man a friend or an enemy is *per se* to suggest a program of action with regard to him. An important ingredient in the meaning of such words is precisely the attitudes and acts which go with them. Regardless of whether we should call the implicit program of action *adequate* (as when speech aids a primitive tribe to organize a successful fishing expedition) or *inadequate* (as when speech confuses our handling of non-racial issues by stimulating racial persecution) these emotional or moral weightings inherent in spontaneous speech tend to re-enforce the act itself, hence making the communicative and active aspects of speech identical. Such speech is profoundly *partisan.* And it was precisely this partisan quality in speech which Bentham, who specifically formulated the project for a neutral vocabulary, would eliminate. He rightly discerned in it the "poetry" of speech, and resented its "magical" powers in promoting unreasoned action.

Naturally, with such an information-giving ideal as the basis of scientific effort, and with science enjoying prestige as the basic ideal of modern effort, the poet often felt his trade in jeopardy, a misgiving which he sometimes symbolized by despair, and sometimes by effrontery. In any event he knew—without telling himself in so many words —that this was not *his* kind of communication. It was not his business to give information about objects: he communicated when he established a moral identity with his group by using the same moral weightings as they used (for instance, a war poem in wartime). Add now the fact that this communalty of moral weightings was itself impaired, and you see the magnitude of his problems.

The proletarian morality advocated by Marx is an attempt to found such communalty of attitude upon a class basis instead of considering society as a homogeneous whole. It seeks to found a new system of partisanship—and in this sense, although it is considered scientific by its adherents, it tends to replace the strictly scientific hopes for a neutral vocabulary by a new weighted vocabulary, which would be moral, or poetic. Probably the entire project for a neutral attitude towards the matter of experience is but transitional, resulting from the fact that so much new matter had come forward for inclusion in our scheme of judgments.

Language and the Communication of Thought[1]

JEAN PIAGET

Language would seem to enable the individual to communicate his thoughts to others. But the matter is not so simple. In the first place, the adult conveys different modes of thought by means of speech. At times, his language serves only to assert, words state objective facts,

[1] From *The Language and Thought of the Child*. New York: Harcourt, Brace and Company, 1926, pp. 1–4. Reprinted by permission of Routledge and Kegan Ltd.

they convey information, and are closely bound up with cognition. "The weather is changing for the worse," "Bodies fall to the ground." At times, on the other hand, language expresses commands or desires, and serves to criticize or to threaten, in a word to arouse feelings and provoke action—"Let's go," "How horrible!" etc. If we knew approximately in the case of each individual the proportion of one type of speech to another, we should be in possession of psychological data of great interest. But another point arises. Is it certain that even adults always use language to communicate thoughts? To say nothing of internal speech, a large number of people, whether from the working classes or the more absent-minded of the intelligentsia, are in the habit of talking to themselves, of keeping up an audible soliloquy. This phenomenon points perhaps to a preparation for social language. The solitary talker invokes imaginary listeners, just as the child invokes imaginary playfellows. This is perhaps an example of that return shock of social habits which has been described by Baldwin; the individual repeats in relation to himself a form of behaviour which he originally adopted only in relation to others. In this case he would talk to himself in order to make himself work, simply because he has formed the habit of talking to others in order to work on them. Whichever explanation is adopted, it would seem that language has been sidetracked from its supposed function, for in talking to himself, the individual experiences sufficient pleasure and excitement to divert him from the desire to communicate his thoughts to other people. Finally, if the function of language were merely to "communicate," the phenomenon of verbalism would hardly admit of explanation. How could words, confined as they are by usage to certain precise meanings (precise, because their object is to be understood), eventually come to veil the confusion of thought, even to create obscurity by the multiplication of verbal entities, and actually to prevent thought from being communicable? This is not the place to raise the vexed question of the relation between thought and language, but we may note in passing that the very existence of such questions shows how complex are the functions of language, and how futile the attempt to reduce them all to one—that of communicating thought.

The functional problem therefore exists for the adult. How much more urgently will it present itself in case of defective persons, primitive races and young children. Janet, Freud, Ferenczi, Jones, Spielrein, etc., have brought forward various theories on the language of savages,

imbeciles, and young children, all of which are of the utmost significance for an investigation such as we propose to make of the child
mind from the age of six.

M. Janet, for example, considers that the earliest words are derived
from cries with which animals and even savages accompany their
action—threats, cries of anger in the fight, etc. In the earliest forms of
social activity, for instance, the cry uttered by the chief as he enters
into battle becomes the signal to attack. Hence the earliest words of
all, which are words of command. Thus the word, originally bound
up with the act of which it is an element, at a later stage suffices alone
to release the act. The psycho-analysts have given an analogous explanation of word magic. The word, they say, having originally
formed part of the act, is able to evoke all the concrete emotional
contents of the act. Love cries, for instance, which lead up to the
sexual act are obviously among the most primitive words; hencefor-
ward these and all other words alluding to the act retain a definite
emotional charge. Such facts as these explain the very wide-spread
tendency of primitive thought to look upon the names of persons and
objects, and upon the designation of events as pregnant with the
qualities of these objects and events. Hence the belief that it is possible
to work upon them by the mere evocation of words, the word being
no longer a mere label, but a formidable reality partaking of the
nature of the named object. Mme. Spielrein has endeavoured to find
the same phenomena in an analysis of the very earliest stages of child
language. She has tried to prove that the baby syllables, "mama,"
uttered in so many tongues to call the mother, are formed by labial
sounds which indicate nothing more than a prolongation of the act
of sucking. "Mama" would therefore be a cry of desire, and then a
command given to the only being capable of satisfying this desire. But
on the other hand, the mere cry of "mama" has in it a soothing element;
in so far as it is the continuation of the act of sucking, it produces a
kind of hallucinatory satisfaction. Command and immediate satisfaction are in this case therefore almost indistinguishable, and so inter-
mingled are these two factors that one cannot tell when the word is
being used as a real command and when it is playing its almost
magical role.

Maumann and Stern have shown that the earliest substantives of
child language are very far from denoting concepts, but rather express
commands or desire; and there are strong reasons for presuming that

primitive child language fulfils far more complicated functions than would at first appear to be the case. Even when due allowance is made for these theories in all their details, the fact remains that many expressions which for us have a purely conceptual meaning, retain for many years in the child mind a significance that is not only affective but also well-nigh magical, or at least connected with peculiar modes of behaviour which should be studied for themselves and quite apart from adult mentality.

The Condition of Clarity [1]

RUDOLF CARNAP

The cardinal point about which we must become clear is that logic is not concerned with human behavior in the same sense that physiology, psychology, and social sciences are concerned with it. These sciences formulate laws or universal statements which have as their subject matter human activities as processes in time. Logic, on the contrary, is concerned with *relations* between factual sentences (or thoughts). If logic ever discusses the truth of factual sentences it does so only *conditionally,* somewhat as follows: *if* such-and-such a sentence is true, *then* such-and-such another sentence is true. Logic itself does not decide whether the first sentence *is* true, but surrenders that question to one or the other of the empirical sciences. Consequently, since the rules of logic refer simply to various *relations* between sentences (or thoughts), we can distinguish between thinking which is in accordance with these rules and thinking which violates them. The former we shall call *logical thinking,* the latter *illogical.* On the other hand, although logic itself is not concerned with facts, a process of

[1] Reprinted by permission of the publishers from Rudolf Carnap, "Logic" from *Factors Determining Human Behavior,* Cambridge, Mass.: Harvard University Press, 1937, pp. 107–112. Copyright, 1937, by the President and Fellows of Harvard College.

thought, whether it be logical or illogical, is an actual fact. And it is a question of greatest importance, both for the individual and for society, whether our thinking is logical or not. . . .

The condition of clarity may be formulated as follows. We must become clear as to what is the subject of our talking and thinking. Although this requirement may seem trivial, in practice it is often not observed. The most serious and frequent breaches of this rule occur whenever sentences are uttered which are taken to assert something, although in fact nothing is asserted, whether truly or falsely. Such self-deceptions have their source, for the most part, in the structure of our common-day language. For our common language is well adapted for obtaining the gross agreements necessary in practical affairs; but when employed in theoretical pursuits to formulate and communicate knowledge, it is very often not merely inadequate but even seriously misleading.

A little reflection will therefore show that we must distinguish between two main functions which expressions may have. Certain expressions in our language assert something, and are therefore either true or false. Such expressions exercise a *cognitive function* and have a cognitive meaning. On the other hand, certain expressions express the emotions, fancies, images, or wishes of the speaker, and under proper conditions evoke emotions, wishes, or resolutions in the hearer. Such expressions will be said to exercise an *expressive function,* and it is possible to subdivide them further into expressions with pictorial, emotional, and volitional functions. An expression may exercise these different expressive functions simultaneously; and it often is the case that a sentence with cognitive meaning may also possess one or more of the expressive functions. It is of prime importance to note that not all expressions of our language possess a cognitive meaning, so that we must distinguish between those which do and those whose function is solely expressive.

This distinction is frequently concealed by the fact that sentences with solely expressive functions sometimes have the grammatical form of statements which are either true or false. Hence we are led to believe, quite mistakenly, that such sentences do have cognitive meaning. When a lyric poet sings of the melancholy forest or the friendly gleam of moonlight, his utterances take the form of factual statements. However, everyone realizes that the poem is not to be taken as a factual description of the forest or the moon; for it is tacitly understood that the lyric poem is simply expressive of a mood, exactly as music is. But what is so evident in poetry is often far from clear in philosophy. Careful logical analysis has shown that many sentences uttered by trans-empirical metaphysicians appear to have cognitive meaning simply because their grammatical form is that of genuine assertions, although in fact these utterances exercise a solely expressive function. For example, a metaphysician may say, "The fact that all objects in nature, down to the smallest particles of matter, attract and repel one another, is to be explained by the love and hate which these objects bear toward one another." If such a metaphysician supposes that his explanation adds anything to our knowledge of the empirical facts of attraction and repulsion, he is grossly in error, misled by his language. For his statement (or better, pseudo-statement) asserts nothing whatsoever, and simply associates certain images and sentiments with our knowledge of the attraction and repulsion of bodies. His statement has, therefore, no cognitive meaning, although it has a pictorial and emotional function. It is neither true nor false, and belongs to poetry, not to science. Without question, many metaphysical utterances of this type influence our lives by stimulating our emotions and springs of action. Nevertheless, when such utterances are taken to be assertions and arguments are offered for them either *pro* or *con,* the partners to the controversy are deceiving themselves.

Unfortunately, this type of illogical thinking occurs also in fields other than philosophy. Philosophers constitute only a small proportion of mankind; and their doctrines and the confusions arising from their failure to distinguish between the cognitive and expressive function of sentences produce relatively little harmful effects upon human destiny. In any case, their influence is considerably less than is often alleged by many philosophers and philosophical historians. The consequences of the indicated confusion are much more serious when it occurs in discussions concerning individual or political conduct. When I say to some one "Come here!" it is evident that my words exercise a volitional function, and express my desire in order to evoke a certain response in my hearer. My utterance is not an assertion, and any debate about its truth or falsity would clearly be irrelevant. If a theoretical discussion were to arise concerning it, the debate would be significant only if it were to deal with such questions as whether the person addressed will obey me or what the consequences of his decision will be.

But although the matter is obvious for this simple case, the situation is not so readily apprehended when sentences expressing a command have the grammatical form of assertions. Frequent illustrations of this are found in politics, with serious practical consequences. For example, suppose that the following creed is promulgated in a certain country: "There is only one race of superior men, say the race of Hottentots, and this race alone is worthy of ruling other races. Members of these other races are inferior, so that all civil rights are to be denied them so long as they inhabit the country." This pronouncement certainly has the appearance of an assertion. Some of those who dissent from it, taking the grammatical form at face value, may regard it as a genuine assertion and may therefore propound a doctrine in opposition to it. In fact, however, the pronouncement has no cognitive meaning and exercises merely a volitional function. The true nature of the doctrine (or better, pseudo-doctrine) is made clear if we state the pronouncement in the imperative form, to reveal its exclusively volitional function. It then reads as follows: "Members of the race of Hottentots! Unite and battle to dominate the other races! And you, members of other races! Submit to the yoke or fly from this land!" It is now obvious that the political creed is a command, concerning which it is not significant to raise questions of truth or falsity. It is, of course, true that it is possible to raise cognitively significant issues in connection with such a command. But these will involve questions such as whether and to what degree the command will be executed, and what the consequences will be of obeying it or not. It is also possible to debate the factual statements about races, which are usually connected with the command; these are clearly scientific issues belonging to anthropology, and must be critically investigated by specialists in this field. It is, however, of great practical importance for understanding the effective appeal of political war-cries like the above to note that they take the form of misleading pseudo-assertions. This is to be explained by the fact that many men respond less readily to what are obviously commands than to such assertions or pseudo-assertions, especially when the latter are accompanied by powerful emotional appeals.

The Functions of Poetry [1]

F. S. C. NORTHROP

Poetry is one of the arts. Any art functions in two ways, either in and for itself, or as the means to an end defined by some other subject or science.

It is a characteristic of the arts when they function in and for themselves that they are concerned with immediately experienced materials. This is especially evident in the case of painting. In conveying color and form the painter places before us the immediately experienceable blues and reds and greens. It is true, also, of music. The composer may work with black marks arranged on horizontal bars ordered at intervals much after the manner of the symbols of the mathematician. Yet he would hardly be called an artist were not the symbolic form of his score embodied in and presented with the sensuous content of the immediately heard sounds at the symphony concert.

Literature, in the form either of written poetry or prose, may seem upon first thought to be an exception to this rule. When the literary masterpieces are not read aloud the artist has presented merely the symbols on the page and not the actual people or elements of experience to which the symbols refer. A closer examination of his artistry will indicate, however, that he achieves the status of an artist only if, by means of these symbols, he succeeds in bringing into concrete vividness in the reader's imagination that which he purports to convey with all the freshness of color, the vital movement of the emotions, and the sensitivity of feeling which an immediate experience of the imagined subject matter, were it possible, would exhibit.

This becomes clear if we note the difference in the treatment of the same phenomenon, for example, a flowing brook, by the poet and by the scientist. The poet refers to it as the "babbling brook." If he achieves his purpose with us by his use of these words in the context of his verse,

[1] From "The Functions and Future of Poetry," *Furioso*, Vol. I, No. 4, Summer Issue, 1941, pp. 71–74. Reprinted by permission.

we experience ourselves in imagination, immediately confronted with the rippling sounds and the broken, flashing surfaces of the waves of shining water as they flow over the stones and incline gradually between the banks of the stream to disappear into an immediately intuited vagueness in the periphery of our consciousness. The scientist, on the other hand, referring to the same phenomenon, would speak of molecules falling from the top of one stone to a stone below and moving in a path which is a parabola, compounded out of an inertial force with a constant velocity in a horizontal straight line, and an accelerated motion perpendicular thereto defined by the constant of gravitation. There would be further statements concerning the angle of deflection which defines the paths of the molecules as they bound from the second stone to inaugurate another parabolic path on their way to the sea. It is quite clear even to an observer immediately confronted with an actual brook that neither these individual paths nor the particles themselves are seen. What one immediately observes are the babbling sounds and the shining, moving surfaces which the poet portrays. Were science the mere description of what is immediately observable, poetry, rather than physics, would be the better science of the brook. These considerations make it evident that the poet, even though he operates mediately through symbols, provides no exception to our general rule that the arts when they function in and for themselves are concerned with immediately apprehendable materials.

It becomes clear, also, that the symbols of the artist and the symbols of the physicist, even when they refer to what may be termed, speaking somewhat loosely, the "same" phenomenon, are different in kind. It is important that we have names and precise definitions for these two kinds. Symbols, like those used by the poet, when poetry functions in and for itself, we shall term concepts by intuition. *A concept by intuition is one the complete meaning of which is given by something immediately apprehendable.* "Brook," in the sense of the babble of sounds and the sequence of shining surfaces, is an example of a concept by intuition. Symbols, like those employed by the physicist, when science has experimentally confirmed, deductively-formulated theory rather than mere natural history description, we shall call concepts by postulation. *A concept by postulation is one designating something in whole or part not immediately observable, the meaning of which is prescribed for it by the postulates of the scientific theory in which the symbol occurs.* "Brook," in the sense of the collection of molecules moving in paths with the form of the parabola, is an example of a concept by postulation. Electrons, electro-magnetic waves, and Einstein's tensor equation for gravitation are additional examples, since what these scientific concepts designate is not immediately observable and can be known only by theory, which is experimentally confirmed, in a somewhat complicated but none the less trustworthy manner, through its deductive consequences.

This distinction between concepts by intuition and concepts by postulation shows that what in some sense is the same world is known by man in two different ways. It is important that we have names for the two aspects or components of reality which these two ways of knowing anything give us. *That factor of anything which is denoted by a concept by intuition* we shall call *the aesthetic component of reality, or reality in its aesthetic aspect;* that designated by *a concept by postulation, the theoretical component, or reality in its postulated or theoretical aspect.*

Since these two components are in some sense components of the same thing, it is important to designate the relation between them which defines this sameness. The common-sense man, most literary critics, and even scientists who are not too critical and informed in their analysis of what they are doing, suppose that this relation is one of identity. It is easy to fall into this error because linguistically scientists and laymen use the same symbol to designate the radically different types of concepts. For example, the word "blue" is used both for the concept by intuition, which is the immediately-sensed color presented by the painter, and the concept by postulation, which is the number for an unobserved wave length in electro-magnetic theory postulated by the physicist. It is clear, however, that the relation between these two factors is not one of identity. Even the scientist and the man of common sense appreciate this. Both realize it to be nonsense to assert that the wave length is blue. It would be equally meaningless to say that electrons are noisy. Such nonsense always occurs when concepts by intuition and concepts by postulation are treated in the same sentence, as if they belonged to a single rather than to two different worlds of discourse.

But if the relation between the immediately-apprehended, aesthetic, and the scientifically-postulated and experimentally-confirmed, theoretical components of reality is not that of identity, then what is it? The answer is epistemic correlation. *An epistemic correlation is a relation,* preferably, but not always, one-one, *joining a theoretically-known factor designated by a concept by postulation to its immediately apprehendable, aesthetic correlate denoted by a concept by intuition.* This relation is termed epistemic, from the word "epistemology," referring to knowledge, because it relates items of reality which are known in two different ways. These epistemic correlations both (1) distinguish the aesthetic component of reality denoted by the concepts by intuition with which the poet operates from the theoretical component of reality designated by the concepts by postulation which only the scientist and the scientific philosopher are competent to determine and (2) relate these two diverse factors. In short, epistemic correlations both separate and connect the real as known aesthetically with immediacy and the real as known scientifically through deductively-formulated, experimentally-verified theory.

In this dual role of the epistemic correlations, art in its two functions has its basis. By distinguishing concepts by intuition from concepts by postulation and thereby preventing the identification of reality as scientifically and truly thought with reality as immediately and aesthetically intuited, the epistemic correlation permits the aesthetic, purely empirical component of reality to be treated by itself and thereby makes possible the pursuit of art in and for itself without any dependence upon or reference to scientific theory or philosophical, political, or religious doctrine. By relating, but not identifying, concepts by intuition with concepts by postulation the epistemic correlations also indicate that the aesthetic component of reality points beyond itself to the theoretically-postulated. Thus, providing the epistemic correlations are made one-one, they permit the poet to convey analogically in terms of immediately-experienceable materials, the unobservable theoretical component of reality which can be literally expressed only by the technical concepts by postulation of science and scientifically-formulated philosophy. Thus arises art in its second function as the instrument or handmaid for metaphorically and analogically conveying a theoretical doctrine, the truth of which can be determined correctly only outside of art by some other subject or science.

The poetry of the "babbling brook" illustrates art in its first function. Clearly this poetic treatment of the sequence of sounds and shining surfaces is quite independent of any scientific theory concerning molecules. The concept by intuition denoting the aesthetic component of reality is here treated by itself apart from the epistemic correlation which joins it to the theoretical component. This is art in and for itself.

Art in its second function is exemplified in Dante's *Divine Comedy*. Here, as in the poem of the "babbling brook," the artist is using concepts by intuition conveying vivid, immediately-experienceable elementary emotions and impressions. Up to this point it is art in and for itself. It can be so treated as mere poetry. But there is more in the poem, and it is this additional factor which gave this poem its influence in its period and its importance in Western culture. Dante had studied the *Summa Theologica* of Saint Thomas. This opus in eight volumes is a theoretical treatise in science, philosophy, and theology formulated technically in dry, formal definitions and with syllogistic reasoning in terms of concepts by postulation. Its propositions made the theological doctrine of the Catholic Church articulate in terms of the science and purely scientific metaphysics of Aristotle. This Aristotelian, inductively-verified, scientific and philosophical theory defined the conception of the theoretical component of reality as determined by the scientific knowledge acquired up to its time.

But the theory, like all scientific and philosophical theories, was technical, difficult for anyone but the expert to comprehend, and required for its appreciation a tremendous amount of empirical knowledge in mathematics, physics, astronomy, and especially biology, in which Aristotle excelled. The problem was to convey this doctrine which defined the idea of the good for informed scientific and philosophical minds to the general masses, who were incapable then, as they are now, of grasping the fundamental ideas of systematic scientific and philosophical theory literally. The general public, like all but a few of our contemporary professors of psychology and education, are incapable of using concepts by postulation with their technical definitions and logical deductions; they must have bells rung for them while they salivate, and have vivid images instead of postulationally-prescribed scientific concepts. Dante solved this problem for his time by epistemically correlating the vivid images denoted by the poet's concepts by intuition with the technical concepts by postulation of Saint Thomas' *Summa*. Then he moved the images about as the technical doctrine of Saint Thomas related their correlated concepts by postulation. Thus in his poem, to people who could not grasp the technical doctrine literally in terms of its concepts by postulation, Dante conveyed an analogue of this doctrine metaphorically in terms of the vivid, immediately-apprehendable aesthetic materials denoted by the poet's concepts by intuition.

This is art in its second function as the instrument or handmaid of some other subject or science.

What Is Poetry? [1]

GERTRUDE STEIN

What is poetry and if you know what poetry is what is prose.

There is no use in telling more than you know, no not even if you do not know it.

But do you do you know what prose is and do you know what poetry is.

I have said that the words in plays written in poetry are more lively than the same words written by the same poet in other kinds of poetry. It undoubtedly was true of Shakespeare, is it inevitably true of every- body. That is one thing to think about. I said that the words in a play written in prose are not as lively words as the words written in other prose by the same writer. This is true of Goldsmith and I imagine it is true of almost any writer.

There again there is something to know.

One of the things that is a very interesting thing to know is how you are feeling inside you to the words that are coming out to be out- side of you.

Do you always have the same kind of feeling in relation to the sounds as the words come out of you or do you not. All this has so much to do with grammar and with poetry and with prose.

Words have to do everything in poetry and prose and some writers write more in articles and prepositions and some say you should write in nouns, and of course one has to think of everything.

A noun is a name of anything, why after a thing is named write

[1] From *Lectures in America.* New York: Random House, 1935, pp. 209–210, 228–234. Copyright, 1935 by Modern Library, Inc. Reprinted by permission of Random House, Inc.

about it. A name is adequate or it is not. If it is adequate then why go on calling it, if it is not then calling it by its names does no good.

People if you like to believe it can be made by their names. Call anybody Paul and they get to be a Paul call anybody Alice and they get to be an Alice perhaps yes perhaps no, there is something in that, but generally speaking, things once they are named the name does not go on doing anything to them and so why write in nouns. Nouns are the name of anything and just naming names is alright when you want to call a roll but is it any good for anything else. To be sure in many places in Europe as in America they do like to call rolls.

As I say a noun is a name of a thing, and therefore slowly if you feel what is inside that thing you do not call it by the name by which it is known. Everybody knows that by the way they do when they are in love and a writer should always have that intensity of emotion about whatever is the object about which he writes. And therefore and I say it again more and more one does not use nouns. . . .

Nouns as you all know are the names of anything and as the names of anything of course one has had to use them. And what have they done. And what has any one done with them. That is something to know. It is as you may say as I may say a great deal to know.

Nouns are the name of anything and anything is named, that is what Adam and Eve did and if you like it is what anybody does, but do they go on just using the name until perhaps they do not know what the name is or if they do know what the name is they do not care about what the name is. This may happen of course it may. And what has poetry got to do with this and what has prose and if everything like a noun which is a name of anything is to be avoided what takes place. And what has that to do with poetry. A great deal I think and all this too has to do with other things with short and long lines and rhymes.

But first what is poetry and what is prose. I wonder if I can tell you.

We do know a little now what prose is. Prose is the balance the emotional balance that makes the reality of sentences and having realized completely realized that sentences are not emotional while paragraphs are, prose can be the essential balance that is made inside something that combines the sentences and the paragraphs, examples of this I have been reading to you.

Now if that is what prose is and that undoubtedly is what prose is you can see that prose real prose really great written prose is bound to be made up more of verbs adverbs prepositions prepositional clauses and conjunctions than nouns. The vocabulary in prose of course is important if you like vocabulary is always important, in fact one of the things that you can find out and that I experimented with a great deal in How to Write vocabulary in itself and by itself can be interesting and can make sense. Anybody can know that by thinking of words. It is extraordinary how it is impossible that a vocabulary does not make sense. But that is natural indeed inevitable because a vocabulary is that by definition, and so because this is so the vocabulary in respect to prose is less important than the parts of speech, and the internal balance and the movement within a given space.

So then we understand we do know what prose is.

But what is poetry.

Is it more or is it less difficult to know what poetry is. I have sometimes thought it more difficult to know what poetry is but now that I do know what poetry is and if I do know what poetry is then it is not more difficult to know what it is than to know what prose is.

What is poetry.

Poetry has to do with vocabulary as prose has not.

So you see prose and poetry are not at all alike. They are completely different.

Poetry is I say essentially a vocabulary just as prose is essentially not.

And what is the vocabulary of which poetry absolutely is. It is a vocabulary entirely based on the noun as prose is essentially and determinately and vigorously not based on the noun.

Poetry is concerned with using with abusing, with losing with wanting, with denying with avoiding with adoring with replacing the noun. It is doing that always doing that, doing that and doing nothing but that. Poetry is doing nothing but using losing refusing and pleasing and betraying and caressing nouns. That is what poetry does, that is what poetry has to do no matter what kind of poetry it is. And there are a great many kinds of poetry.

When I said.

A rose is a rose is a rose is a rose.

And then later made that into a ring I made poetry and what did I do I caressed completely caressed and addressed a noun.

Now let us think of poetry any poetry all poetry and let us see if this is not so. Of course it is so anybody can know that.

I have said that a noun is a name of anything by definition that is what it is and a name of anything is not interesting because once you know its name the enjoyment of naming it is over and therefore in writing prose names that is nouns are completely uninteresting. But and that is a thing to be remembered you can love a name and if you love a name then saying that name any number of times only makes you love it more, more violently more persistently more tormentedly. Anybody knows how anybody calls out the name of anybody one loves. And so that is poetry really loving the name of anything and that is not prose. Yes any of you can know that. . . .

Poetry did then in beginning include everything and it was natural that it should because then everything including what was happening could be made real to anyone by just naming what was happening in other words by doing what poetry always must do by living in nouns.

Nouns are the name of anything. Think of all that early poetry, think of Homer, think of Chaucer, think of the Bible and you will see what I mean you will really realize that they were drunk with nouns, to name to know how to name earth sea and sky and all that was in them was enough to make them live and love in names, and that is what poetry is it is a state of knowing and feeling a name. I know that now but I have only come to that knowledge by long writing.

So then as I say that is what poetry was and slowly as everybody knew the names of everything poetry has less and less to do with everything. Poetry did not change, poetry never changed, from the beginning until now and always in the future poetry will concern itself with the names of things. The names may be repeated in different ways and very soon I will go into that matter but now and always poetry is created by naming names the names of something the names of somebody the names of anything. Nouns are the names of things and so nouns are the basis of poetry.

Behavior That Language Makes Possible [1]

ALDOUS HUXLEY

Human behaviour as we know it, became possible only with the establishment of relatively stable systems of relationships between things and events on the one hand and words on the other. In societies where no such relationship has been established, that is to say, where there is no language, behaviour is nonhuman. Necessarily so; for language makes it possible for men to build up the social heritage of accumulated skill, knowledge and wisdom, thanks to which it is possible for us to profit by the experiences of past generations, as though they were our own. There may be geniuses among the gorillas; but since gorillas have no conceptual language, the thoughts and achievements of these geniuses cannot be recorded and so are lost to simian posterity. In those limited fields of activity where some form of progress is possible, words permit of progress being made.

Nor is this all. The existence of language permits human beings to behave with a degree of purposefulness, perseverance and consistency unknown among the other mammals and comparable only to the purposefulness, perseverance and consistency of insects acting under the compulsive force of instinct. Every instant in the life, say, of a cat or a monkey tends to be irrelevant to every other instant. Such creatures are the victims of their moods. Each impulse as it makes itself felt carries the animal away completely. Thus, the urge to fight will suddenly be interrupted by the urge to eat; the all-absorbing passion of love will be displaced in the twinkling of an eye by a no less absorbing passion to search for fleas. The consistency of human behaviour, such as it is, is due entirely to the fact that men have formulated their desires,

---

[1] From *Words and Their Meanings*. Los Angeles: The Ward Ritchie Press, 1940, pp. 13–16. Copyright, 1940, by the Ward Ritchie Press. Reprinted by permission of the author and publisher.

and subsequently rationalized them, in terms of words. The verbal
formulation of a desire will cause a man to go on pressing forward
towards his goal, even when the desire itself lies dormant. Similarly,
the rationalization of his desire in terms of some theological or philosophical system will convince him that he does well to persevere in
this way. It is thanks to words and to words alone that, as the poet says:

> Tasks in hours of insight willed
> May be in hours of gloom fulfilled.

And let us remember incidentally that by no means all of our tasks
are willed in hours of insight. Some are willed in hours of imbecility,
some in hours of calculating self-interest, some under the stress of
violent emotion, some in mere stupidity and intellectual confusion. If
it were not for the descriptive and justificatory words with which we
bind our days together, we should live like the animals in a series of
discrete and separate spurts of impulse. From the psychological point
of view, a theology or a philosophy may be defined as a device for
permitting men to perform in cold blood and continuously actions
which, otherwise, they could accomplish only by fits and starts and
when the impulse was strong and hot within them. It is worth remark-
ing, in this context, that no animals ever make war. They get into
individual squabbles over food and sex; but they do not organize
themselves in bands for the purpose of exterminating members of their
own species in the name of some sacred cause. The emphasis here must
be placed on the word "name." For, of course, animals have no lack
of sacred causes. What could be more sacred to a tiger than fresh meat
or tigresses? What is lacking in the animal's world is the verbal ma-
chinery for describing and justifying these sacred causes. Without
words, perseverance and consistency of behaviour are, as we have
seen, impossible. And without perseverance in slaughter and consistency in hatred there can be no war.

For evil, then, as well as for good, words make us the human beings
we actually are. Deprived of language we should be as dogs or monkeys.
Possessing language, we are men and women able to persevere in crime
no less than in heroic virtue, capable of intellectual achievements beyond the scope of any animal, but at the same time capable of systematic silliness and stupidity such as no dumb beast could ever dream of.

Talking About the Weather [1]

HOLBROOK JACKSON

When the Lords of Sun and Wind and Cloud have been more than usually capricious, as they are very often, to talk about the weather is permissible. The best people do it — they who sit in the front seats of Olympus wagging tongues about that only which is high and authoritative and remote. In some circumstances everybody does it: superior and inferior alike, everybody does it openly and without apology; at other times and in other circumstances superior people discuss the weather guiltily, with a sense of sin, fearing to be thought commonplace. They miss much, those fearful ones, for the weather is a very proper topic: a topic of incalculable variety, immemorial usage, exalted authority, and infinite jest. We have, in fact, discussed the weather for so many generations that the subject has become the raw material of national small-talk and not a little of our art.

It is easier to sneer at small-talk than to explain it away. Small-talk is a social necessity, if only because it helps to bridge the gaps between thought and thought, and silence and silence. But it does more than that. Small-talk may be the noise made by the human rattle, but it is also one of the disguises of the thoughtful . . . and the cunning. But talk about the weather is not always small-talk in an eccentric climate like ours; it is very often the one topic of enthralling interest.

How soon do we tire of other topics: politics, one's back garden, race-suicide, the latest novel, the newest art, one's ailments, one's servants, that cat Mrs. de Jones-Brown, or that cad Smith-Robinson, or the latest in hats! But the weather as a conversational subject is eternal; it is our national topic. . . .

Even the War, which destroyed so many ideas and made so many topics obsolete, has left the weather topic unscathed. We still discuss the weather. No longer do we inquire eagerly after each other's health,

---

[1] From *Occasions*. New York: Charles Scribner's Sons, 1922, pp. 151–156. Reprinted by permission.

and "How do you do?" is a form of greeting surviving only among the *nouveaux riches*. Now and then, to be sure, Dame Nature or the newspapers may distract us with pyrotechnics, but let them be never so captivating, they cannot decoy us far or for long from the true faith. We always return to the weather. It is our topical anchorage; the sanctuary of the short of speech; the scratching-post of small-talk. When we British discuss the weather we purr.

One might be disposed in one's enthusiasm to conclude that so great a subject needed no advocacy: it has survived the War—it will survive anything. True: but there are, as we have seen, ill-disposed persons, clever folk, barren of goodwill, who for the sake of cleverness would rob us of our topical birthright. True, also, they have proved impotent; but to be forewarned is to be forearmed. We must not sell our birthright for a mess of brilliance. . . . References to the weather would seem to indicate the existence of two very admirable qualities—goodwill and wonder. When men who pass in the street salute each other with a hurried "It's a fine day!" or its contrary, it is not out of idleness or shortage of ideas; it is merely a short way, suitable to the occasion, of saying "God be with you, sir! On such a glorious and invigorating day as this it is more than good to be alive!" If the contrary, say, "Filthy weather!" it is an intimation of the desire for communal disgruntlement, "let us talk of graves" as it were; sympathy in sorrow, the *camaraderie* of gloom. Such sentiments can no more be dull than they can grow old. They are the vocal symbols of goodwill, the sounds of sociability.

As to the wonder, is it not the key of our happiness, the corner-stone of our romance? Without wonder we should scarcely live, and without the weather we should rarely wonder. Proof? Look at the races of man; has ever an equable climate produced an active or an imaginative race? It is equable in the Arctic zone, but does poetry or progress flourish among the Esquimaux? It is equable in Sahara—what then? In England the weather is so variable that every morning brings a renascence of wonder and every night the possibility of climatic adventure; and in this land of meteorological inventiveness has grown up the most acquisitive and imaginative people in the world. The English people have achieved the two most amazing things in history—they have given to the world Industrialism and Shakespeare, and probably, they would have done neither if their interests and enthusiasms, their sense of wonder had not been sharpened by a climate which made the

weather of such infinite variety that the national mind is kept from
rusting by the mere contemplation of it.

Classic Speech[1]

THORSTEIN VEBLEN

"Classic" always carries this connotation of wasteful and archaic,
whether it is used to denote the dead languages or the obsolete or
obsolescent forms of thought and diction in the living language, or to
denote other items of scholarly activity or apparatus to which it is
applied with less aptness. So the archaic idiom of the English language
is spoken of as "classic" English. Its use is imperative in all speaking
and writing upon serious topics, and a facile use of it lends dignity to
even the most commonplace and trivial string of talk. The newest form
of English diction is of course never written; the sense of that leisure-
class propriety which requires archaism in speech is present even in
the most illiterate or sensational writers in sufficient force to prevent
such a lapse. On the other hand, the highest and most conventionalized
style of archaic diction is—quite characteristically—properly employed
only in communications between an anthropomorphic divinity and his
subjects. Midway between these extremes lies the everyday speech of
leisure-class conversation and literature.

Elegant diction, whether in writing or speaking, is an effective means
of reputability. It is of moment to know with some precision what is
the degree of archaism conventionally required in speaking on any
given topic. Usage differs appreciably from the pulpit to the market-
place; the latter, as might be expected, admits the use of relatively new
and effective words and turns of expression, even by fastidious persons.
A discriminate avoidance of neologisms is honorific, not only because

[1] From *The Theory of the Leisure Class* by Thorstein Veblen, pp. 398–400. Copyright
1899, 1912 by The Macmillan Company. Reprinted by permission of The Viking Press,
Inc., New York.

it argues that time has been wasted in acquiring the obsolescent habit of speech, but also as showing that the speaker has from infancy habitually associated with persons who have been familiar with the obsolescent idiom. It thereby goes to show his leisure-class antecedents. Great purity of speech is presumptive evidence of several successive lives spent in other than vulgarly useful occupations; although its evidence is by no means entirely conclusive to this point.

As felicitous an instance of futile classicism as can well be found, outside of the Far East, is the conventional spelling of the English language. A breach of the proprieties in spelling is extremely annoying and will discredit any writer in the eyes of all persons who are possessed of a developed sense of the true and beautiful. English orthography satisfies all the requirements of the canons of reputability under the law of conspicuous waste. It is archaic, cumbrous, and ineffective; its acquisition consumes much time and effort; failure to acquire it is easy of detection. Therefore it is the first and readiest test of reputability in learning, and conformity to its ritual is indispensable to a blameless scholastic life.

On this head of purity of speech, as at other points where a conventional usage rests on the canons of archaism and waste, the spokesmen for the usage instinctively take an apologetic attitude. It is contended, in substance, that a punctilious use of ancient and accredited locutions will serve to convey thought more adequately and more precisely than would the straightforward use of the latest form of spoken English; whereas it is notorious that the ideas of today are effectively expressed in the slang of today. Classic speech has the honorific virtue of dignity; it commands attention and respect as being the accredited method of communication under the leisure-class scheme of life, because it carries a pointed suggestion of the industrial exemption of the speaker. The advantage of the accredited locutions lies in their reputability; they are reputable because they are cumbrous and out of date, and therefore argue waste of time and exemption from the use and the need of direct and forcible speech.

PART III

Matters of Fact, Fiction and Opinion

Discussions of the question, "What is a fact?" are sometimes unduly complicated by the failure to distinguish between whatever facts the talk is about and statements made about those facts. Then, sometimes, statements are made about what facts should be like, which are not differentiated from those which intend to describe what can be observed. Often, statements are fictional even though they look or sound factual. To add to the possibilities of confusion, statements can be made which seem to refer to facts but which refer rather to assumptions, theories, judgments, and opinions; and often the same statement may unwittingly or by design do both. Each of these modes has a purpose and a necessary role in human communication, and each ought to be kept from doing more than it can, from poaching on the role of the others. What is troublesome, of course, is that the taxonomy of statements is ever so much more difficult than the making of the statements. Considerations of difficulty should not, however, be permitted to affect the necessity of establishing the distinctions, for as George Santayana put it, "The ruin of empires and religions has repeatedly admonished mankind, if they have any wit at all, to distinguish fact from fable."

Matters of Fact and Opinion [1]

GEORGE CORNEWALL LEWIS

By a Matter of Fact I understand anything of which we obtain a conviction from our internal consciousness, or any individual event or phenomenon which is the object of sensation. It is true that even the simplest sensations involve some judgment: when a witness reports that he saw an object of a certain shape and size, or at a certain distance, he describes something more than a mere impression on his sense of sight, and his statement implies a theory and explanation of the bare phenomenon. When, however, this judgment is of so simple a kind as to become wholly unconscious, and the interpretation of the appearances is a matter of general agreement, the object of sensation may, for our present purpose, be considered a *fact*. A fact, as so defined, must be limited to individual sensible objects, and not extended to general expressions or formulas, descriptive of classes of facts, or sequences of phenomena, such as that the blood circulates, the sun attracts the planets, and the like. Propositions of this sort, though descriptive of realities, and therefore in one sense, of matters of fact, relate to large classes of phenomena, which cannot be grasped by a single sensation, which can only be determined by a long series of observations, and are established by a process of intricate reasoning.

Taken in this sense, matters of fact are decided by an appeal to our own consciousness or sensation, or to the testimony, direct or indirect, of the original and percipient witnesses. Doubts, indeed, frequently arise as to the existence of a matter of fact, in consequence of the diversity of the reports made by the original witnesses, or the suspiciousness of their testimony. A matter of fact may again be doubtful, in consequence of the different constructions which may be put upon admitted facts and appearances, in a case of proof by (what is termed)

[1] From *An Essay on the Influence of Authority in Matters of Opinion*. London: John W. Parker, 1849, pp. 1–3.

circumstantial evidence. Whenever such doubts exist they cannot be settled by a direct appeal to testimony, and can only be resolved by reasoning; instances of which are afforded by the pleadings of lawyers and the disquisitions of historians upon contested facts. When an individual fact is doubted upon reasonable grounds, its existence becomes a matter of opinion. The existence of such a fact, however, is not a general or scientific truth, but a question to be decided by a consideration of the testimony of witnesses.

Matters of Opinion, not being disputed questions of fact, are general propositions or theorems relating to laws of nature or mind, principles and rules of human conduct, future probabilities, deductions from hypotheses, and the like, about which a doubt may reasonably exist. All doubtful questions, whether of speculation or practice, are matters of opinion. With regard to these, the ultimate source of our belief is always a process of reasoning.[2]

[2] "I remember it was with extreme difficulty that I could bring my master to understand the meaning of the word *opinion,* or how a point could be disputable; because reason taught us to affirm or deny only where we are certain, and beyond our knowledge we cannot do either. So that controversies, wranglings, disputes, and positiveness in false or dubious propositions, are evils unknown among the Houyhnhnms."—Swift.

The essential idea of *opinion* seems to be that it is a matter about which doubt can reasonably exist, as to which two persons can without absurdity think differently. The existence of an object before the eyes of two persons would not be a matter of opinion, nor would it be a matter of opinion that twice two are four. But when testimony is divided, or uncertain, the existence of a fact may become doubtful, and, therefore, a matter of opinion. For example, it may be a matter of opinion whether there was a war of Troy, whether Romulus lived, who was the man in the iron mask, who wrote Junius, etc. So the tendency of a law or form of government, or social institution, the probability of a future event, the quality of an action or the character of an historical personage, may be a matter of opinion.

Any proposition, the contradictory of which can be maintained with probability, is a matter of opinion.

The distinction between matters of fact and matters of opinion is recognized by Bacon, *Advancement of Learning,* vol. ii, p. 42, ed. Montague. See also Locke, *Essay on the Understanding,* B. IV. c. xvi. § 5: *On the Conduct of the Understanding,* § 24; and Whately, *Rhetoric,* Part. I. c. iii. § 3.

In the language of jurists, questions of fact are opposed to questions of law. Hence the maxim of our law: *"De jure respondent judices, de facto jurati."* On this subject, see Bentham *On Judicial Evidence by Dumont,* B. I. c. v.

The Semantic Conception of Truth [1]

ALFRED TARSKI

2. THE EXTENSION OF THE TERM "TRUE"

We begin with some remarks regarding the extension of the concept of truth which we have in mind here.

The predicate *"true"* is sometimes used to refer to psychological phenomena such as judgments or beliefs, sometimes to certain physical objects, namely, linguistic expressions and specifically sentences, and sometimes to certain ideal entities called "propositions." By "sentence" we understand here what is usually meant in grammar by "declarative sentence"; as regards the term "proposition," its meaning is notoriously a subject of lengthy disputations by various philosophers and logicians, and it seems never to have been made quite clear and unambiguous. For several reasons it appears most convenient to *apply the term "true" to sentences,* and we shall follow this course.

Consequently, we must always relate the notion of truth, like that of a sentence, to a specific language; for it is obvious that the same expression which is a true sentence in one language can be false or meaningless in another.

Of course, the fact that we are interested here primarily in the notion of truth for sentences does not exclude the possibility of a subsequent extension of this notion to other kinds of objects.

3. THE MEANING OF THE TERM "TRUE"

Much more serious difficulties are connected with the problem of the meaning (or the intension) of the concept of truth.

The word *"true,"* like other words from our everyday language, is certainly not unambiguous. And it does not seem to me that the philosophers who have discussed this concept have helped to diminish its

[1] From "The Semantic Conception of Truth and the Foundations of Semantics," *Philosophy and Phenomenological Research*, Vol. IV, No. 3, March, 1941, pp. 343–345. Reprinted by permission.

ambiguity. In works and discussions of philosophers we meet many different conceptions of truth and falsity, and we must indicate which conception will be the basis of our discussion.

We should like our definition to do justice to the intuitions which adhere to the *classical Aristotelian conception of truth*—intuitions which find their expression in the well-known words of Aristotle's *Metaphysics:*

> *To say of what is that it is not, or of what is not that it is, is false, while to say of what is that it is, or of what is not that it is not, is true.*

If we wished to adapt ourselves to modern philosophical terminology, we could perhaps express this conception by means of the familiar formula:

> *The truth of a sentence consists in its agreement with (or correspondence to) reality.*

(For a theory of truth which is to be based upon the latter formulation the term "correspondence theory" has been suggested.)

If, on the other hand, we should decide to extend the popular usage of the term "designate" by applying it not only to names, but also to sentences, and if we agreed to speak of the designata of sentences as "states of affairs," we could possibly use for the same purpose the following phrase:

> *A sentence is true if it designates an existing state of affairs.*

However, all these formulations can lead to various misunderstandings, for none of them is sufficiently precise and clear (though this applies much less to the original Aristotelian formulation than to either of the others); at any rate, none of them can be considered a satisfactory definition of truth. It is up to us to look for a more precise expression of our intuitions.

4. A CRITERION FOR THE MATERIAL ADEQUACY OF THE DEFINITION

Let us start with a concrete example. Consider the sentence *"snow is white."* We ask the question under what conditions this sentence is true or false. It seems clear that if we base ourselves on the classical conception of truth, we shall say that the sentence is true if snow is white, and that it is false if snow is not white. Thus, if the definition of truth is to conform to our conception, it must imply the following equivalence:

The sentence "snow is white" is true if, and only if, snow is white.

Let me point out that the phrase *"snow is white"* occurs on the left side of this equivalence in quotation marks, and on the right without quotation marks. On the right side we have the sentence itself, and on the left the name of the sentence. Employing the medieval logical terminology we could also say that on the right side the words *"snow is white"* occur in *suppositio formalis,* and on the left in *suppositio materialis.* It is hardly necessary to explain why we must have the name of the sentence, and not the sentence itself, on the left side of the equivalence. For, in the first place, from the point of view of the grammar of our language, an expression of the form *"X is true"* will not become a meaningful sentence if we replace in it *"X"* by a sentence or by anything other than a name—since the subject of a sentence may be only a noun or an expression functioning like a noun. And, in the second place, the fundamental conventions regarding the use of any language require that in any utterance we make about an object it is the name of the object which must be employed, and not the object itself. In consequence, if we wish to say something about a sentence, for example, that it is true, we must use the name of this sentence, and not the sentence itself. It may be added that enclosing a sentence in quotation marks is by no means the only way of forming its name. For instance, by assuming the usual order of letters in our alphabet, we can use the following expression as the name (the description) of the sentence *"snow is white":*

The sentence constituted by three words, the first of which consists of the 19th, 14th, 15th, and 23rd letters, the second of the 9th and 19th letters, and the third of the 23rd, 8th, 9th, 20th, and 5th letters of the English alphabet.

We shall now generalize the procedure which we have applied above. Let us consider an arbitrary sentence; we shall replace it by the letter *'p.'* We form the name of this sentence and we replace it by another letter, say *'X.'* We ask now what is the logical relation between the two sentences *"X is true"* and *'p.'* It is clear that from the point of view of our basic conception of truth these sentences are equivalent. In other words, the following equivalence holds:

(T)   *X is true if, and only if, p.*

We shall call any such equivalence (with '*p*' replaced by any sentence of the language to which the word *"true"* refers, and '*X*' replaced by a name of this sentence) an *"equivalence of the form* (T)."

Now at last we are able to put into a precise form the conditions under which we will consider the usage and the definition of the term *"true"* as adequate from the material point of view: we wish to use the term "true" in such a way that all equivalences of the form (T) can be asserted, and *we shall call a definition of truth "adequate" if all these equivalences follow from it.*

It should be emphasized that neither the expression (T) itself (which is not a sentence, but only a schema of a sentence) nor any particular instance of the form (T) can be regarded as a definition of truth. We can only say that every equivalence of the form (T) obtained by replacing '*p*' by a particular sentence, '*X*' by a name of this sentence, may be considered a partial definition of truth, which explains wherein the truth of this one individual sentence consists. The general definition has to be, in a certain sense, a logical conjunction of all these partial definitions.

(The last remark calls for some comments. A language may admit the construction of infinitely many sentences; and thus the number of partial definitions of truth referring to sentences of such a language will also be infinite. Hence to give our remark a precise sense we should have to explain what is meant by a "logical conjunction of infinitely many sentences"; but this would lead us too far into technical problems of modern logic.)

5. TRUTH AS A SEMANTIC CONCEPT

I should like to propose the name *"the semantic conception of truth"* for the conception of truth which has just been discussed.

Semantics is a discipline which, speaking loosely, *deals with certain relations between expressions of a language and the objects* (or "states of affairs") *"referred to" by those expressions.* As typical examples of semantic concepts we may mention the concepts of *designation, satisfaction,* and *definition* as these occur in the following examples:

   the expression "the father of his country" designates (denotes) George Washington;

snow satisfies the sentential function (*the condition*) "*x is white*";
the equation "$2.x = 1$" defines (*uniquely determines*) the number $\frac{1}{2}$.

While the words "*designates*," "*satisfies*," and "*defines*" express relations (between certain expressions and the objects "referred to" by
these expressions), the word "*true*" is of a different logical nature: it
expresses a property (or denotes a class) of certain expressions, viz., of
sentences. However, it is easily seen that all the formulations which
were given earlier and which aimed to explain the meaning of this
word (cf. Sections 3 and 4) referred not only to sentences themselves,
but also to objects "talked about" by these sentences, or possibly to
"states of affairs" described by them. And, moreover, it turns out that
the simplest and the most natural way of obtaining an exact definition
of truth is one which involves the use of other semantic notions, e.g.,
the notion of satisfaction. It is for these reasons that we count the concept of truth which is discussed here among the concepts of semantics,
and the problem of defining truth proves to be closely related to the
more general problem of setting up the foundations of theoretical
semantics.

Scientific Observation [1]

WILLIAM H. GEORGE

It is well known that in scientific research much use is made of
instruments and apparatus to aid the senses. Direct observation is not
always used. The sensitive photographic surface, the photo-electrical
cell, and the thermo-electric couple are often substituted for direct vision.
Sound vibrations are converted into electrical oscillations and are analyzed and measured in that form by instruments having a range far
beyond that of the human ear. The balance is substituted for the kines-

[1] From *The Scientist in Action*. New York: Emerson Books, Inc., 1938, pp. 92–95,
99–104. Copyright, 1938, by Emerson Books, Inc. Reprinted by permission.

thetic muscular sensations in the estimation of relative weight. Thermometers and pyrometers are substituted for the sense of touch in estimating warmth and coldness. Where a phenomenon occurs rarely and then only for a short time as in solar eclipses, recording instruments are substituted almost entirely for direct visual observation. With the added complication of unexpectedness, as in earthquakes, the seismograph continually waits ever ready to make records upon which observations can be made later. In direct observation the eye is often aided by the metre-rule, the lens, microscope, telescope, and other optical instruments.

COINCIDENCE OBSERVATION

Let us examine a little more carefully what kind of human judgments have to be made when direct observation is aided by various instruments. Attention has already been directed to the unreliability of judgments of the warmth or coldness of objects touched. The sensations got through the two hands of the same observer may lead to contradictory results. If, however, a simple thermometer such as a clinical thermometer is used, the actual observation is not a judgment of warmth. The act of taking a patient's temperature consists in seeing against which mark on the glass the mercury comes to rest. The observer has to judge with which mark the end of the mercury column coincides or if it lies between two marks he may judge to which it is nearer. This is a typical judgment of coincidence. In weighing with the chemical balance the observer has to alter the weights in one of the scale pans until a pointer, which moves over a scale whilst the balance is swinging, comes to rest opposite one mark on the scale. In many of the balances now used in shops a scale marked on a cylinder moves behind a line marked on a glass window, and the same judgment of the coincidence of two marks has to be made. A similar kind of judgment is necessary to the fine tuning of many radio reception sets. It is in this kind of observation that something like universal agreement can be reached. It is not here necessary to consider the distance apart of the various marks of a scale or the numbers placed against the various marks. It is sufficient to note that this kind of judgment is one which can be made readily by all normal human beings. No elaborate training is necessary. The shop assistant and the analytical chemist in making weighings both have to make the same simple judgments of coincidence.

It is, then, from this kind of observation that impersonal data can be got to form the basis of scientific knowledge. The method does not eliminate the human observer, but he is given a task which from experience is found to be well within the powers of the majority of men upon the majority of occasions. The making of judgments of co-incidence seems to include all the judgments in which universal agreement between men is ever found. If men are asked to judge values of truth, beauty, goodness, importance, merit, or in fact values of any kind, not even an approximation to universal agreement is in practice found, and we enter a world of constant conflict. If the same men are asked to judge coincidences, we get the nearest to universal agreement that is ever found in working with biological material. Any man who can tell the time of day by the clock can judge coincidences and in so doing he is making coincidence observations whether or not he is a scientist.

In the so-called exact sciences this type of observation is always used and is often combined with more complex processes, including counting. The results are then called measurements. The tendency in all scientific work is to try to devise methods of observing the phenomenon studied so that the final observations are judgments of coincidence of two things. Familiar examples are in the use of the rule in measuring lengths, the clock, the balance, the measuring cylinder, flask, burette or pipette, the galvanometer, the spectrometer, and the thermometer. One type of exposure meter used in photography depends on a matching process. In the use of all these instruments the judgment of coincidence is made by eye.

It is not necessary here to consider whether or no a judgment of coincidence is the simplest which can be made by man or whether it can be analyzed into or related to, for example, judgment of one thing being between two others, or judgment of one thing being nearer to another than to a third thing. In the laboratory there is always a stage before the final observation when two lines or marks do not coincide or when two luminous areas are not matched. Adjustments are made to the apparatus and then the judgment of coincidence is made by the observer. In the "null" method of using some scientific instruments the observer has always to make three judgments for each "reading." These three are, that when certain alterations are made to the apparatus a pointer or an optical image, thrown onto a scale, in turn is on one or the other side of a reference line or coincides with the line.

Similar judgments of coincidence can be made by the use of other senses. Whether two sounds occur together or whether they can be distinguished as two separate sounds can be judged by ear. It is interesting to note that in his experiments on falling bodies Galileo used this method of coincidences of sounds to tell whether two bodies reached the ground together, by allowing them to fall onto an iron plate. When our eyes are fully occupied in the laboratory so that a stop-watch cannot be observed, the power of judging coincidences with other senses can be used by fitting muscular actions into the time pattern set by a ticking metronome. By this means visual observations can be taken at times marked by the sounds heard. Outside the laboratory in dancing to music bodily movements are continually fitted into coincidence with time patterns. With the sense of touch, whether or no two coins fit together and are of the same size can be judged, and a blind man can similarly tell the time by judging the fit of the hands of a watch with raised marks on the watch face. Although visual judgment of coincidence is more widely used in research than is any other, any such observation is in this book referred to as a judgment of coincidence irrespective of whether sight or hearing or any other of the senses are used.

. . . .

SUMMARY OF THE TECHNICAL DEFINITION OF A *FACT*

An examination of human observation shows that agreement between different observers is readily reached without the use of threats or torture if the different observers are set to judge coincidences. These elementary human judgments give the nearest to universal agreement that is ever reached, and are called either coincidence observations or facts. . . .

(1) A common example of the use of coincidence observation in everyday life is in telling the time indicated by a clock, when the observer judges whether or no a hand of the clock coincides with a mark on the clock face.

(2) No measurement can be made without the use of coincidence observation, but coincidence observation is *not* necessarily a measurement. Hence . . . , the subsequent reading of the number against the mark on the clock face is not here regarded as part of the elementary judgment involved in using coincidence observation. The clear distinc-

tion between making an elementary judgment of coincidence and the more complex processes, including combining this with counting to give measurement, is essential for an understanding of parts of this book.

(3) An object is said to be observable by the coincidence method *only* when it can serve as one of the two things between which coincidence is judged. That is, the thing to which the name of the object is attached must directly give sense data; an electron, for example, cannot by definition be observed by the coincidence method.

(4) Coincidence observation is used as a means of separating the sense data usable as basic in science from other sense data and from inference. . . .

(5) . . . The term coincidence observation is used for any observation which, with the current laboratory or field technique, could be observed by judgments of coincidence, no matter whether it has actually been so observed or not. The method is actually applied wherever convenient and is invariably applied in cases of doubt or controversy. In the latter case it serves as the final arbiter at the time it is applied. A dispute about what can be observed in an experiment "is to be decided not by discourse, but by new trial of the experiment." [2]

These statements may be roughly summarized as: Science is based upon human judgments of coincidence. This form differs profoundly from the statement: Science is based upon measurement.

INTERNAL OR PERSONAL OBSERVATION

It may seem on first thoughts irrelevant to consider here another kind of observation which cannot be made by judgment of coincidences and which is not used as a tool in scientific observation. But again it must be remembered that research work is done by human beings, not by machines, and consciousness is a property of man. Stimulus of sense organs may not give an observation if the observer is not paying attention; that is, if he is not aware or conscious of the stimulus. In making observations either with or without the aid of instruments are we conscious of nothing more than the things which can be examined by judgment of coincidences? In practice it is found that we are conscious of other things and that in the present stage of knowledge these other things cannot be examined by coincidence methods. As these other things seem to exert a powerful influence

[2] Newton in a letter dated November 13, 1675.

upon us, and seem very close and "real" to us, they may possibly affect what is done with coincidence observations. It will therefore be regarded as relevant to consider them here. For convenience of reference all such observations which can be studied only by the method of introspection, will be called personal or internal observations to distinguish them from coincidence observations which might be called impersonal or external observations. One or two examples will suffice.

Suppose a man observes a scarlet anemone. He may be conscious of its form and colour and texture and all of these can be studied as coincidence observations. If attention be confined to, say, one of these, the colour, a petal may be illuminated by white light and examined by the spectroscope or with the aid of the photo-electric cell and other instruments, but the sum total of all these coincidence observations of the colour of the petal does not represent all of which the man is conscious relating to the petal before him. To take another example, if a man is suffering from toothache he is certainly conscious of something other than the currents passing along the tooth nerves. He is in fact not conscious of these currents as such. The nerve currents, if they can be observed, are impersonal observations, and the pain is a personal or internal observation which only the man himself can observe. Anger and fear can be similarly examined. In the angry man the external observer may observe such things as a stiffening of the body, flushing, loud speech, temporary holding of the breath, increased blood pressure and pulse rate, and possibly an increase in the amount of blood sugar and in the secretion from the adrenal glands. Some of these changes could be observed by the angry man himself, but in addition he would be conscious of other things about his anger which could not be observed by coincidence methods. These other things would be the personal and internal observations, and whether they are called anger or whether the term is applied to the sum of both the types of observation is a matter of definition. For the present purpose it is enough to note that two different kinds of observation can be made upon an angry man and that one type can be made only by the man himself. Except in the study of introspection the internal type of observation is not consciously used in scientific research. Whether or no it is supposed to have any influence upon the actual carrying out of research depends upon what theory of human action is used. In the formal study of scientific method no account is consciously taken of internal observation, but it would appear that formal scientific method would only yield scientific research results if pure-reason machines were available to apply the method to nature. As it is, research is done by human beings, and they cannot avoid making these internal observations as well as the external or coincidence observations.

This brief discussion of internal observation serves as a caution against saying that in observation, nothing else matters but coincidence observations. To remain scientific, no such extravagant claim must be made. It may be said that men have so far found no other method of observation which in practice leads to such complete agreement between different observers. It is unscientific, however, to say that any object or phenomenon is *nothing but* the aspects of it which can be studied by the coincidence method. When an observer looks at a bed of primroses in a sunlit wood in springtime he must quite frankly admit that some of the things of which he is conscious, and some of which he is not conscious, can in the present state of knowledge be studied by the coincidence method, but others cannot. It may be human, but it is certainly unscientific to refuse to make this admission.

ANALYSIS OF STATEMENTS OF OBSERVATION

The statements of results of observations obtained in scientific research are by no means always given as coincidence observations. In the original publication in scientific journals they can often be found in this form in measurements, but even there the observations are discussed and "interpreted." Later the interpretations are said to have been observed. The more familiar the interpretation becomes, the more are observations which fit into the interpretation referred to in terms of the interpretation alone. Gradually as more and more experimental results fitting the original interpretations are obtained, general terms are necessary for enumeration. There is then a danger that those who are not intimately familiar with what the research workers have done in the laboratory may be unable to separate observation from interpretation. Such difficulty has been found in quantum physics and in certain branches of psychology.

It will be found that wherever statements made about complex scientific observations lead to apparent anomalies these statements can be analysed into three parts. This analysis will often help in clarifying thought about the subsequent use to which the observations are put. The three parts are:

(1) Statements of the external or coincidence observations; that is, the judgments of coincidence made with the aid of one or more of the sense organs.

(2) Statements of the internal or personal observations; those things connected with the subject observed, of which the individual observer alone is conscious and which cannot be observed as coincidences. (These data are used by some psychologists.)

(3) General terms used either to refer to collections of all the separate types of coincidence observations (1) so as to avoid the necessity of enumerating each in turn when the whole group is referred to, or alternatively general terms relating to hypotheses or theories into which the observations are fitted.

Every Man His Own Historian[1]

CARL BECKER

I ought first of all to explain that when I use the term history I mean knowledge of history. No doubt throughout all past time there actually occurred a series of events which, whether we know what it was or not, constitutes history in some ultimate sense. Nevertheless, much the greater part of these events we can know nothing about, not even that they occurred; many of them we can know only imperfectly; and even the few events that we think we know for sure we can never be absolutely certain of, since we can never revive them, never observe or test them directly. The event itself once occurred, but as an actual event it has disappeared; so that in dealing with it the only objective reality we can observe or test is some material trace which the event has left—usually a written document. With these traces of vanished events, these documents, we must be content since they are all we have; from them

[1] From *The American Historical Review*, Vol. XXXVII, No. 2, January, 1932, pp. 221–222, 223–225, 231–232. Reprinted by permission.

we infer what the event was, we affirm that it is a fact that the event was so and so. We do not say "Lincoln is assassinated"; we say "it is a fact that Lincoln was assassinated." The event *was,* but is no longer; it is only the affirmed fact about the event that *is,* that persists, and will persist until we discover that our affirmation is wrong or inadequate. Let us then admit that there are two histories: the actual series of events that once occurred; and the ideal series that we affirm and hold in memory. The first is absolute and unchanged—it was what it was whatever we do or say about it; the second is relative, always changing in response to the increase or refinement of knowledge. The two series correspond more or less, it is our aim to make the correspondence as exact as possible; but the actual series of events exists for us only in terms of the ideal series which we affirm and hold in memory. This is why I am forced to identify history with knowledge of history. For all practical purposes history is, for us and for the time being, what we know it to be. . . .

Since we are concerned with history in its lowest terms, we will suppose that Mr. Everyman is not a professor of history, but just an ordinary citizen without excess knowledge. Not having a lecture to prepare, his memory of things said and done, when he awakened this morning, presumably did not drag into consciousness any events connected with the Liman von Sanders mission or the Pseudo-Isidorian Decretals; it presumably dragged into consciousness an image of things said and done yesterday in the office, the highly significant fact that General Motors had dropped three points, a conference arranged for ten o'clock in the morning, a promise to play nine holes at four-thirty in the afternoon, and other historical events of similar import. Mr. Everyman knows more history than this, but at the moment of awakening this is sufficient: memory of things said and done, history functioning, at seven-thirty in the morning, in its very lowest terms, has effectively oriented Mr. Everyman in his little world of endeavor.

Yet not quite effectively after all perhaps; for unaided memory is notoriously fickle; and it may happen that Mr. Everyman, as he drinks his coffee is uneasily aware of something said or done that he fails now to recall. A common enough occurrence, as we all know to our sorrow— this remembering, not the historical event, but only that there was an event which we ought to remember but can not. This is Mr. Everyman's difficulty, a bit of history lies dead and inert in the sources, unable to do any work for Mr. Everyman because his memory refuses to bring it alive in consciousness. What then does Mr. Everyman do? He does what any historian would do: he does a bit of historical research in the sources. From his little Private Record Office (I mean his vest pocket) he takes a book in MS., volume XXXV, it may be, and turns to page 23, and there he reads: "December 29, pay Smith's coal bill, 20 tons, $1017.20." Instantaneously a series of historical events comes to life in Mr. Everyman's mind. He has an image of himself ordering twenty tons of coal from Smith last summer, of Smith's wagons driving up to his house, and of the precious coal sliding dustily through the cellar window. Historical events, these are, not so important as the forging of the Isidorian Decretals, but still important to Mr. Everyman: historical events which he was not present to observe, but which, by an artificial extension of memory, he can form a clear picture of, because he has done a little original research in the manuscripts preserved in his Private Record Office.

The picture Mr. Everyman forms of Smith's wagons delivering the coal at his house is a picture of things said and done in the past..But it does not stand alone, it is not a pure antiquarian image to be enjoyed for its own sake; on the contrary, it is associated with a picture of things to be said and done in the future; so that throughout the day Mr. Everyman intermittently holds in mind, together with a picture of Smith's coal wagons, a picture of himself going at four o'clock in the afternoon to Smith's office in order to pay his bill. At four o'clock Mr. Everyman is accordingly at Smith's office. "I wish to pay that coal bill," he says. Smith looks dubious and disappointed, takes down a ledger (or a filing case), does a bit of original research in his Private Record Office, and announces: "You don't owe me any money, Mr. Everyman. You ordered the coal here all right, but I didn't have the kind you wanted, and so turned the order over to Brown. It was Brown delivered your coal: he's the man you owe." Whereupon Mr. Everyman goes to Brown's office; and Brown takes down a ledger, does a bit of original research in his Private Record Office, which happily confirms the researches of Smith; and Mr. Everyman pays his bill, and in the evening, after returning from the Country Club, makes a further search in another collection of documents, where, sure enough, he finds a bill from Brown, properly drawn, for twenty tons of stove coal $1017.20. The research is now completed. Since his mind rests satisfied, Mr. Everyman has found the explanation of the series of events that concerned him.

Mr. Everyman would be astonished to learn that he is an historian, yet it is obvious, isn't it, that he has performed all the essential operations involved in historical research. Needing or wanting to do something (which happened to be, not to deliver a lecture or write a book, but to pay a bill; and this is what misleads him and us as to what he is really doing), the first step was to recall things said and done. Unaided memory proving inadequate, a further step was essential—the examination of certain documents in order to discover the necessary but as yet unknown facts. Unhappily the documents were found to give conflicting reports, so that a critical comparison of the texts had to be instituted in order to eliminate error. All this having been satisfactorily accomplished, Mr. Everyman is ready for the final operation—the formation in his mind, by an artificial extension of memory, of a picture, a definitive picture let us hope, of a selected series of historical events— of himself ordering coal from Smith, of Smith turning the order over to Brown, and of Brown delivering the coal at his house. In the light of this picture Mr. Everyman could, and did, pay his bill. If Mr. Everyman had undertaken these researches in order to write a book instead of to pay a bill, no one would think of denying that he was an historian. . . .

History as the artificial extension of the social memory (and I willingly concede that there are other appropriate ways of apprehending human experience) is an art of long standing, necessarily so since it springs instinctively from the impulse to enlarge the range of immediate experience; and however camouflaged by the disfiguring jargon of science, it is still in essence what it has always been. History in this sense is story, in aim always a true story: a story that employs all the devices of literary art (statement and generalization, narration and description, comparison and comment and analogy) to present the succession of events in the life of man, and from the succession of events thus presented to derive a satisfactory meaning. The history written by historians, like the history informally fashioned by Mr. Everyman, is thus a convenient blend of truth and fancy, of what we commonly distinguished as "fact" and "interpretation." In primitive times, when tradition is orally transmitted, bards and story-tellers frankly embroider or improvise the facts to heighten the dramatic import of the story. With the use of written records, history, gradually differentiated from fiction, is understood as the story of events that actually occurred; and with the increase and refinement of knowledge the historian recognizes that his first duty is to be sure of his facts, let their meaning be what it may. Nevertheless, in every age history is taken to be a story of actual events from which a significant meaning may be derived; and in every age the illusion is that the present version is valid because the related facts are true, whereas former versions are invalid because based upon inaccurate or inadequate facts.

Literature as Revelation[1]

GILBERT MURRAY

The great difference, intellectually speaking, between one man and another is simply the number of things they can see in a given cubic yard of world. Do you remember Huxley's famous lecture on *A Piece of Chalk,* delivered to the working men of Norwich in 1868, and how the piece of chalk told him secrets of the infinite past, secrets of the unfathomed depths of the sea? The same thing happens with a book. I remember once picking up a copy of *Macbeth* belonging to the great Shakespearian scholar, Andrew Bradley, and reading casually his pencilled notes in the margin. The scene was one which I knew by heart and thought I understood; but his notes showed me that I had missed about half a dozen points on every page. It seems to me that the writers who have the power of revelation are just those who, in some particular part of life, have seen or felt considerably more than the average run of intelligent human beings. It is this specific power of seeing or feeling more things to the cubic yard in some part of the world that makes a writer's work really inspiring.

To have felt and seen more than other people in some particular region of life: Does that give us any sort of guarantee that the judgments which a man passes are likely to be true? Not in the least. Suppose a man has seen and experienced some particular corner of, say, the Battle of the Somme and can give you a thrilling and terrific

[1] From *Tradition and Progress.* Boston: Houghton Mifflin Company, 1922, pp. 131–136. Reprinted by permission of Gilbert Murray.

account of it, that is no particular reason for expecting that his views about the war as a whole will be true. It is on the whole likely that he will see things in a wrong proportion. The point in his favour is only that he does really know *something,* and, whatever his general views are, he can help you to know something. I will confess my own private belief, which I do not wish anyone to share, that of all the books and all the famous sayings that have come as a revelation to human beings, not one is strictly true or has any chance of being true. Nor, if you press me, do I really think it is their business to be strictly true. They are not meant to be statements of fact. They are cries of distress, calls of encouragement, signals flashing in the darkness; they seem to be statements in the indicative mood, but they are really in the imperative or the optative—the moods of command or prayer or longing; they often make their effect not by what they say but by the tone in which they say it, or even by the things they leave unsaid.

Do you remember Garibaldi's speech to his men when his defense of Rome had proved fruitless, and the question was whether to make terms with the Austrians or to follow him? "Let those who wish to continue the War against the stranger come with me. I offer neither pay nor quarters nor provisions. I offer hunger, thirst, forced marches, battles and death." The force of that appeal was in what he did not say. He obviously offered them something else too; something so glorious that as a matter of fact most of them followed him; but he did not mention it.

Sometimes the word of revelation is a metaphor; the speaker knows he cannot attain exact truth, he can only, as it were, signal in the direction of it. There is a wonderful story in a little-read Saxon historian, who wrote in Latin, the Venerable Bede, about the conversion of the Saxons to Christianity. The King was debating whether or no to accept the new religion, and consulted his counsellors. And one old Pagan warrior said: "Do you remember how last midwinter King Edwin held festival in the great hall, with brands burning and two huge fires on the hearths, while outside there was storm and utter darkness? And the windows by the roof being open, a bird flew suddenly from the darkness outside into the warm and lighted place and out on the other side into the outer darkness. Like that bird is the life of man."

Or what again shall we say of the following? A message sent many years ago by the famous Russian revolutionary, Katherine Breshkovsky

—the grandmother of the Revolution as she is called; a message smuggled out of prison and sent to her friends and followers bidding them not to despair or to think that nothing was being accomplished: "Day and night we labour; instead of meat, drink and sleep we have dreams of Freedom. It is youth calling to youth through prison walls and across the world." It seems like a series of statements which it is hard to describe as either true or not true. Yet I doubt if it is really a statement; it is more like a call in the night.

Or take the saying of one of the ancient rabbis after the fall of Jerusalem, when the heathen had conquered the holy places and to a pious Jew the very roots of life seemed to be cut: "Zion is taken from us; nothing is left save the Holy One and His Law." Nothing is left save the Holy One and His Law. Does it not seem at the same time to say two things: that nothing is left, and that everything is left that really matters? All is lost, and nothing that matters is lost. The message has just that quality of self-contradiction which shows that it is not saying all it means, that it is pointing to something beyond itself, calling the hearer's attention not to a fact but to a mystery.

Or take one of the greatest and simplest of all these burning words, the word of a Greek philosopher of a late and decadent period, who has nevertheless made a great stir in the world: "Though I speak with the tongues of men and of angels, and have not charity, I am but a sounding brass or a tinkling cymbal. Though I give my body to be burned, and have not charity, it profiteth me nothing." Who can analyse that into a statement of fact?

By now, I think, we have reached a point where we can formulate a further conclusion about these words of inspiration or revelation. They never are concerned with direct scientific fact or even with that part of experience which is capable of being expressed in exact statement. They are concerned not with that part of our voyage which is already down in the Admiralty charts. They are concerned with the part that is uncharted; the part that is beyond the mist, whither no one has travelled, or at least whence no one has brought back a clear account. They are all in the nature of the guess that goes before scientific knowledge; the impassioned counsel of one who feels strongly but cannot, in the nature of things, prove his case. This fact explains three things about them: their emotional value, their importance, and their weakness. Their weakness is that they are never exactly true, because they are never based on exact knowledge. Their importance is that they are dealing with the part of the journey that is just ahead of us, the hidden ground beyond the next ridge which matters to us now more than all the rest of the road. Their emotional value is intense just because they are speaking of the thing we most long to know, and in which the edge of the emotion is not dulled by exact calculations. A good Moslem believes in Mohammed far more passionately than any one believes in the multiplication table. That is just because in the case of the multiplication table he *knows* and is done with it; in the case of Mohammed he does not *know,* and makes up for his lack of knowledge by passionate feeling.

Knowledge by Definition [1]

VILHJALMUR STEFANSSON

It is said that Bacon considered all knowledge his province. But the sciences of to-day are so many and complex that a single Baconian view of them is no longer possible, and perversions of thought and action result because our intellectual horizon has been narrowed to a part of the field. From a realization of this have come various attempts to co-ordinate the sciences to permit a unifying view of the whole. The French philosopher, Comte, made one of these a century ago in his Positive Philosophy. There have been many since.

But if we pause to state clearly the case against the standardization of knowledge, the essential absurdity becomes so patent that we have to recall the numerous failures to convince ourselves that anyone was ever foolish enough even to try it.

Consider for instance the physiology of the human skin or the composition of a dust nebula. In these fields, among others, the accepted facts of a dozen years ago have become the error and folk-lore of to-

[1] From *The Standardization of Error.* London: Kegan Paul, Trench, Trubner & Co., Ltd., 1928, pp. 7–23. Copyright, 1936, by Vilhjalmur Stefansson. Reprinted by permission.

day. You standardize knowledge, and while you are at the job the knowledge changes. Long before the thing can be adequately done it has ceased being worth doing at all.

Then why are we continually attempting this hopeless task? Partly, let us say, from irrepressible human optimism, which leads us to think that any desirable thing is possible. Partly, also, because of unclear analogizing from fields that seem related but are not. One of these analogies is from business. If you have on hand, on July 1st, a pair of socks, you will have them still on hand on August 1st, or else cash in your till to correspond, assuming honest and successful management. But, in spite of unlimited honesty and efficiency, you have no guarantee that an idea on hand on July 1st may not have been simply removed by August 1st without any equivalent remaining on hand. You may have discovered that month, for instance, reasonable assurance that the moon is *not* made of green cheese, without being able to get any clear idea as to what it *is* made of.

The reader may here jump to the conclusion that we are arriving at a philosophy of pessimistic hopelessness. That is not the way of the true philosopher. His ideal is the *tabula rasa*. He sweeps away the systems of others, that he may build his own on a smooth foundation.

Realizing simultaneously the insatiable craving of the human mind for order and the impossibility of bringing order into the chaos of knowledge, we appear to be faced with a dilemma no less distressing than insoluble. But on looking deeper we find the dilemma apparent only. This will become clear when we consider the essential nature of knowledge.

The thoughtless among us may speak, for instance, of a red cow, and naively imagine we could prove our point with the testimony of a witness or two. But the philosophers have long ago made it clear that a cow would not be red but for the presence of someone to whom it looks red. Having established that point, the deeper of the philosophers go on to prove that the cow would not only not be red, but would not even exist, were it not for the presence of someone who thinks he sees a cow. In our argument the position is even stronger than this, for we have two lines of defence. First, we agree with the philosopher that you cannot prove of any given cow that it is red, or even that it exists at all; secondly, we insist that an idea is so much less stable than a cow that, even were the philosophers wrong about the cow not being red, they might easily be right about an idea not being right or not existing. Take an example. The philosophers of the Middle Ages demonstrated both that the earth did not exist and also that it was flat. Today they are still arguing about whether the world exists, but they no longer dispute about whether it is flat. This shows the greater lasting power of a real thing (whether it exists or not, for that point has not yet been settled) as compared with an idea, which may not only not exist, but may also be wrong even if it does exist.

We have now come in our discussion to the point where we see the absurdity of supposing ourselves to have any knowledge, as knowledge is ordinarily defined—or at least we would have come to that point but for lack of space which prevents us from making the subject really clear. However, it doesn't matter from a practical point of view whether you have followed this philosophical reasoning. Perhaps you are not a philosopher. In that case, and in the homely phrase of the day, I ask you, what's the good of an Englishman's learning, first, that all Americans speak through their noses, and, secondly, why they do so, when he has to find out eventually that they do not? What's the good, again, of learning that most Eskimos live in snow houses, when you may discover later that most of them have never seen a snow house?

Such things do not always go in triplets of (1) so it is, (2) why it is, and (3) it is not—but that is a common order.

The reader may here protest that we are not getting much nearer our promised emancipation from the dilemma between our passion for system and the impossibility of systematizing knowledge. We have hinted above that the solution lies in finding a new basis for knowledge, and this we now proceed to do.

So long as you believe in them, the nasality of American speech and the prevalance of snow houses among the Eskimos are fragments of knowledge capable of being arranged in a system. The trouble comes when you discover that they are "untrue."

This gives the solution of our problem. We must have knowledge that is incapable of being contradicted. On first thought this seems impossible, but on second thought we realize that such facts do exist in the domain of mathematics. Two and two make four.

But why do two and two make four? Obviously because we have agreed that four is the name for the sum of two and two. That principle has been applied in mathematics to such advantage that it is rightly called the science of sciences; and this is the principle which, now at length, we propose to apply to all knowledge. Through it every science will become a pure science, and all knowledge as open to systematization as mathematics.

The trouble with facts, outside mathematics, has been inherent in the methods of gathering information. We call these methods *observation* and *experiment,* and have even been proud of them—not realizing their clumsy nature, the unreliability of the findings, the transient character of the best of them, and the essential hopelessness of classifying the results and thus gratifying the passion of the human intellect for order and symmetry in the universe.

Take an example. A man comes from out-of-doors with the report that there is a red cow in the front yard. Neglecting for the moment the philosophical aspect of the case—as to whether the cow would be red if there were no one to whom she seemed red, and also the more fundamental problem of whether there would have been any cow at all if no one had gone out to look—neglecting, as I say, the deeper aspects of the case, we are confronted with numerous other sources of error. The observer may have confused the sex of the animal. Perhaps it was an ox. Or if not the sex, the age may have been misjudged, and it may have been a heifer. The man may have been colour-blind, and the cow (wholly apart from the philosophical aspect) may not have been red. And even if it was a red cow, the dog may have seen her the instant our observer turned his back, and by the time he told us she was in the front yard, she may in reality have been vanishing in a cloud of dust down the road.

The trouble lies evidently in our clumsy system of observing and reporting. This difficulty has been obviated in the science of mathematics. A square is, not by observation but by definition, a four-sided figure with equal sides and equal angles. No one has denied that and no one can, for the simple reason that we have all agreed in advance that we will never deny it. Nay more, we have agreed that if anyone says that a square has three or five sides we will all reply in chorus: "If it has three or five sides it is not a square!" That disposes of the matter for ever.

Why not agree similarly on the attributes of a front yard?—making it true by definition that, among other things, it contains a red cow. Then if anyone asserts, for reasons of philosophy, colour-blindness, or the officiousness of dogs, that there is no red cow in the yard, we can reply, as in the case of the square: "If it does not contain a red cow, it is not a front yard!"

The author feels at this point a doubtless unwarranted concern that he is not being taken seriously. Or perhaps the plan proposed is not considered practical. But the proof of the pudding is in the eating. The thing has been tried, and successfully—not in the systematic way now proposed, but sporadically. Some instances are well known and convincing.

Take the assertion that a Christian is a good man. If you attempt to deny this on the ground that Jones, a deacon in the church, ran off with some public funds, your stricture is at once shown to have been absurd by the simple reply: "If Jones was a thief, he was *not* a Christian." A Christian is, not by observation but by definition, a good man; if you prove that a certain man was not good you merely show that he was not a Christian. Thus we have established once and for ever the fact that a Christian is a good man. It is like a square having four sides.

But if someone asserts that a Bolshevik, a Conservative, or a chemist is a good man, you can soon confute him; for the members of these classes have neglected to define themselves as good. Thus their attributes have to be determined by observation and experiment (after you have first run the gauntlet of the philosophers who ask whether the Bolsheviks could be good without the presence of someone who considers them good, and further whether any Bolsheviks would exist at all but for certain people who think they exist). It is highly probable that evidence could be brought against almost any given Bolshevik and even some Conservatives to show that they are not good men. At any rate, we have here no such clarity of issue as in things that are true by definition—as the four-sidedness of a square or the goodness of a Christian.

Through some experience of arguing this case in the abstract I have learned that its essential reasonableness can best be established from concrete examples. Let us, then, take cases at random from various fields of knowledge.

Consider first the ostriches of Africa. These birds have been studied in the wild by sportsmen and zoologists, and as domestic animals by husbandmen who tend them in flocks like sheep. There are accordingly thousands of printed pages in our libraries giving what purports to be information upon their habits. Besides being indefinite and in many ways otherwise faulty, this alleged information is in part contradictory.

Having studied the bird of Africa, let us turn next to the ostrich of literature, philosophy, and morals. Instead of the confusion in the case of the ostrich of zoology, we have clarity and precision. This is because the ostrich of literature exists by definition only. He is a bird that hides his head when frightened. You may too precipitately object that men would not accept universally this definition of the ostrich of literature if it did not fit also the zoological ostrich. The answer is that the definition has never received any support from zoologists, hunters, or owners of the domesticated birds, and yet it has been accepted universally throughout Europe since Pliny's time (about 50 B.C.). It has survived all attacks from science and from the bigoted common-sense of those who did not recognize its true nature. Like the definition of a four-sided square or a good Christian, it has survived because it was useful. Can you imagine any real attribute more instructive than the head-burying of the ostrich-by-definition? As a text for moralists, as an epithet that politicians use for their opponents, as a figure of speech generally, what could serve as well? Our literature is richer, our vocabulary more picturesque through this beneficent bird of hypothesis. He has many inherent advantages that no real bird could have. Since his habits are defined we need not waste time studying him first hand, nor in trying to adjudicate at second hand between books about him that disagree. Since he never existed as a beast, he is in no danger of the extinction that is said to threaten the lion and swan.

Consider next what trouble we should get into if we did not have the literary ostrich and wanted to convey picturesquely the idea of that sort of wilful blindness from which we ourselves never suffer, but which curiously afflicts our opponents. In pursuit of suitable analogy we might vainly canvass the whole animal kingdom. The ostrich-by-definition is, therefore, not only less trouble to deal with than a real bird; he is actually more useful and instructive than any real bird or beast. When we consider how often he has been used in sermon and precept we must admit that this model creature has contributed substantially, not only to the entertainment and instruction of nations, but also to the morality and general goodness of the world.

The ostrich is but one of several useful birds of definition. But we must be careful not to confuse these with real birds or their value is lessened. An example is the stork that brings babies. By a confusion of thought which identifies this stork with real storks, and through the pernicious birth-control propaganda which insists on rationalizing everything, the baby-bringing stork has ceased to be useful except in conversation with children, in the symbolism of the movie, and in the picture post-card industry.

The wolves of literature are among the most picturesque and useful of our definitions. Zoological wolves go in pairs or families, never above a dozen. It is obvious how inadequate this would be for modern movie purposes, where they should run in packs of scores or hundreds. Even in a novel or short story of Siberia or Canada you need packs large enough for the hero to kill fifteen or twenty, with enough left over to eat or to be about to eat his sweetheart. This is easily accomplished by employing a wolf of the general type we advocate—having no relation to the so-called realities but possessing by definition all the required characteristics (habit of running in packs of any desired size, willingness to eat, or attempt to eat, the heroine, etc.).

Another useful definition has long been that of Arctic, Canadian, and Siberian cold. The danger and disadvantage of confusing this hypothetical with a so-called real climate are best seen if we compare the facility with which people who have never been in these countries use the weather in conversation, speeches, and books, and contrast that facility with the awkwardness of travellers and natives. An example is a story by Tolstoi. Great as he was, he failed to realize the advantage in simplicity and vividness of postulating that Siberia is always cold, and actually allowed himself to be led into the artistic blunder of having the convicts in one of his novels die of sunstroke. An acquaintance of mine was filming this story. He realized the pictorial ease of "putting over" drifting snow as compared with heat waves—the snow could be managed with confetti and an aeroplane propeller, but how would one photograph heat waves? But he realized still more clearly that the public is wedded to the defined, as opposed to the "real" climate of Siberia, and did what Tolstoi would have done in the first place had he lived in London—changed the scene from summer to winter, and then froze to death as many convicts as the picture required.

These few examples from among many will suffice to show not only that the method of knowledge-by-definition is and long has been in standard use, but also that it has the advantages of being easily grasped, picturesque, and of a higher average moral value than the so-called "real" knowledge. It is inherent in the genesis and nature of defined facts that they can be made picturesque in proportion to the ingenuity of the one who defines them, and as moral as necessary. This is a striking advantage over empirical knowledge, which cannot always be relied on to support the fashion of the time or even the moral system of the community.

Physics and Reality [1]

ALBERT EINSTEIN AND LEOPOLD INFELD

━━━━━━━━━━━━━━━━━━

Science is not just a collection of laws, a catalogue of unrelated facts. It is a creation of the human mind, with its freely invented ideas and concepts. Physical theories try to form a picture of reality and to establish its connection with the wide world of sense impressions. Thus the only justification for our mental structures is whether and in what way our theories form such a link.

We have seen new realities created by the advance of physics. But this chain of creation can be traced back far beyond the starting point of physics. One of the most primitive concepts is that of an object. The concepts of a tree, a horse, any material body, are creations gained on the basis of experience, though the impressions from which they arise are primitive in comparison with the world of physical phenomena. A cat teasing a mouse also creates, by thought, its own primitive reality. The fact that the cat reacts in a similar way toward any mouse it meets shows that it forms concepts and theories which are its guide through its own world of sense impressions.

"Three trees" is something different from "two trees." Again "two trees" is different from "two stones." The concepts of the pure numbers 2, 3, 4 . . . , freed from the objects from which they arose, are creations of the thinking mind which describe the reality of our world.

The psychological subjective feeling of time enables us to order our impressions, to state that one event precedes another. But to connect

[1] From *The Evolution of Physics*. New York: Simon and Schuster, 1938, pp. 310–313. Copyright, 1938, by Albert Einstein and Leopold Infeld. Reprinted by permission of Leopold Infeld.

every instant of time with a number, by the use of a clock, to regard time as a one-dimensional continuum, is already an invention. So also are the concepts of Euclidean and non-Euclidean geometry, and our space understood as a three-dimensional continuum.

Physics really began with the invention of mass, force, and an inertial system. These concepts are all free inventions. They led to the formulation of the mechanical point of view. For the physicist of the early nineteenth century, the reality of our outer world consisted of particles with simple forces acting between them and depending only on the distance. He tried to retain as long as possible his belief that he would succeed in explaining all events in nature by these fundamental concepts of reality. The difficulties connected with the deflection of the magnetic needle, the difficulties connected with the structure of the ether, induced us to create a more subtle reality. The important invention of the electromagnetic field appears. A courageous scientific imagination was needed to realize fully that not the behavior of bodies, but the behavior of something between them, that is, the field, may be essential for ordering and understanding events.

Later developments both destroyed old concepts and created new ones. Absolute time and the inertial co-ordinate system were abandoned by the relativity theory. The background for all events was no longer the one-dimensional time and the three-dimensional space continuum, but the four-dimensional time-space continuum, another free invention, with new transformation properties. The inertial co-ordinate system was no longer needed. Every co-ordinate system is equally suited for the description of events in nature.

The quantum theory again created new and essential features of our reality. Discontinuity replaced continuity. Instead of laws governing individuals, probability laws appeared.

The reality created by modern physics is, indeed, far removed from the reality of the early days. But the aim of every physical theory still remains the same.

With the help of physical theories we try to find our way through the maze of observed facts, to order and understand the world of our sense impressions. We want the observed facts to follow logically from our concept of reality. Without the belief that it is possible to grasp the reality with our theoretical constructions, with the belief in the inner harmony of our world, there could be no science. This belief is and always will remain the fundamental motive for all scientific creation. Throughout all our efforts, in every dramatic struggle between old and new views, we recognize the eternal longing for understanding, the ever-firm belief in the harmony of our world, continually strengthened by the increasing obstacles to comprehension.

On the Logic of Fiction [1]

MORRIS R. COHEN

=====

THE LOGIC OF METAPHORS—FIGURATIVE TRUTH

To appreciate the intellectual or scientific function of metaphors the reader had better begin with an experiment. Let him pick out a page or two of philosophic prose in any classical treatise or modern discussion. Let him read this extract carefully and mark the number of passages in which the meaning is suggested metaphorically rather than literally. Let him then read the passage a second time and reflect how many of the passages first taken as literal truths are really metaphors to which we have become accustomed. I mean such expressions as "the root of the problem," "the progress of thought," "the higher life," "falling into error," "mental gymnastics," and the like. Indeed, whenever we speak of the mind doing anything, collecting its data, perceiving the external world, and the like, we are using the metaphor of reification, just as we use the metaphor of personification whenever we speak of bodies attracting and repelling each other. The third stage of the experiment is to try to rewrite the passage in strictly literal terms without any metaphors at all. I believe that the result of such experiment will confirm the conclusion that to eliminate all metaphors is impossible. This is especially clear when we try to express general considerations of a novel or unfamiliar character. For, how can we apprehend new relations except by viewing them under old categories? At any rate, the experi-

---

[1] From *A Preface to Logic* by Morris R. Cohen, pp. 82–90. Copyright, 1944, by Henry Holt and Company, Inc. Reprinted by permission.

ment will make more plausible the view that metaphors are not merely artificial devices for making discourse more vivid and poetical, but are also necessary for the apprehension and communication of new ideas. This is confirmed by the history of language and of early poetry as well as by the general results of modern psychology.

The prevailing view since Aristotle's *Rhetoric* regards every metaphor as an analogy in which the words of comparison, *like* or *as,* etc., are omitted. This presupposes that the recognition of the literal truth precedes the metaphor, which is thus always a conscious transference of the properties of one thing to another. But history shows that metaphors are generally older than expressed analogies. If intelligence grows from the vague and confused to the more definite by the process of discrimination, we may well expect that the motion common to animate and inanimate beings should impress us even before we have made a clear distinction between these two kinds of being. Thus it is not necessary to suppose that the child that kicks the chair against which it has stumbled personifies the chair by the process of analogy. The reaction is clearly one arising on the undifferentiated level.

Metaphors may thus be viewed as expressing the vague and confused but primal perception of identity which subsequent processes of discrimination transform into the clear assertion of an identity or common element (or relation) which the two different things possess. This helps us to explain the proper function of metaphors in science as well as in religion and art, and cautions us against fallacious arguments for or against views expressed in metaphorical language.

1. The Function of Metaphors in Science.

If it is true that the first perceptions of the new in experience tend to assume metaphoric expression, metaphors must play a large part in opening up new fields of science. In its search for the truth science must formulate some anticipation of what it expects to find. Such anticipation is clearly not fictional even if it turns out to be false, provided it has been held as an hypothesis to be tested. In trying to visualize the unknown, the imagination must clothe it with attributes analogous to the known. That this is actually the case a few examples will indicate:

(a) In the science of electricity the notion of an electric fluid was really never more than a metaphor. But it suggested many fruitful analogies, such as differences of level, direction of flow, etc. Faraday's suggestion of lines or tubes of force may have been taken by many in a more or less literal sense, but the present electron theory shows that it was a metaphor, justified in its day by the fruitful analogies to which it led.

(b) In psychology the metaphor of "states of mind" led to analogies such as the association of ideas, which laid the beginning of modern psychology. James' metaphor of "stream of consciousness" has led to an emphasis on the more continuous aspects of mental life. His analogy between habit and the way paper creased on a given line will always fold more readily on that line, illustrates the power as well as the snares of metaphoric illumination in science.

(c) In metaphysics the idea that the world is a machine working according to mechanical laws, or that it is an organism developing according to a fixed plan, is clearly metaphoric. So is the analysis of everything into substance and inherent qualities, analogous to a man and his possessions or clothes. It is well known that the categories of cause, force, law, are anthropomorphic in origin and were thus originally metaphors.

Each of these, like the various mechanical models of ether or of various unknown physical processes, suggests verifiable analogies and thus directs research. If these directions turn out false, our analogy has acted like a false hypothesis. But the term *fiction* may be applied to certain imaginary and unverifiable entities that vivify our conceptions but are strictly irrelevant to the truth or falsity of our conclusions. Thus Helmholz's and Poincaré's one- and two-dimensional beings, Maxwell's "sorting demon," and similar entities in social science, are really metaphors to express abstract relations. Where one of the figures is used any one of an infinity of others could be substituted, just as, according to Poincaré's proof, wherever a mechanical model is used an infinity of others is possible. When, therefore, these metaphors are taken literally we have the myths of which popular science is full.

It must be recognized, however, that metaphors are not always invented to vivify discourse. They are often the way in which creative minds perceive things, so that the explicit recognition that we are dealing with an analogy rather than a real identity comes later as a result of further reflection or analysis. Though undiscriminating, such primitive perception is likely to be most vivid and its apt expression becomes current coin, so that it becomes difficult if not impossible to distinguish between metaphor and literal truth.

As the essence of science is the search for truth, it seeks to eliminate these irrelevant fictions through the use of technical terms or symbols that denote the abstract relations studied and nothing else. But as no human terms can adequately express (though they can point to or adumbrate) the unknown, science is engaged in an endless process of self-correction and revision of its language. Such a process is irksome to popular discourse and to the social sciences to the extent that they depend on the latter. Hence our language becomes a prolific source of mythology.

2. Practical Value of Metaphors.

The fact that metaphors express the primal perception of things with something of its undifferentiated atmosphere gives these metaphors an emotional power which more elaborate and accurate statements do not have. This is perhaps best seen in the profoundly simple metaphors of the New Testament. "Feed my sheep" is more potent than "teach my doctrine" because it carries with it the atmosphere of suggestion which those genuinely moved to preaching feel before they can formulate it— the tender sympathy to the helpless, the distress of the spiritually hungry, shown especially in the tense, open-mouthed faces of an oriental audience, etc. The same is true of the simile "sowing the seed of truth," or St. Paul's metaphor of preaching as "edification," of the righteous life as "girding on the armor of light," "garrisoning or fortifying the heart." Goethe's metaphor "Gray is all theory" is a vivid expression of what it would require considerable reflection to formulate in purely literal terms. So in practical affairs, the personifying of cities or nations, the likening of the state to a ship ("don't rock the boat"), or of changes of attitude to "the swing of the pendulum," contains a potency which literal statements do not have.

3. Fallacies.

Various fallacies result from the inadequate realization of the metaphoric character of many propositions. Locke's metaphor of the mind as a *tabula rasa* illustrates the general principle. It is obviously fallacious to argue against this, as some have done, that the mind is neither a *tabula* nor *rasa* and that nothing literally makes impressions on the mind, as a stylus on a wax tablet. If there is any respect in which the metaphor can be transformed into a true analogy all these arguments are futile. Obviously there are many such analogies: e.g., the greater vividness of the first impressions, or the greater receptivity of the original state. But it is obvious, also, that this metaphor leads to many false analogies, e.g., the conception of the mind as purely passive or receptive in sensation.

Similar considerations hold with respect to such metaphors as social organism, social forces, or the external world.

This point of view will prevent us from misunderstanding the influence of symbols, and from committing the fallacy involved in the ordinary contemptuous reference to fetishism. The Hebrews could not understand the psychology of Greek and Roman "idol" worshipers, simply because the Greek idols were not to the Hebrews familiar symbols carrying with them vital penumbras of meaning. The Hebrews themselves, of course, had their own symbolic objects, the stones in the ark of the covenant, the scroll of the law (in later times), etc. That a sharp distinction between any symbolic object and that which it symbolizes is not primary, is illustrated by a debate in our own House of Representatives. Upon being pressed as to his attitude to the country's flag, the Socialist Congressman replied that he regarded the flag as but the symbol of the life of the people and that he respected the people, etc. The distinction was entirely too subtle for a Democratic congressman from Texas, who kept on pressing Congressman London as to his attitude to the flag itself.

CEREMONIAL EXPRESSIONS

1. Literal and Conventional Meanings.

Though it cannot be denied that every proposition is either true or false, a great many fallacies result if we ignore conventional meaning. Thus medieval poetry is full of allusions to the fragrance of the daisy. But it would be erroneous to argue that Chaucer did not know that actual daisies have no scent. The expression is conventional, like *"my dear sir,"* or *"your humble servant will meet you on the field of honor."*

It is well known that just as men and women will not wear the same clothes on radically different occasions, they will not use the same modes of expression. We do not use precisely the same language in public address as in private conversation, in writing as in speech, in poetry as in prose. This is generally recognized, but its logical significance has not been sufficiently attended to. Thus the common courtesy which refers to persons or groups by the characteristics which they would like or ought to have, is fruitful of much intellectual confusion. Many, for example, have built elaborate arguments on the assumption that Christian nations are monogamous and that Mohammedans are polygamous, though it is extremely doubtful whether in point of fact there is any great actual difference other than the question of legal status. This is true of the old arguments from the maxim that the king could do no wrong, or the modern ones that in a democratic country the law is the will of the people, that law leaves everyone free, that it protects the poor equally as well as the rich, etc. These statements are in a sense true, but are dubious on the ordinary factual level. Sometimes it is, of course, doubtful whether expressions are or are not intended to be taken literally, e.g., when the Japanese admiral attributes a victory to the virtue of the emperor, or when army bulletins attribute victories to "the will of God and the courage of our troops."

The role of ceremonial expressions in the outer forms of make-believe is as important in social life generally as in the games of children and of primitive man. The social life of a country like England may be viewed as a game that requires among other things that the people should speak of His Majesty's army, navy, or treasury (though the debt is national), and that the actual leaders of the government should speak of "advising" the king where the latter has practically no choice but to obey.

2. Euphemisms.

Ceremonial expressions are often attacked as conventional lies when they are intended not to deceive but to express the truth euphemistically. Courtesy or politeness demands the elimination not necessarily of the truth, but of certain unpleasant expressions that are for some reason or other taboo. This is readily explained by the fact that words have emotional effects on their own account. Thus it is permissible to refer to a female (or lady) dog, but bad taste to use the single-syllabled word. It is proper for the stage pirates in *Peter Pan* to refer to a future meeting "below," but they would shock the audience if they used the more realistic and theologically canonical word. It is a similar desire to avoid the direct admission of a disagreeable truth, *viz.,* that judges are not merely umpires but also make the law, that has led to the great host of legal fictions in the Anglo-American common law. It would be absurd to regard these fictions as false propositions. They are rather resolutions to extend certain legal rights. When the courts insist that the high seas are in the parish of Mary Le Bone in London, they mean to assert not an absurd impossibility, but merely that they will take jurisdiction of acts occurring on the high seas as if they had occurred in London; and in doing so they may be perfectly consistent. An adopted son is not a natural son, but he is entitled to the same rights. So with the fiction of the legal (not natural) personality of corporations. Though these fictions border on, they can be distinguished from, myths which are genuinely believed, and from pious frauds which are intended to deceive in the aid of a good cause. The Roman jurists explained such fictions by means of the Greek philosophic distinction between convention and nature.

Why, however, does not the law use accurate expressions instead of asserting as a fact that which need not be so? Why assert that a corporation *is* a person, instead of saying that a certain group of rights and duties are analogous, to some extent, to those of a natural person? Why say that the United States Embassy in China or on a boat at sea is on American soil, when we mean that certain legal relations in or concerning it are to be treated according to the law of the United States? The answer, in part, is that the practical convenience of brevity outweighs the theoretic gain of greater accuracy. But more important is the fact that at all times, and not merely in "primitive" society where legislatures are not functioning, the law must grow by assimilating the new to old situations, and in moments of innovation we cling, all the more, to old linguistic forms.

From the point of view of social policy fictions are, like eloquence, important in giving the emotional drive to propositions that we wish to see accepted. They can be used to soften the shock of innovation (as when the courts protect a man's vines by calling them *trees*), or to keep up a pleasant veneration for truths which we have abandoned (as when we give new allegoric meaning to old theologic dogmas that are no longer tenable). The confusions, however, between the literal and conventional meaning have been a fruitful source of fallacious reasoning. For if fictions sometimes facilitate change they often hinder it by cultivating an undue regard for the past. If social interest in truth were to prevail, we should in our educational and social policies encourage greater regard for literal accuracy even when it hurts national pride and social sensibilities. But no one has seriously suggested penalizing rhetoric and poetic eloquence in the discussion of social issues. The interest in truth is in fact not as great as in the preservation of cherished beliefs, even though the latter involve ultimate illusions whose pleasantness is more or less temporary.

Fictions, Hypotheses and Dogmas [1]

JEROME FRANK

Hans Vaihinger suggests a new and fruitful classification which divides all ideas, theories, into "fictions," "hypotheses," and "dogmas." A dogma is an idea unhesitatingly accepted as a correct statement about reality; as Vaihinger uses the word, it means what we often call a "fact" or a "law." Where some doubt as to the "objective reality of an idea exists, it is an hypothesis—a statement of what is perhaps "objectively" correct. Where, however, we use an idea as a means to aid thinking, but with no belief that it does or will ever correspond to reality, then it is a fiction. A dogma says, "This is so." An hypothesis says, "Perhaps this is so, let's see if it is." A fiction says, "This isn't so, but let's pretend that it is, let's act 'as if' it were so." An hypothesis, says Vaihinger, "hopes" to coincide with reality; it demands verification; it is an assumption" which, it is expected, will probably turn out to correspond to the truth. A fiction "is not concerned to assert a real fact but to assert something by means of which reality can be dealt with and grasped"; it is a statement of an erroneous fact with knowledge of its falsity. It is a "useful lie" recognized as such; if put forward in an effort to deceive, it is a "lie" in the usual sense; and if men generally believe it, it is a dogma or "myth." Now, says Vaihinger, the history of thought shows, curiously, that a given idea may be first expressed as a fiction, subsequently become an hypothesis, and later turn into a myth, a dogma, a "law," or even a "fact"; the shift may subsequently be from dogma, myth, or law to mere fiction.

Vaihinger has been criticized because, at times, he seems to suggest that all thought is "fictional," that thinking consists entirely of "useful lies." Yet his position, while an exaggeration, nevertheless can be taken as a helpful restatement of the attitude of undogmatic scientists towards scientific theories and "self-evident" truths. For, as those scientists

---

[1] From *Fate and Freedom*, pp. 184–187. Copyright, 1945, by Jerome N. Frank. Reprinted by permission of Simon and Schuster, Inc.

recognize, thinking about nature, so far as it rests on the assumption that man knows, or will someday know, all the facts about nature, is fictional—which is to say that that assumption is not self-evident.

The fictionizing does not stop with that assumption. All thinking starts with some earlier idea which has proved satisfactory and has become familiar. The thinker employs this idea as a model, uses it as an "analogy"; he makes comparisons with it, "reduces the un-known to the known," thinks "as if" the unfamiliar were the same as the familiar. Thus a physiologist says that the human body is like a machine; a sociologist says that a human society is like an organism, treating it "as if" it were a single living body made up of a vast number of different kinds of cells. Obviously, the human body is not a machine, nor is a society a many-celled animal. But, for some purposes, such an "as if" or "let's pretend" may be useful; up to a point, the resemblance holds good, suggesting that what has been learned about machines may turn out to be true of the human body and that our knowledge of the behavior of organisms may be instructive in studying social groups.

In this sense, all scientific theories, being inexact and incomplete analogies, are "fictional." Newton's gravitational theory employed a "force" or "pull" which resembled the "forcing" or "pulling" of things with which all men are familiar in their daily activities—in opening a bureau drawer or digging in a garden. Einstein's revision of Newton's theory substitutes as an analogy a sort of picture of space being warped by the presence of matter—an image, as someone has suggested, of space as a stretched-out sheet onto which some object is thrown, causing the sheet to assume a curved, bent shape. In both instances there is an "as if" which invokes a resemblance to the familiar. Such resemblances are indispensable—especially in science. The waves of the ocean suggested the theory of sound waves; the sound waves suggested light waves; both those waves suggested the theory that physical energy of all kinds is wave-like. But, since no resemblance—analogy—used in picturing nature is ever perfect, none is ever entirely correct. It always turns out, sooner or later, that the analogy limps; if the limp is too great, a new analogy is invented.

So it is with the notion of determinism in physics. It was a fiction, an "as if." Until most of the "laws" of physics proved to be statistical, that "as if" satisfied physicists. Now, to many of them, it no longer does so.

The physicists' facts are those of a faction, a group of men with a distinctive professional purpose. Their facts have a highly selective character; their "metonymy" takes the quantitative part for the whole; they paint portraits of the world in numbers, symbolize with nothing but the measurable. But the physicists' quantitative facts are no more "real" than the qualitative facts on which they turn their backs. The physicists' dogma, which excludes the qualitative from the realm of "real" facts, is now fortunately coming to be regarded, by many physicists, as a fiction, a "useful lie." Dickens expressed his scorn of that dogma in his description of Mr. Gradgrind, "with a rule and pair of scales, and the multiplication table always in his pocket, ready to weigh and measure any parcel of human nature, and tell you exactly what it comes to." Mr. Gradgrind, reports Dickens, found it disheartening to learn that the people of Coketown "persisted in wondering. They wondered about human nature, human passions, human hopes and fears, the struggles, triumphs and defeats, the cares and joys and sorrows, the lives and deaths of common men and women. They sometimes, after fifteen hours of work, sat down to read mere fables about men and women, more or less like themselves."

Legal Fictions [1]

EDWARD STEVENS ROBINSON

Such catch-all concepts as *reasonable, equitable, fair, just, Christian,* offer excellent services to large and general interests like property rights of women and political independence of industrialists. Yet the very vagueness of these terms may limit the judge in his use of them. When they are suggested by the arguments of one of the contesting parties, the judge will frequently prove resistant to the suggestion. Throughout judicial discourse there is the motive to give expression to a law that

[1] From *Law and the Lawyers,* pp. 226–231. Copyright, 1935, by The Macmillan Company. By permission of The Macmillan Company, publishers.

is certain and definite. Never use a general rule where the same result can be obtained by the use of a more specific one; this seems to be an effective axiom permeating the judicial process. This bias toward the limited rule is a technique in addition to that of the natural-law terminology which tends to give this barrier a considerable permeability. This is the technique of the so-called legal fictions.

A judge may extend the scope of a rule simply by giving an unusual meaning to one of its terms. Suppose that a man, legally within a building, breaks through a partition to commit a theft. The seriousness of the offense renders it desirable to apply the law of burglary. One alternative is a frank extension of the law justified in terms of a *reasonable* interpretation of the *spirit* of the law or of the *intentions* of the lawmakers. But such a procedure has the disadvantage that it makes the literal rule look uncertain and subject to the whims of the judges. Another alternative is that of calling the partitioned space itself a building. The suggestion is thus given that the established rule may stand without any modification of its wording. In the employment of such a technique courts have been known to say that a fence, a tent, a railroad car, may be a building. In order to disqualify Chinamen as witnesses against white men a California court is said to have held that Chinamen are Indians. In another instance it was held that the falling of a steam shovel upon a motor truck is a collision.

We may distinguish between those fictions employed by the judge to meet a special circumstance and others of more permanent character which become established by radical changes in social relations. When social adjustment requires a new distribution of the costs of injury and the enforcement of a "liability without fault," a term like "intent" comes to take on new legal meanings; and these new meanings become thoroughly established as a legal way of thinking. Now the question that arises here is why, since laymen still maintain the older understanding of the word, judges do not find a terminology which will make clear the actual changes that have taken place in juristic thought. The answer is at least partially to be found in the ideal of a stable and certain law. If the judges can alter their own understanding of an old term and thus save the term itself, this seems preferable to the more radical, if more intelligible, step of so changing their terms as to keep all men informed of the changes taking place in judicial thinking.

The most naïve generalization to be made regarding the presence of fictions in the law is that they are essentially immoral. "A fiction of law," said Bentham, "may be defined a willful falsehood, having for its object the stealing of legislative power, by and for hands which durst not, or could not, openly claim it; and, but for the delusion thus produced, could not exercise it." A result of these fictions, in Bentham's mind, is to make the law incomprehensible and thus to create a sinister monopoly for those who know the language. Even juries, he thought, are rendered powerless to resist judicial bidding for the simple reason that the real meaning of the law is obscured by its fictions. He had little patience for the claim that these fictions often accomplish useful purposes.

". . . The virtues of an useful institution will not be destroyed by any lie or lies that may have accompanied the establishment of it; but can they receive any increase? The virtues of a useful medicine will not be destroyed by pronouncing an incantation over it before it is taken; but will they be increased?

"Behold here one of the artifices of lawyers. They refuse to administer justice to you unless you join with them in their fictions; and then their cry is, see how necessary fiction is to justice! Necessary indeed; but too necessary; but how come it so, and who made it so?

"As well might the father of a family make it a rule never to let his children have their breakfast till they had uttered, each of them, a certain number of lies, curses, and profane oaths; and then exclaim, 'You see, my dear children, how necessary lying, cursing and swearing are to human sustenance.'"

Such a judgment is clearly hot-headed, though possibly it was justified by the intellectual habits of the bench and bar in Bentham's day. In refuting such condemnation of legal fictions other writers have stressed the convenience of the fictional technique. It is relatively easy for a judge to adjust himself to the idea that "daughter" in some circumstances also means "son," that the "foreigner" may be a citizen, but many difficulties are involved in pronouncing a decision that does not agree with any rule or in going to the lawmakers and getting the rule changed. Then too it is pointed out that legal fictions may perform a simple psychological service. They may function as convenient symbols of ideas and thus facilitate the manipulation of those ideas. "The fiction is the algebra law and a picturesque form of algebra besides." All that is required, according to Professor Tourtoulon, is that the judge keep clearly in mind the difference between his system of notation and that for which it stands.

The employment of a fiction may also serve legitimate emotional ends. "Thus the idea of a Roman citizen taken prisoner by the enemy and led into slavery was too hard on Roman pride. Existence of such a fact was not admitted. If the citizen died a slave it was said that he died in war and was killed on the field of battle; if he regained his liberty, he was supposed to have been at home all of the time and at the head of his family and his business." One is reminded of the verbal formulas by means of which American parents, whose boys died of influenza at the camps in 1918, explained that their sons had really been killed in action.

Among those who are not so naïve as to hold that all lawyers are consciously deceptive, the point is often made that the law is at any rate stubbornly conservative. Legal fictions are condemned because they are said to be an aid in holding to the past at times when the past should be frankly left behind. This contention has a degree of justification. The persistence of the word "intent" in complex social problems where conscious intent is either irrelevant or indeterminable probably retards legal progress. The cloudy ethical atmosphere that hovers about this term tends to make difficult the introduction of psychological, psychiatric, economic, and sociological factors which ought to dominate in the composition of social conflicts. The fact that judges still pretend that corporations are persons has introduced into the field of corporate control ideas applicable to individuals but largely ineffective in the control of modern business organizations.

The charge that fictions encourage the fundamental conservatism of legal minds, is, however, a little too general to be quite accurate. Remember that the fiction, like the natural-law term, tends to be utilized when the judge wishes to express an idea for which the conventional legal language contains no literal provision. "They satisfy the desire for improvement, which is not quite wanting, at the same time that they do not offend the superstitious disrelish for change which is always present." Whether the use of a fiction by a particular judge at a particular time is desirable or undesirable can hardly be decided until one has examined the particular circumstances. Would the judge have been capable of entertaining the new idea without the metaphorical employment of old, familiar, words? Is the new idea, itself, desirable or undesirable? (Careful thinkers are not likely to accept mere novelty any more than mere antiquity as a criterion of desirability.) Is there a new idea involved? Or does the judge use the fiction simply because he is too lazy to call a situation by its real name? Questions like these must be answered before the matter of desirability can be settled. We have in the legal fiction a device prevalent throughout the entire of human thinking. Physics with its ether, and mathematics with its irrational quantities are indulging in fictions. Like most intellectual devices these fictions are in themselves neither good nor bad, nor are they the constant accessories of either invention or conservatism.

PART IV

Questions and Answers

In studies of the kinds of sentences appearing in public discussions, questions are usually found to be the least numerous, but easily among the most important in keeping those discussions going. The question is, indeed, a kind of gadfly, annoying and persistent, which has to be dealt with. However, one rarely finds people asking questions about the business of asking questions. Those who do take the trouble have uncovered a number of varieties: stupid questions, meaningless questions, pseudo questions, footless questions. It is apparent, further, that these should perhaps not be answered in the same way as those listed under significant categories. The study of questions thus moves into the examination of the character of an answer. Under what conditions can a question be answered? What does one do when he makes an explanation?

The Nature of a Question[1]

HANS REICHENBACH

One of the foremost results of . . . scientific philosophy is the clarification of the nature of a question. The adage that a fool can ask more than a wise man can answer finds its logical equivalent in the distinction between meaningful and meaningless questions. A question is meaningful only if it is so asked that before we can give the true answer we at least can tell how a possible answer would look. Thus to ask for the origin of the terrestrial globe is a reasonable question, because we can imagine an answer, for instance in the form of a theory according to which the earth was originally part of the sun and then detached by centrifugal forces; whether this answer is true remains to be found out by scientific investigation. But to ask for the origin of the universe is an unreasonable question; it is meaningless because we cannot say how a possible answer would look. Any answer would make the universe the product of some other occurrence which in turn would have to be included in the universe and therefore could not be the source of the universe. A review of philosophical systems shows that many so-called philosophical questions are of the meaningless type. No wonder that a great many of the philosophical controversies are so empty and futile. The distinction between meaningful and meaningless questions is the scientific form of a criticism which common sense has always raised against philosophy. "Where concepts are missing, the word is right at hand," says Goethe. The term "metaphysics" is now often used, by its opponents, to indicate what they consider to be an empty brand of philosophy.

Not all philosophical questions are meaningless, however. Some have remained unanswered because their answer required a scientific

[1] From "Philosophy: Speculation or Science?" *The Nation,* Vol. 164, No. 1, January 4, 1947, pp. 19–21. Copyright, 1947, by the Nation Associates, Inc. Reprinted by permission.

technique which up to now had not been developed. The question of the origin of life, for instance, has found a new approach through Darwin's theory of evolution; and the near future may perhaps supply us with the proof that living cells may be constructed from inorganic matter. The question of the nature of space and time has found an answer in certain mathematical and physical discoveries, reaching a climax in Einstein's theory of relativity. We have learned to distinguish between mathematical space, a conceptual construction open to various geometrical forms, and physical space, which is part of the structure of the universe; and we know that space and time, in the physical sense, express some very general features of the physical world, such as are given in the behavior of solid bodies and light rays. Some of the answers thus supplied by science to philosophical questions have turned out to be surprising even to the scientist. Thus the question of the nature of cause and effect has found a negative answer, in that it has been shown that there exists no strict causality in the physical world, that the future is indeterminate, and that the dream of a predetermination of the future and of a possible strict prediction of future events must forever be abandoned. Only statistical predictions are possible.

The concept of probability which thus has received a legitimate place in the system of physics has likewise turned out to be indispensable for the solution of a problem which the history of philosophy had faced for about two hundred years without the hope of a solution —the problem of the inductive inference. This problem, which found its critic in David Hume, is now accessible to an answer based on probability notions; it turns out that the procedure of inductive knowledge is more closely related to the betting of the gambler than to the rationalized conception of knowledge which so far has been the basis of philosophic investigation.

In addition to answering old questions, the philosophy of science has learned to ask new questions of which the philosophical systems had never thought. That there is more between heaven and earth than was dreamed of in traditional philosophy has found a vivid demonstration in the results of modern quantum physics, according to which the elementary physical particles, when unobserved, behave in an irrational way, so that the world of unobserved objects cannot be constructed along the lines of macroscopic phenomena. The critique of the foundations of mathematics, furthermore, has led to the discovery of concepts incomprehensible to traditional logic. That the whole need not be larger than its part was shown in the theory of sets; that logic is not restricted to the alternative true-false but can be replaced by a multi-valued logic, which possesses more than the two truth values of truth and falsehood, was shown in mathematical logic. One of these non-Aristotelian logics, a three-value system, has been used for the interpretation of quantum physics.

Questioning Questions [1]

A. B. JOHNSON

LECTURE XIX

§1.—Questions Have Interrogated Everything Except Themselves

No subject is less understood than questions. They constitute a field which is not ungleaned merely, but unreaped. Every thing pertaining to them is unmarked by the feet of curiosity and untrained by the hand of cultivation. As the eye sees every thing but itself, so questions have interrogated every thing but themselves. To supply this deficiency is the object of the present discourse.

§2.—All Questions Which Relate to the External Universe Must Be Directed to Our Senses

What is the shape of a taste, or the colour of a sound? The questions are insignificant. They inquire after no information of our senses. Every interrogation which possesses a similar defect is equally trifling, provided it relates to the external universe, our senses being the only means we possess of knowing the external universe.

[1] From *A Treatise on Language: or the Relation Which Words Bear to Things*. New York: Harper & Brothers, 1836. After the text printed by Stillman Drake, San Francisco, 1940, pp. 171–181; used with his permission.

§3.—Should a spark of fire fall amid a room full of gunpowder, what effect will occur? Should a spark of fire fall amid the satellites of Jupiter, what effect will occur? These questions are grammatically alike; yet the last is insignificant, while the first is significant. The significant question inquires after information which my senses can furnish, while the insignificant question inquires after no information which the senses can furnish. What if the sun should wander from the zodiac? This question was propounded once in ridicule by Sterne. Every person knows it to be insignificant, though perhaps few persons can tell what constitutes the insignificance.

§4.—When the Lord answered from the flaming bush the inquiry of Moses by saying, "I am that I am," the answer was wonderfully expressive of the nature of language, which can in no instance accomplish more than it effected in that. We may say to life, What art thou? and to death, What art thou? and we may address a like inquiry to the sun, the earth, the sea, the revolution of the seasons, the alternations of day and night, the fluctuation of the tides, the attraction of magnetism, and the gravitation of stones; but language can furnish them with no better answer than I am that I am. Would we learn more in relation to them, we must seek it from our senses. Every sight, sound, taste, feel, and smell which an object exhibits spontaneously, or which it can by any art be made to exhibit, is an answer to our question; but we may as well attempt to enlarge our family by multiplying the names of our children as increase our knowledge of an external existence by multiplying words upon it. What our senses discover we may relate, and in such language as we deem most appropriate; but the moment we attempt to make our answers more comprehensive, we are employing language for purposes that are beyond its capacity. We may fabricate theories and definitions, but we cannot enlarge our knowledge of the external universe by an arrangement of words, any more than a conjurer can look into futurity by arranging the figures of a pack of cards.

§5.—How does a magnet attract iron? Exhibit the magnet and the iron, and let the querist see the operation; he can receive no reply which will be so authoritative. But he sees the fact only, and not the cause. Let him examine further, and see every thing that is visible, touch every thing that is tangible, and employ similarly all his senses; if he wants to find what his senses cannot discover, his search is not only fruitless, but it is unmeaning. When he would speak of the object of such a search, language itself fails him. His sentences may be grammatical, but they will possess no sensible signification. When a blind man talks of colours, the word is sensibly insignificant to him; and every word is equally insignificant to us when it refers to the external universe, and attempts to speak of what our senses cannot discover.

§6.—Nero threatened to decapitate a painter unless he should produce three pictures on subjects that should be given to him. The first was the emperor's favourite horse. The painter finished the likeness, and it was satisfactory. He was then required to paint the emperor, and in this he also succeeded. But the last requirement was that he should paint the sound of the emperor's flute. The requirement was not within the power of colours, and the painter was beheaded.

§7.—That colours are unable to depict sounds, tastes, and smells, we are aware; but we know not that words are unable to discourse of any thing external which is not a sight, sound, taste, feel, or smell. The inability in both cases possesses the same foundation in nature. Colours are sights; hence no combination of them can represent what is not visible. In the same way, words which relate to the external universe are in effect sights, sounds, tastes, feels, and smells; hence no combination of them can discourse of what is not sight, sound, taste, feel, or smell.

§8.—An External Thing That Is Not Sensible Is as Incongruous a Thing as an Insensible Elephant

Even to speak of any thing external which my senses cannot discover is a contradiction; because the word thing, when it refers to the external universe, signifies some revelation of my senses. Endeavour to teach a Frenchman the meaning of the word thing. If you cannot speak French, nor he English, no ingenuity of yours, and no aptness of his, can enable you to convey to him a meaning of the word thing unless you make him understand that it signifies some sight, sound, taste, feel, or smell which you may present to his senses. An external thing which the senses cannot discover is a word divested of signification. We may as well talk of an insensible horse as an insensible external thing; both words admit equally the existence of a sensible revelation.

§9.—The same difficulty occurs, employ what word you will in place of thing. You cannot more readily teach the Frenchman a meaning of the word existence than of the word thing. You must appeal to his senses for the meaning of existence, precisely as you must for the meaning of the word horse or elephant; hence an insensible external existence is a contradiction, for the word external existence admits the cognizance of your senses as much as the word horse.

§10.—What is lightning? The phrase is elliptical. It means what thing is lightning; and we have already shown that the word thing signifies a sensible existence; hence the question truly inquires after the information of the senses, and can be answered by their information only. The same result follows if you supply the ellipsis with the word existence, or with whatever other word you may substitute as the substantive of the pronoun what.

§11.—We are situated in relation to the senses like St. Paul in relation to evil. He says, "when I attempt to do good, evil is present with me." So, when we attempt to forsake sensible information, it is still present with us. Apple is the name of something that can be seen, felt, and tasted. The word admits these qualities; hence to speak of an insensible apple is to contradict what must be admitted to make the word significant. A like difficulty occurs with every word. External existence names something that can be seen, felt, tasted, heard, or smelled; hence to speak of an insensible external existence is to contradict the admission which gives signification to the phrase. We may, with no greater impropriety, speak of an invisible brilliancy, or an inaudible noise, or any other contradiction. Boys in the country wear attached to their shirts a false collar, which is called a dickey. This is usually much starched, and sometimes surrounds the boy's neck so as to bury his chin and mouth. A boy who was thus annoyed was seen by his schoolmaster to jump repeatedly; and, on being asked why he jumped, said he was attempting to spit over his dickey. The boy's attempts are analogous to ours when we endeavour to exalt our meaning beyond our senses. The sensible meaning of words cannot be detached in our flights, any more than the boy could jump up without carrying his dickey upwards with him.

§12.—Diminution Is One of the Means by Which We Attempt to Conceal the Absurdity of Employing the Names of Sensible Existences Where the Existences Are Not Discoverable

The original of all matter is, we are told, atoms, which are so small that millions of them must be aggregated before the mass becomes sensible. Still, these little insensible primitives are atoms. Were we told that they are gwho, we should scorn the unmeaning affirmation. Atoms seems intelligible, though we forget that it is applied where our senses can discover none of the sensible information which gives the word its signification; hence that the word, when thus used, has no more signification than gwho.

§13.—Subtilization Is Another Means So Used

Attraction is attenuated as we discover it in magnetick and electrick experiments; but when we wish to predicate attraction where our senses cannot discover it, we are forced to substitute it verbally till it becomes too subtile for our senses. In this condition, it is the most potent agent that is employed in verbal philosophy. It not only holds together the insensible atoms which constitute a diamond, but it upholds the earth, sun, and planets. The only difficulty is that when we subtract from the word attraction its sensible qualities, we leave an empty sound—as empty as the word apple, when we abstract from that word its sensible references.

§14.—Insensible evaporation, insensible perspiration, insensible heat, etc., are agents by which also we attempt to penetrate beyond the sensible realities of the universe. By affixing to them the adjunct insensible, we endeavour to account for our inability to discover them by our senses; but insensibility is as much a negation of all which gives signification to the words as death is a negation of life. We read in the *Arabian Nights* of a facetious rich man who tendered a sumptuous entertainment to a hungry mendicant: "Eat, brother, of this ragout, and spare not this stewed lamb and pistachio nuts." To the poor man's senses, the table was unfurnished with viands of any kind, and though his complaisance induced him for a period to accompany his host in the evolutions of eating, his stomach gave him practical admonitions of the nature of insensible ragouts. Evaporation, perspiration, attraction, etc., are so subtile in their sensible form that we see not the inanity of depriving them entirely of their sensible properties; but the same principle which nullifies an insensible ragout nullifies an insensible vapour, etc.

§15.—Finally, all that Providence has placed within our power in relation to the external universe is to note and record what our senses discover. To this end, we may compound elements and analyze compounds; we may examine causes and trace effects. While our language is confined to what our senses disclose, every word is significant.

Within this circle, we may propose significant questions and receive significant answers. But the moment we step beyond the circle, we can neither propound a significant question, nor frame a significant answer. We are worse than blind men when they try to talk about colours; for though their language is sensibly insignificant to themselves, it is significant to others; but when we attempt to discourse about external realities which no person's senses can discover, language itself fails us, and becomes insignificant. Our language may retain a verbal meaning, but it will lose its sensible meaning; it may be significant of theories, definitions, mathematical calculations, and other verbal processes, but it will not be significant of the realities of the external universe.

§16.—If we examine the speculations of philosophers, we shall find that no truth is so little known as the above. As the stars appear at sunset to supply the light of the absent sun, so philosophy commences its revelations where our senses terminate theirs. But here the parallel ceases. The stars possess a little light that is inherent and independent of the sun; but words possess no inherent meaning in any case, and no external meaning independent of the senses.

§17.—To deem ourselves shut up in the universe with no capacity to know or even speak any thing of it but what our senses reveal seems a narrower range than we are accustomed to attribute to our knowledge. Still, such is our situation. Language cannot enable us to pass the barrier of our senses. We may as well attempt to construct a dwelling house which shall be undiscoverable by the senses as construct a proposition which shall signify something of the external universe that cannot be discovered by the senses. The same difficulty obstructs both attempts. We possess for the house no materials but such as are sensible, and we possess no words for the proposition but such as refer for their signification to sensible information.

§18.—I have now, I trust, shown that every question which relates to the external universe is insignificant if it cannot be answered by our senses. It is insignificant because we can frame no question that will not, in its terms, relate to sensible information, and secondly because we possess no means of knowing any thing of the external universe but what our senses reveal.

LECTURE XX

§1.—Having shown in my last discourse that every question which relates to the external universe is insignificant if it cannot be answered by our senses, I must add that every question which relates to the universe within ourselves is insignificant if it cannot be answered by our consciousness.

§2.—When a flash of lightning crosses the horizon, it appears as vividly to persons around you as to you; hence, when you attach a name to it, every person knows what the name signifies. But when you become conscious of some phenomenon within yourself, and wish to speak of it, much difficulty occurs in making other persons know the phenomenon to which you allude. This difficulty embarrasses all discourse which relates to what we experience internally.

§3.—If you ask me to tell you how I felt at beholding the decapitation of a felon, I may be unable to give you any verbal definition of my feeling, or any verbal description of it; still, I know precisely what I experienced on the occasion.[2] The feeling may say to me, I am that I am. You cannot transmute me into words. You may reflect on me, and note in relation to me all that you experience. You may refer to me in any words that you deem appropriate, but your words are not me. I am myself alone. Your words cannot alter me, or enlarge or abridge me. They are the breath of your own body. So far as they refer to me, you must look to me alone as the only true expositor of myself.

§4.—What constitutes personal identity? What enables you to know that you are the individual who, thirty years ago, arrived in this city? The usual answer to this question would be words; but the true answer is independent of all words. It is simply what you discover it to be. A dumb mute possesses on this subject all the knowledge which you possess; and usually in much greater clearness and purity than you possess it, for with you the answer is probably so confounded with words that the phenomena of nature (which constitute the real answer) are but little regarded.

§5.—What are thoughts? What is memory? What is an idea? What are conscience and consciousness? They may severally answer, I am that I am. No answer is so good as this, because none is so little likely to mislead the inquirer. Would we know further what they are, we must resort to our experience, and in its mute revelations alone can we receive the answer. What is lightning? Should the clouds exhibit to me a flash, it would constitute the best answer that the question is susceptible of. Precisely thus, when I ask what is memory. Should the

[2] Or I knew while I was experiencing the feeling.

recollection occur to me of a flash of lightning, the recollection would constitute the best answer which the question about memory is susceptible of.

§6.—To experience a recollection of a flash of lightning will tell you only what the word memory names. You may say that you wish to know how memory is caused, and what constitutes its nature. Recur, then, again, to your consciousness. Experience all which you can in relation to memory, and receive the experience as the only answer which the questions admit. If experience will not answer the questions, language cannot; for language possesses no signification in the premises, except what it derives from its reference to your experience.

§7.—We can answer every question which inquires after any thing that we can experience, either by our senses or our consciousness; but a question which inquires after none of these is an inquiry after nothing. How would memory look if we could see it? How would it feel, taste, smell, or sound? Does it die, or continue to live in the soul after the death of the body? If it is a property of the soul, why does it decay in old men? If it is a property of matter, is confined to a particular piece? Does it possess gender and number? We may form as many such questions as we can form syntactical sentences, but the questions are like a numerical sum whose figures refer to nothing. The figures may be multiplied, divided, added, and subtracted, according to the rules which figures obey, but if they possess no ulterior reference, their product will possess no ulterior signification. Our questions also may be subjected to all the rules of logick that are applicable to the words; but so long as the words possess no ulterior reference, the answers which may be elaborated from them will possess no ulterior signification.

"Footless" Questions [1]

P. W. BRIDGMAN

An honest question, as distinguished from a rhetorical question, implies an answer, and "answer" implies the property of being "right" or "wrong," and "right" or "wrong" operationally implies the possibility of making some sort of test to determine whether the answer is right or wrong (at least I find this implication in the way that people ordinarily use the words right and wrong). Now it is possible to frame questions in such form that the very wording itself rules out, either explicitly or implicitly, the possibility of making any test to determine whether an answer is "right" or "wrong." There is, for example, the celebrated question of W. K. Clifford: "May not the entire universe be uniformly contracting in dimensions, everything together, our standards of length as well as everything else?" The physicist reacts to this question without the slightest hesitation, for the operations by which he defines length demand comparison with a standard, and if the standards themselves are "changing," what shall we mean by a change of length? In other words, the question is so framed as to make impossible any check of the correctness of the answer, and it thus defeats its ostensible purpose. The physicist would describe such a question as "meaningless." If he asked such a question in the first place, this analysis would show him that he did not accomplish what he wanted to with the question, for the question fails to correspond in an important respect to the actual situation. The physicist has come to recognize that it is unpleasantly easy to put words together into formal questions which admit of no possible operational check on the correctness of the answer, and in making this recognition and in learning to avoid "meaningless" questions he has acquired an important tool in aid of precise thinking. He recognizes, furthermore, that this is

[1] From P. W. Bridgman: *The Intelligent Individual and Society*, pp. 75-79. Copyright, 1938, by The Macmillan Company and used with their permission.

merely a special case of the more general fact that words sometimes become our master.

How will the theologian or mystic react to Clifford's question? At least some will say that there is perfectly definite meaning in the question, because there is such a thing as absolute length, independent of any standards of length, namely the length perceived in the mind of God. As before, the meaning of "perceived in the mind of God" must be sought operationally in what the mystic does in applying this concept to the present situation. The meaning which the mystic attaches to length is also operational, as well as the meaning of the physicist, but the operations and therefore the meanings are different. Observation will show that the operations of the mystic include arguing for some system of philosophy. An important difference between the physicist and the mystic is to be found in their estimates of the significance of the respective operations and in their underlying purposes. The purpose of the physicist is tacitly to find some method of dealing "correctly" with the "external" world. His experience as a physicist has so convinced him of the futility of the method of the mystic for this purpose that it simply does not occur to him as a possibility, and he brusquely characterizes the question "meaningless."

This is doubtless an extreme example, but it makes the point. As long as one is dealing with as homogeneous a body of people as physicists with as definitely understood a common purpose, one may profitably talk about "meaningless" questions in the sense just discussed. This was the sense in which I used "meaningless" in my "Logic of Modern Physics" and in some of my subsequent writing. But now that the inquiry is to be extended to cover activities so remote from physics as that of the mystic I believe that the use of "meaningless" in this somewhat technical sense may sometimes lead to confusion, for obviously the mystic did "mean" something by his question in spite of the fact that it would have been impossible for a physicist to go on asking the question after he had discovered the implications. Accordingly I propose sometimes to replace the word "meaningless" by the less aggressive word lifted from American slang: "footless." A question is "footless" if it implies within itself the impossibility of meeting the purpose for which the question was ostensibly asked. A man who asks a footless question has *failed*. "Footless" is obviously not a sharp designation, but whether it is applied or not will depend on the purpose, and on the estimate of the questioner, derived from his own experience of the sort of operation that is profitable in attaining the purpose. We can to a certain extent tell what kind of person one is by observing the kind of question that he will call footless; the physicist will call Clifford's question footless, the mystic will not.

We have perhaps conceded more to the mystic than the physicist will feel to be profitable. But even the mystic will admit that he too can sometimes put words together in ways that at first have an appearance of being satisfactory, but which more careful analysis discloses not to be what he wants.

Questions may fail in other ways to achieve their purpose than by involving contradiction. Thus many questions which on their face have some "objective" significance, turn out on analysis to be concerned with verbalisms. For instance, the question "What is life?" turns out on analysis not to be a question about the external world alone, but a question as to the adequacy of our classification of the objects of the external world into living and dead. Or when we ask "Is this or that lowly form vegetable or animal?" we may not be asking something about the form, but we may be asking whether our classification of living things into vegetable and animal is adequate.

Questions and Answers [1]

CASSIUS JACKSON KEYSER

No reader who will reflect a little upon the matter can fail to see clearly that any question that he or another has asked or can ask belongs to one or the other of two immense classes, kinds, or types: Questions concerning things that constitute the Actual world; and questions relating to the world of the Possible. Under each of those great types

---

[1] From "Science and Mathematics," *Humanism and Science*. New York: Columbia University Press, 1931, pp. 57–68. Copyright, 1931, by Columbia University Press. Reprinted by permission of the Editor of *Scripta Mathematica*.

there are, of course, many subtypes of questions, but with that fact we are not now concerned. I shall not tarry here to tell, or try to tell, precisely what is meant by the Actual world or what by the Possible; for, in any discourse, some terms must be taken for granted, and I am going to assume that, for the purpose of this discussion, the terms in question are sufficiently understood or will become so in the light of what remains to be said.

Questions about the Actual world are such as these: What is the specific gravity of iron? What are the essential functions of government? What is the shape of the Earth's orbit? What are the social values of the human sense of "right" and "wrong"? What is the velocity of light? What are the cardinal factors constraining humans to live in society instead of isolation? What is the weight of the sun? What are the causes of war? How big is the universe? What are the agencies that produce disease and death? What are the offices of speech? What is the origin and essential nature of municipal law? What are the societal effects of mechanical invention? What are the factors that beget, establish, and transform a people's mores? What is it that produces, and what that destroys, belief in the existence of malign spirits, in magic, in immortality, in hells and heavens? What is the distance of the moon from the earth, and what are the effects of moonlight upon poetry, love, and agriculture? And so on endlessly.

Questions about the world of the Possible are commonly of the form: If such-and-such supposable things were actual, then what other things would, by logical necessity, be so, too? Even when not in that form, they can always be put in it. Examples are: If the axioms of Euclid were valid statements about our actual space, what additional statements about it would then, of logical necessity, be likewise valid? If the affairs of a universe were actually administered by an all-wise, all-powerful and perfectly benevolent Being, then what, by logical implication, would the characteristics of the administration have to be? If there be a four-dimensional space related to our ordinary space as this is related to a plane immersed in it, what conclusions logically follow regarding the structure of that higher space? If a tribe of primitive people actually believe that their environment is perpetually occupied by a host of malignant spirits having dispositions fashioned on the pattern of hostile humans as known to the tribe and if the tribe believe that their own welfare depends on their constantly making suitable adjustments to the demands of the demonic world, what conclusions logically follow as to the means the tribe will employ for making the required adjustments? If all the people of the world were embraced in one vast fraternity for friendly coöperation in the interest of the common weal, what advantages would necessarily accrue therefrom? If a municipal law be such an expression of the people's will that it can be enforced, what conclusion follows, by logical necessity, as to whether a non-enforceable statute is or is not a law? And so on ad infinitum.

ANSWERS AND PROPOSITIONS

A question leads sooner or later to a proposition purporting to answer it. I do not mean to assert that answers are always given in the form of articulate propositions. Far from it. If, for example, a blacksmith be asked how one shoes a horse, he may answer, quite without words, by actually shoeing a horse in the presence of the asker. The example is but one of millions familiar to all. Such an answer in the form of speechless action, in the form of wordless behavior, may be regarded as a kind of inarticulate proposition or propositions—it is, for one beholding it attentively, a species of inarticulate discourse, which, if we will, can be translated into words. Henceforth, in speaking of propositions, I shall always mean articulate propositions. For (1) it is these that respond to questions born of intellectual curiosity, or wonder, great mother of knowledge-seeking for the sake of knowledge; (2) it is in the form of articulate propositions that answers can be permanently recorded, stored up, communicated through space, transmitted to succeeding generations of mankind; and (3) articulate propositions afford the only forms in which answers can be subjected to the processes and scrutinies of logic. As forms for answering questions propositional forms are so superior to all others that they may properly be regarded as *the* forms for that purpose.

THE GREAT PROPOSITIONAL TYPES

It is essential to note very attentively that, corresponding to the great question types above signalized as fundamental, there are two great propositional types no less fundamental.

Propositions purporting to answer questions about the Actual world are of a form stating that *Such-and-such is the case or fact.* They will be called Categorical propositions.

Propositions purporting to answer questions about the world of the

Possible are commonly of a form equivalent to this: *If such-and-such propositions be true, then, by logical necessity, such-and-such additional propositions are true.* Statements of that form will be called Hypothetical propositions.

So fundamentally important are the two propositional types that it is desirable to define them sharply before illustrating them by concrete examples. I will give such a definition presently but it will come better after a few words of explanation. Let p denote one or more propositions, let q denote one or more other propositions, and consider the additional proposition: *p implies q.* We are to understand that to assert "*p implies q*" is equivalent to asserting that q is logically deducible from p. The form, p implies q, is the best form, and should be regarded as the normal or standard form, forestating Hypothetical propositions; p being the implier or hypothesis, and q the implicate or conclusion. It is prudent to note that the familiar form—if p, then q—may or may not assert an implication. It does so when and only when the assertor of it thereby intends to assert that q is logically deducible from p; which, obviously, he does not intend to do when asserting such a proposition as: If it lightens, then it will thunder. We are now prepared for the promised Definition: *If a proposition, P, is such that to assert it is equivalent to asserting that a proposition or propositions* q *can be logically deduced from a proposition or propositions* p *or—what is tantamount—that* p *implies* q, *then* P *is a Hypothetical proposition; otherwise,* P *is a Categorical proposition.* By this definition it is seen that a Categorical proposition, even though it be in the if-then form, never asserts an implication, and, on the contrary, that a Hypothetical proposition always does so. The two great types may be helpfully illustrated by some concrete specimens of them.

A few examples of Categorical propositions, chosen at random, are these: the velocity of light exceeds all other actual velocities; among the planets of the solar system the earth is the only one inhabitable by living creatures; a hydrogen atom consists of a negative electron revolving about a positive nucleus; A cannot be at once both A and not-A; denoting by S_1, S_2, S_3 the sensations due to three different amounts of stimulus (in a given department), it may happen that S_1 is indistinguishable from S_2 and that S_2 is indistinguishable from S_3 but that nevertheless S_1 and S_3 are distinguishable from one another; malaria is due to a germ carried by a certain kind of mosquito; the radius of a circle is equal to one side of the regular inscribed hexagon; the number found by counting the objects of a group is the same for all the possible orders of counting them; in the evolution of animal life, "struggle for existence" has included both competition and coöperation; liquids submitted to pressure transmit it undiminished equally in all directions; economic competition spontaneously established in a market establishes there a stable price at which supply equals demand; transformations of energy from kind to kind neither increase nor decrease the total energy of the universe. The foregoing Categoricals, all of which say that such-and-such is the case, will, I hope, sufficiently exemplify the sort of propositions that purport to answer questions relating to no matter what aspect of the world of Actuality.

How sharply and how radically those Categoricals contrast with the following random examples of the Hypothetical type: if John Doe was in Chicago at the time he is alleged to have stabbed Richard Roe in New York, then John Doe is not guilty as charged (that is, the proposition—John Doe was in Chicago, etc.—*implies* the proposition—John Doe was not guilty, etc.); the primitive propositions or axioms of Euclidean geometry imply that the sum of the angles of a triangle is 180 degrees; the axioms of Lobachevskian geometry imply that the angle sum is greater than 180 degrees; the proposition, an American law is such an expression of the people's will as to be enforceable, implies the proposition, an unenforceable *statute* or Constitutional amendment is not an American law; the proposition that entropy always increases—the second Law of Thermodynamics—implies that in the course of time the last erg of energy will have reached the zero of availability, whereupon the universe will be dead; if the dogma of The Fall of Man and the dogma of total human Depravity were true, then the love and pity and benevolence of "natural" men and women would be but forms of sin; if 2 were 3, then a fifth of 40 would be 12; if the General Theory of Relativity has for its aim to establish propositions that shall be valid for all observers, whatever their times or places, and if nearly all that seems true for an individual human so seems because of its special relation to what is unique in his experience and personality, then that Theory is restricted to an exceedingly minute part of what can seem true to any normal man, woman or child. And so on and on.

WHAT AN "ESTABLISHED" PROPOSITION IS

It will frequently be convenient or even necessary to speak of a proposition as established or not established. What is meant by the familiar phrase, an established proposition? In asking that question I am not asking what is meant by the phrase, a true proposition; for a proposition may be true without being established, and it may be established without being true. The question must be answered in accord with prevailing usage, and the answer is this: An established proposition is a proposition that is so spoken of, so described, by all or nearly all expert authorities in the subject or field to which the proposition belongs. In other words, a proposition has the status of an established proposition when and only when it is credited by the consensus of competent opinion. It is plain that the element of time is involved: an established proposition owns a date or dates. The history of thought makes it abundantly evident that a given proposition may be, for a longer or shorter time, an established proposition, and then cease to be such. And it is noteworthy that the status of being an established proposition may hold for the Occident only or for the Orient only or for the entire world. For examples, consider such famous propositions as the following:

(1) Heat, light and electricity are imponderable *substances.*
(2) The Newtonian law of gravitation.
(3) The nebular hypothesis of Kant and Laplace.
(4) The earth is flat.
(5) The world was created in six days by divine fiat 4004 years before the birth of Christ.
(6) Jesus was born of a virgin.
(7) Faith is essential to salvation but Reason is not.
(8) Any whole is greater than any one of its parts.
(9) Every continuous curve admits a tangent at each of its points.
(10) As God's vice-regent on earth, a Pope is infallible.

Such are only a familiar few of many notable propositions that were once established propositions but now are not.

The How and the Why of Things [1]

CLAUDE BERNARD

The nature of our mind leads us to seek the essence or the *why* of things. Thus we aim beyond the goal that it is given us to reach; for experience soon teaches us that we cannot get beyond the *how,* i.e., beyond the immediate cause or the necessary conditions of phenomena. In this respect the limits of our knowledge are the same in biological as in physico-chemical sciences.

When, by successive analyses, we find the immediate cause determining the circumstances in which a phenomenon presents itself, we reach a scientific goal beyond which we cannot pass. When we know that water, with all its properties, results from combining oxygen and hydrogen in certain proportions, we know everything we can know about it; and that corresponds to the *how* and not to the *why* of things. We know how water can be made; but why does the combination of one volume of oxygen with two volumes of hydrogen produce water? We have no idea. In medicine it is equally absurd to concern one's self with the question "why." Yet physicians ask it often. It was probably to make fun of this tendency, which results from lack of the sense of limits to our learning, that Molière put the following answer into the mouth of his candidate for the medical degree. Asked why opium puts people to sleep, he answered: *"Quia est in eo virtus dormitiva, cujus est natura sensus assoupire."* This answer seems ludicrous and absurd; yet no other answer could be made. In the same way, if we wished to answer the question: "Why does hydrogen, in combining with oxygen, produce water?" we should have to answer: "Because hydrogen has the quality of being able to beget water." Only the question "why," then, is really absurd, because it necessarily involves a naïve or ridiculous answer. So we had better recognize that we do not

[1] From *An Introduction to the Study of Experimental Medicine.* New York: The Macmillan Company, 1927, pp. 80–83. Reprinted by permission of The General Education Board, owners of the copyright.

know; and that the limits of our knowledge are precisely here.

In physiology, if we prove, for instance, that carbon monoxide is deadly when uniting more firmly than oxygen with the hemoglobin, we know all that we can know about the cause of death. Experiénce teaches us that a part of the mechanism of life is lacking; oxygen can no longer enter the organism, because it cannot displace the carbon monoxide in its union with the hemoglobin. But why has carbon monoxide more affinity than oxygen for this substance? Why is entrance of oxygen into the organism necessary to life? Here is the limit of our knowledge in our present state of learning; and even assuming that we succeed in further advancing our experimental analysis, we shall reach a blind cause at which we shall be forced to stop, without finding the primal reason for things.

Let us add that, when the relative determinism of a phenomenon is established, our scientific goal is reached. Experimental analysis of the conditions of the phenomenon, when pushed still further, gives us fresh information, but really teaches us nothing about the nature of the phenomenon originally determined. The conditions necessary to a phenomenon teach us nothing about its nature. When we know that physical and chemical contact between the blood and the cerebral nerve cells is necessary to the production of intellectual phenomena, that points to conditions, but it cannot teach us anything about the primary nature of intelligence. Similarly, when we know that friction and that chemical action produce electricity, we are still ignorant of the primary nature of electricity.

We must therefore, in my opinion, stop differentiating the phenomena of living bodies from those of inorganic bodies, by a distinction based on our own ability to know the nature of the former and our inability to know that of the latter. The truth is that the nature or very essence of phenomena, whether vital or mineral, will always remain unknown. The essence of the simplest mineral phenomenon is completely unknown to chemists and physicists today as is the essence of intellectual phenomena or of any other vital phenomenon to physiologists. That, moreover, is easy to apprehend; knowledge of the inmost nature or the absolute, in the simplest phenomenon, would demand knowledge of the whole universe; for every phenomenon of the universe is evidently a sort of radiation from that universe to whose harmony it contributes. In living bodies absolute truth would be still harder to attain; because, besides implying knowledge of the universe outside a living body, it would also demand complete knowledge of the organism which, as we have long been saying, is a little world (microcosm) in the great universe (macrocosm). Absolute knowledge could, therefore, leave nothing outside itself; and only on condition of knowing everything could man be granted its attainment. Man behaves as if he were destined to reach this absolute knowledge; and the incessant *why* which he puts to nature proves it. Indeed, this hope, constantly disappointed, constantly reborn, sustains and always will sustain successive generations in the passionate search for truth.

Our feelings lead us at first to believe that absolute truth must lie within our realm; but study takes from us, little by little, these chimerical conceits. Science has just the privilege of teaching us what we do not know, by replacing feeling with reason and experience and clearly showing us the present boundaries of our knowledge. But by a marvellous compensation, science, in humbling our pride, proportionately increases our power. Men of science who carry experimental analysis to the point of relatively determining a phenomenon doubtless see clearly their own ignorance of the phenomenon in its primary cause; but they have become its master; the instrument at work is unknown, but they can use it. This is true of all experimental sciences in which we can reach only relative or partial truths and know phenomena only in their necessary conditions. But this knowledge is enough to broaden our power over nature. Though we do not know the essence of phenomena, we can produce or prevent their appearance, because we can regulate their physico-chemical conditions. We do not know the essence of fire, of electricity, of light, and still we regulate their phenomena to our own advantage. We know absolutely nothing of the essence even of life; but we shall nevertheless regulate vital phenomena as soon as we know enough of their necessary conditions. Only in living bodies these conditions are much more complex and more difficult to grasp than in inorganic bodies; that is the whole difference.

To sum up, if our feeling constantly puts the question *why,* our reason shows us that only the question *how* is within our range; for the moment, then, only the question *how* concerns men of science and experimenters. If we cannot know *why* opium and its alkaloids put us to sleep, we can learn the mechanism of sleep and know *how* opium or its ingredients puts us to sleep; for sleep takes place only because an active substance enters into contact with certain organic substances which it changes. Learning these changes will give us the means of

producing or preventing sleep, and we shall be able to act on the phenomenon and regulate it at pleasure.

The Nature of Explanation [1]

C. J. DUCASSE

It is sometimes said that science does not explain but only describes—
that it does not tell us why things happen as they do, but only how they
happen. But obviously this is not true unless, to begin with, we force
upon the question "Why?" some mystical or foolish meaning not intended by those who, day in and day out, ask it and get it satisfactorily
answered. I recently had occasion to ask, for instance, why my oil-
burning furnace failed to start when the thermostat called for heat,
and my question was eventually answered by the statement that it was
because the contact points in the electrical relay had become corroded,
and whenever this occurs the electric current no longer passes through.
This was exactly the sort of information that my demand for an explanation, through the question "Why?" was meant to elicit. To say
that even if that information was true it did not constitute explanation
would be simply to refuse to use the word "explanation" in the sense
it has in ordinary English, and to force upon it instead, *ad damnandum,*
some unusual one. Again, the particular fact that a given piece of wax
has melted can be explained, for instance, by supposing that the sun
has been shining upon it, and recalling that exposure of wax to heat
regularly causes it to melt, can be explained, although the explanation
of it would be more esoteric. Without attempting to give it here, we
can say that it would consist of a statement that the structure of wax
is molecular, and of a description of heat and of melting in terms of
molecular behavior.

[1] From *Philosophy as a Science.* New York: Oskar Piest, 1941, pp. 162–164. Copyright, 1941, by Oskar Piest. Reprinted by permission.

We may be told, however, that when the explanations offered in these or any other cases are examined, they are found to consist only of descriptions of the *explicandum* in more general terms. But to say this is obviously to abandon the claim that science does not explain but only describes, and to substitute for it the admission that science does explain, together with the claim that explanation consists of description in more general terms. Even this claim, however, is hardly admissible. To explain the fact that a given piece of wax melted by saying that it was exposed to heat is not to describe in more general terms its having melted; it is to assert the antecedent occurrence of a particular event of another kind, already known to be capable of causing wax to melt. Again, to explain in terms of molecular changes the law that exposure of wax to heat regularly causes it to melt, is to define and postulate a respect of identity between being heated and melting, and to do this could only very elliptically be called describing that law in more general terms.

The essential nature of explanation is much rather that, given an *explicandum* Q, an explanation of it always has the form: Because P, and if P, then Q. That is, the *explicans* of a given *explicandum* always consists of the major and minor premises of some hypothetical syllogism in the *modus ponens*, having the *explicandum* as conclusion.[2]

---

[2] The major premise of the hypothetical syllogism must consist of some law of connection, whether causal or conceptual. That is, no basis for explanation is provided by a law of mere joint incidence. For example, that giraffes have cloven hoofs is not explained by the fact that giraffes are ruminants and the conjecture that all ruminants have cloven hoofs.

PART V

The Ambiguous Word

Define your terms!" has in many quarters become a disruptive tactic, a useful way of breaking off an argument, something to be avoided since the very effort itself is an invitation to disagreement. Nevertheless, the theory and practice of definition have been the object of much study in spite of John Wilkins' assertion in 1668 that "the business of Defining, [is] amongst all others the most nice and difficult," and, perhaps, because of C. I. Lewis' statement in 1946 that "what are most commonly called definitions are a class of statements which are peculiarly liable to ambiguity." And even when some word has been defined another issue must be faced: where does the process stop?

The opening sentence of Chapter VI of the seventh edition of *The Meaning of Meaning* is the same as it was in the first: "There is at present no theory of Definition capable of practical application under normal circumstances."

In the face of all this, it is still valuable to recognize that ambiguity, indefiniteness, vagueness and equivocation are ever with us. We may, if sensitive to the possibilities of confusion, learn to curb the arrogance, the presumption that we necessarily know what we or others are saying. When we have become conscious of the danger, we may even search for methods of prevention.

On Definition [1]

BLAISE PASCAL

The true method, which would furnish demonstrations of the highest excellence, if it were possible to employ the method fully, consists in observing two principal rules. The first rule is not to employ any term of which we have not clearly explained the meaning; the second rule is never to put forward any proposition which we cannot demonstrate by truths already known; that is to say, in a word, *to define all the terms,* and *to prove all the propositions.* But, in order that I may observe the rules of the method which I am explaining, it is necessary that I declare what is to be understood by *Definition.*

We recognise in Geometry only those definitions which logicians call *Nominal Definitions,* that is to say, only those definitions which impose a name upon things clearly designated in terms perfectly known; and I speak only of those definitions.

[Their value and use is to clear and abbreviate discourse by] expressing in the single name which we impose what could not be otherwise expressed but in several words; provided nevertheless that the name imposed remain divested of any other meaning which it might possess, so as to bear that alone for which we intend it to stand.

For example, if we need to distinguish among numbers those which are divisible into two equal parts, from those which are not so divisible, in order to avoid the frequent repetition of this distinction, we give a name to it in this manner: we call every number divisible into two equal parts an *Even Number.*

This is a geometrical definition, because after having clearly designated a thing, namely any number divisible into two equal parts, we

[1] Originally called "Réflexions sur la Géométrie en Général." This "free translation of the more important parts of this fragment" was made by W. Stanley Jevons and is to be found in his *Elementary Lessons in Logic: Deductive and Inductive,* Lesson XIII. London: Macmillan and Co., Limited, 1871.

give it a name divested of every other meaning, which it might have, in order to bestow upon it the meaning designated.

Hence it appears that definitions are very free, and that they can never be subject to contradiction, for there is nothing more allowable, than to give any name we wish to a thing which we have clearly pointed out. It is only necessary to take care that we do not abuse this liberty of imposing names, by giving the same name to two different things. Even that would be allowable, provided that we did not confuse the results, and extend them from one to the other. But if we fall into this vice, we have a very sure and infallible remedy; it is, to substitute mentally the definition in place of the thing defined, and to hold the definition always so present in the mind, that every time we speak, for instance, of an even number, we may understand precisely that it is a number divisible into two equal parts, and so that these two things should be so combined and inseparable in thought, that as often as one is expressed in discourse, the mind may direct itself immediately to the other.

For geometers and all who proceed methodically only impose names upon things in order to abbreviate discourse, and not to lessen or change the ideas of the things concerning which they discourse. They pretend that the mind always supplies the entire definition of the brief terms which they employ simply to avoid the confusion produced by a multitude of words.

Nothing prevents more promptly and effectively the insidious fallacies of the sophists than this method, which we should always employ, and which alone suffices to banish all sorts of difficulties and equivocations.

These things being well understood, I return to my explanation of the true method, which consists, as I said, in defining everything and proving everything.

Certainly this method would be an excellent one, were it not absolutely impossible. It is evident that the first terms we wished to define would require previous terms to serve for their explanation, and similarly the first propositions we wish to prove, would presuppose other propositions preceding them in our knowledge; and thus it is clear that we should never arrive at the first terms or first propositions.

Accordingly in pushing our researches further and further, we arrive necessarily at primitive words which we cannot define, and at principles so clear, that we cannot find any principles more clear to prove them by. Thus it appears that men are naturally and inevitably incapable of treating any science whatever in a perfect method; but it does not thence follow that we ought to abandon every kind of method. . . . The most perfect method available to men consists not in defining everything and demonstrating everything, nor in defining nothing and demonstrating nothing, but in pursuing the middle course of not defining things which are clear and understood by all persons, but of defining all others; and of not proving truths known to all persons, but of proving all others. From this method they equally err who undertake to define and prove everything, and they who neglect to do it in things which are not self-evident.

Third Meaning of the Word "Is": Definition[1]

GEORGE SANTAYANA

[Philosophers] are always asking you to tell them *what* some natural object is—man, matter, time, God—as if any definition whatever which you might offer of such deep-lying realities would be likely to come nearer to the thing as it is than do current names, sundry indications, or even the sum total of your discourse on that subject. Man, they say, *is* a rational animal: a circle *is* a plane figure bounded by a curve every part of which is equally distant from a point within called the centre. These definitions may be correct; but if I had no independent knowledge of what a man or a circle was, I could not judge whether they were correct or not. Pure discourse likes to take the bit in its teeth; and a geometer might tell me that he need have no notion whatever of the circle save that which the definition gives him, and that all his deductions would follow just as well from that premise; indeed, it is only from that premise that they must follow if they are to be valid mathe-

[1] From "Some Meanings of the Word 'Is,'" *The Journal of Philosophy*, Vol. XXI, No. 14, July 3, 1924, pp. 369–370. Reprinted by permission.

matically. The definition of the circle *is* the circle for the geometer. It would therefore be better, and worthier of the purity of deductive science, to drop such terms as circle, which suggests wheels, round eyes, and other vulgar objects, and to invent a symbol or formula to express the definition only, without any images borrowed from sense.

I believe this is the right method of dialectic; and if it is rigorously employed, it keeps discourse revolving about essences alone, and only about such essences as it has explicitly selected. But then, let it be remembered, these essences are not alleged to be the essences of anything existing. What follows from the algebraic formula for the circle is not alleged to hold good of hoops or rose-windows or the course of the planets. So that when any material, visible, or imagined circle is said to *be* a circle in the mathematical sense, the assertion is worse than false: it is irrelevant. Nothing can *be* the definition of it: at best the definition may be true of it. No definition, and no dialectic proceeding from the definition, can vouch for this natural truth. Only animal faith, trust in appearances, or experience in practical arts can justify such a presumption, or can even propose it. Definition is therefore perfectly useless for natural knowledge; but it is, when strictly adhered to, a fountain of deductions which are unimpeachable in themselves, although their relevance to matters of fact is problematical, and can only be asserted by one who knows those facts independently.

Definitions are complex names and they have the same function as names. They can not repeat the essence of a thing, because its essence is its whole texture and character. An adequate definition of any existing thing would be as complicated as the thing itself, and true only of that individual, or of such others, if any, as were indistinguishable from it internally. Nevertheless, like names, definitions are sometimes useful. If I asked a man "Who are you?" he might not unreasonably think the question impertinent, seeing that I was in his presence, and he might reply "I am myself." So when I ask of a thing, "What is that?" if the thing could overhear me, it might justly retort, "I am that I am." If, however, the man I challenged was of a mild and affable temper, and explained that he was Jenkins, that name might not be unmeaning to me. I might instantly conclude that I had not heard of him before, and should probably not hear of him again. So if I learned that the tome before me was a work of poetry, although poetry is proverbially difficult to define, I should know that all further consideration of it on my part was optional. Definitions may inform me of the place in which con-

ventional discourse puts the object before me, and if I trust the wisdom
of the definer, I shall have a useful hint concerning the ways of that
object. A card may suffice to tell me the sex, rank, and nationality of
the person whose name it bears, and may even enable me to guess
whether he comes to pay his compliments or to solicit a subscription.
Though a name seems to report who a man is, and a definition what
a thing is, yet the thing no more is its definition than the man is his
name.

Nominal and Real Definitions [1]

A U G U S T U S   D E   M O R G A N

When a name is complex, it frequently admits of definition, nominal
or real. A name may be said to be *defined nominally* when we can of
right substitute for it other terms. In such a case, a person may be made
to know the meaning of the word without access to the object of which
it is to give the idea. Thus, an *island* is completely defined in "land
surrounded by water." In definition, we do not mean that we are necessarily to have very precise terms in which to explain the name defined:
but, as the terms of the definition so is the name which is defined; according as the first are precise or vague, clear or obscure, so is the
second. Thus there may be a question as to the meaning of *land:* is a
marsh sticking up out of the water an island? Some will say that, as
opposed to water, a marsh is land, others may consider marsh as inter-
mediate between what is commonly called (dry) land and water. If
there be any vagueness, the term island must partake of it: for island
is but short for "land surrounded by water," whether this phrase be
vague or precise. This sort of definition is *nominal,* being the substitution of names for names. It is complete, for it gives all that the name is

[1] From *Formal Logic.* London: The Open Court Company, 1926, pp. 40–41. Copyright by The Open Court Company, Illinois. Reprinted by permission.

to mean. An island, as such, can have nothing necessarily belonging to it except what necessarily belongs to "land surrounded by water." By *real* definition, I mean such an explanation of the word, be it the whole of the meaning or only part, as will be sufficient to separate the things contained under that word from all others. Thus the following, I believe, is a complete definition of an elephant: "an animal which naturally drinks by drawing the water into its nose, and then spirting it into its mouth." As it happens, the animal which does this is the elephant only, of all which are known upon the earth: so long as this is the case, so long the above definition answers every purpose; but it is far from involving all the ideas which arise from the word. Neither sagacity, nor utility, nor the production of ivory, are necessarily connected with drinking by help of the nose. And this definition is purely objective; we do not mean that every idea we could form of an animal so drinking is to be called an elephant. If a new animal were to be discovered, having the same mode of drinking, it would be a matter of pure choice whether it should be called elephant or not. It must then be settled whether it shall be called an elephant, and that race of animals shall be divided into two species, with distinctive definitions; or whether it shall have another name, and the definition above given shall be incomplete, as not serving to draw an entire distinction between the elephant and all other things.

It will be observed that the nominal definition includes the real, as soon as the terms of substitution are really defined: while the real definition may fall short of the nominal.

When a name is clearly understood, by which we mean when of every object of thought we can distinctly say, this name does or does not, contain that object—we have said that the name applies to everything, in one way or the other. The word man has an application both to Alexander and Bucephalus: the first *was* a man, the second *was not*. In the formation of language, a great many names are, as to their original signification, of a purely negative character: thus, parallels are only lines which do *not* meet, aliens are men who are *not* Britons (that is, in our country). If language were as perfect and as copious as we could imagine it to be, we should have, for every name which has a positive signification, another which merely implies all other things: thus, as we have a name for a tree, we should have another to signify every thing that is not a tree. As it is, we have sometimes a name for the positive, and none for the negative, as in *tree:* sometimes for the negative and none for the positive, as in *parallels:* sometimes for both, as in a frequent use of *person* and *thing*.

How is "Exactness" Possible? [1]

F. C. S. SCHILLER

It is amazing what a spell the ideal of exactness has cast upon the philosophic mind. For hundreds, nay thousands, of years philosophers seem to have been yearning for exactness and hoping that, if only they can attain it, all their troubles will be over, that all the pitfalls in the way of philosophic progress will be circumvented and that every philosophic science, from psychology and logic to the remotest heights of metaphysics, will become accessible to the meanest understanding.

Yet what a gap there is between these professions and the practice of philosophers! Despite all their zeal for exactness, what body of learned men is more careless in their terminology and more contemptuous of all the devices which seem conducive to exactness?

Experience shows that it is quite impossible to pin any philosophic term down to any single meaning, even for a little while, or even to keep its meanings stable enough to avoid gross misunderstanding. Even the most express and solemn definitions are set at naught by the very writers who propounded them. The most famed philosophers are the very ones who have been the worst offenders. For example, Kant's fame rests in no small measure on the tricks he played with words like *"a priori,"* "category," "object," and his systematic confusion of "transcendental" and "transcendent." There is hardly a philosophy which does not juggle thus with ambiguous terms. If the theories of philosophers may be interpreted in the light of their practice, they should be the last persons in the world to laud "exactness."

On the other hand, they might fairly be expected to inform us what "exactness" means or at least what they wish it to mean. I do not find, however, that they are at all eager to do this. Apparently they are content to refer to mathematics as an "exact" science and to admonish philosophy to respect and aspire to the mathematical ideal.

To understand "exactness," therefore, we must go to mathematics and inquire whether and in what sense mathematics is "exact." Now it is clear that mathematics is not exact in the sense that mathematical objects exactly reproduce physical realities; nor do physical realities exactly exemplify mathematical ideals. There are no straight lines or circles to be found in nature, while all the physical constants, like the year, month, and day, are inexact. Plato knew this, but yet thought of God as a mathematician; he should have added that when God geometrizes, he does so very inexactly.

Hence, if the relation between realities and mathematical ideals is conceived as a copying or reproduction, it cannot possibly be "exact." Which is the archetype and which the copy does not matter; whether the real copies the mathematical ideal or the latter is moulded upon the former, no exactness can be found.

There is, however, a sense in which exactness depends on definition; and mathematicians take great pride in the exactness of their definitions. A definition can be exact, because it is as such a command addressed to nature. It sounds quite uncompromising. If the real will not come up to the definition, so much the worse for the real! In-so-far therefore as exactness depends on definitions, mathematics can be exact. It can be as exact as anything defined exactly.

But there appear to be limits to the exactness thus attainable. The exactness of a definition is limited by two difficulties: (a) In the first place things must be found to which the definition, when made, does actually apply; and secondly (b) the definition has to be maintained against the growth of knowledge. Both these difficulties may easily prove fatal to exactness.

As to (a), it is clear that we cannot arbitrarily "define" the creatures of our fancy, without limits. Definitions which apply to nothing have no real meaning. The only sure way, therefore, of securing a definition which will be operative and will have application to the real, is to allow the real, idealized if necessary, to suggest the definition to the mathematician. The mathematician was sensible enough to adopt this procedure. He allowed a ray of sunlight to suggest the definition of a straight line, and this assured to Euclidean geometry a profitable field of application.

But it did not render the definition immutable and immune to the growth of knowledge. The mathematical definition remains dependent on the behaviour of the real. If, therefore, rays of light are found to curve in a gravitational field, a far-reaching doubt is cast on the use of Euclidean geometry for cosmic calculations.

As to (b), the definer retains the right to revise his definitions. So the very framing of his definition may suggest to the mathematician the idea of developing it in some promising and interesting direction. But this procedure may entail a further definition or re-definition which destroys the exactness of the first formula. Thus, when he has accomplished the "exact" definition of a circle and an ellipse, it may occur to a mathematician that after all a circle may be taken as a special case of an ellipse and that it would be interesting to see what happens if he followed out this line of thought. He does so, and arrives at "the points of infinity," with their paradoxical properties. Again the development of non-Euclidean geometries has rendered ambiguous and inexact the Euclidean conception, for example, of "triangle." Even so elementary and apparently stable a conception as that of the unit of common arithmetic undergoes subtle transformations of meaning as others beyond the original operation of addition are admitted.

In mathematics then, as in the other sciences, it is inevitable that the conceptions used should grow. It is impossible to prohibit their growth and to restrict them to the definitions as they were conceived at first. Indeed the process of stretching old definitions so as to permit of new operations is particularly evident in mathematics.

The method by which it is justified is that of analogy. If an analogy can be found which promises to bridge a gap between one notion and another, their identity is experimentally assumed. And if the experiment works for the purposes of those who made it, the differences between them are slurred over and ignored. If it were not possible to take the infinitesimal, now as something, now as nothing, what would be left of the logic of the calculus? But the logician at least should remind himself that analogy is not an exact and valid form of argument.

Can exactness be said to inhere in the symbols used by mathematicians? Hardly. $+$ and $-$, and even $=$, have many uses and therefore senses, even in the exactest mathematics.

The truth is that mathematical definitions cannot be more exact than our knowledge of the realities to which, sooner or later, directly or indirectly, they refer. Nor can mathematical symbols be more exact than words. It is sheer delusion to think otherwise.

And what about words? Whence do they get their meanings, and how are they stabilized and modified? Words get their meaning by being used successfully by those who have meanings to convey. *Verbal* meaning, therefore, is derivative from *personal* meaning. Once a verbal meaning is established and can be presumed to be familiar, personal meaning can employ a word for the purpose of transmitting a new meaning judged appropriate to a situation in which a transfer of meaning is always experimental, and generally it is problematic and inexact.

Moreover the situation which calls for it is always more-or-less new. Hence a successful transfer, that is, the understanding of a meaning, always involves an extension of an old meaning; and in the course of time this may result in a complete reversal of the initial definition. For example, when the "atom" was first imported into physics, it was defined as the ultimate and indivisible particle of matter. Now, notoriously, it has been subdivided so often that there seems to be room in it for an unending multitude of parts; and its exploration is the most progressive part of physics. The word remains, but its definition has been radically changed. For the scientist always has an option when he finds that his old words are no longer adequate: he can change either his terms or his definitions. But there is and can be no fixity and no exactness about either.

There is a further difficulty about definitions. Not all words can be defined. Wherever the definer begins or ends he makes use of terms not yet defined, or has recourse to definitions revolving in a circle. So, if he hankers after exactness, he declares that some terms are indefinable and need no definition. This subterfuge is utterly unworthy of an exact logician. For if he holds that these indefinables are yet intuitively understood or apprehended, he enslaves his "logic" to psychology. If he admits that he cannot guarantee that any two reasoners will understand the indefinables alike, he explodes the basis of all exactness. Thus even the exactest definitions are left to float in a sea of inexactitude.

The situation grows still more desperate if the logician realizes that to achieve exactness he must eradicate and overcome the potential ambiguity of words. He must devise words which exactly fit the particular situation in which the words are used. For otherwise the same word will be permitted to mean one thing in one context, another in another. It will be what logicians have been wont to call "ambiguous." However, they may have been mistaking for a flaw the most convenient property of words, namely, their plasticity and capacity for repeated use as vehicles of many meanings.

For the alternative of demanding a one-one correspondence between words and meanings, seems incomparably worse. I remember this was tried once by Earl Bertrand Russell, in a sportive mood. It was not long after the War, and he had just emerged from the dungeon to which he had been consigned for an ill-timed jest, that he came to Oxford to read a paper to a society of undergraduate philosophers on what he called "vagueness." I was requested to "open the discussion" on this paper, and so obtained what in Hollywood is called a "preview" of it. What was my amazement when I found that Russell's cure for "vagueness," that is, the applicability of the same word to different situations, was that there should be distinctive words enough for every situation! Certainly that would be a radical cure; but in what a state would it leave language! A language freed from "vagueness" would be composed entirely for nonce-words, *hapex legomena,* and almost wholly unintelligible. When I pointed out this consequence, Russell cheerfully accepted it, and I retired from the fray.

Russell had rightly diagnosed what was the condition of exactness. But he had ignored the fact that his cure was impracticable and far worse than the alleged disease. Nor had he considered the alternative, the inference that therefore the capacity of words to convey a multitude of meanings must not be regarded as a flaw, but that a distinction must be made between plurality of meanings and actual ambiguity.

It is vital to logic that the part words play in transmitting meaning from one person to another should be rightly understood; but does not such understanding reduce the demand for "exactness" to a false ideal?

What finally is the bearing of these results on the pretensions of logistics? It seems to reduce itself to a game with fictions and verbal meanings. It is clear that it is a fiction that meanings can be fixed and embodied in unvarying symbols. It is clear that the verbal meanings to be fixed are never the personal meanings to be conveyed in actual knowing. The assumption that they can be identified is just a fiction too. There appears to be no point of contact between the conventions of this game and the real problems of scientific knowing. This is the essential difference between logistics and mathematics. Pure mathematics is a game too, but it has application to reality. But logistics seems to be a game more remote from science than chess is from strategy. For in a science the meanings concerned are those of the investigators, that is, they are personal. They are also experimental. They respond to every advance in knowledge and are modified accordingly. Their fixity would mean stagnation and the death of science. Words need have only enough stability of meaning, when they are used, for the old senses (which determine their selection) to yield a sufficient clue to the new senses to be conveyed, to render the latter intelligible. In their context, not in the abstract. In the abstract they may remain infinitely "ambiguous," that is, potentially useful. This does no harm, so long as it does not mislead in actual use. And when an experimenter ventures on too audacious innovations upon the conventional meanings of his words, the right rebuke to him is not "You contradict the meaning of the words you use," but "I do not understand; what do you mean?"

I am driven then to the conclusion that logistics is an intellectual game. It is a game of make-believe, which mathematically trained pedants love to play, but which does not on this account become incumbent on every one. It may have the advantage that it keeps logisticians out of other mischief. But I fail to see that it has either any serious significance for understanding scientific knowing or any educational importance for sharpening wits.

Definitions and Reality [1]

LOUIS DE BROGLIE

May it not be universally true that the concepts produced by the human mind, when formulated in a slightly vague form, are roughly valid for Reality, but that when extreme precision is aimed at, they become ideal forms whose real content tends to vanish away? It seems to me that such is, in fact, the case, and that innumerable examples can be found in all spheres, particularly in those of Psychology and Ethics, as well as of everyday life.

Let us take an example from the ethical field and consider the concept of an honest man. Let us begin with a somewhat vague definition; let us say that an honest man is a man of great probity, who always tends to do what he considers his duty and to resist all temptations drawing him in the opposite direction. We shall find around us— for we must not be too pessimistic—a certain number of people who fulfill this definition. But if we were to insist that the crown of honesty is to be awarded only to a man who never, in any circumstances, at any moment of his life, experienced the slightest temptation to disobey his conscience, then no doubt we shall find a striking diminution—since human nature is full of frailty—in the number of men to whom our definition will apply. The more precise and rigid the concept becomes, that is to say, the more restricted becomes its sphere of application. Like the plane monochromatic wave, absolute virtue, if defined with too exacting a precision, is an idealization the probability of whose full realization tends to vanish away.

Examples of this kind are, it should be repeated, innumerable. In the psychological, ethical, and social sphere an uncompromisingly rigid definition or argument often leads away from, rather than towards, Reality. It is true that the facts tend to assume a certain

[1] Reprinted from *Matter and Light* by Louis de Broglie by permission of W. W. Norton & Company, Inc., New York, copyright, 1939. Pp. 280–282 in the 1946 Dover Publications edition.

order within the framework supplied by our reason; but it is no more than a tendency, and the facts invariably overflow if the framework is too exactly defined.

Thus in the region of the inexact sciences of human conduct, the strictness of the definitions varies inversely as their applicability to the world of Reality. But now the question arises, whether we have any right to compare this fact with those encountered during the development of modern Physics. Admittedly we are dealing with nothing more than an analogy whose applicability must not be overstressed; yet I believe that it is less superficial than might at first be thought. Whenever we wish to describe facts, whether of a psychological or an ethical nature, or belonging to the sphere of the physical or natural sciences, we are inevitably dealing with a Reality which is always infinitely complex and full of an infinity of shades on the one hand, and on the other with our understanding, which forms concepts which are always more or less rigid and abstract. A confrontation between Reality and understanding is inevitable, and as far-reaching a reconciliation as possible, desirable. It is certain that our concepts are capable of adaptation to Reality to a considerable extent, provided that we allow them a certain margin of indeterminateness: if it were otherwise, no argument relating to real facts could be effected on the basis of any order of ideas. What is more doubtful is whether such a correspondence can be maintained to the end, if we insist on eliminating the margin of indeterminateness and on effecting extreme precision in our concepts. Even in the most exact of all the natural sciences, in Physics, the need for margins of indeterminateness has repeatedly become apparent—a fact which, it seems to us, is worthy of the attention of philosophers, since it may throw a new and illuminating light on the way in which the idealizations formed by our reason become adaptable to Reality.

What has been said also throws light on the parts played respectively by the spirit of geometry, and that of intuition, in the development of human knowledge. The spirit of geometry is needed, for without it we could give no degree of precision to our ideas and arguments; our knowledge, without it, would always remain vague and merely qualitative. But there is a need also for the spirit of intuition; it is required to recall to us without ceasing that reality is too fluid and too rich to be contained in its entirety within the strict and abstract framework of our ideas. These are certainly familiar notions to all who have given any thought to the progress and value of human knowledge; yet it seems to me that the development of Physics might suggest to such thinkers some new reflections in the sense which it has been the aim of these pages to indicate.

The Patient's Language [1]

FREDERICK C. REDLICH

Any physician who listens to the stories of patients and explains the nature of their illness to them becomes aware of frequent misunderstandings between patient and physician. In bedside teaching, on the presentation of patients to students, and on ward rounds one is often struck by the anxiety and confusion of patients which follow a partial or complete misunderstanding of the physician's words on such occasions. At times serious maladjustment of the patient has resulted from such inadequate communication. . . .

C. W. Morris in agreement with Carnap postulates three dimensions of semiotics: The relations of signs to other signs, or syntactics; the relation of signs to objects, or semantics; and the relation of signs to its interpreters, or pragmatics. Naturally these dimensions are intimately interconnected, as Morris points out repeatedly.

No systematic empirical investigation of the subject of the meaning of medical terms to patients has been made. The purpose of the present investigation was to study responses of patients to medical terms. In terms of semiotics this study deals with the following problems: How do patients respond to medical terms; what are their verbal habits if asked to define such signs? What do definitions, i.e., substitutions of signs by other signs which are presumably better "understood," teach us about such interpretations? Can any statement about

[1] From *The Yale Journal of Biology and Medicine*, Vol. 17, No. 3, January, 1945, pp. 427–453. Reprinted by permission of the editor and author.

such "understanding" be made? Can any conclusions as to the patient-physician relationship be drawn from this material?

METHOD

The following report is based on the data obtained from 25 patients to whom 60 medical terms were presented and who were asked to define these terms. The patients were chosen in a neuropsychiatric hospital practice by random sample. Every fourth case was used for this study, excluding patients with sweeping personality changes, marked deterioration, feeble-mindedness, and aphasias. All patients were literate; none of them had more than a high school education; all came from an urban environment and were born in the United States.

A survey of the patient's diagnosis, sex, age, education, occupation, intelligence quotient (obtained by the Wechsler-Bellevue Test—verbal scale—for adults), emotional status, and a test score for medical vocabulary [was] made. . . .

An attempt to score the patient's definitions was made in the following manner: The patients' definitions of all words which can be objectively (operationally) defined were compared with definitions given by physicians. The scoring was done by two physicians; in cases of doubt and contradiction comparisons were made with definitions as they are given in the American Medical Dictionary. To achieve a crude quantitative analysis, such terms were scored in the following manner: The score plus (+) was given when the definition was identical with a reasonably full definition as given by an expert. The score plus-minus (±) was given when the statements were true though incomplete as judged by an expert. The score minus (−) was given when statements were either very incomplete or false. The score (0) designated the lack of any response, or acknowledgment of ignorance of the sign. Such comparisons between statements of experts and the statements of patients and subsequent rating will necessarily be inadequate and arbitrary; nevertheless they will determine roughly what the patient knows and what he does not know.

The following words were used in the test in the given order: infection, spinal fluid, prognosis, spine, nerve, deterioration, feeble-minded, convulsions, schizophrenia, dementia praecox, tuberculosis, moron, pathology, syphilis, lesion, tumor, gonorrhea, lues, I.Q., hysteria, G.C., Ca., neurosis, Wassermann, metastasis, cancer, paralysis, psychoanalysis, functional, organic, psychogenic, hypnosis, diagnosis, psychopathic, physiotherapy, psychotherapy, nervous disease, mental disease, neurologist, psychiatrist, psychologist. . . .

The patient was asked to define these words in a simple manner. He was encouraged to speak freely without regard to elegance of form, but rather to express whatever occurred to him when he heard such a word. Patients were told that they were expected not to know a number of these words because they were technical terms, mostly known only to physicians and medical students. In all cases good cooperation was assured; whenever it was necessary the patient was encouraged and praised for his achievements. The atmosphere of an examination was avoided as much as possible and all patients were told that this was not an intelligence test, but just served the purpose of seeing whether patients understand certain medical terms. The patients were all well known to the examiner at the time of this examination and no particular resistance or anxiety about the whole test was encountered. All patients were tested privately in the form of a casual interview; the responses of the patient were recorded verbatim.

Semiotics employs certain terms which will be used in the following sections: Such basic terms occurring in the process of semiosis are: 1. The sign vehicle or word (in the case of language) or mediator of a sign; in this paper referred to as sign, term, or word. 2. The designatum or what is taken account of (if the designatum refers to an actual existant semiotics speaks of a denotatum). 3. The interpreter and its response or the interpretation; such responses are complexes of cognitive, emotive, and conative behavior and experiences.

OBSERVATIONS

In the following paragraphs the most typical and interesting definitions of the terms of this study are quoted. It is impossible to quote all definitions as this would make the study too bulky.[2] On the other hand, hardly any attempt at quantitative appraisal has been made as only 25 patients were studied.

Infection:

The sign is known to physician and patients. Denotations are rare (10 per cent), but approximate definitions were given by 86 per cent. It is a sign which is apt to lead to some confusion and possibly to

---

[2] Of the 60 terms investigated only 4 are presented here [Editor's note].

anxiety. It expressed (a) sepsis, (b) destruction of tissue, to most patients. Recurrent definitions are: (patient L) "if you scratch or cut yourself"; (patient C) "something that got into the blood stream from the skin"; (patient J) "something that has gotten into the blood stream which causes poisoning of the body"; (patient A) "it's poison, blood poisoning, skin wounds cause it."

Nerve:

This term is one of the most interesting ones. It is used by physicians and patients very frequently in their discourse on neuropsychiatric disease and is the root word for a number of other words as nervous, nervous disease, nervous breakdown, etc. Wide discrepancies in its usage by physicians and patients result in considerable confusion and possibly consequent maladjustment. Not a single patient gave a complete or essential definition, while three-fourths of the patients stressed one or the other properties. To all patients the sign expressed something. The majority of the patients tried to describe (a) the appearance and location; (b) functions. As no patient had any concrete experience with the anatomy and physiology of nerves, most statements were based on hearsay, vague general assumptions with little cognitive and many emotional interpretations. Descriptions of nerves referred to threads, wires, which run all over the body. (Patient A) "A tiny thread all over your body"; (patient E) "it goes to the spine, I never saw it, like a little vein"; (patient H) "a delicate tissue in the brain, the brain is the central nerve, the nerves are all at the back of the brain"; (patient K) "it's the entire wiring of the nervous system"; (patient Q) "a telephone line from body to brain"; (patient V) "parts of your body; the main nerve in the back, the pulse nerve." It is noteworthy that the sensory function of nerves is much stressed, while the motor role is hardly mentioned. The description of functions pertains to feelings, vague notions on coordination, "life," "nervousness." (Patient B) "something you have all over, I think it's microscopic, they give you feelings or if they go dead, if they are upset it makes you bad"; (patient D) "nerves is something in the system; if they get irritated you can't find peace and you worry"; (patient F) "feels like strings and gives sharp sensation all over the body"; (patient I) "stands all over the body for feeling, tasting, smelling, is very sensitive; the main line runs to the brain"; (patient J) "it's the background of the whole body"; (patient M) "a tendon that carries currents to the brain";

(patient N) "a nerve would be what shakes; you have nervous headaches, a nervous stomach"; (patient S) "they keep you alive"; (patient R) "they are controlled by our mind"; (patient U) "you have to have them, they keep you excited"; (patient W) "something inside you, it makes you nervous."

Paralysis:

The sign is used by physicians and patients. All patients had heard of the sign. The most important reference is to "immobility"; (patient B) "it makes you stiff so you can't move"; (patient E) "loss of limb or speech"; (patient G) "when the nerves of the body go dead"; (patient R) "when one has no control over extremities"; (patient W) "is when you are rigid"; (patient Y) "when the nerves become dead." Shock, stroke, infantile paralysis are mentioned as causes. (Patient A) "like a shock"; (patient L) "a stroke you get"; (patient U) "is infantile paralysis; could be in a part of the body; caused by a cold or shock; a fall paralyzes you."

Neurosis:

The sign is used widely by physicians, less so by patients. One-fourth of the cases never heard of the term and only one-fourth referred to some significant features. Some of the definitions referred to it as a "disease of the nerves"; (patient A) "a breaking down of the nerves"; (patient K) "is a nerve disease; it might reveal itself often physically"; (patient H) "it is neurotic pain, neuralgia." In other definitions this is not clear, because patients refer to the pragmatically hazy concept of "nerves." (Patient R) "something to do with the nerves"; (patient D) "is something to do with the nerves, a nervous condition." Other definitions stress psychological aspects—(patient G) "is a mental state; anxiety neurosis; you have to do certain things, a compulsion state of mind that pins down actions"; (patient H) "means you are extremely nervous"; (patient I) "is a form of illness confined to the mind; it may be in existence, but the mind helps it along." . . .

ANALYSIS AND DISCUSSION

A definition as a conscious verbal response is certainly only one of many responses. All definitions remain incomplete, if only for the reason that an infinity of existants corresponds to a finitude of words, or to put it differently there are more things than words. This is particularly true when short definitions are demanded in a test situation. Many definitions are unsatisfactory because people who are not accustomed to expressing themselves in such a manner are unable to verbalize sufficiently for linguistic reasons or because consciously or unconsciously they do not wish to verbalize. To determine more adequately an individual's response to a sign, it would be necessary to observe the individual over a period of time and in various situations. It is quite obvious that such studies would be very laborious and complex. The present study with all its insufficiencies seems to be at least a beginning in the direction of a study of medical signs and their interpretations.

The test scores on medical terms of 25 patients were expressed on a 0–100 scale; they varied from a minimum of 10 to a maximum of 63 with a mean of 30 and a standard deviation of 12. The I.Q. of these patients, determined by the Wechsler-Bellevue (verbal scale), varied from a minimum of 80 to a maximum of 134, with a mean of 110 and a standard deviation of 16. The correlation between knowledge of medical terms and I.Q. is $+ 0.3$.

It is quite evident that, in addition to general intelligence and general vocabulary of the patient, other factors determine the test scores. Interest in the disease, the degree of anxiety, hypochondriacal tendencies, curiosity, as well as the age of the patient, cultural and ecological background, duration of the disease and reward or punishment of previous explorations seem to play a role.

The impression was gained that patients get most of their medical knowledge from observation of other patients and discussions among themselves. Twelve of the 25 patients thought they obtained some information from their physicians. Thirteen thought their information about their own disease and medical matters in general was not adequate. General school education seemed to contribute very little to the patients' knowledge of disease. Only 10 of 25 listed radio and books as sources of information. Only one patient thought he gained medical knowledge in school. Discussions of medical matters in the family and with friends received low ratings, though it seemed patients underrated such sources.

The ignorance and the confusion as regards medical terms make one wonder whether our system of education fulfills its function of teaching the population certain minimal requirements regarding health and disease. An investigation of this topic might be of equal importance for educators, public health officials, and physicians and might become the basis for certain changes in the teaching of hygiene.

. . . Hardly any term was generally known. As was expected, highly technical terms and medical jargon expressions were virtually unknown in the cultural and educational group which was represented by the 25 patients. Such expressions were: prognosis, schizophrenia, dementia praecox, pathology, lesion, lues, G.C., Ca., metastasis.

A more important and much larger group were definitions of terms which gave rise to "semantic confusion." Such definitions by patients were different from definitions made by physicians, and the inference is drawn that such confusion might lead to definite maladjustment on the side of the patient. Such terms were: infection, tuberculosis, syphilis, gonorrhea, tumor, cancer, paralysis, spine, spinal fluid, nerve, functional, organic, psychogenic, hypnosis, psychologist, neurologist, psychiatrist.

A third group consisted of terms which led to a more or less outspoken fear response. Such an emotional response was inferred either from the content of the response or from concomitant reactions of the patients. Some of these terms were comparatively well known, as: infection, cancer, paralysis, fit, tumor, syphilis, mental disease. Others were only vaguely known, often ill-defined, as: degeneration, psychopathic, moron, schizophrenia, hypnosis.

No attempt is made to present the histories of the patients with the full protocols of their definitions of medical terms. Naturally great differences in knowledge and in the type of response were encountered even in the small group of patients under investigation. It was felt, however, that in many cases important knowledge in regard to the patient's illness and his "experiencing" of it was gained from his definitions. Definitions of such signs as neurosis, mental disease, nervous disease, psychiatrist, neurologist, and psychotherapy proved to be interesting material in the case study and became helpful for future relationships. Generally speaking, it was felt that most patients could be helped considerably in their attitude by a rational discussion, with elimination of certain fears and doubts and other irrational attitudes arising from ignorance and misunderstanding of medical terms. Two-thirds of the 25 patients knew too little about medical matters, their illnesses, and the implications of their illnesses. A small group possibly knew "too much," but their knowledge was rather erratic, poorly integrated, and often quite irrational. Both groups might be helped considerably by sensible information. However, it should be stressed that adjustment is possible without any adequate knowledge of the processes involved, as our every-day life shows. Most persons handle money, play radios, take care of their bodily needs, etc., without much of an idea of economic, physical, or physiological laws or of the nature of the things involved. An operating knowledge usually is sufficient.

Questions posed were whether patients "understand" the language of their physicians, whether physicians "understand" their patients' language, and whether both are aware of any limitation of such "understanding." "Understanding" can be defined in syntactic, semantic, and pragmatic rules. Understanding pre-supposes the proper observation of formation and transformation, or syntactic rules, by users of a language. The semantic dimension of understanding refers to operational acts which intend to determine actual existants. In pragmatics, however, "understanding" occurs when identical expectations are raised by the same sign in its different users. In trying to deduct such expectations from definitions given by patients one becomes aware that patients often do not understand medical terms as they are used by physicians and even more often have confusing and misleading concepts, causing inadequate behavior, unnecessary suffering, and a poor physician-patient relationship. Naturally a physician ought to expect such ignorance of medical terms, but actually physicians are not sufficiently aware of these misunderstandings.

Some of these misunderstandings can be explained in syntactic-semantic terms though, as Morris says, all rules when actually in operation contain a pragmatic component. To my knowledge, syntax, as developed by Carnap, Tarski, etc., has chiefly dealt with scientific languages and very little with every-day language. It will be the future task of some logician to subject the every-day language to a syntactical analysis; but some crude observations may be made even without such analysis. The amount of circular definitions in our material (with consequent confusion and maladjustment) is amazing. Few patients observed the fundamental rule of definition to establish a familiar starting point and to define outside the speech situation, i.e., to denote. Besides, unfamiliar signs very often are defined on grounds of their phonetic similarity to other familiar signs and thus are not properly denoted. "Paralysis" is equated with "infantile paralysis"; "feeble-minded" is defined as a "feeble mind"; "psychoanalysis" is defined as "analysis of the mind." Such violation of formation rules and neglect of significations occur with the signs "nerve," "nervous," "nervous disease." The denotation of "nerve" is not well known to laymen and on the ground of similarity of these signs with the vague designation "nervous," the sign "nervous disease" acquires a very peculiar significance for patients, and even "nerve" itself tends to be defined in terms of the designation "nervous." A totally inadequate orientation results. . . .

The different interpretations of medical terms by physicians and laymen must be recognized. To physicians, medical terms are, or ought to be at least, "significata," the content of which has been determined by operational procedures. Laymen in most cases, as it has been demonstrated, are not aware of such denotations and their underlying operational principles; their responses to medical terms are predominantly emotional. If physicians are not aware of such responses, they will not be understood, and the doctors will not understand patients or be able to alleviate the patients' anxiety and maladjustment. . . .

The results of this study might be of some interest to the teaching physician. In bedside teaching, in lectures, and on ward rounds, it is often unavoidable that some statements about the patient's illness are made to students in front of the patient. This need not be harmful to the patient; it may even happen that when no statements are made anxiety is aroused over such silence. The teaching clinician ought to be aware of the impression which his behavior and his remarks make on the patient. This problem has found too little attention in medical circles. . . .

Interpretation [1]

I. A. RICHARDS AND CHRISTINE GIBSON

We have all suffered from the kind of confusion illustrated by the exclamation, "What a (w)hole Harvard is!" The speaker had one idea in his mind and his hearer another. Most of us, too, have our stories about children's misunderstandings of prayers: "Lead us not into Thames Station," and so on. (Shades of the deep Shelter! What division will there be between those who had to go through all that and those who did not?) These mishearings come at the foot of a ladder that reaches up as high as Jacob's. On the lower rungs of it we are most of us fairly safe, though children are not. A little girl meeting for the first time

> *There is a green hill far away*
> *Without a city wall*

was deeply (and rightly) puzzled as to why a green hill should have a wall at all. *Without* as "outside" had not yet come within her ken. There might be these notable differences, however, between our examples. In the first, there could be solid grounds of prejudice to explain the mistaking of *whole* for hole. In the second, mere unfamiliarity with the word *temptation* might be enough. But in the third, the word *without* was familiar enough in one of its senses. In fact it was this very familiarity which prevented the possibility of another sense from coming up. Had the word been quite new, had it been *ayont*, say, there would have been no trouble. Context would have made the reader take it in her stride. It was because the word was already reserved and booked for another sense that the relevant sense was turned away.

A similar case higher up the ladder occurred when Chateaubriand translated Milton's *fast* in *Paradise Lost* (I:11–12)

> *Siloa's brook that flow'd*
> *Fast by the oracle of God*

[1] Reprinted from *Learning Basic English* by I. A. Richards and Christine Gibson, pp. 87–89, by permission of W. W. Norton & Company, Inc., New York. Copyright, 1945, by W. W. Norton & Company, Inc.

by *rapidement*. Milton meant "béside, close to, hard by" though "hard" would probably have confirmed Chateaubriand in his impression. Translation from other languages constantly brings up this sort of mistake. Teachers and students generally understand them very well and know how to be on the lookout for them. Indeed, mistakes of this sort commonly announce themselves as resoundingly as fog signals—to others, who know the language better. In general they do no great damage to human understanding—unless they get into translations of peace treaties or similar places. And if that happens we will usually be right in suspecting that more than mere ignorance was responsible for the mistake. We shall probably find that it was as much a twist as a slip.

Mistakes due to mere ignorance, to insufficiently wide acquaintance with a language, to unfamiliar words, and so forth, come within the routine of learning. The remedy is as simple as the fault—a careful look at the right part of the right article in Webster's will supply the missing bit or clean up the confusion. We may note in passing that this *acquaintanceship* with words is a surface matter. It does not go deeper than the sort of acquaintance we may have with thousands of people: We know their names, can recognize their faces or voices, we may know broadly what they do and who they are—but we do not *really know* them. We have no need to. Acquaintanceship is enough.

The really serious misunderstandings (from the lost point to the quarrel) concern those other words we all think we do really know—the familiar, friendly, incessantly useful key words which take a part in all our doings and in every third sentence.[2] In general the more useful a word is the more dangerous it can be. This is important—and particularly for Basic, since so many Basic words are certainly among the most useful. What we have just said may seem to hand enemies of Basic a magnificent weapon, but Basic supplies its own remedy here—through giving so much *intensive experience* with these words. The foreign learner is given this in learning his Basic, the English speaker through learning to keep within it. Both are better placed than a similar student without the experience to deal "justly, skillfully and magnanimously" with these handiest if trickiest of words.

No reader who has worked through our Chapter V, the one previous, is very likely to think at this point that we are scaremongering, or

[2] For a list of 100 such key words, and a discussion of our means of mastering them, see *How To Read a Page* by I. A. Richards (Norton, 1942), pp. 22, 108, and Chapter VII, "The Choice of the Key Words."

exaggerating these losses and dangers. For his eyes will not be on problems like the use of *lay* and *lie, infer* and *imply, ingenuous* and *ingenious, awake* and *waken* or similar malapropistic and stylistic hazards. As we have remarked above, these are not the troublemakers. A certain sort of language study—well understood by every good language teacher—can deal with them. Dictionary exercises can handle all confusions between different words or between those senses of one word which a dictionary can list. The trouble is more widespread, since the mistakes that matter most are mistakes as to *the jobs a word may be doing at a place in a passage.* The senses of a word (as we are using "sense" here) are limited—much as a man's official positions are limited. (Even Poo Bah's ministerial appointments were limited.) But his jobs may be endless, covering everything he can successfully turn his hand to. Senses are relatively settled things. Jobs can be indefinitely various and shifting. It is useful, of course, to know that Poo Bah is at once First Lord of the Treasury, Lord Chief Justice, Commander in Chief, Lord High Admiral, Master of the Buckhounds, Groom of the Back Stairs, Archbishop of Tipper, Lord Mayor both Acting and Elect, Lord Chamberlain, Attorney-General, Chancellor of the Exchequer, Privy Purse, Private Secretary, Leader of the Opposition, Paymaster General, Lord High Auditor, and First Commissioner of Police, and you may suffer if you forget it. But over and above this you need to be able to see whether it is a pencil or his knife which he is sharpening and he may be doing either in any or none of his official capacities. So, too, a word's job—what it is doing at a place in a passage—is not settled simply by its dictionary sense or senses; it is settled by what the occasion and the rest of the passage hands it to do then and there. In brief, its job is what the situation requires of it.

Now the jobs that words do are the really neglected part of most studies of reading and writing. To study their jobs we have, of course, to know the senses of the words, but too often our studies stop right there. That is not enough. For real understanding we must go further and look closer, and this is where Basic can be a help—chiefly through forcing us, as no less limited medium will, to concern ourselves with the context.[3] It is the context always that assigns a word's job and it is only through the context that we can discover what it is doing.

[3] A set of first exercises of this sort for school use is *Words at Work* by Christine Gibson, which may be obtained from the Harvard Commission on English Language Studies, 13 Kirkland Street, Cambridge, Massachusetts.

A current example will make this distinction between the *senses* and the *jobs* of words clear. Take the word *fear*. No dictionary will tell us what sort of fear is in question when we meet the word. Fear of what, and how or why felt? A good dictionary can separate for us:

1. A painful sort of emotion, or an instance of it.
2. A state or habit of fearing.
3. Awe or reverence, e.g. for the Supreme Being.
4. That which causes fear or toward which fear is felt.

It can and does indicate something of the possible range of the word's jobs by listing other words, *anxiety, cowardice, timidity* . . . which may in various contexts take over its work. But when we have consulted the dictionary and absorbed all it says, we still have, in connection say with "freedom from fear," to consider for ourselves what job *fear* has here—in view of the relevant context of situation— immense though this job is and reaching, of course, far beyond the accompanying words. We have to decide (a) what sorts of fears, (b) felt in what measure, (c) about what, (d) by whom, (e) under what conditions, (f) when, (g) where, and (h) why—at least.

This looks absurdly overcomplicated—but in fact most people do all this in a flash as easily and unconsciously as they turn their eyes in the direction of a sound—which would look a hopelessly complicated business, too, if we were to start writing out the *how* of it. Most people know pretty well what this ideal means. And they know very well that Mr. Roosevelt in formulating the Four Freedoms was not recommending, under the heading of "Freedom from Fear," any blind optimism or ostrichism, any form of anodyne or alcohol, any neglect of preparations for defense or lack of realism in foreign affairs. They know, too, that he was not inhibiting either the pursuit of wisdom (fear of the Lord is its beginning; *Proverbs* 9:10) or true courage (the knowledge of what is truly to be feared, as Plato defined it; *Republic* 430).

Fear is a big word. As things have been, are, and probably will be, it is one of the most useful of words. And though states of anxiety and dread need to have their inner and outer causes seen to, heaven defend us from becoming less apt in our necessary fears! The main thing is to have the right fears—which may imply being freed from obsessive fears and distracting physical threats. But to help us much in the choice and control of our fears is hardly yet within the sphere of government action.

Ambiguity and Its Avoidance [1]

JAMES MACKAYE

STANDARD FORM FOR THE AVOIDANCE OF AMBIGUITY

Arnauld has very truly remarked that "some of the greatest controversies would cease in a moment, if one or other of the disputants took care to make out precisely, and in a few words, what he understands by the terms which are the subject of dispute," words which are peculiarly applicable to the fallacy of ambiguity. That fallacy indeed is so important in connection with reasoning, and defeats the purpose thereof throughout such a wide realm of thought, that it seems well to formulate a standard form in which ambiguities and the mode of avoiding them may find expression. Five steps in the process may be conveniently distinguished.

First, the difficulty always arises in connection with some issue, and this issue should first be stated, either in the form of a categorical or interrogative proposition. The latter form is very convenient, and when possible the questions should be so phrased as to be answerable "Yes" or "No." This is usually feasible; perhaps always so. Thus, suppose the question at issue is, Does the compass point north? This might very well be a disputed question, and its statement is the first step in the process of avoiding the ambiguity which causes the dispute.

The second step is recognition and record of the ambiguous word or words which lead to disagreement, and in this case it is rather easy to recognize the word "north" as the culprit because of the two meanings which would be most likely to be confounded in connection with compass readings, viz. (1) geographic north, and (2) magnetic north.

The third step is to recognize and record a meaning of the ambiguous word (or words) which *fails* to make the distinction required to resolve the dispute; a meaning which slurs over the essential issue involved,

[1] From *The Logic of Language.* Hanover, New Hampshire: Dartmouth College Publications, 1939, pp. 125–130, 135–136, 143–146. Copyright, 1939, by Dartmouth College. Reprinted by permission.

and is presumably the meaning which neither party would dispute. I say presumably, because it usually happens that such a meaning must be guessed at, or inferred from inconclusive evidence, since it is characteristic of verbal disputes that the definitions of the words which cause them are either not stipulated at all, or stipulated with insufficient intelligibility, and hence subject to conjecture. It may not always be possible, therefore, to take this third step in the process. Often indeed it is difficult to decide what the inadequate definition may be; but usually a more or less plausible guess is possible, and it is fair to presume that it is some customary and loose meaning to be found in a dictionary, or one approximating thereto. In the example under discussion, it is a fair inference that such a definition as the following would meet the requirements: North means the direction at the right hand of the setting sun. This definition would not suffice to settle the issue in dispute, since *both* the geographic and magnetic north would conform to it.

The fourth step is to recognize and separately record the two (or more) meanings which *are* sufficient to resolve the dispute, and the failure to distinguish which has caused it. This also is a matter of conjecture, and sometimes requires much ingenuity, depending upon the subtlety of the distinctions which have been confounded. In the case of our example, however, this fourth step is easy. The two definitions are: (1) North (a) means "the direction of the north geographic pole," and (2) North (b) means "the direction of the north magnetic pole." These definitions, being stipulated, may be distinguished from each other in any convenient manner, either by calling them north (a) and north (b), as above, or north′ and north″, or north [1] and north [2], etc., or, qualifying adjectives may be employed. Thus north (a) may be called geographic north, and north (b) magnetic north, and this latter expedient, when feasible, is likely to be the most convenient, since the qualifying adjectives, if properly selected, can be made to suggest the meanings of the words, as is done in the present example.

The fifth and last step consists in, (1) multiplying the original question so as to ask the two (or more) questions required by the split or divided meanings formulated in the fourth step, and substituting one of the sufficiently defined terms in each of them, and (2) answering them, preferably by "Yes" or "No." The disagreement in the answers will disclose the ambiguity simulating a contradiction which is the cause of the original dispute.

In the manner described above the originally unanswerable question is converted into two (or more) answerable ones. Throwing the example here cited into this standard form will illustrate the general rule, and indicate how to apply it in other cases:

    I Ambiguous question:
      Does the compass point to the north?
   II Ambiguous word:
      North.
 III Insufficient definition:
      North means "a direction to the right hand of the setting sun."
 IV Sufficient definitions:
      North (a) (geographic north) means "the direction of the north geographic pole."
      North (b) (magnetic north) means "the direction of the north magnetic pole."
   V Multiplied questions and answers:
      Does the compass point to north (a) (geographic north)? Answer, No.
      Does the compass point to north (b) (magnetic north)? Answer, Yes.

When once the meanings of the numerals I, II, III, IV, V, are understood, it is unnecessary to state them on each occasion when the form is used, because it is understood that I stands for the ambiguous question, II for the ambiguous word, III for the insufficient definition, IV for the sufficient definitions, and V for the multiplied questions and their answers.

It is obvious that the process is one, not of word-splitting, but of meaning-splitting. The more the meanings are divided, the more the questions are multiplied. It might indeed be called a process of meaning splitting, or a process of dividing meanings and multiplying questions, or perhaps the best name would be the process of definitional analysis. The comprehension of the process is more important than its name. When the meanings divide into more than two there will be more than two definitions under IV, and more than two questions under V. Sometimes it is difficult to ascertain III, but this is not really necessary to the success of the process. It is usually only a matter of conjecture in any event. Resourcefulness in discovering the definitions expressed in IV is the essential matter. It is indeed of an importance hard to exaggerate. A knack for detecting the two (or more) meanings which are being confused in a disputed verbal question is of more service in reasoning than the most thorough knowledge of the moods and figures of the syllogism. Failure to acquire this knack is accountable for numberless disputes and futilities among thinkers, and the chief lesson to be taught by the examples which follow is the supreme usefulness of acquiring it.

A question in which an ambiguous word occurs is in reality more than one question disguised as one, and hence requires more than one answer. Of such questions Aristotle remarks:

> Several questions put as one should be at once decomposed into their several parts. Only a single question admits of a single answer: so that neither several predicates of one subject, nor one predicate of several subjects, but only one predicate of one subject, ought to be affirmed or denied in a single answer.

The decomposition of ambiguous questions thus referred to is obviously the purpose of the standard form here described.

CONFUSION OF TWO "JOHNS"

We may begin our illustrations of the confusion caused by ambiguity with a few trivial examples, the first of which will be particularly obvious. Two men are disputing about the color of John's hair. One of them has in mind a boy named John with black hair, the other a boy, also named John, with red hair. As the boys are called by a common name, the disputants suppose the same boy is being referred to. One contends that John's hair is black; the other that it is not black, but red. Thus they appear to be contradicting each other, and as long as the ambiguity of the name *John* is not recognized, no way of settling the dispute is available. The question of how John's hair can be black and yet not black at the same time remains a mystery. When it is recognized that there are two Johns, however, John Jones and John Smith, the mystery is at once resolved; the apparent contradiction is seen to be no more than an ambiguity posing as a contradiction, and the dispute is settled. Clarity takes the place of confusion. Both disputants are in the right. John Jones' hair is black and John Smith's hair is not black. Thus no citation of evidence except about meanings is required, because the whole dispute is verbal. Throwing the issue into the standard form; it appears thus:

   I Ambiguous question:
      Is John's hair black?
  II Ambiguous word:
      John.
 III Insufficient definition:
      John means "a person whose name is John."
 IV Sufficient definitions:
      John (a) means "John Jones."
      John (b) means "John Smith."
   V Multiplied questions and answers:
      Is John (a)'s (John Jones') hair black? Answer,
      Yes.
      Is John (b)'s (John Smith's) hair black? Answer,
      No.

In most philosophical disputes, not to mention those which are not philosophical, the apparent contradictions are similar ambiguities simulating contradictions. There are two (or more) Johns, and their hair is not of the same color.

. . . .

CONFUSION OF TWO "SOUNDS"

A very simple example of ambiguity is that contained in the question, Does the fall of a tree in an uninhabited wilderness cause a sound? The natural impulse of most people to answer this question in the affirmative receives the reply that, as there is no one present to hear the crash, no sound can result, since a sound which nobody hears would be a contradiction. It is indeed of the nature of sound that it shall be heard. This seems a very simple controversy to settle, yet it is sometimes argued with the same inconclusiveness as the "goes round" question, for, strange as it may seem, this question is not always recognized as a verbal one. The fact is, no uncustomary meanings need to be stipulated in this case, since the two definitions which are being confused can be found distinguished in any good sized standard dictionary. Adopting these distinctions in IV, and throwing the issue into the usual standard form, it appears as follows:

   I Does a tree falling in an uninhabited wilderness cause a sound?
  II Sound.
 III Sound means "noise or acoustic phenomena."

iv Sound (a) means "an audible sensation."
Sound (b) means "a series of waves in the air which are capable of causing sound (a) when they impinge on the human ear."

v Does a tree falling in an uninhabited wilderness cause a sound (a)? Answer, No.
Does a tree falling in an uninhabited wilderness cause a sound (b)? Answer, Yes.

Thus it is entirely true that the nature of sound (a) is that it shall be heard, but it is not true of the nature of sound (b). The disputants are talking about two Johns, only John has changed his name to Sound.

. . . .

CONFUSION OF TWO "KNOWLEDGES"

Mediaeval philosophers spent most of their time discussing verbal questions, and in this respect did not differ much from modern ones. . . . Hence, few of their controversies were ever settled. The disputants were always confident that their opponents were mistaken about the color of John's hair, but neither could convince the other, because it was not recognized that there were two Johns. Exceptions to this rule are sometimes encountered, however, and our next example will be taken from the writings of the schoolman, John Scotus Eriugena, who flourished in the ninth century. A favorite theme among these scholastics was the relation of God to man; whether they were of the same substance or only of similar substance, and like verbal questions. The dialogue form of exposition was common among them, and in the course of one of these dialogues between master and disciple, the following example of the application of the process of definitional analysis is to be found:

Disc. Why is it, then, since you have spoken of it for a long time now, that the human mind has the idea by which it knows itself, and the discipline by which it learns itself, and now you assert on the other hand that it can be known neither by itself nor by any other creature?

Mast. Reason teaches that both are true: that the human mind assuredly knows itself and does not know itself. For it knows that it is, but it does not know what it is. And through this circumstance, as we have taught in the previous books, the image of God is shown most of all to be in man.

For as God is comprehensible in that one deduces from creation that he is, and is incomprehensible because what he is can be comprehended by no understanding, human or angelic, nor even by himself because he is not a *what*, but is superessential: so it is given to the human mind to know only this, that it is, but it is in no way granted to it to know what it is; and, what is even more to be wondered at and more beautiful to those who contemplate themselves and their God, the human mind is more to be praised in its ignorance than in its knowledge. . . . The divine likeness in the human mind, therefore, is recognized most clearly in that it is known only to be; but what it is is not known.

This passage draws a distinction between two kinds of knowledge; what may be called existential knowledge on the one hand and essential knowledge on the other. The first is knowledge of the existence of a thing, the second knowledge of the essence or nature of a thing. Thus of the hypothetical planet supposed by some astronomers to exist between Mercury and the sun we have essential knowledge, but not existential knowledge. We know its nature because we know the nature of planets in general, but we do not know that it exists. Of the cause of magnetic attraction, on the other hand, we have existential knowledge, but not essential knowledge. We know that a cause of the attraction exists, as we know that a cause of all such phenomena must exist, but we do not know the nature of the cause. This is evidently the distinction made by Eriugena in order to show that the apparent contradiction, "the human mind assuredly knows itself and does not know itself," is only an ambiguity simulating a contradiction. That it is a typical "two Johns" settlement of the question is plain from its expression in standard form, thus:

I Can mind, human or divine, have knowledge of itself?
II Knowledge.
III Knowledge means "a state of awareness of fact or meaning."
IV Knowledge (a) (existential knowledge) means "a state of awareness of the existence of a thing."
Knowledge (b) (essential knowledge) means "a state of awareness of the essence of a thing."
V Can mind, human or divine, have existential knowledge of itself? Answer, Yes.
Can mind, human or divine, have essential knowledge of itself? Answer, No.

If this explicit expression of the ambiguity and the method of avoiding it is compared with the obscure expression of the same process embodied in Eriugena's own words, the usefulness of employing the standard form will be apparent. In the foggy statement of the process by the scholastic, it is none too easy to recognize what is really happening. In thus expressing Eriugena's solution in standard form, of course, I am not taking any position on the material issues raised by his answers under V. Material issues are not being discussed in this chapter, and it would certainly be a futile digression to discuss those he raises. The normal character of his method of avoiding a metaphysical dispute "that otherwise might be interminable" is all to which attention is here directed.

PART VI

The Recognition of Differences

In the 4th century, B.C., Aristotle noted that

Science arises whenever from a multitude of notions given in experience a universal conception is formed comprising all similar cases. . . . The reason for this is that experience is knowledge of individual cases, whereas science is knowledge of universal principles, and every action and every creative process has to do with individual cases.

In 1940 Albert Einstein pursued the issue in these terms:

Science is the attempt to make the chaotic diversity of our sense-experience correspond to a logically uniform system of thought. In this system single experiences must be correlated with the theoretic structure in such a way that the resulting coordination is unique and convincing.

An interest in the individual case, the single experience, the recognition of differences among things and people is something which, nevertheless, may have to be cultivated. As Coleridge put it, "For one error resulting from excess of distinguishing the indifferent, I could show ten mischievous delusions from the habit of confounding the diverse." Somehow, it has seemed easier to speak in "universal conceptions" without caring for the correlation with the specific case. This is not to say that the emphasis on similarities has no role. It is to say that the differences must not be lost in the process.

Of General Terms [1]

JOHN LOCKE

All things that exist being particulars, it may perhaps be thought reasonable that words, which ought to be conformed to things, should be so too; I mean in their signification: but yet we find the quite contrary. The far greatest part of words, that make all languages, are general terms; which has not been the effect of neglect or chance, but of reason and necessity.

First, It is impossible that every particular thing should have a distinct peculiar name. For the signification and use of words, depending on that connexion which the mind makes between its ideas and the sounds it uses as signs of them, it is necessary, in the application of names to things that the mind should have distinct ideas of the things, and retain also the particular name that belongs to every one, with its peculiar appropriation to that idea. But it is beyond the power of human capacity to frame and retain distinct ideas of all the particular things we meet with: every bird and beast men saw, every tree and plant that affected the senses, could not find a place in the most capacious understanding. If it be looked on as an instance of a prodigious memory, that some generals have been able to call every soldier in their army by his proper name, we may easily find a reason, why men have never attempted to give names to each sheep in their flock, or crow that flies over their heads; much less to call every leaf of plants, or grain of sand that came in their way, by a peculiar name.

Secondly, If it were possible, it would yet be useless; because it would not serve to the chief end of language. Men would in vain heap up names of particular things, that would not serve them to communicate their thoughts. Men learn names, and use them in talk with

[1] From *Essay Concerning Human Understanding,* Book III, Chapter III, Sections 1–6, 9, 11. New York: Valentine Seaman, 1824.

others, only that they may be understood: which is then only done, when by use or consent the sound I make by the organs of speech, excites in another man's mind, who hears it, the idea I apply it to in mine, when I speak it. This cannot be done by names applied to particular things, whereof I alone having the ideas in my mind, the names of them could not be significant or intelligible to another, who was not acquainted with all those very particular things which had fallen under my notice.

Thirdly, But yet granting this also feasible (which I think is not) yet a distinct name for every particular thing would not be of any great use for the improvement of knowledge: which, though founded in particular things, enlarges itself by general views: to which things reduced into sorts under general names, are properly subservient. These, with the names belonging to them, come within some compass, and do not multiply every moment, beyond what either the mind can contain, or use requires: and therefore, in these, men have for the most part stopped; but yet not so as to hinder themselves from distinguishing particular things, by appropriated names, where convenience demands it. And therefore in their own species, which they have most to do with, and wherein they have often occasion to mention particular persons, they make use of proper names; and there distinct individuals have distinct denominations. . . .

The next thing to be considered, is, how general words come to be made. For since all things that exist are only particulars, how come we by general terms, or where find we those general natures they are supposed to stand for? Words become general, by being made the signs of general ideas; and ideas become general, by separating from them the circumstances of time, and place, and any other ideas, that may determine them to this or that particular existence. By this way of abstraction they are made capable of representing more individuals than one; each of which having in it a conformity to that abstract idea, is (as we call it) of that sort. . . .

. . . He that thinks general natures or notions are any thing else but such abstract and partial ideas of more complex ones, taken at first from particular existences, will, I fear, be at a loss where to find them. For let any one reflect, and then tell me, wherein does his idea of man differ from that of Peter and Paul, or his idea of horse from that of Bucephalus, but in the leaving out something that is peculiar to each individual, and retaining so much of those particular complex ideas of several particular existences, as they are found to agree in? Of the complex ideas signified by the names man and horse, leaving out but those particulars wherein they differ, and retaining only those wherein they agree, and of those making a new distinct complex idea, and giving the name animal to it; one has a more general term, that comprehends with man several other creatures. Leave out of the idea of animal, sense and spontaneous motion; and the remaining complex idea, made up of the remaining simple ones of body, life, and nourishment, becomes a more general one, under the more comprehensive term *vivens*. And not to dwell longer upon this particular, so evident in itself, by the same way the mind proceeds to body, substance, and at last to being, thing, and such universal terms which stand for any of our ideas whatsoever. To conclude, this whole mystery of genera and species, which make such a noise in the schools, and are with justice so little regarded out of them, is nothing else but abstract ideas, more or less comprehensive, with names annexed to them. In all which this is constant and unvariable, that every more general term stands for such an idea, and is but a part of any of those contained under it. . . .

To return to general words, it is plain by what has been said, that general and universal belong not to the real existence of things; but are the inventions and. creatures of the understanding, made by it for its own use, and concern only signs, whether words or ideas. Words are general, as has been said, when used for signs of general ideas, and so are applicable indifferently to many particular things: and ideas are general, when they are set up as the representatives of many particular things: but universality belongs not to things themselves, which are all of them particular in their existence; even those words and ideas, which in their signification are general. When therefore we quit particulars, the generals that rest are only creatures of our own making; their general nature being nothing but the capacity they are put into by the understanding, of signifying or representing many particulars. For the signification they have is nothing but a relation, that by the mind of man is added to them.

Realists and Nominalists[1]

H . G . W E L L S

There is a natural tendency in the human mind to exaggerate the differences and resemblances upon which classification is based, to suppose
that things called by different names are altogether different, and that
things called by the same name are practically identical. This tendency
to exaggerate classification produces a thousand evils and injustices. In
the sphere of race or nationality, for example, a "European" will often
treat an "Asiatic" almost as if he were a different animal, while he will
be disposed to regard another "European" as necessarily as virtuous
and charming as himself. He will, as a matter of course, take sides with
Europeans against Asiatics. But, as the reader of this history must
realize, there is no such difference as the opposition of these names
implies. It is a phantom difference created by two names. . . .

The main mediæval controversy was between the "Realists" and the
"Nominalists," and it is necessary to warn the reader that the word
"Realist" in mediæval discussion has a meaning almost diametrically
opposed to "Realist" as it is used in the jargon of modern criticism.
The modern "Realist" is one who insists on materialist details; the
mediæval "Realist" was far nearer what nowadays we should call an
Idealist, and his contempt for incidental detail was profound. The
Realists outdid the vulgar tendency to exaggerate the significance of
class. They held that there was something in a name, in a common
noun that is, that was essentially real. For example, they held there was
a typical "European," an ideal European, who was far more real than
any individual European. Every European was, as it were, a failure, a
departure, a flawed specimen of this profounder reality. On the other
hand the Nominalist held that the only realities in the case were the
individual Europeans, that the name "European" was merely a name
and nothing more than a name applied to all these instances.

[1] From *The Outline of History.* Garden City, N. Y.: Garden City Publishing Co., Inc.,
1929, pp. 726–728. Copyright, 1920, by H. G. Wells. Reprinted by permission.

Nothing is quite so difficult as the compression of philosophical controversies, which are by their nature voluminous and various and tinted by the mental colours of a variety of minds. With the difference of Realist and Nominalist stated baldly, as we have stated it here, the modern reader unaccustomed to philosophical discussion may be disposed to leap at once to the side of the Nominalist. But the matter is not so simple that it can be covered by one instance, and here we have purposely chosen an extreme instance. Names and classifications differ in their value and reality. While it is absurd to suppose that there can be much depth of class difference between men called Thomas and men called William, or that there is an ideal and quintessential Thomas or William, yet on the other hand there may be much profounder differences between a white man and a Hottentot, and still more between *Homo sapiens* and *Homo neanderthalensis*. While again the distinction between the class of pets and the class of useful animals is dependent upon very slight differences of habit and application, the difference of a cat and dog is so profound that the microscope can trace it in a drop of blood or a single hair. When this aspect of the question is considered, it becomes understandable how Nominalism had ultimately to abandon the idea that names were as insignificant as labels, and how, out of a revised and amended Nominalism, there grew up that systematic attempt to find the *true*—the most significant and fruitful—classification of things and substances which is called Scientific Research.

And it will be almost as evident that while the tendency of Realism, which is the natural tendency of every untutored mind, was towards dogma, harsh divisions, harsh judgments, and uncompromising attitudes, the tendency of earlier and later Nominalism was towards qualified statements, towards an examination of individual instances, and towards inquiry and experiment and scepticism.

On Knowing the Difference [1]

ROBERT LYND

It was only the other day that I came upon a full-grown man reading with something like rapture a little book—*Ships and Seafaring Shown to Children*. His rapture was modified, however, by the bitter reflection that he had already passed so great a part of his life without knowing the difference between a ship and a barque; and, as for sloops, yawls, cutters, ketches, and brigantines, they were simply the Russian alphabet to him. I sympathise with his regret. It was a noble day in one's childhood when one had learned the names of sailing-vessels, and, walking to the point of the harbour beyond the bathing-boxes, could correct the ignorance of a friend: "That's not a ship. That's a brig." To the boy from an inland town every vessel that sails is a ship. He feels he is being shown a new and bewildering world when he is told that the only ship that has the right to be called a ship is a vessel with three masts (at least), all of them square-rigged. When once he has learned his lesson, he finds an unaccustomed delight in wandering along the dirtiest coal-quay, and recognising the barques by the fact that only two of their three masts are square-rigged, and the brigs by the fact that they are square-rigged throughout—a sort of two-masted ships. Vessels have suddenly become as real to him in their differences as the different sorts of common birds. As for his feelings on the day on which he can tell for certain the upper fore topsail from the upper fore top-gallant sail, and either of these from the fore skysail, the crossjack, or the mizzen-royal, they are those of a man who has mastered a language and discovers himself, to his surprise, talking it fluently. The world of shipping has become articulate poetry to him instead of a monotonous abracadabra.

It is as though we can know nothing of a thing until we know its name. Can we be said to know what a pigeon is unless we know that it

[1] From *The Pleasures of Ignorance*. New York: Charles Scribner's Sons, 1921, pp. 82–90. Reprinted by permission.

is a pigeon? We may have seen it again and again, with its bottle-shoulders and shining neck, sitting on the edge of a chimney pot, and noted it as a bird with a full bosom and swift wings. But if we are not able to name it except vaguely as a "bird," we seem to be separated from it by an immense distance of ignorance. Learn that it is a pigeon, however, and immediately it rushes towards us across the distance, like something seen through a telescope. No doubt to the pigeon-fancier this would seem but the first lisping of knowledge, and he would not think much of our acquaintance with pigeons if we could not tell a carrier from a pouter. That is the charm of knowledge—it is merely a door into another sort of ignorance. There are always new differences to be discovered, new names to be learned, new individualities to be known, new classifications to be made. The world is so full of a number of things that no man with a grain of either poetry or the scientific spirit in him has any right to be bored, though he lived for a thousand years. Terror or tragedy may overwhelm him, but boredom never. The infinity of things forbids it. I once heard of a tipsy young artist who, on his way home on a beautiful night, had his attention called by a maudlin friend to the stars, where they twinkled like a million larks. He raised his eyes to the heavens, then shook his head. "There are too many of them," he complained wearily. It should be remembered, however, that he was drunk, and that he did not know astronomy. There could be too many stars only if they were all turned out on the same pattern, and made the same pattern on the sky. Fortunately, the universe is the creation not of a manufacturer but of an artist.

There is scarcely a subject that does not contain sufficient Asias of differences to keep an explorer happy for a lifetime. It would be easy to do nothing but chase butterflies all one's days. It is said that thirteen thousand species of butterflies have been already discovered, and it is suggested that there may be nearly twice as many that have so far escaped the naturalists. After so monstrous a figure, we are not surprised to learn that there are sixty-eight species of butterflies in Great Britain and Ireland. We should be astonished, however, had we not already expended our astonishment on the large number. How many of us are there who could name even half-a-dozen varieties? We all know the tortoiseshell and the white and the blue—the little blue butterflies that flutter over the gold and red of the cornfields. But the average man does not even know by name such varieties as the Camberwell Beauty, the Dingy Skipper, the Pearl-bordered Fritillary, and the White-letter

Hairstreak. As for the moth, are there not as many sorts of moths as there are words in a dictionary? Many men give all the pleasant hours of their lives to learning how to know the difference between one of them and another. One used to see these moth-hunters on windless nights in a Hampstead lane pursuing their quarry fantastically with nets in the light of the lamps. In pursuing moths, they pursue knowledge. This, they feel, is life at its most exciting, its most intense. They regard a man who does not know and is not interested in the difference between one moth and another as a man not yet thoroughly awakened from his pre-natal sleep. And, indeed, one could not conceive a more appalling sort of blank idiocy than the condition of a man who could not tell one thing from another in any department of life whatever. We would rather change lives with such a man. This luxury of variety was not meant to be ignored. We throw ourselves into it with exhilaration as a swimmer plunges into the sea. There are few forms of happiness I know which are more enviable than that of those who have eyes for birds and flowers. How they rejoice on learning that, according to one theory, there are a hundred and three different species of brambles to be found in these islands! They would not have them fewer by a single one. It is extraordinarily pleasant even for one who is mainly ignorant of the flowers and their families to come on two or three varieties of one flower in the course of a country walk. As a boy, he is excited by the difference between the pinheaded and the thrum-headed primrose. As he grows older, he scans the roadside for little peeping things that to a lazy eye seem as like each other as two peas—the dove's foot geranium, the round-leaved geranium and the lesser wild geranium. "As like each other as two peas," we have said; but *are* two peas like each other? Who knows whether the peas have not the same difference of feature among themselves that Englishmen have? Half the similarities we notice are only the results of our ignorance and idleness. The townsman passing a field of sheep finds it difficult to believe that the shepherd can distinguish between one and another of them with as much certainty as if they were his children. And do not most of us think of foreigners as beings who are all turned out as if on a pattern, like sheep? The further removed the foreigners are from us in race, the more they seem to us to be like each other. When we speak of Negroes, we think of millions of people most of whom look exactly alike. We feel much the same about Chinamen and even Turks. Probably to a Chinaman all English children look exactly alike, and it may be that all

Europeans seem to him to be as indistinguishable as sticks of barley-sugar. How many people think of Jews in this way! I have heard an Englishman expressing his wonder that Jewish parents should be able to pick out their own children in a crowd of Jewish boys and girls.

Thus our first generalisations spring from ignorance rather than from knowledge. They are true, so long as we know that they are not entirely true. As soon as we begin to accept them as absolute truths, they become lies. One of the perils of a great war is that it revives the passionate faith of the common man in generalisations. He begins to think that all Germans are much the same, or that all Americans are much the same, or that all Conscientious Objectors are much the same. In each case he imagines a lay figure rather than a human being. He may hate his lay figure or he may like it; but, if he is in search of truth, he had better throw the thing out of the window and try to think about a human being instead. I do not wish to deny the importance of generalisations. It is not possible to think or even to act without them. The generalisation that is founded on a knowledge of and a delight in the variety of things is the end of all science and poetry. Keats said that he sought the principle of beauty in all things, and poems are in a sense simply beautiful generalisations. They subject the unclassified and chaotic facts of life to the order of beauty. The mystic, meditating on the One and the Many, is also in pursuit of a generalisation—the perfect generalisation of the universe. And what is science but the attempt to arrange in a series of generalisations the facts of what we are vain enough to call the known world? To know the resemblances of things is even more important than to know the difference of things. Indeed, if we are not interested in the former, our pleasure in the latter is a mere scrap-book pleasure. If we are not interested in the latter, on the other hand, our sense of the former is apt to degenerate into guesswork and assertion and empty phrases. Shakespeare is greater than all the other poets because he, more than anybody else, knew how very like human beings are to each other and because he, more than anybody else, knew how very unlike human beings are to each other. He was master of the particular as well as of the universal. How much poorer the world would have been if he had not been so in regard not only to human beings but to the very flowers—if he had not been able to tell the difference between fennel and fumitory, between the violet and the gilly-flower!

The Passion for Parsimony [1]

WILLIAM JAMES

The facts of the world in their sensible diversity are always before us, but our theoretic need is that they should be conceived in a way that reduces their manifoldness to simplicity. Our pleasure at finding that a chaos of facts is the expression of a single underlying fact is like the relief of the musician at resolving a confused mass of sound into melodic or harmonic order. The simplified result is handled with far less mental effort than the original data; and a philosophic conception of nature is thus in no metaphorical sense a labor-saving contrivance. The passion for parsimony, for economy of means in thought, is the philosophic passion *par excellence;* and any character or aspect of the world's phenomena which gathers up their diversity into monotony will gratify that passion, and in the philosopher's mind stand for that essence of things compared with which all their other determinations may by him be overlooked.

More universality or extensiveness is, then, one mark which the philosopher's conceptions must possess. Unless they apply to an enormous number of cases they will not bring him relief. The knowledge of things by their causes, which is often given as a definition of rational knowledge, is useless to him unless the causes converge to a minimum number, while still producing the maximum number of effects. The more multiple then are the instances, the more flowingly does his mind rove from fact to fact. The phenomenal transitions are no real transitions; each item is the same old friend with a slightly altered dress.

Who does not feel the charm of thinking that the moon and the apple are, as far as their relation to the earth goes, identical; of knowing respiration and combustion to be one; of understanding that the

---

[1] From "The Sentiment for Rationality," *The Will to Believe.* New York: Longmans, Green and Co., 1897, pp. 65–70. Copyright, 1896, by William James. Reprinted by permission.

balloon rises by the same law whereby the stone sinks; of feeling that
the warmth in one's palm when one rubs one's sleeve is identical with
the motion which the friction checks; of recognizing the difference
between beast and fish to be only a higher degree of that between
human father and son; of believing our strength when we climb the
mountain or fell the tree to be no other than the strength of the sun's
rays which made the corn grow out of which we got our morning
meal?

But alongside of this passion for simplification there exists a sister
passion, which in some minds—though they perhaps form the minority
—is its rival. This is the passion for distinguishing; it is the impulse to
be *acquainted* with the parts rather than to comprehend the whole.
Loyalty to clearness and integrity of perception, dislike of blurred outlines, of vague identifications, are its characteristics. It loves to recognize particulars in their full completeness, and the more of these it
can carry the happier it is. It prefers any amount of incoherence, abruptness, and fragmentariness (so long as the literal details of the separate
facts are saved) to an abstract way of conceiving things, that while it
simplifies them, dissolves away at the same time their concrete fulness.
Clearness and simplicity thus set up rival claims, and make a real
dilemma for the thinker.

A man's philosophic attitude is determined by the balance in him
of these two cravings. No system of philosophy can hope to be universally accepted among men which grossly violates either need, or
entirely subordinates the one to the other. The fate of Spinoza, with
his barren union of all things in one substance, on the one hand; that
of Hume, with his equally barren "looseness and separateness" of
everything, on the other—neither philosopher owning any strict and
systematic disciples to-day, each being to posterity a warning as well as
a stimulus—show us that the only possible philosophy must be a compromise between an abstract monotony and a concrete heterogeneity.
But the only way to mediate between diversity and unity is to class the
diverse items as cases of a common essence which you discover in them.
Classification of things into extensive "kinds" is thus the first step; and
classification of their relations and conduct into extensive "laws" is the
last step, in their philosophic unification. A completed theoretic philosophy can thus never be anything more than a completed classification of the world's ingredients; and its results must always be abstract,
since the basis of every classification is the abstract essence embedded

in the living fact—the rest of the living fact being for the time ignored by the classifier. This means that none of our explanations are complete. They subsume things under heads wider or more familiar: but the last heads, whether of things or of their connections, are mere abstract genera, data which we just find in things and write down.

When, for example, we think that we have rationally explained the connection of the facts A and B by classing both under their common attribute x, it is obvious that we have really explained only so much of these items as *is* x. To explain the connection of choke-damp and suffocation by the lack of oxygen is to leave untouched all the other peculiarities both of choke-damp and of suffocation—such as convulsions and agony on the one hand, density and explosibility on the other. In a word, so far as A and B contain $l, m, n,$ and $o, p, q,$ respectively, in addition to x, they are not explained by x. Each additional particularity makes its distinct appeal. A single explanation of a fact only explains it from a single point of view. The entire fact is not accounted for until each and all of its characters have been classed with their likes elsewhere. To apply this now to the case of the universe, we see that the explanation of the world by molecular movements explains it only so far as it actually *is* such movements. To invoke the "Unknowable" explains only so much as is unknowable, "Thought" only so much as is thought, "God" only so much as is God. *Which* thought? *Which* God? —are questions that have to be answered by bringing in again the residual data from which the general term was abstracted. All those data that cannot be analytically identified with the attribute invoked as universal principle, remain as independent kinds or natures, associated empirically with the said attribute but devoid of rational kinship with it.

Hence the unsatisfactoriness of all our speculations. On the one hand, so far as they retain any multiplicity in their terms, they fail to get us out of the empirical sand-heap world; on the other, so far as they eliminate multiplicity the practical man despises their empty barrenness. The most they can say is that the elements of the world are such and such, and that each is identical with itself wherever found; but the question Where is it found? the practical man is left to answer by his own wit. Which, of all the essences, shall here and now be held the essence of this concrete thing, the fundamental philosophy never attempts to decide. We are thus led to the conclusion that the simple classification of things is, on the one hand, the best possible theoretic philosophy, but is, on the other, a most miserable and inadequate substitute for the fulness of the truth. It is a monstrous abridgment of life, which, like all abridgments, is got by the absolute loss and casting out of real matter. This is why so few human beings truly care for philosophy. The particular determinations which she ignores are the real matter exciting needs, quite as potent and authoritative as hers. What does the moral enthusiast care for philosophical ethics? Why does the *Æsthetik* of every German philosopher appear to the artist an abomination of desolation?

> *Grau, theurer Freund, ist alle Theorie*
> *Und grün des Lebens goldner Baum.*

The entire man, who feels all needs by turns, will take nothing as an equivalent for life but the fulness of living itself. Since the essences of things are as a matter of fact disseminated through the whole extent of time and space, it is in their spread-outness and alternation that he will enjoy them. When weary of the concrete clash and dust of pettiness, he will refresh himself by a bath in the eternal springs, or fortify himself by a look at the immutable natures. But he will only be a visitor, not a dweller in the region; he will never carry the philosophic yoke upon his shoulders, and when tired of the gray monotony of her problems and insipid spaciousness of her results, will always escape gleefully into the teeming and dramatic richness of the concrete world.

So our study turns back here to its beginning. Every way of classifying a thing is but a way of handling it for some particular purpose. Conceptions, "kinds," are teleological instruments. No abstract concept can be a valid substitute for a concrete reality except with reference to a particular interest in the conceiver. The interest of theoretic rationality, the relief of identification, is but one of a thousand human purposes. When others rear their heads, it must pack up its little bundle and retire till its turn recurs. The exaggerated dignity and value that philosophers have claimed for their solutions is thus greatly reduced. The only virtue their theoretic conception need have is simplicity, and a simple conception is an equivalent for the world only so far as the world is simple—the world meanwhile, whatever simplicity it may harbor, being also a mightily complex affair. Enough simplicity remains, however, and enough urgency in our craving to reach it, to make the theoretic function one of the most invincible of human impulses. The quest of the fewest elements of things is an ideal that some will follow, as long as there are men to think at all.

The Individuality of Things and the Generality of Language[1]

A. B. JOHNSON

An infusion of words constitutes nearly all instruction—an ability to repeat them, nearly all learning. I say this not to disparage learning or instruction, but to manifest the importance of understanding words. To a portion of this science, not embraced in my former publication, I now beg your attention.

Nine hundred and ninety-seven millions of beings exist, to whom we apply the word man. Amid their varieties of complexion, stature, hair, features, age, sex, structure, habits, and knowledge, they possess similarities which make the word man appropriate to all. No two of them are, perhaps, identical in their general appearance, or in the appearance of any particular part. They differ, also, individually from each other, in many qualities besides the appearance.

The word man, therefore, refers to a mass of individuals. Every word is equally general in its signification. By means of their generality, a few thousand words comprehend all creation, though created existences are infinitely numerous. Nature, then, is truly a congregation of individual existences, and language a collection of general terms.

This distinction is obvious, still, when we wish to disparage Napoleon, we say, he was but a man; and when we wish to exalt stupidity, we say, he is a man as well as Napoleon. The alleged identity is correct, if we interpret it by the similarities that we discover in the compared individuals; but the identity is alleged to imply a similarity beyond what we discover in the two individuals, and even to control the differences that they exhibit. This is an insidious error, and it constitutes a principal subject of the present discourse.

You perceive, we disregard the individuality of nature, and substitute a generality which belongs to language. The generality is an indispensi-

[1] From *A Discourse on Language*. Utica: William Williams, 1832, pp. 10 ff.

ble defect of the finitude of language; but creation is subject to no such circumscription. Creation exhibits John, Charles, and nine hundred and ninety-seven millions of other equally varying individuals. Language alone makes them identical. Measure, then, no longer, creation by the poverty of a human vocabulary. The change is simple, but it will emancipate us from errors which are associated with all our learning.

Medical science long suffered by the delusion which we are investigating. It still suffers measurably. Diseases possess sufficient resemblances, to be classed under general names; hence we possess the words perepneumony, pleuresy, rheumatism, &c. I censure not physicians for constructing the names, nor for deciding that Thomas and Henry are severally afflicted with pleuresy; but their diseases are not as identical in nature as in language. The verbal identity is the contrivance by which language comprehends the infinity of creation. The verbal identity is perfect, while in nature, similarities at most exist, and with only various approximations to an entire identity.

No two parcels of calomel possess the perfect identity which the sameness of their name implies. No two men possess the perfect identity which the sameness of their manhood implies, nor possesses any one man, at all times, and under all circumstances, the complete identity with which language invests his individuality.

The identity which language implies, is responded to by nature very nearly, or we could possess no medical science; but the most skilful physician is often defeated by the subtle individualities of nature. Physicians have long detected these individualities, and deemed them anomalies of nature. The anomaly is, however, in language, which unites under one name what is only partially identical. Individuality is no anomaly of nature. It is nature's regular production, and boundless richness.

Having distinguished the identity which nature exhibits, from the identity that language implies—I wish to shew, that, while language implies always a perfect identity, nature exhibits in some cases more identity than in other cases: for instance—

In two flakes of snow, the snow presents an identity, which is almost complete; but in a whale and anchory the fish of both animals presents a very incomplete identity. The fish of the whale and anchory is, however, as identical verbally, as the snow of the two flakes.

Again, a polypus and an elephant are animals, and the animality of both is identical in language. In nature, the identity is less than even the identity of the fish.

Iron is matter—a sun-beam is matter. Their materiality is identical in language, while in nature we discover in it less identity than we discover in even the animality of the polypus and elephant.

I complain not of language for its implied identities. Utility justifies them; and a whale and an anchory present sufficient similarities to render the word fish appropriate to both: still the complete identity is artificial and verbal, and we need not confound it with the realities of nature. In nature, the identity is just as we discover it to be. It must not be measured by names, but ascertained by observation. I shall shew that we reverse this rule: we interpret the natural identity by the verbal.

For instance, some water is salt, some sulphurous, some sweet, and some chalybeate. It is found cold, tepid, and hot.

Shall we believe language, which, by naming them all water, makes them identical? or shall we believe nature, which teaches us they are diverse? We believe language, and with an entire unconsciousness of the delusion that arises from testing nature by the identities of language, we believe that the saltness of the sea is adventitious—the heat of hot springs is adventitious—the sulphureousness of sulphur springs, and the iron of chalybeate springs, are adventitious. We accordingly teach, as the pryings of our sagacity, that internal fires, or chemistry, heat the springs, and beds of sulphur and iron impregn them. Unshocked by the extent of the absurdity, we even maintain that stupendous reservoirs of salt must be laved by the ocean.

The salt springs of Salina, in our vicinity, are also supposed to result from recesses of salt; and our legislature have sanctioned experiments to discover the salt. Salt may be discovered. It is certainly adequate to the assigned effect, as are sulphur and iron in the other cases; but to suppose their presence indispensible is a delusion. All the fluids which we name water, possess sufficient similarities to make the name appropriate; but we should not forget that the nominal identity is a human contrivance, and must be controlled bv the discoverable realities of nature.

Sweetness we deem as identical in nature as in name. We call it sacharine, and say it is the ingredient which makes honey sweet, fruit, beets, &c.: hence if we can remove from them every thing but the sacharine, we shall obtain an identical remainder.

This remainder is not realized by our experiments, though we obtain sugar and various concretions. The failure has not taught us that the verbal identity of sacharine is more complete than the natural identity of different sweets; nor are we taught this by the more glaring discrepancy of some sweet liquids which cannot be concreted. We attribute the variance to any cause but the diversity of nature; so inveterate is the practice of interpreting nature by the identities of language.

No man observes so superficially as not to discover in natural productions an endless diversity. Children say, that no two blades of grass are alike. Still the differences in the blades we estimate as not effecting their identity as grass. But what is the identity of grass, beyond the sensible resemblances of the different blades? Nothing but the name grass. We deem the identity a hidden property of nature, while it is only a property of language.

Botanists say, that oats, barley, and wheat, are also grass: and when we become botanists we see that the name is appropriate. We are, however, deceived, if we suppose that in these different existences some property is as identical as the identity of the word grass. We are transferring to nature a generalization of language.

The question is deemed profound which asks how the soul is united to the body; how the movements of a man's limbs are united to his volition; how heat and light are united in flame; how coldness and hardness are united in ice?

The union, in the above cases, is deemed identical with the union of the arm to the shoulder; and hence the wonder and the fallacy. Coincidences enough exist to make the word union applicable in all the cases; but if we look among them for an identity, we are looking for what exists in language only. In nature, the union of each case is just what we discover.

A spark causes gun powder to explode. This is curious. But speculation wonders not at the explosion, but that we can discover no necessary connexion between the touch of the spark and the explosion.

Mankind would not have attached the word connexion to the spark and explosion, if the word was not appropriate; but if we infer that the connexion is identical with the connexion exhibited by two links of a chain, we are deluded. Nature is boundlessly diverse; and all that we can accomplish, is, to refer to the diversities, by such language as we deem most analogous.

A man who is blind from his birth knows roundness by the feel. Should he attain sight, and see a ball, he will not recognize it as the round object of his former amusements. When, however, he shall have learnt roundness by the sight, he may inquire how the visible ball and the tangible are identical?

Their identity is wholly different from the identity of his person now, and his person a few moments ago. The identity of John, an infant, and the same John, a decriped old man, differs from both the other identities. If he seeks, in all these cases, for an identity which is as similar in nature as in language, he is seeking in nature for what is only a property of language.

The identity of the Holy Trinity is, by this error, unnecessarily mysticised as a tenet of revelation. Objectors to the identity, disbelieve that three men can be distinct and still identical. The objectors are correct, so far as they refer to three men; but the objectors are incorrect, when they suppose that the identity of the Trinity must be interpreted by any other identity. Such an interpretation, places on the identity of the Trinity a restriction, to which the identity of no created existences is subjected.

After an assayer pronounces two bars to be gold, I shall know but little correctly of even their identity, till he shows me the phenomena to which his decision refers. Their identity possesses not the unqualified sameness which exists in the name gold.

Men agree on the standard which decides whether two bars are gold, but a like agreement exists not in every other alleged identity. One man will deem no two things identical, unless they exhibit the phenomena which constitute his personal identity. Every disputant supposes that the identity is a property of nature, instead of a human contrivance, by which an infinitely diverse creation is comprehended by a finite vocabulary: comprehended as well as we can, in groups of much similarity, under the word gold; in groups of less similarity under the word metal; and in groups of but little similarity, under the word mineral.

Heat, whether solar or culinary, chemical or animal, is deemed as identical in nature as in language. So far the fallacy is free from much absurdity. But the prepossession which induces us to deem all heats identical, induces us to deem their causes equally identical; hence, solar heat is either chemical or igneous. An alternative is pleasant, but philosophers are almost unanimous that the sun is fire. Even the years are numbered which must elapse before its combustible parts will be exhausted. Whether this continues the scientific romance of the day, I know not, and care not. The theory may be changed, but the error which originated it remains. Pursuing the verbal identity, astronomers find that some planets, by approaching the sun, become periodically hotter than iron in fusion, and comets accumulate enough heat to retain, after a century's absence, a sufficiency for comfort.

These are the calculations of men with whom I presume not to contend, except where they delusively impute to nature the identity which exists only in language—a delusion which has been indulged by astronomers, till they have fabricated wilder romances than ever fiction created intentionally.

Again, stone is matter, air, light, water, man, earth, and sun, are severally matter. That matter is as identical in nature as in language, is believed with all the simplicity of an undisturbed prepossession in favor of the error. Creation displays in vain its diversities. The variety only augments our admiration at the implied identity.

So far, however, the absurdity is moderate compared with the chimeras which we produce, when, in pursuance of the implied identity of matter, we invest a sun-beam with the properties of rock. Gravity, we are taught, is a concomitant of all matter that we can subject to fair experiment; consequently, that we may properly deem gravity a concomitant of every particle of matter, and hence of a ray of light. I speak from memory, but the reasoning is Newton's.

The process is continued till light is invested with hardness, bulk, particles, resistance, and every other essential property of stone. We are then taught to admire that light, so constituted, can pervade solid crystal—nay, can fall with a velocity almost inconceivable, and from a height almost inexpressible, and leave our houses unbattered, and our eyes unconscious even of the blows which they sustain. These difficulties vanish before the following astonishing explanation: the particles of light are so small, that in the sixteenth part of a minute, a candle emits more particles of light than ten hundred thousand million times the number of sands which exist in the whole earth![2]

Light moves from the sun to the earth, and a coach moves from Utica to Albany. The word motion is proper in both phrases, but when we deem the motions as identical in nature as in language, we are transferring to nature what is simply a property of language. The mistake is unimportant, till, by virtue of the supposed identity, we attribute to the motion of light the concomitants of the coach's motion. Proceeding thus, we calculate that during one vibration of a clock's pendulum,

[2] *Rees' Cyclopedia*—Tit. Light.

light moves, as consecutively as the coach, one hundred and sixty thousand miles.

I lately saw a little book[3] which teaches children occult doctrines. The child's curiosity is excited by the information that he and stones possess many properties in common—color, form, substance, hardness, bulk, resistance, mobility, &c.

That the child and the stone are identical in some particulars, is, you perceive, the marvel and the fallacy. So far as the identity is verbal, the child knows the identity. So far as you wish him to impute to nature the identity which exists in the words, you are deluding him. This delusion may pass for science now, but it will not always. It may be deemed salutary for children, big and little—but I admit no warrant for error.

In the same way, youth are not taught by botanists that male and female, when applied to plants, are not identical in meaning with male and female when applied to animals. That the identity is as complete in nature as in language, is inculcated, and thus we obtain from youth an interest for botany at the cost of their understanding.

We teach a child that certain stars are suns. We court his belief that the identity is as complete naturally, as verbally. Beyond all ordinary visibility and all telescopic, other suns, we say, exist; still wishing him to believe that the identity of language and of nature are one. This verbal delusion, to which teachers and scholars are usually alike victims, exalts, we say, creation. Miserable compliment! The stupendousness of creation needs not romance for its exaltation, nor the perversion of reason for its glory.

We tell a pupil that the earth travels with various velocities, and various motions, wishing him to believe that the motions and velocities are identical in nature with the motions and velocities of a steamboat. This error is so monstrous and so general, that it presents a wonderful example of the delusion by which we transfer to nature the identity of language. . . .

In the use of general propositions, much misunderstanding occurs from not distinguishing between the identity of language and the diversity of nature. If I assert that George is good, you may assent. Under this verbal identity, I may refer to actions of George that are unknown to you; and you may refer to actions unknown to me. Nay, the actions to which I refer, might cause you to reprobate George.

[3] *The Child's Book on the Soul.*

You and I may be well acquainted with Thomas; still, when we see his portrait, you may deem the likeness excellent, while I may call it execrable. While we speak of the appearance of Thomas, our knowledge seems identical; but our different estimations of the portrait, prove that our knowledge is diverse. When we view Thomas, we take not necessarily the same view. I may habitually contemplate his profile, and you his bust; I may notice his chin, and you his forehead.

I attempt not to enumerate all the cases in which the identity of language conflicts with the diversity of nature. My remarks are merely elucidations of a principle.

Dismissing then the present topic, I will proceed to shew, that language implies also a oneness, to which nature presents no corresponding unit. I am speaking. This is a truth. I am standing, is a truth. That several persons are present, is a truth. If we seek among these truths for truth itself, believing it to be a unit, we are seeking for what is merely a contrivance of language.

What is truth? said Pilate. He supposed truth to be a unit, and hence the difficulty of his question. To comprehend creation, language adopts two expedients: it deems identical, existences that are only semilar; and it deems a unit, existences which are only aggregated.

Temperature is hot, cold, and tepid. Temperature seems to be a unit, but these examples exhibit it tri-corporal. Shall we believe nature, and interpret the oneness of temperature by the multiformity of the above examples; or shall we believe language, and interpret hot, cold, and tepid by the oneness of the word temperature? We believe language, and perplex ourselves to discover in hot, cold, and tepid, the oneness which language says they constitute.

The delusion by which we transfer to nature the oneness of language, is exhibited strongly in treatises on our faculties and passions. Certain phenomena are enumerated; not as the meaning of the word love, but as the acts of a mysterious unit. Conscience is deemed a unit as literally as our head. Indeed conscience is one of the little sprites which we have crowded into the head, that general receptacle of verbal personages, where, on invisible tripods are seated reason, judgment, mind, instinct, soul, shame, and numerous kindred individuals.

The word soul signifies many phenomena, and many definitions; hence the soul is not in nature a unit. In revelation, however, the soul is referred to as a unit, and its oneness doubtless exists in the sense which revelation intends. The word God, while we refer to nature, means the mass of phenomena to which we refer. The oneness exists in the name only. This is the God of natural theology. When, however, we refer to the Holy Scriptures, God is a unit, for revelation declares the oneness. All my remarks then, will exclude the oneness to which revelation refers. I shall speak of unscriptural language solely, and unscriptural applications.

The health of a country is as much a unit in language as the health of Thomas. In nature, the oneness of the two cases is dissimilar. Even Thomas' general health is less a unit in nature, than his health at the present moment. The oneness which language implies is, you perceive, always entire; while nature presents but different approximations to a complete oneness. The shape of the earth is as much a unit in language, as the shape of a pin's point; while in nature the oneness of the earth's shape is less simple than the oneness of the point's. The saltness of the ocean is a unit in language, and the saltness of any given drop of the ocean is another unit; but plainly the oneness is more unique in the drop than in the ocean.

In these cases, experience neutralizes the implied oneness; but the delusion is subtle, where we cannot obviously compare the multiformity of nature with the oneness of language: for instance, wisdom is as much a unit in language as the moon. The countless actions, &c. which constitute wisdom, possess a homogeneity which makes the word wisdom applicable to them all; but to impute to these actions the oneness of the word wisdom, is as delusive as to impute to a whale and anchory the identity of the word fish.

A shadow possesses more natural oneness than a triangle. The shadow is discoverable by sight only, but a triangle by the sight and touch; and discoverable so diversely, that a blind man, and a man void of the sense of feeling, (if we may suppose such a man,) can both recognize a triangle, while their knowledge of it will be different and reciprocally incommunicable.

Even a triangle possesses more natural oneness than water, for while a triangle is cognizable by only the sight and touch, water is cognizable by these and by the taste; and so diversely that a man void of sight, and another void of taste, and another of feeling, might know water without the least similarity in their knowledge.

To escape delusion then, we must construe nature by nature itself. This obvious precept is unknown to philosophy. We estimate nature by the oneness and other properties of language, and hence, when we investigate nature verbally, valuable results are rare: witness all the labors that have been wrecked on metaphysics. Where men investigate nature experimentally, they escape the delusions of language, and the results are valuable: for instance, the operations of mechanism and chymistry.

The medical question of contagion, is embarrassed by not discriminating the oneness of language from the plurality of nature. The contagiousness of cholera, generally, may be less a unit in nature, than the contagiousness of a single case; even the contagiousness of a single case, during its whole continuance, may be less a unit in nature, than its contagiousness on any given moment.

But cholera itself is not a unit—it is a succession of many phenomena. Whether medical science suffers not by the implied oneness of each disease, may deserve consideration. The phenomena which constitute an attack of gout, we do not deem gout, but attendants of the mysterious unit gout. I speak hypothetically—physicians may not think thus.

Is a man a unit as strictly as language implies? Should I attempt to discover wherein his oneness exists, (and volumes have been written on the subject,) I might seem to discuss humanity very profoundly, but I should be discussing it very ignorantly. I should be seeking in nature, for a mere contrivance of language.

For instance, amputate one of Peter's arms, will the remainder of Peter be a man? How much excision of his body must occur before the remainder will cease to be a man? These questions are not deemed trifling. Their answer is usually some theory, which reconciles the oneness that is supposed to pertain unquestionably to Peter, with the phenomena that conflict with his oneness. We interpret nature by the oneness of the word man, instead of interpeting the oneness of the word man by the exhibitions of nature.

Statistical Thinking [1]

GEORGE BOAS

Aristotelian thinking could ask only one question, "What is the *nature,* or *essence,* of this thing?" Statistical thinking, on the other hand, asks, "What are its *relations* in so far as they are measurable?" Thus the Greek, like the American fundamentalist, believed that all animals and plants fall into fixed and permanent groups, called "species." Within any group the individuals are all alike, in so far as they are members of that group. For instance, men and women are both human beings; they are identical in their humanity, though permissibly different in their sexuality. When the group characteristics are known, the characteristics of the individuals are automatically known. People grew to believe that the discovery of the group characters was all-important. As late as Buffon one finds descriptions of "The Camel," "The Bear," "The Hummingbird," though curiously enough in one of Buffon's most important predecessors, Claude Perrault, one finds an insistence on the fact that the descriptions are of individuals, and only of groups to the extent that the groups vary but slightly. The great scientific products of this type of thinking, however, neglected Perrault's caution, as one can see in reading them: Buffon's natural history and Linnæus's system of nature and classification of plants.

The same method was followed in all the sciences. In medicine physicians wrote books on the specific—the class—properties of the various diseases, three-day fever, biliousness, malaria. Every case of malaria was like every other case, every case of biliousness like every other. Similarly in psychology appeared accounts of "the angry man," "the melancholy man," "the sanguine man." One had only to classify and all was done. Once an object was classified, its essence, its nature was known. And since it came to be believed that these classes could be

[1] From *Our New Ways of Thinking,* pp. 12–24. Copyright, 1930, by Harper & Brothers. Reprinted by permission.

grouped together hierarchically, from the most inclusive class, God, to the most particular, it was immediately seen that a knowledge of the more general "natures" would permit one to deduce by the use of the reason alone a knowledge of the less general "natures." For what good was observation? Observation could no more penetrate to the "nature" of things than it could perceive a perfect (*i.e.*, a mathematical) circle. Hence mankind came to believe that the world in which we live was a bad copy of a perfect world beyond the reach of his sense organs and, if observation did not square with reasoning, it—not reasoning—had to be corrected.

What was done with exceptions? They were either called "accidental," if they were slight, or "monstrous," if they were great. By using these words one seemed to eliminate the necessity of explaining them. It is, however, at least curious that in an Aristotelian universe, which had to be absolutely "logical" and consistent, there should have been any accidents or monsters. The Greeks, like some of our contemporaries, tried to squirm out of this difficulty by calling them "unnatural" or "contrary to nature." But how anything in nature could be unnatural, no one has ever been able to explain. Today we use the term "abnormal." But all that term properly means is "unusual." When we say that two-headed calves, or homosexual men and women, or hard-hearted parents are "unnatural," we mean simply that they are infrequent. But, as there is a definite tendency to appraise the frequent more highly than the infrequent, we often still read into the word something of a derogatory nature. The Greek implied that they were logically inexplicable, for they did not have the characteristics of the group to which they seemed most obviously to belong. Today we expect variation within groups; our fathers felt that they must explain it away.

Nowadays who outside the states of Tennessee and Florida would dream of classifying animals, plants, diseases, and temperaments, and imagine that he was doing more than indicating a rough practical sort of grouping? A biological species was seen even in Huxley's day to be a great collection of individuals amongst which monsters find their natural place. (For that matter Lamarck in the eighteenth century said the term had outlived its usefulness.) "The Camel," so to speak, is the "average" camel; if you had to bet on the characteristics of a camel chosen at random, you would put your money on him. The notion that all camels are alike is as absurd as the notion that all dollars are alike. In fact, their differences are carefully measured, like the differences of all animals, and the measurements carefully recorded. The biometrist does little else than collect such figures and he knows that two extreme members of two similar species may be in some respects more alike than two extreme members of the same species. Thus a human idiot is probably—I am guessing here—more like a clever chimpanzee, than he is like Goethe, as far as his reactions to intelligence tests are concerned. In fact, the discovery of biological variation was one of the bases for Darwin's theory that species had an origin and were not created as they are today. . . .

In medicine, again, a disease has normal characteristics, but these cannot be expected to be present in every case of it. As Dr. Joseph Collins pointed out in *Harper's Magazine* a few years ago, physicians are coming to recognize that a patient may have a very common disease in his own very personal way. It is not so important to know what disease a man has as how he has it. We are all aware of the havoc caused by ignorant doctors who plot their cures after the names of illnesses. They are like judges who decide cases after the names of crimes. We ought to conclude, if we still stuck to Aristotelian logic, that there are no specific diseases or else recognize that each individual has his own brand of disease.

It is easy to see why in Aristotelian thinking the first question that popped into everyone's head was, "What is it? What class does it belong to?" For if these questions were answered, all that is important would be known, as we have said above. And if the individual failed to meet the requirements of his class, he could be insulted or punished and the world would be deprecated for having produced him. He would be like George III in the celebrated poem (I quote from memory):

> *George III*
> *Should never have occurred.*
> *One can only wonder*
> *At so grotesque a blunder.*

It is in this spirit that certain discussions arise, such as, "Is cubism really art?" or, "Is Unitarianism really Christianity?" One might as well ask, "What is a mule?" For it ought to be (but isn't) obvious that you can define "art" to include cubism or exclude it at will, and "Christianity" to include or exclude Unitarianism. Definitions are bound to be arbitrary; they are convenient or inconvenient, but never true or false. And nothing is gained in an argument which relies on them by adding the adjective "real" or the adverb "really."

In law such questions are of tragic importance, for on the answer given depend the lives of human beings. Did Aaron Burr *really* commit treason? Did John Doe commit murder or manslaughter? Is such and such an act a case of assault and battery? One is taught that the statutes define such terms so precisely that all the judge has to do is to apply the law. But the fact that courts of appeal exist show that such an application is sometimes not so easy as it looks. A "human being" or a "person" ought to be fairly clear and distinct in meaning. But when does fertilized egg begin to be a person? An unborn child is a person for some purposes but not for others. He can inherit property and sue for the infringement of his property rights just as an infant can. But can he sue for injury to his life? In Drobner *v.* Peters (232 N. Y. 220, 1922) Mr. Justice Holmes was cited as declaring that the great weight of authority was against the contention that an unborn child had a right of immunity from personal harm. In the particular case the pregnant mother was injured by falling down a coalhole left open through the negligence of the defendant. The baby was born eleven days after the accident and was injured by the fall. Yet it was not considered a person. At the same time it was admitted that in criminal law it would have been a person, for it would have been a crime to kill it, and if the child had died after birth from injuries prenatally received, the individual who caused the injury would have been guilty of murder. Therefore an unborn child can inherit property and can be murdered, but it cannot be injured or maimed.[2]

It is clear that if words have fixed meanings revealing the essence or nature of the things they denote, one ought to be able to tell whether a piece of flesh and blood is a person or not, for it would have the stigmata of personality or not and that would be all there would be to it. But we forget that words are names, are symbols, and that the fact of their being given to certain things is simply an historical fact, like the name given to a child, which can be explained by historical and not by innate logical reasons. Consequently, the shift in the meaning of words and their consequent ambiguity are to be expected and not

[2] People who are fond of legal curiosities should read Johnson *v.* Cadillac Motor Co., 261 Fed. 878, 1919, in which the U. S. Circuit Court of Appeals reversed its decision in a case involving the term "inherently dangerous instrument."

wondered at. That the word "novel" means a variety of things is as normal an occurrence as that the children of one set of parents should not all be doubles. The problem is not why words vary in meaning, but why they retain the same meaning; so the problem in the study of nature is not why "things" in general differ, but why they are alike.

Statistical descriptions were discovered, I believe, in the seventeenth century. At that time they were applied especially to social phenomena. They were gradually extended, going into psychology and biology, until at the present day they are used even in physics. Clerk Maxwell, if I am not mistaken, is usually given the credit of introducing statistics into physics; today dynamics is full of it. Gilbert Lewis, whose authority as a scientist few would care to dispute, points out that one can calculate the probability of what would be called levitation in large material bodies, and indicates that we can even calculate the chances of freezing a kettle of water by putting it on the stove. To be sure, his words are not mine; they are exact, whereas mine are pictorial. But they are not contradicted by what I have said. I should not advise ice-cream manufacturers to count on the chance reduction of entropy to save them money on their ice bills, for it occurs so rarely as to be what is properly called impossible.[3] For further details the curious are referred to Professor Lewis's *The Anatomy of Science*. Here we must be content with noting that it recognizes the world to be made up of *individual events,* no two of which are exactly alike, but any selected class of which acts with statistical regularity. This means that physical law, which in the nineteenth century was looked upon as a symbol of the irrevocable and immutable, to be divine in its purity and eternality, is really a set of generalizations which actual events only approximate in their behavior and never completely reflect.

It is worth observing that the history of science began with astronomy and geometry and went on to physics, subject matters in which there is but a minimum of variation. Where variation did occur, it was explained away. It was against the background of such sciences that Aristotelian logic was developed. The tendency was, therefore, to seek in all fields of observation the same uniformity which was characteristic of the sciences already known. When such uniformity could not be observed, it was, as the French philosopher, Meyerson, has so brilliantly shown, invented. One had to have uniformity in order to have science

---

[3] "An event the probability of which is exceedingly small we designate as being *impossible.*"—A. Haas, *The New Physics,* p. 39.

and one had to have science. Even when statistical regularity was discovered, the emphasis was upon the regularity, not upon the variation.
It arose in a field where regularity was hardly suspected of existing, and
statistics are used even today by some people to show that a kind of
"physical law" reigns even in the acts of men seemingly free to do as
they will.

For a number of reasons, however, during the seventeenth century
there developed a cult of variety, and the adherents of this cult have
increased instead of dwindling. Statistics are a perfect tool for handling
the various. Hence the reverse of the past history of science set in and
a movement spread—and how widely we shall see in the second part
of this essay—towards recognizing the "reality" of the multiple. If
statistics are now used in physics and probability has replaced iron
truth, it is because of this movement. Whereas in Greece the traits of
the physical order were held to be typical and fundamental throughout
the whole universe, in modern times the traits of living organisms are
held to be thus typical and fundamental. Whereas variation was shocking in Greece and had to be explained away, uniformity is shocking
today and equally suspect.

In our new thinking, the individual has become the center of our
interest. We shy away from generalizations, modifying our ideas to the
average of our observations. We can define nothing in absolute terms;
art, medicine, science, and morality become relative. If this makes for
confusion at first, for difficulties in settling any given point of fact or
ethics, it is the challenge this generation will be forced to meet. In all
practical issues, the modern man must take as wide a selection of examples as lies within his experience. By ranging them, analyzing the
differences, the likenesses, the average mean tenors, he can draw his
conclusions. He will have confidence in these conclusions only as approximations, more or less accurate. Facts are no longer facts to be
relied upon in the face of all objections; they are probabilities, upon
which in the long run we can depend until fresh data have been observed in sufficient quantities to alter their character. We hesitate to
accept dogma and anticipate the reversal of our decisions. But on the
other hand, we can have a far more workable hypothesis about the phenomena of nature than was ever conceived by our Aristotelian-minded
forebears.

PART VII

Verbal Fascination

What are words for?

Those marks on paper or vibrations in the air are not *triangles, guns, butter, sadness, hatred, old age,* but ways of pointing to, representing, calling attention to the things, feelings, relationships, etc., and to the words which are used in connection with *them*. They name things, feelings, relationships, etc. They are *about* things and other words in the way a map is about a countryside or a blueprint is about a structure or a temperature chart is about what happened inside a man or a box score is about what happened in the field.

Anybody can give a name to anybody or anything. But is one name as good as another? Is it possible that some words have a deep connection with some things? Are there ways of naming which can affect the character of the things named? Or are people only affected? In spite of what they actually do, most people are likely to agree that Wycherley's attitude is the sensible one: "I weigh the man, not his title: 'Tis not the king's stamp that can make the metal better."

That a man will respond to some words while remaining indifferent to others is a well-known phenomenon which influences the course of human affairs. It is recognized by the student of salesmanship, oratory, medical practices, magic, social control. It is an open question whether the use of such a weapon should be deplored or used against the users or merely recognized when it is used to exploit those who do not know what is being done to them. Another position says that it is more important to teach people to face up to Pavlov's assertion "that men are more influenced by words than by the facts of the surrounding reality."

The Attributive Attitude[1]

ELLIS FREEMAN

A necessary part of any study of the profound influence of language in the shaping and perpetuation of our cultural ideas is the determination of the precise psychological mechanism by means of which this influence operates. In the first place, language as experience and behavior is employed in two different types of functions. Primarily words have an independent existence as objects or things perceived by means of audition, vision, or kinesthesis. In this sense they are precisely like any other environmental object and possess like psychological properties. They are in this regard subject to the basic operation of the senses which has already been described. Moreover, in this quality they operate upon the individual as simple stimulating situations very much like colors and pitches, and produce relatively constant perceptions in all participants.

But they possess also an externally attached property consisting of a complex of associated meanings and references, a symbolic function which gives them a much more involved character. As symbols they are significant, not for what they immediately and intrinsically are, but for what they represent and in themselves are not. True language is synonymous with symbolism, and as such is to be conceived of broadly and not necessarily restricted to words, for in this sense mathematical and other symbols are also language. A cry or gesture of pain in automatic response to injury is not a symbol or a part of true language because in purpose it is not communicative; it is not uttered to direct or refer a hearer to something which it itself is not. To be sure the hearer may infer from its occurrence that pain has been suffered, but in this case the cry is merely an integral part of the pain situation, without any communicative intention on the part of the utterer. Before any perceptual

[1] From *Social Psychology* by Ellis Freeman, pp. 110–117. Copyright, 1936, by Henry Holt and Company, Inc. Reprinted by permission.

event can become language, or symbol, the intention must be present to communicate a fact through the agency of and distinct from the symbol itself.

It is worth noting in passing that even when a characteristic word sound like "John" is uttered or heard, no one need necessarily apprehend it as an arbitrary symbol in order to behave effectively. By conditioning, individuals have come to handle it automatically. One unhesitatingly calls "John" if he desires John's attention, and John automatically responds and makes as much of a reflex move and is as little engaged in using language as when contracting his pupil. This behavior is representative of the manner in which we habitually treat nearly all words in ordinary situations, and it seems to contradict the view of language as symbolism which has here been advanced. But the contradiction is more apparent than real, for the fact remains that, however reflexive our use of words may have become through conditioning in habitual situations, normal adults are always at least potentially capable of regarding the words purely as symbols. Once a normally intelligent person's attention is called to this symbolic attribute of language, he can immediately perform the necessary intellectual operation required for viewing words as symbols. This, which no other animal can do, fundamentally differentiates man from all other creatures. Not even the parrot who utters recognizably human words can therefore be said to employ language. He is merely articulating certain sounds which we happen to be capable of regarding as symbols but which he has merely associated with objects and persons. He is not employing symbols because he is incapable of realizing that the sound is a surrogate for the object. While most of the speech behavior of man is of this automatic parrot-like behavior, the distinction remains that man as a class is potentially capable of distinguishing between the object and its representative symbol. Since the parrot cannot do so, he is not employing language, however much the sounds he produces may be words.

Accordingly symbols may be any convenient thing, although ordinarily they are restricted to spoken and written words and mathematical signs. In practice these are found to offer the most economical means of indicating objects which they themselves are not.

In many respects symbols are notably like tools, for the use of both depends ultimately on the capacity to employ means for an end which is different from the means. The use of a word-symbol in communication is of advantage only in so far as it enables us to behave in some measure as if the object named were present and susceptible to manipulation. The use of a chisel is of advantage only in so far as it contributes to the realization of a cabinet, for instance. Both symbol and tool mediate in the realization of ends with which they are not identical. But since each is part of a more general and inclusive configuration, which involves the means as well as the object or end result, this contiguity produces a fixed association between both factors. Here we note, as elsewhere, the process of conditioning or habit formation under the influence of functional significance. And thus in language we have the remarkable phenomenon of the universal and habitual identification of word-symbols with objects into an inseparable unity. This identification greatly economizes our responses (whenever I hear the call "John," I turn immediately, and am not obliged to stop and reason, " 'John'—that is a word-symbol referring to a person, namely, me; and I shall therefore look back"). But it also involves certain hazards in that it leads to the ascription of false properties to objects and persons by the simple means of attaching to them the characteristics and emotions which are associated with their symbols.

The process of the attribution of foreign properties by means of language consists of the application of the ordinary psychological rules of frequency, contiguity, and habit.

If, for instance, from infancy upward a German child is permitted to associate nothing but inferiority with the name *French* and superiority with the name *German* in his school exercises; if the numerous formal and informal propagandistic influences of the home, play-group, church, press, radio, and cinema reënforce this association through interminable repetition; and if, moreover, the child loses caste among his fellows should he venture to question it, he cannot escape the weaving of these concepts into the very fabric of his entire consciousness. This will be the more true to the degree that the emotions related to these verbal concepts have been evoked, sedulously cultivated, and strongly linked with the words. Long after the concrete verbal expression of these ideas has become lost the feeling tone will remain and will evoke a sense of ill, hostility, and negation with the word *French,* and a sense of good and affection with the word *German.* So deep will it be, that should the enlightenment of subsequent experience of a less prejudiced nature oblige him to reverse or modify his views intellectually, he will never succeed completely in throwing off the emotional tonal accompaniment of these names. However much he may become prepared to entertain more rational views toward the French, a vague sense of discomfort, at least, will always arise to plague him in dealing with the concept. In this manner propaganda may irrationally pervade the life of a large group. It is, therefore, not surprising that, in accordance with the views of the psychologically uninformed and the loose terminology of the somewhat better informed, that such a purely conditioned emotional response should come to be regarded as deeply inbred and indicative of an intrinsic racial hostility based upon blood and instinct. Much in the American attitude toward the Negro is founded on a similar irrational basis.

But there is a still subtler property of language which fosters such a deep-seated association. Wertheimer [2] has observed a curious tendency of language to develop two functional aspects, or two almost qualitatively different properties for the individual as he matures intellectually. In this Wertheimer has made a very helpful advance over the purely mechanistic view that the growth of language in the individual is exclusively a quantitative matter of increasing the number of objects to which one attaches words. He has observed that in primitives and the children of civilized peoples names are intimately fused with the objects to which they are literally thought of as "belonging." It will be serviceable if we term this initial use of words as *attributive language,* for the primitive and the child literally regard words as attributes of associated objects, very much like their color, size, taste, etc. Hence arises the primitive's notion that his name is an integral part, an attributive essence, of his personality, and hence his earnest concern over what may be done with it in some magical ceremony designed to injure him. If the reader will pause to reflect, he will discover a sufficient residual of the primitive in himself, and recognize a similar perturbation, of which he may not intellectually approve, over a like treatment of his name among enemies. In discussing Wertheimer's views, Koffka [3] cites an enlightening instance of the deep-rooted tendency to identify an object with its name as if the name were an essential property. It also demonstrates the tendency to associate nationalistic emotions with one's own language. An Englishman undertook to prove that English is the best language, for, said he, "take the word knife; the French call it *couteau;* the Germans *Messer;* the Danes *kniv;* while the English say

[2] M. Wertheimer, "Uber das Denken der Naturvölker, I. Zahlen und Zahlgebilde," *Zeitschr. f. Psychol.,* 60, 1912.
[3] K. Koffka, *The Growth of the Mind,* New York, 1925, p. 324.

knife, and that's what it really is." Even in the speech of civilized adults the object and name, especially of common things, do not invariably stand in such an arbitrary external relationship as to have become liberated from the attributive character. Similarly when a child learns the word for apple he does not, to his thinking, realize that he is learning to associate an arbitrary symbol with the fruit. What he does, as far as he knows, is to make the discovery of a new attribute of the apple which had hitherto eluded him, an attribute to be added to the color, shape, and taste of the apple. However much he may later mature intellectually, the word for apple in any other language will never have quite the same closely knit intimacy with the apple, nor will it be as convincingly appropriate, as the one which he first learned. In this sense the term "mother tongue" represents the fundamental bonds which are established early in life. But it also facilitates erroneous and emotional notions concerning the superiority and inevitability of these particular associations.

The student of social psychology cannot fail to detect in facts such as these a basis for the emotionality and persistence of economic, religious, racial, and chauvinistic bigotry. When in one's thinking the commendatory words and ideas by which one's religion, race, and country are characterized have become attributively and inseparably attached to the ideas of these institutions, it is almost impossible to dislodge them intellectually on the grounds that they are merely childish habit formations. This formation of profound attributive ties between the familiar institutions of childhood and emotional ideas in large measure accounts for the persistence of the institutions even when outmoded or actually detrimental. It is as difficult then for the adult to distinguish between economic status quo and good, white-race and superiority, American and superiority, as it is for the child to distinguish between the object apple and its name, and for the Englishman to distinguish between a cutting instrument and the word knife. When the emotional associates of our ideas of institutions have become exceedingly strong they may excite attitudes that will appear to more sober reflection as a travesty of patriotism and as a repulsive spirit of jingoistic aggression.

Not only is this attributive character assigned to the ordinary names of things and institutions, but the primitive and child assign it to number-words like those used in counting and designating groups. A cue to this lies in the fact that many primitive peoples have different terms for ordinal than for cardinal numbers. This indicates that they conceive counting and group designation as functionally different configurations of behavior which therefore should possess different name-attributes. But better still, different words will be used ordinally and cardinally for different types of objects even. Thus the *two* used in designating two men will be different from the *two* used in designating two trees. So it is with the young child. Although, by imitation he is confined to the use of identical number-words of cardinal and ordinal functions and for a variety of objects, he will treat them as very different and appear to be quite surprised on learning that in themselves the words used in different situations are identical, term for term. The reason for this is that counting and group-designation are to him *functionally* different configurations of performance in which all attributes, including those of name, must necessarily be different. Furthermore if he establishes a certain order in counting his fingers, say from the thumb out, he cannot make a reversal, because the number *one,* say, is an attribute already appropriated by the thumb and cannot be transferred to something different like the little finger. To make such a transfer would be to him the equivalent of calling his father by the name of mother.

Only with intellectual maturation, and then only under the most favoring educational conditions, may the civilized individual realize that objects and names possess but an external arbitrary relationship; that the word is but a symbol, a convenient representative, having no attributive union with the object and capable of being replaced by any other which has been equally arbitrarily assigned. This aspect of language we may appropriately term *symbolic.* It appears when the individual has been enabled to accomplish the intellectual advance of apprehending the representative character of words, and becomes capable of distinguishing between arbitrary representation and the attributive residuals from his more primitive use of language. It must not be assumed, however, that with this accomplishment he succeeds in divesting his use of language of all attributive residuals in all situations. Enough has been suggested to demonstrate that in ordinary activity he does not succeed in making this change complete. But at least he has made this intellectual advance: he can on occasion apprehend the notion that words are *not* properties of things and that they may be used more and more symbolically. The latter capacity grows at the expense of the former which however is never fully overcome, even with the greater refinement and exploitation of initially sound individual intelligences. Thus the achievement of such relatively purely symbolic disciplines as mathematics is reserved for the few. But in the functions of life taken as a whole, even for the mathematician, a purely symbolic contemplation of language never occurs, and to some degree attributive language must as a matter of convenience in conditioned responses continue to operate.

However, for most individuals, the attributive attitude governs the larger part of their use of language. For still great numbers of others, particularly those whose intelligence is too limited or whose formal education has been too restricted, the concept of language as symbolic must forever remain foreign, a complete mystery.

If then we consider the force of emotional attitudes which are daily being woven attributively into words by the conditioning processes of formal and informal education; if we recall that these attributive emotional complexes in turn become the felt attributes of the institutions they represent; if to this we add the general power of the attributive use of language to cement and perpetuate the bonds between ideas and emotions; and if further we add the fact that only a rare few, who appreciate the symbolic aspect of language, can even in part emancipate themselves from the effects of this process, we may better evaluate the power of language to shape concepts and cultural institutions. Far from being an inert mechanical device for the communication of ideas concerning a culture, it impregnates and to a large degree actively modifies and determines the nature of that culture.

Reification[1]

J A M E S   W .   W O O D A R D

Reification . . . means any unwarranted extension of reality in the thing perceived or conceived. The first syllable of the word (Latin *res,* thing) is the same root as the first syllable of the word "real"; and to re-ify is therefore to take as real something which is not real or to confer a greater reality upon something than that which it has. Thus reification means the taking as real that which is only apparently real; the taking as objectively real that which is only subjectively real; the taking as factual, concrete, or perceptual that which is only conceptual; the taking as absolute that which is only relative, etc.

It must be evident that a tendency toward reification is ever present in mental functioning. And much of what follows flows from the ubiquity of this tendency, even though in many particular instances the tendency does not carry on to what might more strictly be termed an actual case of reification. In a sense, all misconceptions, mistakes, misunderstandings, and errors are taking for real what is not real and so illustrate the ubiquity of the *tendency.* However, there is in the case of these, from experience, a certain tenuousness of belief, a certain implicit recognition that one may be mistaken. Even so, to apply the term indiscriminately to the whole gamut of error in human mental functioning would not be so much amiss, as, practically, to explain so much that it would explain nothing. While many of the illustrations which follow have been chosen from instances of as slight a degree of the working of the tendency as is contained in these concepts, this has been done to show the ubiquity of the *tendency.* The strict definition of the term, however, is best drawn at that point where something definite can be said as to the way in which the reality of the perceptual or conceptual object has been extended, and where there is a definite rigidifying of the erroneous perceptual pattern so that it resists correc-

[1] From *Intellectual Realism and Culture Change.* Hanover, New Hampshire: The Sociological Press, 1935, pp. 8–13. Reprinted by permission of James W. Woodard.

tion. The tendency thus reaches its logical ultimate when the erroneous conception becomes a rigid preconception or pattern of perception itself (*gestalt*) such that all further experience is filtered through it smoothly and automatically, and when the inner preconception of things is "projected" into the reality of the universe, it appearing, subjectively, that reality is self-evidently what the individual or group preconceives it to be—that is, when a preconception or a fragmentary and relative perception are taken as absolutes.

One may distinguish at least the following "directions" in which reality is sometimes extended at the hands of reification. (1) *The conceptual is taken as the perceptual;* that is, there occurs an extension of the reality of the object in the direction of a greater concreteness and tangibility than really exists. Hypostatization (and reification as traditionally defined) are terms which express this sort of reification. Examples of it are the reality and power given to names by primitive peoples and young children; conceptual realism in science; philosophic idealism; the failure to remember the fictional character of methodological fictions in science and philosophy; the taking of such concepts as atoms, forces, faculties, instincts, endopsychic censors, and the like as if they represented concrete entities which, if we had powerful microscopes or subtle enough techniques, we could actually perceive; and many similar forms.

(2) Affiliated with this mechanism is a further tendency; *the relational is taken as if it had an existence, not necessarily a tangible existence, of its own.* The conceptions of *mana* among primitives and of religious blessings among some moderns are examples. Another example is the tendency to regard such things as the good, the true, and the beautiful as realities in their own right, though not necessarily tangible realities. It is a distortion *in the direction of* a concretizing, going at least so far as to posit entity where it does not exist, though not necessarily positing a material entity. It need not go beyond positing the self-sufficient nature of what, on closer analysis, appears to be entirely relational and derivative.

Thus, early in the child's development, he has no conception that certain ideas which are necessarily relative in their connotations for adults, are other than independent. For example, it is not apparent to him that a brother must necessarily be a brother of somebody, that a part must necessarily be part of a whole, or that the description of an object as being right or left can only be in terms of its being to the

right or left of some other object. He thinks of all of these characteristics as existing in themselves and absolutely.[2]

Such behavior is universal among children and lingers on among
the adults and the sophisticated. It is even sometimes necessary to
elucidate this matter to students at the university level. But among
children, primitives, and the uneducated, this error is very common.
Friend and enemy, for example, are apt to be devoid of relativity to
the child of 7; an enemy is "a soldier," "someone who fights," "a horrid person," "someone who is horrid," "someone who wants to hurt us,"
etc. That is, he is not defined as enemy in relation to someone else
but an enemy in himself. Questionnaire results from university students, later referred to, show the same difficulty concerning the word
"alien." At the age of 9 or 10 such words as alien and foreigner are
quite devoid of relativity in the minds of children. The same is true
of spatial positions, M. Reichenbach having supplied Piaget with examples of children who, living south of Berne and knowing that for
them the north wind came from Berne, maintained that the north wind
also came from Berne at Basle, although Basle was in the north. And
Piaget gives instances of children in Geneva who were unable to understand how Switzerland could be both north of Italy and south of Ger-
many. If it is north it is not south! The points of the compass are
also at first absolute values.

To the cultural anthropologist and to the comparative psychologist
and biologist it soon becomes apparent that "good" and "evil" are entirely relative to the needs and situations of the individuals and groups
concerned, and that they must always be defined in relative terms. But
all morals and most ethics treat good and evil as if they had an independent existence; and most laymen think in these terms. Likewise
the "faculties" of the older psychologies, concepts applicable to the
relational products of a functioning organism, were not always given
a concretized reality, but were given an existence of a sort in their
own right. Thought, consciousness, mind, and the soul are similar examples in which the tendency has led sometimes very profound thinkers
quite astray. These are relational, quite, and when the functioning relations that produce them disappear there is no more problem of what
becomes of them than there is of what becomes of a light when it goes
out. Other examples might be the layman's conception of space and
time. It is obvious how closely related this category is to our first

[2] Jean Piaget, *Judgment and Reason in the Child*, p. 131.

category, yet it represents a different degree of the hypostatizing process.

(3) *The quite non-existent is given existence, sometimes also given entity and concreteness.* This involves a graver fallacy than does the distortion expounded in the second category. In the first two types a given reality, real enough in its own relationships, is taken as having a more concrete reality than it has. But here the quite non-existent is given reality. "Projection" and hallucination are current terms applicable to this type of reification. The hallucinations, emotionalized projections, and delusions of insanity, with relation to which the individual lacks insight, are examples of this category. Perhaps no less striking are the gods and demons of religion, at least of all religions except one's own, and the supernatural forces of magic. In all these cases the quite non-existent is given existence and even concrete entity. This is the extreme of this aspect of the extension of reality involved in reification; that is, there is not merely an illegitimate extension of an existing reality, but the quite non-existent is taken as real.

(4) *The subjective is taken as objective.* This is perhaps the most general form of statement applicable to all cases of reification, for all reifications are examples of intellectual realism of one sort or another. However, it is useful to designate this separate aspect of the matter, since, sometimes, as in the category just discussed, there may be no objective correlates whatsoever to the subjective reality. Thus projection, hallucination, and delusion are preeminently cases of mistaking what is subjectively very real as if it were objectively real. Most forms of primitive magic are traditionally defined in these terms. That is, objects, processes, or behavior that are closely associated in the mind of the person are mistakenly taken to be also closely associated in reality. Hence it is that by manipulating the name of his enemy (which is closely associated with him subjectively), the primitive thinks that he can harm him; or by manipulating things that have once been in contact with each other and hence closely associated, thinks that he can affect them at a distance; or, again, thinks that if he can imitate a process that he will induce a similar result in nature itself; or, finally, mistakes the subjective intensity of his desire or effort of will as conducive to the bringing about of a wished-for result. Modern examples are ever so numerous in the realm of superstitions and in the thought-magic and will-magic of prayer. And of course the gods and demons of religion and all so-called animism, primitive and modern, are

similar examples. Likewise the delusions of reference of the paranoiac, etc.

That these are not always, in a strict sense, projected, but sometimes arise from the failure of differentiation, rather than a prior differentiation with a later projection, will presently be seen. But the import to the present purpose remains the same. Perhaps the most generalizable aspect of reification is thus that it is a mistaking of the subjectively true for the objectively true.

An example of extending the bounds of reality in the object, other than in the direction of concreteness, is the overlooking of the temporal and spatial limitations of its existence. This is another form of overlooking its relativity. Here (5) *the boundaries of reality of what are real enough in their local, temporal, and relative situations, are so extended that these things are taken as universal, eternal, absolute, and natural-order intrinsics.* The words naivete, provincialism, ethnocentrism, autistic thinking, automorphism, anthropomorphism, etc. are currently used to apply to this type of reification. Examples of it are the tendencies of groups to hold that their folkways, mores, and institutions are not merely appropriate in the relative sense that they are well adapted to their own particular needs, but to consider them as of absolute merit. What is termed "hundred-percentism" is the current example of this tendency. The reification of the racial or cultural type of beauty or of the aesthetic norms of the current school of art into absolutes is another example. The more intense megalomanias and ethnocentrisms and the more virulent moralities are further examples. Likewise, the extension of the supernatural sanction over the tribal moralities, elevating them into absolutes in the nature of the universe supposedly revealed to man by the creator of the universe, is another example of this same thing. Similarly, the naivete with which people of certain temperaments and backgrounds regard their individual tastes as responses to absolute values. That lack of historical perspective which must inevitably characterize the work of all human students is another example. And that tendency of moralists and ethicists to posit, not merely the separately existing rather than the relational nature of the good, but to define that "intrinsic" good in turn in terms of their own tribal definition, is a still further example.

A variant of this tendency in turn is the following tendency: (6) *the relativity of proof and the debatability of belief, preference, or conviction are lost sight of, so that the reified subjects appear as Selbstver-*

ständlichkeiten. Current terms applicable to this form of reification are dogmatism and mysticism, though we lack a complete battery of terms to show all the nuances involved. Aesthetic reifications and the subtle differences between pure art and reminiscent art are examples of this; also the reification of the implicit, unverbalized, or even unverbalizable orientations contained in ethos, *Weltanschauung,* control shibboleths, religious dogmas, belief systems, value systems, and religious and tribal symbols and ceremonials of various kinds. Also the dogmatic intolerance with which a firmly established moral system looks upon the violator or the questioner of what is felt subjectively to be so self-evidently right and appropriate as not to brook questioning. Reification, in action, is utterly impatient of the dissenter, ruthless in its insistence upon conformity, and given to the single control technique of ordering-and-forbidding.

What may be termed (7) *negative reifications also occur.* Sublation is the concept currently applied to this process. However, on closer analysis, it becomes evident that sublation or negative reification is only an obverse aspect of some one of the above mentioned forms of positive reification. In sublating *a, b* is given a more extended reality; or the more extended reality given to *b* results spontaneously in a sublation of *a,* in accordance with the old German maxim, *"Je höher das Alps, desto tiefer das Tal."* Thus in these negative reifications the object is torn from its class and the generalizability of its characteristics is *de*limited and shorn away to yield the supposedly absolute uniqueness of its positively reified rival. An example of this would be the attitude of the person deeply in love that no love such as his has existed before in history. Another example is religion's claim of exclusive and unique merit and thereby its rejection of the merits of other religious systems and of secular belief-value systems. Another example would be the claims of unique merit (the "merit" itself absolutized, however) that appear in the pathological megalomanias, ethnocentrisms, etc. These sublations or negative forms of reification run the same gamut as do the positive forms. That is, some of them shear away only a little of the realities involved, some of them more, and some of them go to the lengths of negating quite the existent and the demonstrable. Examples of this would be the negativistic blind-spots of the psychopathologies; the denial of the fact of evil in much religious coping with the problem of evil; the blind-spots to facts straight in the face of their rationalizations on the part of moral, supernatural, and virulent ethnocentric belief systems; the sublations involved in various unilateralisms within philosophy and science (for example, the behaviorist's denial of consciousness, and the indeterminist's denial of causality); etc. Perhaps the three-year denial on the part of President Hoover that there was a depression is in point. The denial on the part of many theorists on the family of the fact that sexual morality has changed is another example. Likewise, the denial of the actual existence of many behavior set-ups that continue in full functional adjustment straight in the face of the claim made by our mores-rationalizing ideologies that such behavior will surely be disastrous. The extreme in the so-called normal person is the famous "there ain't no such animal," asserted in its bodily presence.

All of the mechanisms above listed involve an unjustifiable extension of the reality of the conceptual or perceptual object; and it is as a general term to cover this whole group of distortions of perception in this direction that we propose to use the term reification. . . .

Tabooed Words [1]

SIR JAMES GEORGE FRAZER

Unable to discriminate clearly between words and things, the savage commonly fancies that the link between a name and the person or thing denominated by it is not a mere arbitrary and ideal association, but a real and substantial bond which unites the two in such a way that magic may be wrought on a man just as easily through his name as through his hair, his nails, or any other material part of his person. In fact, primitive man regards his name as a vital portion of himself and takes care of it accordingly. Thus, for example, the North American Indian "regards his name, not as a mere label, but as a distinct part of his per-

[1] From *The Golden Bough*, pp. 244–246, 247. Copyright, 1922, by The Macmillan Company. By permission of The Macmillan Company, publishers.

sonality, just as much as are his eyes or his teeth, and believes that injury will result as surely from the malicious handling of his name as from a wound inflicted on any part of his physical organism. This belief was found among the various tribes from the Atlantic to the Pacific, and has occasioned a number of curious regulations in regard to the concealment and change of names." Some Esquimaux take new names when they are old, hoping thereby to get a new lease of life. The Tolampoos of Celebes believe that if you write a man's name down you can carry off his soul along with it. Many savages at the present day regard their names as vital parts of themselves, and therefore take great pains to conceal their real names, lest these should give to evil-disposed persons a handle by which to injure their owners.

Thus, to begin with the savages who rank at the bottom of the social scale, we are told that the secrecy with which among the Australian aborigines personal names are often kept from general knowledge "arises in great measure from the belief that an enemy, who knows your name, has in it something which he can use magically to your detriment." "An Australian black," says another writer, "is always very unwilling to tell his real name, and there is no doubt that this reluctance is due to the fear that through his name he may be injured by sorcerers." Amongst the tribes of Central Australia every man, woman, and child has, besides a personal name which is in common use, a secret or sacred name which is bestowed by the older men upon him or her soon after birth, and which is known to none but the fully initiated members of the group. This secret name is never mentioned except upon the most solemn occasions; to utter it in the hearing of women or of men of another group would be a most serious breach of tribal custom, as serious as the most flagrant case of sacrilege among ourselves. When mentioned at all, the name is spoken only in a whisper, and not until the most elaborate precautions have been taken that it shall be heard by no one but members of the group. "The native thinks that a stranger knowing his secret name would have special power to work him ill by means of magic."

The same fear seems to have led to a custom of the same sort amongst the ancient Egyptians, whose comparatively high civilisation was strangely dashed and chequered with relics of the lowest savagery. Every Egyptian received two names, which were known respectively as the true name and the good name, or the great name and the little name; and while the good or little name was made public, the true or great name appears to have been carefully concealed. A Brahman child receives two names, one for common use, the other a secret name which none but his father and mother should know. The latter is only used at ceremonies such as marriage. The custom is intended to protect the person against magic, since a charm only becomes effectual in combination with the real name. Similarly, the natives of Nias believe that harm may be done to a person by the demons who hear his name pronounced. Hence the names of infants, who are especially exposed to the assaults of evil spirits, are never spoken; and often in haunted spots, such as the gloomy depths of the forest, the banks of a river, or beside a bubbling spring, men will abstain from calling each other by their names for a like reason.

The Indians of Chiloe keep their names secret and do not like to have them uttered aloud; for they say that there are fairies or imps on the mainland or neighbouring islands who, if they know folk's names, would do them an injury; but so long as they do not know the names, these mischievous sprites are powerless. The Araucanians will hardly ever tell a stranger their names because they fear that he would thereby acquire some supernatural power over themselves. Asked his name by a stranger, who is ignorant of their superstitions, an Araucanian will answer, "I have none." When an Ojibway is asked his name, he will look at some bystander and ask him to answer. "This reluctance arises from an impression they receive when young, that if they repeat their own names it will prevent their growth, and they will be small in stature. On account of this unwillingness to tell their names, many strangers have fancied that they either have no names or have forgotten them."

In this last case no scruple seems to be felt about communicating a man's name to strangers, and no ill effects appear to be dreaded as a consequence of divulging it; harm is only done when a name is spoken by its owner. Why is this? and why in particular should a man be thought to stunt his growth by uttering his own name? We may conjecture that to savages who act and think thus a person's name only seems to be a part of himself when it is uttered with his own breath; uttered by the breath of others it has no vital connexion with him, and no harm can come to him through it. Whereas, so these primitive philosophers may have argued, when a man lets his own name pass his lips, he is parting with a living piece of himself, and if he persists in so reckless a course he must certainly end by dissipating his energy and shattering his constitution. Many a broken-down debauchee, many a feeble frame wasted with disease, may have been pointed out by these simple moralists to their awe-struck disciples as a fearful example of the fate that must sooner or later overtake the profligate who indulges immoderately in the seductive habit of mentioning his own name.

. . . When the Sulka of New Britain are near the territory of their enemies the Gaktei, they take care not to mention them by their proper name, believing that were they to do so, their foes would attack and slay them. Hence in these circumstances they speak of the Gaktei as o lapsiek, that is, "the rotten tree-trunks," and they imagine that by calling them that they make the limbs of their dreaded enemies ponderous and clumsy like logs. This example illustrates the extremely materialistic view which these savages take of the nature of words; they suppose that the mere utterance of an expression signifying clumsiness will homeopathically affect with clumsiness the limbs of their distant foemen. Another illustration of this curious misconception is furnished by a Caffre superstition that the character of a young thief can be reformed by shouting his name over a boiling kettle of medicated water, then clapping a lid on the kettle and leaving the name to steep in the water for several days. It is not in the least necessary that the thief should be aware of the use that is being made of his name behind his back; the moral reformation will be effected without his knowledge.

The Context of Associations[1]

MARGARET SCHLAUCH

COMMUNICATION AND MISUNDERSTANDING

Two human beings who talk together are accomplishing an act of "communication," as we defined it. . . . Since the effort succeeds so well in most cases, we are apt to forget that the act is and must always be an approximation. To each of his friends, even to his closest *alter ego,* a man talks out of a private world of his own: the sum total of his memories and experiences. Persons strongly attracted to each other by the emotions are prone to attempt a more intimate approaching of the two worlds, so that by some kind of magic extension of personality each one may reach back into the early days of the other and build the same structure of experience. But despite the torrents of eloquence with which the miracle is sometimes attempted, the isolation remains a dreary fact.

The reason is simple. It is impossible for any two persons ever to have learned the same word under precisely the same circumstances; occupying, as it were, the same space in time, and apprehending the new term with precisely the same background. Therefore each will take it into his consciousness ringed about with a special context of associations, differing from the associations of everyone else hearing it. This is what Hermann Paul means when he says that each linguistic creation—and re-creation—is and remains the work of an individual. Yet procedures repeat themselves and approximations of understanding do occur. Our speech is a compromise between the ultimate incommunicability of one person with another and the conventional communication values attached to certain symbols.

WORDS AND REFERENCES

Let us pause a moment to analyze what happens to us in normal conversation when we employ terms for things. Suppose the subject talked about is a spider. When the word is pronounced the sounds will call up in the mind of the listener a general background of experience, not always very vivid, and not always involving a sharp photographic image of remembered spiders. The background of experience in the listener's mind is called by some writers the *reference*, as distinguished from the *referent*, or the real spider existing in the world outside ourselves. It is important to keep the three elements in the situation quite distinct:

The *word*, which is merely a symbol made up of sounds, like ['spaidə(ɹ)];
The *referent*, or concrete object (a living animal);
The *reference*, or recalled experience of past spiders evoked in the mind of the listener.

Under certain circumstances, however, an extremely vivid image is recalled in connection with a given word. The reference is sharpened. This happens especially when the referent is associated with a strong emotion like love or fear. But the same stimulus, the spoken word ['spaidə(ɹ)], may produce nothing but a vague reference in one listener while it evokes a sharp one in another. Their experiences are by no means identical.

EMOTIONAL ASSOCIATIONS

For instance: when I first learned the word "spider," the circumstances were apparently tranquil. I had no cause for alarm, and my attention, so far as I recall, was chiefly captivated by the spinning activities of the creature. The word had no sinister connotations for me. A playmate of mine in those early days, however, must have learned the word under terrifying circumstances. She was never able to recall them or convey them to me in any way; but the mere pronunciation of the word (not to speak of the sight of an actual arachnidan creature) was enough to induce symptoms of panic amounting almost to a fit. If emotions may strongly color the reference of "spider," they may do so to some slight degree with less concrete terms such as "isosceles triangle." There is the illuminating story of a little girl who, having recently learned to read, was spelling out a political article in the newspaper. "Father," she asked, "what is Tammany Hall?" And father replied in the voice usually reserved for the taboos of social communication, "You'll understand that when you grow up, my dear." Acceding to this adult whim of evasion, she desisted from her inquiries; but something in Daddy's tone had convinced her that Tammany Hall must be connected with

illicit *amour,* and for many years she could not hear this political institution mentioned without experiencing a secret non-political thrill.
Another high school girl reports that the phrase "plane geometry"
was first introduced to her in a context of deprecation, as applying to
a science much less exciting and esoteric than something else (presumably "solid" geometry). So for a long time she understood "plane"
in the sense of "plain"—a semantic confusion heightened by the
homonyms of identical origin—appropriate for an unadorned Cin-
derella among the mathematical sisters; and it was only much later
that she realized with a shock that the key word applied quite color-
lessly to (imaginary) surfaces, having nothing to do with beauty or
complexity.

With such varieties of individual experience in relation to words,
there arise all sorts of *connotations,* as they are called, or nuances of
association around the accepted factual definition. Some connotations
(like the erotic aura around Tammany Hall for the little girl of our
anecdote) remain strictly private and individual, the results of special
accidents; others are coincidental for many persons and hence become
currently attached to the word. If the sound-symbol is "spider," the
situation can be thus represented:

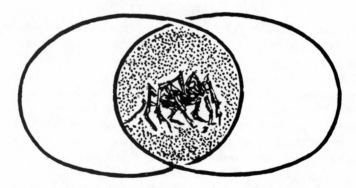

The unshaded sections in the ellipse of associations represent the
special and private associations of the word due to the accidents of
individual experience; the shaded portion represents a common store
of connotations (tactile impressions approximately the same for anyone
who has ever felt an arachnid crawl over his shin, generally current
anecdotes or superstitions about spiders, etc.). In the heart of the over-
lapping associations is the word in its scientific sense: a designation of a

biological type by (so far as possible) a colorless, unemotional scientific label. Even the label is a mere approximation of completely scientific denotation. The connotations cannot be kept away entirely, even from the abstract terms.

Images, Words and Formulas [1]

GUSTAVE LE BON

The power of words is bound up with the images they evoke, and is quite independent of their real significance. Words whose sense is the most ill-defined are sometimes those that possess the most influence. Such, for example, are the terms democracy, socialism, equality, liberty, etc., whose meaning is so vague that bulky volumes do not suffice to precisely fix it. Yet it is certain that a truly magical power is attached to those short syllables, as if they contained the solution of all problems. They synthesise the most diverse unconscious aspirations and the hope of their realisation.

Reason and arguments are incapable of combating certain words and formulas. They are uttered with solemnity in the presence of crowds, and as soon as they have been pronounced an expression of respect is visible on every countenance, and all heads are bowed. By many they are considered as natural forces, as supernatural powers. They evoke grandiose and vague images in men's minds, but this very vagueness that wraps them in obscurity augments their mysterious power. They are the mysterious divinities hidden behind the tabernacle, which the devout only approach in fear and trembling.

The images evoked by words being independent of their sense, they vary from age to age and from people to people, the formulas remaining identical. Certain transitory images are attached to certain words:

the word is merely as it were the button of an electric bell that calls them up.

All words and all formulas do not possess the power of evoking images, while there are some which have once had this power, but lose it in the course of use, and cease to waken any response in the mind. They then become vain sounds, whose principal utility is to relieve the person who employs them of the obligation of thinking. Armed with a small stock of formulas and commonplaces learnt while we are young, we possess all that is needed to traverse life without the tiring necessity of having to reflect on anything whatever.

If any particular language be studied, it is seen that the words of which it is composed change rather slowly in the course of ages, while the images these words evoke or the meaning attached to them changes ceaselessly. This is the reason why, in another work, I have arrived at the conclusion that the absolute translation of a language, especially a dead language, is totally impossible. What do we do in reality when we substitute a French for a Latin, Greek, or Sanskrit expression, or even when we endeavour to understand a book written in our own tongue two or three centuries back? We merely put the images and ideas with which modern life has endowed our intelligence in the place of absolutely distinct notions and images which ancient life had brought into being in the mind of races submitted to conditions of existence having no analogy with our own. When the men of the Revolution imagined they were copying the Greeks and Romans, what were they doing except giving to ancient words a sense the latter had never had? What resemblance can possibly exist between the institutions of the Greeks and those designated to-day by corresponding words? A republic at that epoch was an essentially aristocratic institution, formed of a reunion of petty despots ruling over a crowd of slaves kept in the most absolute subjection. These communal aristocracies, based on slavery, could not have existed for a moment without it.

The word "liberty," again, what signification could it have in any way resembling that we attribute to it to-day at a period when the possibility of the liberty of thought was not even suspected, and when there was no greater and more exceptional crime than that of discussing the gods, the laws and the customs of the city? What did such a word as "fatherland" signify to an Athenian or Spartan unless it were the cult of Athens or Sparta, and in no wise that of Greece, composed of rival cities always at war with each other? What meaning had the same word "fatherland" among the ancient Gauls, divided into rival tribes and races, and possessing different languages and religions, and who were easily vanquished by Caesar because he always found allies among them? It was Rome that made a country of Gaul by endowing it with political and religious unity. Without going back so far, scarcely two centuries ago, is it to be believed that this same notion of a fatherland was conceived to have the same meaning as at present by French princes like the great Condé, who allied themselves with the foreigner against their sovereign? And yet again, the same word had it not a sense very different from the modern for the French royalist emigrants, who thought they obeyed the laws of honour in fighting against France, and who from their point of view did indeed obey them, since the feudal law bound the vassal to the lord and not to the soil, so that where the sovereign was there was the true fatherland?

Numerous are the words whose meaning has thus profoundly changed from age to age—words which we can only arrive at understanding in the sense in which they were formerly understood after a long effort. It has been said with truth that much study is necessary merely to arrive at conceiving what was signified to our great-grand-fathers by such words as the "king" and the "royal family." What, then, is likely to be the case with terms still more complex?

Words, then, have only mobile and transitory significations which change from age to age and people to people; and when we desire to exert an influence by their means on the crowd what it is requisite to know is the meaning given them by the crowd at a given moment, and not the meaning which they formerly had or may yet have for individuals of a different mental constitution.

Thus, when crowds have come, as the result of political upheavals or changes of belief, to acquire a profound antipathy for the images evoked by certain words, the first duty of the true statesman is to change the words without, of course, laying hands on the things themselves, the latter being too intimately bound up with the inherited constitution to be transformed. The judicious Tocqueville long ago made the remark that the work of the consulate and the empire consisted more particularly in the clothing with new words of the greater part of the institutions of the past—that is to say, in replacing words evoking disagreeable images in the imagination of the crowd by other words of which the novelty prevented such evocations. The "taille" or tallage has become the land tax; the "gabelle," the tax on salt; the "aids," the indirect contributions and the consolidated duties; the tax on trade companies and guilds, the license, etc.

One of the most essential functions of statesmen consists, then, in baptizing with popular or, at any rate, indifferent words things the crowd cannot endure under their old names. The power of words is so great that it suffices to designate in well-chosen terms the most odious things to make them acceptable to crowds. Taine justly observes that it was by invoking liberty and fraternity—words very popular at the time—that the Jacobins were able "to install a despotism worthy of Dahomey, a tribunal similar to that of the Inquisition, and to accomplish human hectatombs akin to those of ancient Mexico." The art of those who govern, as is the case with the art of advocates, consists above all in the science of employing words. One of the greatest difficulties of this art is, that in one and the same society the same words most often have very different meanings for the different social classes, who employ in appearance the same words, but never speak the same language.

In the preceding examples it is especially time that has been made to intervene as the principal factor in the changing of the meaning of words. If, however, we also make race intervene, we shall then see that, at the same period, among peoples equally civilised but of different race, the same words very often correspond to extremely dissimilar ideas. It is impossible to understand these differences without having travelled much, and for this reason I shall not insist upon them. I shall confine myself to observing that it is precisely the words most often employed by the masses which among different peoples possess the most different meanings. Such is the case, for instance, with the words "democracy" and "socialism" in such frequent use nowadays.

In reality they correspond to quite contrary ideas and images in the Latin and Anglo-Saxon mind. For the Latin peoples the word "democracy" signifies more especially the subordination of the will and the initiative of the individual to the will and the initiative of the community represented by the State. It is the State that is charged, to a greater and greater degree, with the direction of everything, the centralisation, the monopolisation, and the manufacture of everything. To the State it is that all parties without exception, radicals, socialists, or monarchist, constantly appeal. Among the Anglo-Saxons, and notably in America this same word "democracy" signifies, on the contrary, the intense development of the will of the individual, and as complete a subordination as possible of the State, which, with the exception of the police, the army, and diplomatic relations, is not allowed the direction of anything, not even of public instruction. It is seen, then, that the same word which signifies for one people the subordination of the will and the initiative of the individual and the preponderance of the State, signifies for another the excessive development of the will and the initiative of the individual and the complete subordination of the State.

The Confusion of Likeness with Identity by Means of Comparisons and Other Figures of Speech[1]

JOSHUA ROSETT

In social intercourse, representation and symbolism are employed as means for externalizing—for expressing—the internal state of one's body to one's fellows. Such is the function of gestural, vocal, written, and other modes of expression. Certain internal states, however, do not lend themselves readily to expression. It is impossible, for instance, to convey to another that state of one's body which consists in the experience of a given quality or shade of a sensation, such as a certain kind of sour or sweet or bitter taste, or the exact degree of cold or heat experienced. In such instances appeal is had to the other person's concrete past experiences of a similar kind. Expressions like "sour as vinegar," "sweet as sugar," "bitter as gall," "cold as ice," "warm as toast," are appeals to concrete past experiences of the listener or the

[1] From *The Mechanism of Thought, Imagery and Hallucination*. New York: Columbia University Press, 1939, pp. 141–142. Copyright, 1939, by Columbia University Press. Reprinted by permission.

reader. In a number of instances even such an appeal to the past concrete experiences of one's fellows fails as an expression of the state of one's body. In such instances the next best mode of conveying a meaning is by further symbolization on one's state of being. Such are the expressions "sweet as young love," "a bitter insult," "a mortal injury," "a cold reception." The necessity to which we are frequently driven of resorting to the use of similes, metaphors and even parables, when representation and simple symbolism fail, testifies to the difficulty of externalizing certain internal states. Useful as such expressions may be in conveying meaning, they are capable of profound evil in the course of the extreme evolution of symbols, as will be presently seen.

"Spontaneous" movement is an inalienable attribute of life, but is not exclusively characteristic of it. Fermentation, changes of temperature, and other causes bring about a movement in liquids which appears to be spontaneous. The wind and the waves, by moving solid objects, endow them with the simulacrum of living things. By contrast, immobility is the most prominent gross trait of inanimate things. A number of insects, and even vertebrate animals such as the opossum, when in danger become motionless, "pretending" to be dead. In accordance with these facts, primitive man, to whom movement was a symbol of life, endowed the winds and waves and clouds, and earthquakes and avalanches, as well as the heavenly bodies, with enormous vital powers. In the same manner that the power of his chieftain could by prayer and gifts, be diverted from harmful into beneficial channels, so he employed sacrifice and supplication as means of propitiating the powers of nature and of enlisting them in his cause.[2]

But the evil does not end there. The interposition of analogy and metaphor in the course of the evolution of representation into symbolism operates for the production of identity out of likeness. The chieftain of the tribe, who is at first analogous with the sun, becomes in the course of prayer and flattery, identical with the sun. Having become *the* sun, he becomes the symbol of all power and is worshiped accordingly.[3]

One of the attributes of the chieftain or the king is his form. A stone or wooden image fashioned in his form is therefore a representation of

[2] See, for example, Prescott's description of the devotional rites of the ancient Mexicans.

[3] On a smaller and certainly more ridiculous scale, a superior official is frequently endowed by his subordinates with profound wisdom in all things and is worshiped accordingly, though outside of his particular business that superior may be a perfect ass.

the chief or the king. In the process of reproduction, the form of the image loses its likeness to the chief's form, thus becoming a symbol. A further evolution of the symbol may result in the form of an angel, a devil, or a dragon. In the course of adulation and from habit, this symbol of the chief becomes, by means of analogy and metaphor, and through the gradations of similarity, likeness, and identity, *the* chief, and is respected, feared, and worshiped accordingly. The contention that images have only the power of representation is historically untrue. Having become symbols, they cover a much wider range of significance. The fact is that throughout the ages they have been invested by their votaries with mystical, supernatural powers, capable of accomplishing miraculous cures, of bringing rain, of extinguishing conflagrations, of arresting earthquakes and volcanoes, of offering protection from enemies' missiles—in brief, with the power of averting every calamity and of bringing every possible benefit.

Logotherapy [1]

MALFORD W. THEWLIS, M.D.

Logotherapy (Gk. *logos,* word; *therapia,* healing) might be defined as the therapeutic influence of words upon diseased persons. One's first impression might be that this is a form of psychotherapy which should be employed by psychologists and psychiatrists. This is not the meaning I wish to convey. On the contrary, a careful selection of words may spare the elderly patient much mental suffering, thus making it unnecessary for the psychotherapist to clean up the wreckage physicians have produced by a tyranny of words. It is obvious that severe emotional disturbances are often caused by the wrong choice of words.

The fear that the truth is not being told can cause as much damage

[1] From *The Care of the Aged* (*Geriatrics*), 5th ed. St. Louis: The C. V. Mosby Company, 1946, pp. 109–113. Copyright by the C. V. Mosby Company. Reprinted by permission.

as the blunt facts. I search for words to tell the truth with the least possible injury to the patient.

Medical terms have become more precise, medicine more scientific, and physicians, especially younger ones, are likely to inform patients bluntly of their condition.

Sometimes physicians forget the simpler methods of approach to illness. They are apt to overlook the human side of medicine, that is compassion. I have attempted to interpret patients' reactions to our approach and why it is often unwise to use final, startling, and dramatic words. There is always a coefficient of errors—the possibility of a mistaken diagnosis, or that the patient may live for years, in spite of an "incurable" disease. He may adjust himself so well to pathologic processes that he is able to carry on in spite of them.

Stuart Chase, in *The Tyranny of Words,* showed that words like freedom, liberty, and democracy could not be defined so closely that they would have the same general interpretation. Physicians' words leave no doubt in the patient's mind as to the exact meaning of the terms used. He may not know the exact pathologic implications, but by an "association of words" he can imagine their consequences. The patient associates the words with actual disease conditions in other persons who have been hopelessly ill or crippled by the disease indicated by a word. Thus the word cancer brings to mind all the horrible and shocking manifestations of the disease the patient can think of. The physician utters the word and the patient lies awake worrying about it, building up a picture of a gruesome illness followed by death. The patient associates the word with his own destruction. He practices collateral thinking and, already being in a disturbed mental state because of disease, can develop an emotional condition which may kill him. No one can estimate how many illnesses have been precipitated by an ominous word. Emotional imbalance plays a powerful role in disease.

In wartime, women may show sudden evidence of hyperthyroidism as a result of worry when a son or husband goes into military service. The lack of a word from a son overseas may have as much effect on the nervous system of a parent as actual disaster. A father lost 20 pounds and his hair turned gray when he did not hear for six months from his son stationed in Iran. Physicians may likewise cause intense suffering to patients by maintaining silence at a time when a gentle, kind, and encouraging word is really needed. Physicians may be so absorbed in their work that to them a stimulating word of encouragement seems superfluous. A short note or telephone message to a patient often helps him to recover. Physicians, always overworked, occasionally forget the simple things men live by. Very few of us can live without encouragement and stimulus. Most of us must have it fed at frequent intervals.

Physicians themselves are often the victims of oppressed words. A colleague of mine, aged 68, was really ill, and remained in bed for a week, following his discharge by a family whom he had treated for some years. He was dismissed by a curt statement: "We want a younger man who is more up to date." When I attempted to diagnose his condition, he repeated this sentence; he was a man of few words, and repetition meant to me that this preyed on him. Incidentally that physician had one of the most successful practices I can remember. His success was due in a measure to his gentle, firm manner, and timely use of reassuring words. He talked little, listened much. He never volunteered information to any patient but he was willing to discuss the scientific pattern of the patient's illness, if requested to do so. He was an expert in directing conversation; the patient poured out his troubles, the physician listened attentively and sympathetically. If a patient was critical of him, he listened, objective, detached, convinced that the expression of opinions, normal or not, was beneficial to the patient; it was a release. He expressed himself with clarity, was concise but never curt. When he entered the sickroom his technique was obvious. He diverted the disturbed patient, examined a painting on the wall, or an object in the room the presence of which had some significance. This often led to a short conversation about the patient's interests, friends or relatives, the type of work he did or his hobbies. This approach helped the patient to relax.

Another physician almost retired from practice after being told that he had coronary thrombosis. He had no electrocardiographic proof of the presence of the disease. Pain in his chest subsided when he gave up smoking, in which he overindulged.

If physicians are susceptible to their own funereal diagnoses, what about the layman who is the victim of the physician's careless words?

Few of us have the energy required to speak carefully to people in everyday life. One is apt to disregard the art of speaking properly, and discharge obligations with flowers.

Nurses occasionally depress patients by telling them about past professional experiences—patients they cared for; who, of course, had died. Physicians frequently have to undo the damage done by a kind but tactless nurse.

The average person is unequipped to deal with the ill, too often uttering disturbing words exasperating to the sick.

Unconsciously I wounded a family by telling a daughter that her mother was suffering from premature old age. I forgot the possibility that relatives listen and tell. In this particular instance the woman improved with the use of desiccated thyroid, for she had hypothyroidism. Her anxiety disappeared when her condition was openly discussed and adequately treated. Certainly telling old persons that they are suffering from "old age" can be a legal form of homicide. One should never refer to withering old age in their presence. Better speak to them of advancing years or of ripe maturity. Life is so uncertain that it is unwise for us to risk shortening it by the use of dreadful words.

I am not suggesting the use of dishonest words for diagnostic placebos. It is not good medicine to be vague when one is not certain of the diagnosis. It is much better to confess our ignorance.

To this, one might object that in case another physician is later consulted, and you are quoted, you are exposing yourself to the accusation of "covering yourself" when you do not use academic language. The use of synonyms will not fool another physician; he will readily recognize the code. For example, if one says "anemia" and advises permanent liver therapy, any physician will recognize pernicious anemia. One might ask, why not say pernicious anemia in the beginning? The term "pernicious anemia" is a misnomer anyway, and it has very depressing connotations to most patients.

While physicians are "duty-bound" to tell some responsible member of a family the truth, one must not forget that relatives often dramatize the diagnosis. If they do remain silent, their faces are often a mirror. The physician, always protecting his reputation, may make the diagnosis more serious to impress the family with his importance in diagnostic skill. Instead of being helpful, suggestive, and optimistic, as every physician should, he kills hope. But let him be ill himself, and he will leave orders for every "crepe-hanging" physician-friend to be kept out of the sickroom.

Apoplexy (shock, stroke, paralysis), arteriosclerosis, coronary thrombosis, arthritis, arterial hypertension, arterial hypotension, cancer, cirrhosis of the liver, colitis, and pernicious anemia are known to be incurable. Old age and senility are also destructive words. Many people have logophobia when these terms are mentioned.

These words are symbolic, referring to a single thing—incurability. Symbolization is the study of the influence of language upon thought, according to Ogden and Richards. Perhaps physicians are inclined to affix symbols on their patients. One word can be a simple way to dismiss a person. The references, however, which result from such a symbol are devastating. They have the same effect on the patient as they would have on the physician, if the same symbol were attached to him. The physician must search for those symbols which are least disturbing. This is not too difficult since disease is a complex process, rarely an entity, and medicine never can be an exact science.

Perhaps physicians feel that patients must be impressed by scientific words. In my experience, the patient is favorably impressed before he comes to the physician or he would not consult him. Why then the fireworks of words?

Nowhere in medicine is a bright, cheerful face required more than in surgery. The physician or surgeon must be hopeful and never give up, even in a desperate situation. In postoperative states, above all, soothing words are required since the average patient feels as if he were dying during the first few days following a major operation.

If the patient is worried after the operation, he may be told that all patients are in the same condition for a few days, and suddenly the clouds lift and the patient sees fair weather ahead. One great anesthetist said that he "kissed" the patient before anesthesia. What he meant was that he took plenty of time to condition the patient. Death was rare in his practice. The surgeon for whom he worked is one of the most successful ones I know. He is tactful, clear, makes his diagnosis and prognosis slowly, and uses few, well-chosen words, but these words follow a formula which is used on the patient and his relatives and is clothed in faith-inspiring language. His visits to the patient may be at any hour of the day or night. He routinely drops in the hospital at night to see if all is going well on the floor.

He creates hope. As Cathell said, "Hope creates ideas, generates new expedients, brings up useful reflections and fresh endeavors." This surgeon leaves no doubt in his patient's mind that he will get well. He makes no promises, however. He tells the patient that he will not promise to cure a weeping sinew, but he reassures the patient that he will do the best he can.

He leaves no doubt, by his actions, that he is taking as good care of the patient, millionaire or pauper, as if he were his own relative. He takes time to practice surgery; no abruptness, no chilly or indifferent words. His manner is warm, therefore his words are tender. He makes the patient proud of the fight he is putting up. When the patient leaves the hospital he is devoted to him and remains so. Working constantly against shock, he feels that despairing, dreary, tragic words can contribute as much to shock in the patient as the knife does when it cuts nerves.

Little things make great physicians. These simple suggestions on logotherapy can make practice much more pleasant for the geriatrician and patient and cultivate a more tolerant attitude on the part of the family. Thus the physician is in a favored position to exert an idealistic influence and render a valuable service to his patients and to their families. Logotherapy includes both the words one uses and those one omits.

The physician who is too free in the use of devastating words should bear in mind the following considerations regarding some of the conditions commonly encountered in the aged:

1. Many persons recover full use of their extremities following apoplexy.

2. Arteriosclerosis is one of the most depressing words in the language. It is often used to cover up our ignorance of the actual cause of the illness.

3. Many persons fully recover from an attack of coronary thrombosis.

4. Arterial hypertensive patients often have exaggerated fears which can easily shorten their lives. Some persons live and work for years with a systolic blood pressure over 200, and a diastolic pressure over 120 mm. Hg.

5. Many persons become semi-invalid when told that they have low blood pressure, but good health can be maintained in old age with a systolic blood pressure of 100.

6. The word "arthritis" cripples as many people as the disease itself. Physicians frequently dismiss these patients with the words "nothing will help you." This is not true because many patients are rehabilitated by modern treatment. These patients often fear that they will be crippled. Medical facts allow us to reassure these patients.

7. Cancer is the most dreaded word in the language. Excellent results

are obtained by modern treatment and the physician should be as optimistic about the disease as statistics warrant.

8. Recent work on proteins and vitamins gives encouragement in the treatment of cirrhosis of the liver.

The General Theory of Magical Language[1]

BRONISLAW MALINOWSKI

The mastery over reality, both technical and social, grows side by side with the knowledge of how to use words. Whether you watch apprenticeship in some craft within a primitive community or in our own society, you always see that familiarity with the name of a thing is the direct outcome of familiarity with how to use this thing. The right word for an action, for a trick of trade, for an ability, acquires *meaning* in the measure in which the individual becomes capable to carry out this action. The belief that to know the name of a thing is to get a hold on it is thus empirically true. At the same time, it lends itself to obvious distortions in the direction of mysticism. For the genuineness of the process, that is the genuineness of verbal power over things through manual and intellectual control, is the result of a fine balance. On the one hand we have people who are more effective manually than verbally. This is a handicap. The simple mind, primitive or civilised, identifies difficulty of speech and clumsiness and unreadiness of expression with mental deficiency. In the Trobriands *tonagowa* covers idiocy and defective speech; and among European peasantry the village idiot is very often merely a person who stammers or suffers from inability of clear expression. On the other hand the verbal type and the theoretical type of person surpass in mastery of

---

[1] From *Coral Gardens and Their Magic*. London: George Allen & Unwin, Ltd., 1935, Vol. II, pp. 233–236, 238–239. Copyright by George Allen & Unwin, Ltd. Reprinted by permission.

words while they are backward in manual effectiveness. Even within the most primitive differentiation of activities the man who is better at counsel and advice, at talking and bragging, represents what in more advanced communities will become the schoolman, the talmudist or the baboo. This may be an unhealthy development of learning or of a purely consulting or advisory capacity; but it is rooted in something which functions throughout all human work—I mean the fact that some people must command, advise, plan and co-ordinate.

So far I have been mainly speaking about arts and crafts. Power through speech in the mastery of social relations, of legal rules and of economic realities, is quite as plain. The child who grows up in a primitive community and becomes instructed gradually in the intricacies of kinship, the taboos, duties and privileges of kindred, of clansmen, of people of higher and lower rank, learns the handling of social relations through the knowledge of sociological terms and phrases. The instruction may take place in the course of initiation ceremonies, a great part of which consists in the sociological apprenticeship of the child, boy or girl, youth or maiden, to tribal citizenship. But obviously there is a long educational process between the small infant, who can name and call for the few people of its immediate surroundings, and the adult tribesman or tribeswoman, who must address a score, a few hundred or even a few thousand people in the proper manner, appeal to them through adequate praise, be able to greet, converse and transact business with them. This process again has two sides: experience in "deportment," manners, practices and abstentions, and the capacity to name, describe and anticipate these things, and also the mastery of social aspect and social terminology runs parallel.

If space allowed, I could enlarge on this side of our subject indefinitely. Take, for instance, the problem of law in its verbal and pragmatic aspects. Here the value of the word, the binding force of a formula, is at the very foundation of order and reliability in human relations. Whether the marriage vows are treated as a sacrament or as a mere legal contract—and in most human societies they have this two-fold character—the power of words in establishing a permanent human relation, the sacredness of words and their socially sanctioned inviolability, are absolutely necessary to the existence of social order. If legal phrases, if promises and contracts were not regarded as something more than *flatus vocis,* social order would cease to exist in a complex civilisation as well as in a primitive tribe. The average man, whether civilised or primitive, is not a sociologist. He neither needs to, nor can, arrive at the real function of a deep belief in the sanctity of legal and sacral words and their creative power. But he must have this belief; it is drilled into him by the process whereby he becomes part and parcel of the orderly institutions of his community. The stronger this belief, the greater becomes what might be called the elementary honesty and veracity of the citizens. In certain walks of human life speech may develop into the best instrument for the concealment of thought. But there are other aspects—law, contracts, the formulae of sacraments, oaths—in which a complicated apparatus inviolably based on mystical and religious ideas develops in every community as a necessary by-product of the working of legal and moral institutions and relationships.

This must suffice to establish my proposition that there is a very real basis to human belief in the mystic and binding power of words. We can also see where the truth of this belief really lies. Man rises above his purely animal, anatomical and physiological equipment by building up his culture in co-operation with his fellow-beings. He masters his surroundings because he can work with others and through others. Verbal communication from the earliest infantile dependence of the child on his parents to the developed uses of full citizenship, scientific speech and words of command and leadership, is the correlate of this. The knowledge of right words, appropriate phrases and the more highly developed forms of speech, gives man a power over and above his own limited field of personal action. But this power of words, this co-operative use of speech is and must be correlated with the conviction that a spoken word is sacred. The fact also that words add to the power of man over and above their strictly pragmatic effectiveness must be correlated with the belief that words have a mystical influence. . . .

Having established the two-fold aspect of linguistic development, the sacred and the profane, the mystical and the pragmatic, within the growth of every individual, we should find within every culture a ready-made distinction and traditional cleavage between these two aspects of human speech. In other words, having started by using language in a manner which is both magical and pragmatic, and passed gradually through stages in which the magical and pragmatic aspects intermingle and oscillate, the individual will find within his culture certain crystallised, traditionally standardised types of speech, with the language of technology and science at the one end, and the language of sacrament, prayer, magical formula, advertisement and political oratory at the other.

. . . At the very basis of verbal magic there lies what I have elsewhere called "the creative metaphor of magic." By this I mean that the repetitive statement of certain words is believed to produce the reality stated. I think that if we stripped all magical speech to its essentials, we would find simply this fact: a man believed to have mystical powers faces a clear blue sky and repeats: "It rains; dark clouds forgather; torrents burst forth and drench the parched soil." Or else he would be facing a black sky and repeat: "The sun breaks through the clouds; the sun shines." Or in illness he repeats, like Monsieur Coué: "Every day and in every way it is getting better and better." The essence of verbal magic, then, consists in a statement which is untrue, which stands in direct opposition to the context of reality. But the belief in magic inspires man with the conviction that his untrue statement must become true. How far this is rooted in emotional life, in the power of man to day-dream, in unconquerable human hopes and human optimism, is clear to those who are acquainted with the fact of magic as well as the theoretical literature connected with it. In another place also I have defined magic as the institutionalised expression of human optimism, of constructive hopes overcoming doubt and pessimism.

I would like to add here that when Freud defines this function of magic as the "omnipotence of thought" (*Allmacht der Gedanken*) and tries to find the roots of magical activities in the human tendency idly to day-dream, this view requires a serious correction—a correction which is contained in our theory here. Because—and this is of the greatest importance—man never runs on the side-track of magical verbiage or of magical activities in that idle day-dreaming which stultifies action. Organised magic always appears within those domains of human activity where experience has demonstrated to man his pragmatic impotence. In the measure as humanity, through developing technique, conquers one realm of activity after another, magic disappears and is replaced by science and technique. We do not use magic in agriculture any more, we do not attract shoals of fish by magic nor improve the trajectory of a high explosive by incantations. Aspects of human activity which have been made subject to the control of physics, chemistry or biology, are treated by systems based on reason and experience. And even in primitive communities we find a clear realisation of those phases in fishing, hunting and agriculture which are mastered by man with his implements, his hands and his brains; where man knows that his thought is impotent, there and there only does he resort to magic. Magic is not a belief in the omnipotence of thought but rather the clear recognition of the limitations of thought, nay, of its impotence. Magic, more especially verbal magic, grows out of legitimate uses of speech, and it is only the exaggeration of one aspect of these legitimate uses. More than that: ritual magic and verbal magic are not mere counterparts of idle day-dreaming. In the affirmation of the hopeful aspect magic exercises an integrative influence over the individual mind. Through the fact that this integrative influence is also connected with an organising power, magic becomes also an empirical force. Freud's conception of magic as a type of vicious megalomania would relegate it to the domain of cultural pathology. Frazer's theory that sympathetic magic is due to a mistaken association of ideas, while it explains one aspect of magic, namely the sympathetic principle which underlies the creative metaphor of magic, still does not account for the enormous organising part played by magic. Durkheim's view that the substance of magic, that is *mana* or magical force, is nothing but society personified, explains one mystical attitude by inviting us to assume another.

In my opinion magic has exercised a profound positive function in organising enterprise, in inspiring hope and confidence in the individual. Side by side with this, magical belief has obviously developed an attitude which exerts disturbing and subversive influences, especially in witchcraft and black magic. In the history of culture every phenomenon, I think, has got its constructive and disintegrative sides, its organising functions and its influences which point towards dissolution and decay. Human cultures do not merely grow and develop. They also decompose, die or collapse. Functional anthropology is not magic; it is not a chartered optimism or whitewashing of culture. One of its duties, in the wider cultural sense, is to show that savagery and superstition are not confined to primitive society. If we have insisted on the "white" aspects of magic side by side with its black aspects, it is rather to bring into relief something which has been less fully recognised and elaborated in anthropological literature and in the practical approach to facts. Apart from Frazer's work on *Psyche's Task* (reprinted as the *Devil's Advocate*), the constructive side of magic has not been sufficiently recognised; and even now, when formulated, it meets with vigorous opposition—remarkably enough from the modern theologian.

PART VIII

The Structural Patterns and Implications of a Language

Human beings do not live in the objective world alone, nor alone in the world of social activity as ordinarily understood, but are very much at the mercy of the particular language which has become the medium of expression for their society. It is quite an illusion to imagine that one adjusts to reality essentially without the use of language and that language is merely an incidental means of solving specific problems of communication or reflection. The fact of the matter is that the "real world" is to a large extent unconsciously built up on the language habits of the group. . . . We see and hear and otherwise experience very largely as we do because the language habits of our community predispose certain choices of interpretation.

EDWARD SAPIR

Inferences based on peculiar forms of classification of ideas, and due to the fact that a whole group of distinct ideas are expressed by a single term, occur commonly in the terms of relationship of various languages; as, for instance, in our term *uncle,* which means the two distinct classes of father's brother and mother's brother. Here, also, it is commonly assumed that the linguistic expression is a secondary reflex of the customs of the people; but the question is quite open in how far the one phenomenon is the primary one and the other the secondary one, and whether the customs of the people have not rather developed from the unconsciously developed terminology.

FRANZ BOAS

Perception and Language [1]

GRACE DE LAGUNA

It is to be assumed as a methodological postulate that there is a general correlation between the range of perceptual content of an organism and its behavior-system. This does not mean, of course, that for every possible item of perceptual content there is a corresponding item of response. There is no one-to-one correspondence of element to element. Indeed we cannot think either of perceptual content or of behavior as analyzable into discrete elements. The correlation that is to be postulated is a correspondence of patterning—a correlation of organized functional systems. Any distinction which an animal is able to perceive in its surroundings will, under appropriate conditions, discriminate in its behavior. And any distinction which remains undiscriminated in its behavior we must assume not to characterize its perceptual field. This postulate has usually been applied with reference to sensory discrimination: to determine, for example, the color vision of fish, or the auditory sensitivity of the frog. But the postulate has a much wider applicability than this: namely, to the organization of perceptual content. The type and degree of organization that we can observe in the behavior of an animal is evidence of a corresponding type and degree of organization of its perceptual field.

Speech is a unique form of behavior peculiar to man. It is highly organized. Man does not speak except as he speaks a language, and language has a characteristic and complex structure. Moreover, in speaking man is not indulging in a set of vocal gymnastics. Speech is, as it were, geared to mesh with all other human activities. The language that a man speaks applies to the things and events that he experiences, and its systematic organization reflects the organization of what he sees and hears and feels.

[1] From *Human Biology*, Vol. i, No. 4, December, 1929, pp. 555–558. Reprinted by permission.

It has sometimes been said that an animal psychologist is forced to use indirect methods of investigation because the animal is unfortunately unable to speak and tell him what it experiences. This betrays a curious misapprehension. As if the animal's inability to speak were not itself a positive and significant witness of what it experiences! No one would deny that speech is evidence of conceptual thought. If an animal cannot express its thoughts in language, that is because it has no thoughts to express; for thoughts which are not formulated are something less than thoughts. But it is equally true that if an animal is unable to describe what it sees and hears, that is because what it perceives is essentially inexpressible in the terms of language. If *per impossible* a psychologist were endowed with a magic gift which enabled him to look with a dog's eyes and hear with a dog's ears, he no more than the dog could describe in words what he thus perceived, for the words of human speech apply to a world of things and qualities, acts and relations, which do not exist for the dog either in their distinctiveness or in their interconnections. The patterning of the animal's world is at once vaguer in its outlines and simpler in its design.

We have long been accustomed to think of what we perceive without senses as given once for all, and as essentially distinct from our understanding of it. It has been one of the major problems of epistemology how understanding is related to sense, and conception to perception. Latterly psychologists, at least, have ceased to think in such terminology: but the problem of "meaning" is no less urgent, and it is essentially the same problem. And it will, I venture to believe, prove equally baffling, if we continue to think of perception as containing a hard core of sensation to which a variable "meaning" becomes attached. At the perceptual level what a thing "is" and what it "means" are not distinct from each other. Once we fully accept the doctrine that what is perceived is an organized whole, the problem appears in a new light. When I look under the hood of an automobile I see a mass of dirty black iron dripping with grease, the very shape of which is so ill defined that I could not now sketch in vaguest outline what I saw. But my son sees carburetor and timer, starting motor and exhaust manifold, and could, I have no doubt, draw a clear diagram of these parts and their visible structure, although the blackness and dirtiness that catches my eye evidently escapes his. But I could, with instruction and effort, learn to see these parts in their dynamic structure, just as I now see hood and doors and wheels. The understanding of what one sees is not something externally added on, but it enters into and transforms the whole down to its last details.

Now it does not need argument to prove that without language we should none of us come to understand the sensible world about us. It is through the conceptual analysis effected by language that I may come to understand the construction of the automobile engine, and it has similarly been through the agency of language that we all acquired in childhood an understanding of the common objects of daily life. But the sights and sounds of everyday have not only acquired meaning in this way: they have also, through the analysis and synthesis effected by speech, become perceptually differentiated and organized as the objects and events we now see. Of course it is not language in isolation that has accomplished this transformation. But language does not exist in isolation from the culture of which it forms the chief vehicle. It is impossible to learn the language of an alien culture merely from grammar and dictionary. One really acquires a language only insofar as he acquires a culture. Otherwise, as Rousseau says, one may only speak French in six languages. It might well be argued that men of widely differing cultures and modes of speech perceive in correspondingly different terms. The Eskimo, for example, who discriminates by name a dozen varieties of snow surface and formation, each of which has for him its distinctive significance, must see a different landscape from that which meets the eye of the European traveler to the Arctic. But while this might be argued, the thesis here maintained is simpler: that man's ability to use language implies a perceptual experience fundamentally different in its content and organization from that possessed by any other animal.

Considered merely as a mode of discriminatory response, speech is unique. By speech it is possible to respond directly and specifically to an object as such, or even to a quality or relation as distinguished from what is qualified or related. Even the gesture of pointing cannot discriminate the object as such from its spatial location, while it is obviously impossible to point to a quality or a relation. But a word is not merely a vocal gesture which discriminates an object from its location or a quality from an object. By naming something a "tree," for example, I at once distinguish it as an object from its setting, and identify it as a member of a familiar system, in which "bark," "branches" and "leaves" each has its place, as well as "shade," or "ax" and "firewood," as the case may be. How much of this actually enters into perception at any one time depends on occasion and circumstance. But if I see it as a "tree," the content of my perception is so organized that every sensory detail of hue and brightness and contour is incorporated within it as qualifying just that whole. If I scrutinize it more closely, still regarding it as a "tree," fresh details emerge, each of which continues to have its place within the determining pattern. Thus I perceive more clearly the texture of the "bark," the color and form of the "leaves," etc. In such a case language serves to patternize perception, to determine the general framework into which sensory detail will fit.

But not all our perceptual experience is verbalized in so explicit a fashion. Human perception occurs on different levels. To look at something with a definite view to describing in language what one sees is to see with fresh eyes. What is seen takes on a noticeable transformation. Such explicitly verbalized perception is rare. I may indeed not see the tree as a "tree" at all, but only vaguely as an object to be avoided in my walk, and having no determinate color, shape or size. In such moments we doubtless approach more nearly an animal type of perception. Yet even here there is something distinctly human, in that later I may recall "that I met an obstacle in my path." The influence of language on perception is not limited to what may be termed "verbalization." What as men we see and hear and feel is already such that it *may become* verbalized. The specific organization that accompanies explicit verbalization is not an act of special creation *de novo*. It occurs as a natural development of what is already prepared.

An Experimental Study of the Effect of Language on the Reproduction of Visually Perceived Form [1]

L. CARMICHAEL, H. P. HOGAN, AND
A. A. WALTER

═══════════

II

SPECIFIC PROBLEM AND METHODS OF EXPERIMENTATION

In the investigation here reported an effort was made to direct experimentally the changes in the reproduction of visually perceived form by the use of language. One set of twelve relatively ambiguous figures was prepared. (See Chart I.) Two names were assigned to each of these figures (Word List I and Word List II). The same visual figure was presented to all subjects, but one list of names was given to the figures when they were presented to one group of subjects, and the other list of names was given to the figures when they were presented to a second group of subjects. A small control group was also used to whom the forms were presented without the assignment of any name.

The apparatus used in presenting the visual forms was a modification of the Ranschburg memory apparatus, similar to that described by Gibson.[2] The twelve stimulus-figures were drawn in black upon a white cardboard disk 19 cm in diameter. The disk was divided into 30 sectors and a figure was drawn upon every other sector. At the end of the series a space of 7 empty sectors occurred before the series repeated itself. The exposure apparatus was operated by an electrically activated pendulum. The experimenter sat at one side of the table on which the

---

[1] From *Journal of Experimental Psychology*, Vol. 15, No. 1, February, 1932, pp. 74–82. Reprinted by permission.
[2] J. J. Gibson, "The Reproduction of Visually Perceived Forms," *Journal of Experimental Psychology*, 1929, Vol. XII, p. 6.

Chart I

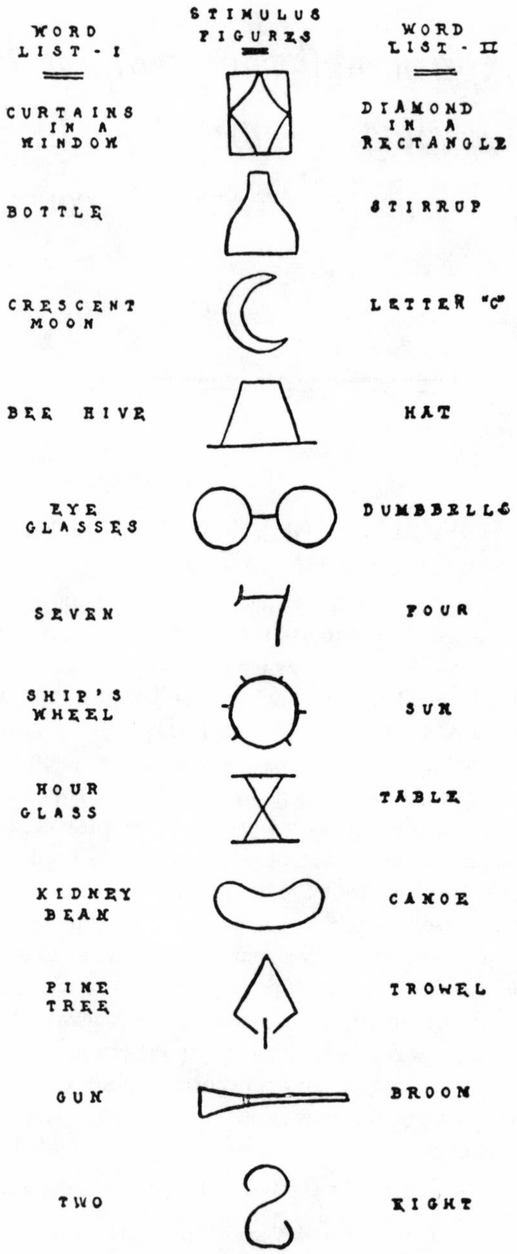

WORD LIST - I	STIMULUS FIGURES	WORD LIST - II
CURTAINS IN A WINDOW		DIAMOND IN A RECTANGLE
BOTTLE		STIRRUP
CRESCENT MOON		LETTER "C"
BEE HIVE		HAT
EYE GLASSES		DUMBBELLS
SEVEN		FOUR
SHIP'S WHEEL		SUN
HOUR GLASS		TABLE
KIDNEY BEAN		CANOE
PINE TREE		TROWEL
GUN		BROOM
TWO		EIGHT

apparatus was placed, and the subject at the other side, where he could conveniently see the exposure apparatus.

By twice listening to the reading of a set of directions, the subjects were first informed that they would be shown a set of figures, and that they were to reproduce them, after the series was over, as accurately as possible, but in any order.

In any given experimental setting the apparatus was then started, and while an empty space was shown in the window of the Ranschburg apparatus, the experimenter said, "The next figure resembles . . ." (giving one of the two names of the figure next to appear). These names were divided into two lists, I and II, respectively, as shown in Chart I.

As noted above, after each presentation of the total list of figures the subject was required to reproduce as accurately as possible all of the figures that he had just seen. If a recognizable representation of each figure was not given, the list was then shown again. This was repeated until a recognizable reproduction of all twelve figures was secured. The number of trials required was between 2 and 8, with an average of 3 trials. The small control group working without names required an average of 4 trials. Any verbal report volunteered by the subject in response to the question, "Will you tell me how you performed this task?" was noted down.

List I was given to 48 subjects, and List II to 38 subjects. As a check upon the naming procedure as already noted, the series of visual forms was presented without names, that is, according to Gibson's technique, to 9 subjects. All subjects were college students or college teachers. Sixty of the subjects were women and 35 men. The sexes were approximately evenly divided between the two experimental groups. Altogether 3576 presentations of separate figures were given, and of this number 3051 were reproduced.

III

RESULTS

After the experimental work had been completed, the papers on which the figures were drawn were studied, without consultation, by two of the authors. The figures were then independently rated upon the following five-degree rating scale:

Quality Step 1.—This group included all figures that were normal or approximately perfectly reproduced.

Quality Step 2.—This group included all figures with very slight changes from the original. Here were included figures which merely showed slight shortening or lengthening of lines, slight changes in curves or angles, or slight changes in the proportion of one part of the figure in relation to some other part of the figure.

Quality Step 3.—This group included all figures showing a noticeable change in the original figure, but which did not mark a complete distortion. Here were included figures showing a rather marked lengthening or shortening of lines, a clearly noticeable change in curves or angles, or a noticeable change in proportion. These figures were in all cases, however, still quite satisfactory reproductions of the original.

Quality Step 4.—This group included all figures showing marked changes such as additions or omissions, and marked changes in proportion. The figures in this group, while still somewhat resembling the original, were changed considerably from it.

Quality Step 5.—This group included figures which were almost completely changed from the original. Here were included inverted figures, and those hardly recognizable in relation to the stimulus-figure.

The basis of rating is inadequately described in the brief verbal description given above. An absolute alteration or addition in measured line might cause one figure to be put in Group 2, while a simpler change would cause it to be put in Group 3 or even in Group 4. Thus an added line in the "sun" or "ship's wheel" figure was much less important than an added line in the letter "C" or "crescent moon" figure. The rating was done independently, and at the time of rating no reference was made to the particular associated word that had been given with the stimulus-form in question. When the judgment of the two raters differed the reasons were discussed, and if a conclusion could not be reached the choice of a third judge, who was also familiar with the rating scale, was accepted. There were very few of these contested decisions.[3] The numerical result of this rating procedure is shown in

[3] The authors are aware of the intrinsic shortcomings of all qualitative rating schemes, and of the fact that the rating procedures employed in this experiment are theoretically open to improvement. The plan of rating used here seemed, however, to be the best device available because of the nature of the data. It can be asserted that those concerned in the experiment felt a greater satisfaction in the result of this rating after it had been performed than had been anticipated before the rating was done. It may be pointed out that the method here used, in spite of all its shortcomings, is less dependent upon one personal opinion than that used in any of the earlier studies noted in the historical introduction to this paper. There are, of course, many methods for attempting to quantify roughly a qualitative series by rating. A number of these methods are dependent upon the training of the one who is to do the rating. This is notably true in much mental testing as, for example, in the Binet-Simon "Ball and Field" test (*cf.* L. M. Terman, *The Measurement of Intelligence*, p. 211). In this test

Table I which presents the numbers of reproductions falling in each of the five quality steps noted above.

TABLE I

Group	Number of Reproductions
1	26
2	285
3	1011
4	1268
5	905

For the purposes of the present study it was decided first to study the figures in Group 5, for these figures by definition showed the greatest amount of change from the stimulus-figure. Subsequent study, not recorded here, of Quality Groups 2, 3, and 4 showed similar relationships but in a less marked degree. It seemed to the present authors that if most of the figures in Quality Group 5 could be shown to have varied from the stimulus-figure without showing any constant relationship to the typical form of the objects represented by the concomitantly presented word of either list, then the conclusion must be accepted that the associated verbal stimulus was unimportant in the modification of form as shown in the reproduction of visual pattern. On the other hand, if the figure in Quality Group 5 appeared more like the object represented by the concomitantly presented word, the assumption of the influence of language would be justified. The observation of this relationship should also throw some light upon the question left unsolved by Gibson as to whether the changes that he observed were caused by the influence of past experience upon the perception or memory of form, or whether evidence can be found that unequivocally shows that the changes were caused, as alleged by Wulf, by the nature of the *structure* of the perceived form itself.

A study of the nature of the variations in Group 5 showed marked differences between different figures. These differences again required rating, which was carried out as before. In Table II the judged amount

there is seldom any difference in opinion in regard to the type of performance of the test when the rating is done by experienced examiners. Much of the success of rating depends upon the suitable training of the "raters" and the possibility of immediately comparing the item under consideration in a qualitative series. These two conditions were met in the present experiment (*cf.* W. F. Dearborn, *Intelligence Tests*, pp. 8ff, and W. S. Munroe, *An Introduction to the Theory of Educational Measurement*, pp. 133–144).

of influence of the two lists is given. It thus appears that of the 905 figures in Group 5 approximately 74 percent were like what may be

TABLE II

Figure	Percent like Figure Named	
	List I	List II
1	47	78
2	100	69
3	65	48
4	69	75
5	45	81
6	87	94
7	54	47
8	83	100
9	90	63
10	86	100
11	76	85
12	87	40
Total percent	74	73

termed *the visual representation of the figure named* in List I, and 73 percent were like the visual representation of the figure named in List II. A comparatively few cases of the control group to whom no verbal associate was given showed a resemblance. to the visual representation of either of the named figures, or only 45 percent. Chart II shows some selected examples of pronounced modification.

It may be seen by an inspection of Table II that all of the figures were not truly ambiguous to the various subjects. It may be that some verbal names were therefore much more effective than others. In some cases, even if the subjects were representing the object named rather than the form visually perceived, there would be little differentiation in the end result. The "stirrup" and "bottle" figure was an example of such a case. If the experiments are repeated, every effort should be made to avoid figure-name constellations of the sort represented by the stirrup-bottle figure.

In spite of these difficulties which were exposed in the course of experimentation, and in spite of the fundamental objections to the rating procedures employed in the experiment, it seems to the authors, on the basis of the examination of the forms in Groups 2, 3, and 4, as well as those considered above, that it may be said with assurance that naming

Chart II

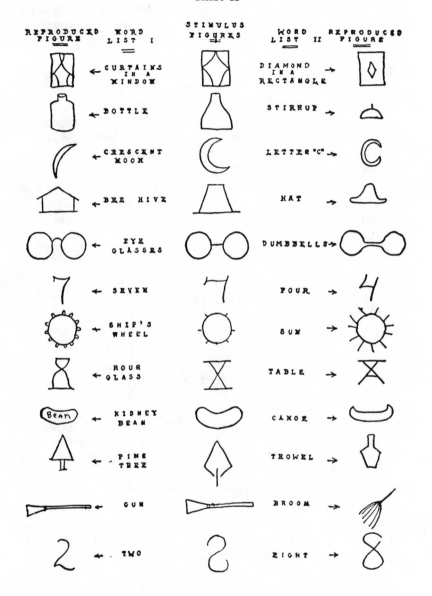

REPRODUCED FIGURE	WORD LIST I	STIMULUS FIGURES	WORD LIST II	REPRODUCED FIGURE
	← CURTAINS IN A WINDOW		DIAMOND IN A RECTANGLE →	
	← BOTTLE		STIRRUP →	
	← CRESCENT MOON		LETTER "C" →	
	← BEE HIVE		HAT →	
	← EYE GLASSES		DUMBBELLS →	
	← SEVEN		FOUR →	
	← SHIP'S WHEEL		SUN →	
	← HOUR GLASS		TABLE →	
	← KIDNEY BEAN		CANOE →	
	← PINE TREE		TROWEL →	
	← GUN		BROOM →	
	← TWO		EIGHT →	

a form immediately before it is visually presented may in many cases change the manner in which it will be reproduced. Besides the major conclusions just noted, the results of the experiment in many ways confirm the conclusions already published by Gibson, and in certain minor respects differ from these conclusions.

Contrary to the assertion of Wulf and Gibson, it was found in certain instances that straight lines were reproduced as curved. An example of this fact is seen in the "table" and "hour-glass" figure. In several instances this "straightline" figure was reproduced in curved lines. Many examples of what Gibson terms "figure assimilation" were observed.

In final conclusion, therefore, it may be said that the present experiment tends to confirm the observations of previous experimenters in this field, and to show that, to some extent at least, the reproduction of forms may be determined by the nature of words presented orally to subjects at the time that they are first perceiving specific visual forms.

Language and a View of the World [1]

E R N S T C A S S I R E R

'By the beginning of the twenty-third month," says D. R. Major, "the child had developed a mania for going about naming things, as if to tell others their names, or to call our attention to the things he was examining. He would look at, point toward, or put his hand on an article, speak its name, then look at his companions." [2] Such an attitude would not be understandable were it not for the fact that the name, in the mental growth of the child, has a function of the first importance to perform. If a child when learning to talk had simply to learn a certain vocabulary, if he only had to impress on his mind and memory a

[1] From *An Essay on Man*. New Haven: Yale University Press, 1944, pp. 132–135. Copyright, 1944, by Yale University Press. Reprinted by permission.
[2] David R. Major, *First Steps in Mental Growth* (New York, Macmillan, 1906), pp. 321f.

great mass of artificial and arbitrary sounds, this would be a purely mechanical process. It would be very laborious and tiresome, and would require too great conscious effort for the child to make without a certain reluctance since what he is expected to do would be entirely disconnected from actual biological needs. The "hunger for names" which at a certain age appears in every normal child and which has been described by all students of child psychology [3] proves the contrary. It reminds us that we are here confronted with a quite different problem. By learning to name things a child does not simply add a list of artificial signs to his previous knowledge of ready-made empirical objects. He learns rather to form the concepts of those objects, to come to terms with the objective world. Henceforth the child stands on firmer ground. His vague, uncertain, fluctuating perceptions and his dim feelings begin to assume a new shape. They may be said to crystallize around the name as a fixed center, a focus of thought. Without the help of the name every new advance made in the process of objectification would always run the risk of being lost again in the next moment. The first names of which a child makes conscious use may be compared to a stick by the aid of which a blind man gropes his way. And language, taken as a whole, becomes the gateway to a new world. All progress here opens a new perspective and widens and enriches our concrete experience. Eagerness and enthusiasm to talk do not originate in a mere desire for learning or using names; they mark the desire for the detection and conquest of an objective world.[4]

We can still when learning a foreign language subject ourselves to an experience similar to that of the child. Here it is not sufficient to acquire a new vocabulary or to acquaint ourselves with a system of abstract grammatical rules. All this is necessary but it is only the first and less important step. If we do not learn to think in the new language all our efforts remain fruitless. In most cases we find it extremely difficult to fulfill this requirement. Linguists and psychologists have often raised the question as to how it is possible for a child by his own efforts to accomplish a task that no adult can ever perform in the same way or as well. We can perhaps answer this puzzling question by looking back at our former analysis. In a later and more advanced state of our

[3] See, for instance, Clara and William Stern, *Die Kindersprache* (Leipzig, 1907), pp. 175ff.

[4] For a more detailed discussion of this problem see Cassirer, "Le langage et la construction du monde des objets," *Journal de Psychologie,* XXXe Année (1933), pp. 18–44.

conscious life we can never repeat the process which led to our first entrance into the world of human speech. In the freshness, in the agility and elasticity of early childhood this process had a quite different meaning. Paradoxically enough the real difficulty consists much less in the learning of the new language than in the forgetting of a former one. We are no longer in the mental condition of the child who for the first time approaches a conception of the objective world. To the adult the objective world already has a definite shape as a result of speech activity, which has in a sense molded all our other activities. Our perceptions, intuitions, and concepts have coalesced with the terms and speech forms of our mother tongue. Great efforts are required to release the bond between words and things. And yet, when we set about to learn a new language, we have to make such efforts and to separate the two elements. Overcoming this difficulty always marks a new and important step in the learning of a language. When penetrating into the "spirit" of a foreign tongue we invariably have the impression of approaching a new world, a world which has an intellectual structure of its own. It is like a voyage of discovery in an alien land, and the greatest gain from such a voyage lies in our having learned to look upon our mother tongue in a new light. *"Wer fremde Sprachen nicht kennt, weiss nichts von seiner eigenen,"* said Goethe.[5] So long as we know no foreign languages we are in a sense ignorant of our own, for we fail to see its specific structure and its distinctive features. A comparison of different languages shows us that there are no exact synonyms. Corresponding terms from two languages seldom refer to the same objects or actions. They cover different fields which interpenetrate and give us many-colored views and varied perspectives of our experience.

This becomes especially clear if we consider the methods of classification employed in different languages, particularly in those of divergent linguistic types. Classification is one of the fundamental features of human speech. The very act of denomination depends on a process of classification. To give a name to an object or action is to subsume it under a certain class concept. If this subsumption were once and for all prescribed by the nature of things, it would be unique and uniform. Yet the names which occur in human speech cannot be interpreted in any such invariable manner. They are not designed to refer to substantial things, independent entities which exist by themselves. They are determined rather by human interests and human purposes. But these

[5] Goethe, *Sprüche in Prosa,* "Werke," XLII, Pt. II, 118.

interests are not fixed and invariable. Nor are the classifications to be found in human speech made at random; they are based on certain constant and recurring elements in our sense experience. Without such recurrences there would be no foothold, no point of support, for our linguistic concepts. But the combination or separation of perceptual data depends upon the free choice of a frame of reference. There is no rigid and pre-established scheme according to which our divisions and subdivisions might once for all be made. Even in languages closely akin and agreeing in their general structure we do not find identical names. As Humboldt pointed out, the Greek and Latin terms for the moon, although they refer to the same object, do not express the same intention or concept. The Greek term (*mēn*) denotes the function of the moon to "measure" time; the Latin term (*luna, luc-na*) denotes the moon's lucidity or brightness. Thus we have obviously isolated and focused attention on two very different features of the object. But the act itself, the process of concentration and condensation, is the same. The name of an object lays no claim upon its nature; it is not intended . . . to give us the truth of a thing. The function of a name is always limited to emphasizing a particular aspect of a thing, and it is precisely this restriction and limitation upon which the value of the name depends. It is not the function of a name to refer exhaustively to a concrete situation, but merely to single out and dwell upon a certain aspect. The isolation of this aspect is not a negative but a positive act. For in the act of denomination we select, out of the multiplicity and diffusion of our sense data, certain fixed centers of perception. These centers are not the same as in logical or scientific thought. The terms of ordinary speech are not to be measured by the same standards as those in which we express scientific concepts. As compared with scientific terminology the words of common speech always exhibit a certain vagueness; almost without exception they are so indistinct and ill-defined as not to stand the test of logical analysis. But notwithstanding this unavoidable and inherent defect our everyday terms and names are the milestones on the road which leads to scientific concepts; it is in these terms that we receive our first objective or theoretical view of the world. Such a view is not simply "given"; it is the result of a constructive intellectual effort which without the constant assistance of language could not attain its end.

Language and Thought[1]

FRANZ BOAS

It may be well to discuss the relation between language and thought. It has been claimed that the conciseness and clearness of thought of a people depend to a great extent upon their language. The ease with which in our modern European language we express wide abstract ideas by a single term, and the facility with which wide generalizations are cast into the frame of a simple sentence, have been claimed to be one of the fundamental conditions of the clearness of our concepts, the logical force of our thought, and the precision with which we eliminate in our thoughts irrelevant details. Apparently this view has much in its favor. When we compare modern English with some of those Indian languages which are most concrete in their formative expression, the contrast is striking. When we say *The eye is the organ of sight,* the Indian may not be able to form the expression *the eye,* but may have to define that the eye of a person or of an animal is meant. Neither may the Indian be able to generalize readily the abstract idea of an eye as the representative of the whole class of objects, but may have to specialize by an expression like *this eye here.* Neither may he be able to express by a single term the idea of *organ,* but may have to specify it by an expression like *instrument of seeing,* so that the whole sentence might assume a form like *An indefinite person's eye is his means of seeing.* Still, it will be recognized that in this more specific form the general idea may be well expressed. It seems very questionable in how far the restriction of the use of certain grammatical forms can really be conceived as a hindrance in the formulation of generalized ideas. It seems much more likely that the lack of these forms is due to the lack of their need. Primitive man, when conversing with his fellow man, is not in the habit of discussing abstract ideas. His interests center around the

[1] From the "Introduction," *Handbook of American Indian Languages,* Smithsonian Institution, U.S. Bureau of American Ethnology. Washington: Government Printing Office, 1911, pp. 64–67. Reprinted by permission of U. S. Bureau of American Ethnology.

occupations of his daily life; and where philosophic problems are touched upon, they appear either in relation to definite individuals or in the more or less anthropomorphic forms of religious beliefs. Discourses on qualities without connection with the object to which the qualities belong, or of activities or states disconnected from the idea of the actor or the subject being in a certain state, will hardly occur in primitive speech. Thus the Indian will not speak of goodness as such, although he may very well speak of the goodness of a person. He will not speak of a state of bliss apart from the person who is in such a state. He will not refer to the power of seeing without designating an individual who has such power. Thus it happens that in languages in which the idea of possession is expressed by elements subordinated to nouns, all abstract terms appear always with possessive elements. It is, however, perfectly conceivable that an Indian trained in philosophic thought would proceed to free the underlying nominal forms from the possessive elements, and thus reach abstract forms strictly corresponding to the abstract forms of our modern languages. I have made this experiment, for instance, with the Kwakiutl language of Vancouver Island, in which no abstract term ever occurs without its possessive elements. After some discussion, I found it perfectly easy to develop the idea of the abstract term in the mind of the Indian, who will state that the word without a possessive pronoun gives a sense, although it is not used idiomatically. I succeeded, for instance, in this manner, in isolating the terms for *love* and *pity,* which ordinarily occur only in possessive forms, like *his love for him* or *my pity for you.* That this view is correct may also be observed in languages in which possessive elements appear as independent forms, as, for instance, in the Siouan languages. In these, pure abstract terms are quite common.

There is also evidence that other specializing elements, which are so characteristic of many Indian languages, may be dispensed with when, for one reason or another, it seems desirable to generalize a term. To use the example of the Kwakiutl language, the idea *to be seated* is almost always expressed with an inseparable suffix expressing the place in which a person is seated, as *seated on the floor of the house, on the ground, on the beach, on a pile of things,* or *on a round thing,* etc. When, however, for some reason, the idea of the state of sitting is to be emphasized, a form may be used which expresses simply *being in a sitting posture.* In this case, also, the device for generalized expression is present, but the opportunity for its application arises seldom, or perhaps never. I think what is true in these cases is true of the structure of every single language. The fact that generalized forms of expression are not used does not prove inability to form them, but it merely proves that the mode of life of the people is such that they are not required; that they would, however, develop just as soon as needed.

This point of view is also corroborated by a study of the numeral systems of primitive languages. As is well known, many languages exist in which the numerals do not exceed two or three. It has been inferred from this that the people speaking these languages are not capable of forming the concept of higher numbers. I think this interpretation of the existing conditions is quite erroneous. People like the South American Indians (among whom these defective numeral systems are found), or like the Eskimo (whose old system of numbers probably did not exceed ten), are presumably not in need of higher numerical expressions, because there are not many objects that they have to count. On the other hand, just as soon as these same people find themselves in contact with civilization, and when they acquire standards of value that have to be counted, they adopt with perfect ease higher numerals from other languages and develop a more or less perfect system of counting. This does not mean that every individual who in the course of his life has never made use of higher numerals would acquire more complex systems readily, but the tribe as a whole seems always to be capable of adjusting itself to the needs of counting. It must be borne in mind that counting does not become necessary until objects are considered in such generalized form that their individualities are entirely lost sight of. For this reason it is possible that even a person who has a flock of domesticated animals may know them by name and by their characteristics without ever desiring to count them. Members of a war expedition may be known by name and may not be counted. In short, there is no proof that the lack of the use of numerals is in any way connected with the inability to form the concepts of higher numbers.

If we want to form a correct judgment of the influence that language exerts over thought, we ought to bear in mind that our European languages as found at the present time have been moulded to a great extent by the abstract thought of philosophers. Terms like *essence* and *existence,* many of which are now commonly used, are by origin artificial devices for expressing the results of abstract thought. In this they would resemble the artificial, unidiomatic abstract terms that may be formed in primitive languages.

Thus it would seem that the obstacles to generalized thought inherent in the form of a language are of minor importance only, and that presumably the language alone would not prevent a people from advancing to more generalized forms of thinking if the general state of their culture should require expression of such thought; that under these conditions the language would be moulded rather by the cultural state. It does not seem likely, therefore, that there is any direct relation between the culture of a tribe and the language they speak, except in so far as the form of the language will be moulded by the state of culture, but not in so far as a certain state of culture is conditioned by morphological traits of the language.

Conceptual Categories in Primitive Languages[1]

EDWARD SAPIR

The relation between language and experience is often misunderstood. Language is not merely a more or less systematic inventory of the various items of experience which seem relevant to the individual, as is so often naively assumed, but is also a self-contained, creative symbolic organization, which not only refers to experience largely acquired without its help, but actually defines experience for us by reason of its formal completeness and because of our unconscious projection of its implicit expectations into the field of experience. In this respect language is very much like a mathematical system, which, also, records experience, in the true sense of the word, only in its crudest beginnings,

[1] From *Science*, Vol. 74, Dec. 4, 1931, p. 578. This is the summary of a paper presented at the Autumn, 1931, meeting of the National Academy of Sciences. Reprinted by permission.

but as time goes on, becomes elaborated into a self-contained conceptual system which previsages all possible experience in accordance with certain accepted formal limitations. Such categories as number, gender, case, tense, mode, voice "aspect" and a host of others, many of which are not recognized systematically in our Indo-European languages, are, of course, derivative of experience, at last analysis, but, once abstracted from experience, they are systematically elaborated in language and are not so much discovered in experience as imposed upon it because of the tyrannical hold that linguistic form has upon our orientation in the world. Inasmuch as languages differ very widely in their systematization of fundamental concepts, they tend to be only loosely equivalent to each other as symbolic devices, and are, as a matter of fact, incommensurable in the sense in which two systems of points in a plane are, on the whole, incommensurable to each other if they are plotted out with reference to differing systems of coordinates. The point of view urged in this paper becomes entirely clear only when one compares languages of extremely different structures, as in the case of our Indo-European languages, native American Indian languages, and native languages of Africa.

Language and the Categorizing of Experience [1]

CLYDE KLUCKHOHN AND DOROTHEA LEIGHTON

Any language is more than an instrument for the conveying of ideas, more even than an instrument for working upon the feelings of others and for self-expression. Every language is also a means of categorizing experience. What people think and feel, and how they report what they think and feel, is determined, to be sure, by their individual physio-

[1] Reprinted by permission of the publishers from Clyde Kluckhohn and Dorothea Leighton, *The Navaho*. Cambridge, Mass.: Harvard University Press, 1947, pp. 197–205. Copyright, 1946, by the President and Fellows of Harvard College.

logical state, by their personal history, and by what actually happens in the outside world. But it is also determined by a factor which is often overlooked; namely, the pattern of linguistic habits which people have acquired as members of a particular society. The events of the "real" world are never felt or reported as a machine would do it. There is a selection process and an interpretation in the very act of response. Some features of the external situation are highlighted; others are ignored or not fully discriminated.

Every people has its own characteristic classes in which individuals pigeonhole their experiences. These classes are established primarily by the language through the types of objects, processes, or qualities which receive special emphasis in the vocabulary and equally, though more subtly, through the types of differentiation or activity which are distinguished in grammatical forms. The language says, as it were, "Notice this," "Always consider this separate from that," "Such and such things belong together." Since persons are trained from infancy to respond in these ways they take such discriminations for granted, as part of the inescapable stuff of life. But when we see two peoples with different social traditions respond in different ways to what appear to the outsider to be identical stimulus-situations, we realize that experience is much less a "given," an absolute, than we thought. Every language has an effect upon what the people who use it see, what they feel, how they think, what they can talk about.

. . . The language of The People delights in sharply defined categories. It likes, so to speak, to file things away in neat little packages. It favors always the concrete and particular, with little scope for abstractions. It directs attention to some features of every situation, such as the minute distinctions as to direction and type of activity. It ignores others to which English gives a place. Navaho focuses interest upon doing—upon verbs as opposed to nouns or adjectives.

Striking examples of the categories which mark the Navaho language are the variations in many of its verb stems according to the types of their subjects or objects. . . . The verb stem used often depends upon whether its subject (or object) is in the long-object class (such as a pencil, a stick, or a pipe), the granular-mass class (such as sugar and salt), the things-bundled-up class (such as hay and bundles of clothing), the animate-object class, and many others.

It must not be thought that such classification is a conscious process every time a Navaho opens his mouth to speak. It would, of course, paralyze speech if one had to think, when about to say a verb, "Now I must remember to specify whether the object is definite or indefinite; whether it is something round, long, fluid, or something else." Fortunately this is no more necessary in Navaho than in English. The Navaho child simply learns that if he is talking about dropping baseballs or eggs or stones he uses a word different from the word he would use if he spoke of dropping a knife or a pencil or a stick, just as the English-speaking child learns to use different words (herd, flock, crowd) in mentioning a group of cows, sheep, or people.

The important point is that striking divergences in manner of thinking are crystallized in and perpetuated by the forms of Navaho grammar. Take the example of a commonplace physical event: rain. Whites can and do report their perception of this event in a variety of ways; "It has started to rain," "It is raining," "It has stopped raining." The People can, of course, convey these same ideas—but they cannot convey them without finer specifications. To give only a few instances of the sorts of discrimination the Navaho must make before he reports his experience: he uses one verb form if he himself is aware of the actual inception of the rain storm, another if he has reason to believe that rain has been falling for some time in his locality before the occurrence struck his attention. One form must be employed if rain is general round about within the range of vision; another if, though it is raining round about, the storm is plainly on the move. Similarly, the Navaho must invariably distinguish between the ceasing of rainfall (generally) and the stopping of rain in a particular vicinity because the rain clouds have been driven off by wind. The People take the consistent noticing and reporting of such differences (which are usually irrelevant from the white point of view) as much as granted as the rising of the sun.

Navaho is an excessively literal language, little given to abstractions and to the fluidity of meaning that is so characteristic of English. The inner classification gives a concreteness, a specificity, to all expression. Most things can be expressed in Navaho with great exactness by manipulating the wide choice of stems in accord with the multitudinous alternatives offered by fusing prefixes and other separable elements in an almost unlimited number of ways. Indeed Navaho is almost overneat, overprecise. There is very little "give" in the language. It rather reminds one of a Bach fugue, in which everything is ordered in scrupulous symmetry.

The general nature of the difference between Navaho thought and English thought—both as manifested in the language and also as forced by the very nature of the linguistic forms into such patterns—is that Navaho thought is prevailingly so much more specific, so much more concrete. The ideas expressed by the English verb "to go" provide a nice example. To Germans the English language seems a little sloppy because the same word is used regardless of whether the one who goes walks or is transported by a train or other agency, whereas in German these two types of motion are always sharply distinguished in the two verbs *gehen* and *fahren*. But Navaho does much more along this line. For example, when one is talking about travel by horse, the speed of the animal may be expressed by the verb form chosen. The following all mean "I went by horseback."

łį́į shił niyá,   (at a walk or at unspecified speed).
łį́į shił yíldloozh,   (at a trot).
łį́į shił neeltą́ą́',   (at a gallop).
łį́į shił yílghod,   (at a run).

When a Navaho says that he went somewhere he never fails to specify whether it was afoot, astride, by wagon, auto, train, or airplane. This is done partly by using different verb stems which indicate whether the traveler moved under his own steam or was transported, partly by naming the actual means. Thus, "he went to town" would become:

kintahgóó 'íiyá,   He went to town afoot or in a non-specific way.
kintahgóó bił 'i'íibą́ą́z,   He went to town by wagon.
kintahgóó bił 'o'oot'a',   He went to town by airplane.
kintahgóó bił 'i'íi'éél   He went to town by boat.
kintahgóó bił 'o'ooldloozh, He went to town by horseback at a run (or perhaps by car or train).
kintahgóó bił 'i'nooltą́ą́',   He went to town by horseback at a gallop.

Moreover, the Navaho language insists upon another type of splitting up of the generic idea of "going" to which German is as indifferent as English. The Navaho always differentiates between starting to go, going along, arriving at, returning from a point, etc., etc. For instance, he makes a choice between:

kintahgi níyá, He arrived at town.
kintahgóó íiyá He went to town and is still there.
kintahgóó haayá, He went to town but is now back where he started.

. . . .

In English one might ask, "Where did he go" and the usual answer would be something like "He went to Gallup." But in Navaho one would have to select one of eight or ten possible forms which, if rendered exactly into English, would come out something like this: "He started off for Gallup," "He left to go as far as Gallup," "He left by way of Gallup," "He left, being bound for Gallup (for a brief visit)," "He left, being bound for Gallup (for an extended stay)," etc.

The People are likewise particular about other differentiation, similar to some of those discussed earlier in this chapter:

kin góne' yah 'iikai, We went into the house (in a group).
kin góne' yah 'ahiikai, We went into the house (one after another).

or:

chizh kin góne yah'íinil, I carried the wood into the house (in one trip).
chizh kin góne yah 'akénil, I carried the wood into the house (in several trips).

It is not, of course, that these distinctions *cannot* be made in English but that they *are not* made consistently. They seem of importance to English-speakers only under special circumstances, whereas constant precision is a regular feature of Navaho thought and expression about movement.

The nature of their language forces The People to notice and to report many other distinctions in physical events which the nature of the English language allows speakers to neglect in most cases, even though their senses are just as able as those of the Navaho to register the smaller details of what goes on in the external world. For example, suppose a Navaho range rider and a white supervisor see that the wire fence surrounding a demonstration area is broken. The supervisor will probably write in his notebook only: "The fence is broken." But if the range rider reports the occurrence to his friends he must say either *béésh 'ałc'ast'i* or *béésh 'ałc'aat'i;* the first would specify that the damage has been caused by some person, the second that the agency was non-human. Further, he must choose between one of these statements and an alternative pair—the verb form selected depending on whether the fence was of one or several strands of wire.

Two languages may classify items of experience differently. The class corresponding to one word and one thought in Language A may be regarded by Language B as two or more classes corresponding to two or more words and thoughts. For instance, where in English one word "rough" (more pedantically, "rough-surfaced") may equally well be used to describe a road, a rock, and the business surface of a file, Navaho finds a need for three different words which may not be used interchangeably. . . . While the general tendency is for Navaho to make finer and more concrete distinctions, this is not invariably the case. The same stem is used for "rip," "light beam," and "echo," ideas which seem diverse to white people. One word is used to designate a medicine bundle with all its contents, the skin quiver in which the contents are wrapped, the contents as a whole, and some of the distinct items of the contents. Sometimes the point is not that the images of Navahos are less fluid and more delimited but rather just that the external world is dissected along different lines. For example, *digóón* may be used to describe both a pimply face and a nodule-covered rock. In English a complexion might be termed "rough" or "coarse" but a rock would never, except facetiously, be described as "pimply." Navaho differentiates two types of "rough rock"—the kind which is rough in the manner in which a file is rough, and the kind which is nodule-encrusted. In these cases . . . the difference between the Navaho and the English ways of seeing the world cannot be disposed of merely by saying that Navaho is more precise. The variation rests in the features which the two languages see as essential. Cases can even be given where Navaho is notably less precise: Navaho gets along with a single word for flint, metal, knife, and certain other objects of metal. . . . This, to be sure, is due to the historical accident that, after European contact, metal in general and knives in particular largely took the place of flint. But in the last analysis most linguistic differentiations, like other sorts of cultural selectivity, rest upon the historical experience of the people.

How the Navaho and English Languages dissect nature differently perhaps comes out most clearly when we contrast verbal statements.

Take a simple event such as a person dropping something. The different "isolates of meaning" (thoughts) used in reporting this identical experience will be quite different in Navaho and in English. . . . The two elements which are the same are "I" and "sh," both of which specify who does the dropping. A single image "drop" in English requires two complementary images (*naa* and *'aah*) in Navaho. English stops with what from the Navaho point of view is a very vague statement—"I drop it." The Navaho must specify four particulars which the English leaves either unsettled or to inference from context:

1. The form must make clear whether "it" is definite or just "something."
2. The verb stem used will vary depending upon whether the object is round, or long, or fluid, or animate, etc., etc.
3. Whether the act is in progress, or just about to start, or just about to stop or habitually carried on or repeatedly carried on must be rigorously specified. In English, "I drop it" can mean once or can mean that it is customarily done (e.g., in describing the process of getting water from my well by a bucket). All the other possibilities are also left by English to the imagination.
4. The extent to which the agent controls the fall must be indicated: *naash'aah* means "I am in the act of lowering the round object" but *naashné* means "I am in the act of letting the round object fall."

To make the analysis absolutely complete, it must be pointed out that there is one respect in which the English is here a bit more exact. "I drop it" implies definitely (with the exception of the use of the "historical present") that the action occurs as the speaker talks or just an instant before, while the two Navaho verbs given above could, in certain circumstances, refer either to past or to future time. In other words, Navaho is more interested in the type of action (momentaneous, progressing, continuing, customary, etc.) than in establishing sequences in time as related to the moving present of the speaker.

Languages and Logic [1]

BENJAMIN LEE WHORF

In English, the sentences "I pull the branch aside" and "I have an extra toe on my foot" have little similarity. Leaving out the subject pronoun and the sign of the present tense, which are common features from requirements of English syntax, we may say that no similarity exists. Common, and even scientific, parlance would say that the sentences are unlike because they are talking about things which are intrinsically unlike. So Mr. Everyman, the natural logician, would be inclined to argue. Formal logic of an older type would perhaps agree with him.

If, moreover, we appeal to an impartial scientific English-speaking observer, asking him to make direct observations upon cases of the two phenomena to see if they may not have some element of similarity which we have overlooked, he will be more than likely to confirm the dicta of Mr. Everyman and the logician. The observer whom we have asked to make the test may not see quite eye to eye with the old-school logician and would not be disappointed to find him wrong. Still he is compelled sadly to confess failure. "I wish I could oblige you," he says, "but try as I may, I cannot detect any similarity between these phenomena."

By this time our stubborn streak is aroused; we wonder if a being from Mars would also see no resemblance. But now a linguist points out that it is not necessary to go as far as Mars. We have not yet scouted around this earth to see if its many languages all classify these phenomena as disparately as our speech does. We find that in Shawnee these two statements are, respectively, *ni-l'θawa-'ko-n-a* and *ni-l'θawa-'ko-θite* (the θ here denotes *th* as in "thin" and the apostrophe denotes a breath-catch). The sentences are closely similar; in fact, they differ only at the tail end. In Shawnee, moreover, the beginning of a con-

[1] Reprinted from *The Technology Review*, Vol. XLIII, No. 6, April, 1941, pp. 250–272, edited at the Massachusetts Institute of Technology. Reprinted by permission.

struction is generally the important and emphatic part. Both sentences start with *ni-* ("I"), which is a mere prefix. Then comes the really important key word, *l'θawa,* a common Shawnee term, denoting a forked outline, like Fig. 3, No. 1. The next element, *-'ko,* we cannot be sure of, but it agrees in form with a variant of the suffix *-a'kw* or *-a'ko,* denoting tree, bush, tree part, branch, or anything of that general shape. In the first sentence, *-n-* means "by hand action" and may be either a causation of the basic condition (forked outline) manually, an increase of it, or both. The final *-a* means that the subject ("I") does this action to an appropriate object. Hence the first sentence means "I pull it (something like branch of tree) more open or apart where it forks." In the other sentence, the suffix *-θite* means "pertaining to the toes," and the absence of further suffixes means that the subject manifests the condition in his own person. Therefore the sentence can mean only "I have an extra toe forking out like a branch from a normal toe."

Shawnee logicians and observers would class the two phenomena as intrinsically similar. Our own observer, to whom we tell all this, focuses his instruments again upon the two phenomena and to his joy sees at once a manifest resemblance. Figure 1 illustrates a similar situation: "I push his head back" and "I drop it in water and it floats," though very dissimilar sentences in English, are similar in Shawnee. The point of view of linguistic relativity changes Mr. Everyman's dictum: Instead of saying, "Sentences are unlike because they tell about unlike facts," he now reasons: "Facts are unlike to speakers whose language background provides for unlike formulation of them."

Conversely, the English sentences, "The boat is grounded on the beach" and "The boat is manned by picked men," seem to us to be rather similar. Each is about a boat; each tells the relation of the boat to other objects—or that's *our* story. The linguist would point out the parallelism in grammatical pattern thus: "The boat is *x*ed preposition *y.*" The logician might turn the linguist's analysis into "*A* is in the state *x* in relation to *y,*" and then perhaps into $f A = xRy$. Such symbolic methods lead to fruitful techniques of rational ordering, stimulate our thinking, and bring valuable insights. Yet we should realize that the similarities and contrasts in the original sentences, subsumed under the foregoing formula, are dependent on the choice of mother tongue and that the properties of the tongue are eventually reflected as peculiarities of structure in the fabric of logic or mathematics which we rear.

In the Nootka language of Vancouver Island, the first "boat" statement is *tlih-is-ma;* the second, *lash-tskwiq-ista-ma.* The first is thus I-II-*ma;* the second, III-IV-V-*ma;* and they are quite unlike, for the final -*ma* is only the sign of the third-person indicative. Neither sentence contains any unit of meaning akin to our word "boat" or even "canoe." Part I, in the first sentence, means "moving pointwise," or moving in a way like the suggestion of the outline in Fig. 3, No. 2; hence "traveling in or as a canoe," or an event like one position of such motion. It is not a name for what we should call a "thing," but is more like a vector in physics. Part II means "on the beach"; hence I-II-*ma*

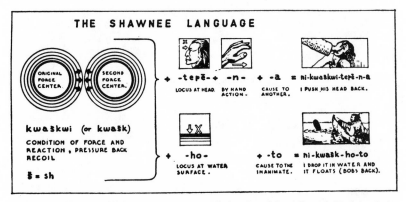

FIG. 1. The English sentences "I push his head back" and "I drop it in water and it floats" are unlike. But in Shawnee the corresponding statements are closely similar, emphasizing the fact that analysis of nature and classification of events as like or in the same category (logic) are governed by grammar.

means "it is on the beach pointwise as an event of canoe motion," and would normally refer to a boat that has come to land. In the other sentence, part III means "select, pick," and IV means "remainder, result," so that III-IV means "selected." Part V means "in a canoe (boat) as crew." The whole, III-IV-V-*ma,* means either "they are in the boat as a crew of picked men" or "the boat has a crew of picked men." It means that the whole event involving picked ones and boat's crew is in process.

As a hang-over from my education in chemical engineering, I relish an occasional chemical simile. Perhaps readers will catch what I mean when I say that the way the constituents are put together in these sentences of Shawnee and Nootka suggests a chemical compound, whereas their combination in English is more like a mechanical mixture. A mixture, like the mountaineer's potlicker, can be assembled out of almost anything and does not make any sweeping transformation of the overt appearance of the material. A chemical compound, on the other hand, can be put together only out of mutually suited ingredients, and the result may be not merely soup but a crop of crystals or a cloud

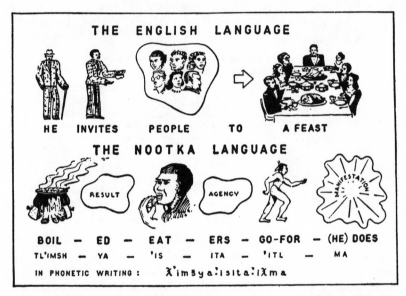

THE ENGLISH LANGUAGE

HE   INVITES   PEOPLE   TO   A FEAST

THE NOOTKA LANGUAGE

RESULT   AGENCY   MANIFESTATION

BOIL — ED — EAT — ERS — GO-FOR — (HE) DOES
TL'IMSH — YA — 'IS — ITA — 'ITL — M A
IN PHONETIC WRITING : $\bar{\lambda}$'im ʃ y aːl s ı t aːl ʌ m a

FIG. 2.   Here are shown the different ways in which English and Nootka formulate the same event. The English sentence is divisible into subject and predicate; the Nootka sentence is not, yet it is complete and logical. Furthermore, the Nootka sentence is just one word, consisting of the root *tl'imsh* with five suffixes.

of smoke. Likewise the typical Shawnee and Nootka combinations appear to work with a vocabulary of terms chosen with a view not so much to the utility of their immediate references as to the ability of the terms to combine suggestively with each other in manifold ways that elicit novel and useful images. This principle of terminology and way of analyzing events would seem to be unknown to the tongues with which we are familiar.

It is the analysis of nature down to a basic vocabulary capable of this sort of evocative recombination which is most distinctive of polysynthetic languages, like Nootka and Shawnee. Their characteristic quality is not, as some linguists have thought, a matter of the tightness or indissolubility of the combinations. The Shawnee term *l'θawa* could probably be said alone but would then mean "it (or something) is forked," a statement which gives little hint of the novel meanings that arise out of its combinations—at least to our minds or our type of logic. Shawnee and Nootka do not use the chemical type of synthesis ex-

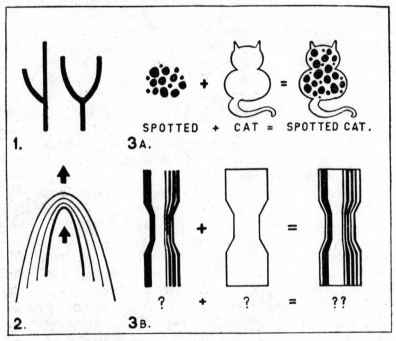

FIG. 3. Suggested above are certain linguistic concepts which, as explained in the text, are not easily definable.

clusively. They make large use of a more external kind of syntax, which, however, has no basic structural priority. Even our own Indo-European tongues are not wholly devoid of the chemical method, but they seldom make sentences by it, afford little inkling of its possibilities, and give structural priority to another method. It was quite natural, then, that Aristotle should found our traditional logic wholly on this other method.

Let me make another analogy, not with chemistry but with art—art of the pictorial sort. We look at a good still-life painting and seem to see a lustrous porcelain bowl and a downy peach. Yet an analysis that screened out the totality of the picture—as if we were to go over it carefully, looking through a hole cut in a card—would reveal only oddly shaped patches of paint and would not evoke the bowl and fruit. The synthesis presented by the painting is perhaps akin to the chemical type of syntax, and it may point to psychological fundamentals that enter into both art and language. Now the mechanical method in art and language might be typified by Fig. 3, No. 3A. The first element, a field of spots, corresponds to the adjective "spotted," the second corresponds to the noun "cat." By putting them together, we get "spotted cat." Contrast the technique in Fig. 3, No. 3B. Here the figure corresponding to "cat" has only vague meaning by itself—"chevronlike," we might say—while the first element is even vaguer. But combined, these evoke a cylindrical object, like a shaft casting.

The thing common to both techniques is a systematic synthetic use of pattern, and this is also common to all language techniques. I have put question marks below the elements in Fig. 3, No. 3B, to point out the difficulty of a parallel in English speech and the fact that the method probably has no standing in traditional logic. Yet examination of other languages and the possibility of new types of logic that has been advanced by modern logicians themselves, suggest that this matter may be significant for modern science. New types of logic may help us eventually to understand how it is that electrons, the velocity of light, and other components of the subject matter of physics appear to behave illogically, or that phenomena which flout the sturdy common sense of yesteryear can nevertheless be true. Modern thinkers have long since pointed out that the so-called mechanistic way of thinking has come to an impasse before the great frontier problems of science. To rid ourselves of this way of thinking is exceedingly difficult when we have no linguistic experience of any other and when even our most advanced logicians and mathematicians do not provide any other—and obviously they cannot without the linguistic experience. For the mechanistic way of thinking is perhaps just a type of syntax natural to Mr. Everyman's daily use of the western Indo-European languages, rigidified and intensified by Aristotle and the latter's medieval and modern followers.

As I said in an article, "Science and Linguistics," in *The Review* for

April, 1940, the effortlessness of speech and the subconscious way we picked up that activity in early childhood lead us to regard talking and thinking as wholly straightforward and transparent. We naturally feel that they embody self-evident laws of thought, the same for all men. We know all the answers! But when scrutinized, they become dusty answers. We use speech for reaching agreements about subject matter: I say, "Please shut the door," and my hearer and I agree that "the door" refers to a certain part of our environment and that I want a certain result produced. Our explanations of how we reached this understanding, though quite satisfactory on the everyday social plane, are merely more agreements (statements) about the same subject matter (door, and so on), more and more amplified by statements about the social and personal needs that impel us to communicate. There are here no laws of thought. Yet the structural regularities of our sentences enable us to sense that laws are *somewhere* in the background. Clearly, explanations of understanding such as "And so I ups and says to him, says I; see here, why don't you . . . !" evade the true process by which "he" and "I" are in communication. Likewise psychological-social descriptions of the social and emotional needs that impel people to communicate with their fellows tend to be learned versions of the same method and, while interesting, still evade the question. In similar case is evasion of the question by skipping from the speech sentence, via physiology and "stimuli," to the social situation.

The *why* of understanding may remain for a long time mysterious; but the *how* or logic of understanding—its background of laws or regularities—is discoverable. It is the grammatical background of our mother tongue, which includes not only our way of constructing propositions but the way we dissect nature and break up the flux of experience into objects and entities to construct propositions about. This fact is important for science because it means that science *can* have a rational or logical basis even though it be a relativistic one and not Mr. Everyman's natural logic. Although it may vary with each tongue, and a planetary mapping of the dimensions of such variation may be necessitated, it is, nevertheless, a basis of logic with discoverable laws. Science is not compelled to see its thinking and reasoning procedures turned into processes merely subservient to social adjustments and emotional drives.

Moreover, the tremendous importance of language cannot, in my opinion, be taken to mean necessarily that nothing is back of it of the nature of what has traditionally been called "mind." My own studies suggest, to me, that language, for all of its kingly role, is in some sense a superficial embroidery upon deeper processes of consciousness which are necessary before any communication, signaling, or symbolism whatsoever can occur and which also can at a pinch effect communication (though not true *agreement*) without language's and without symbolism's aid. I mean "superficial" in the sense that all processes of chemistry, for example, can be said to be superficial upon the deeper layer of physical existence, which we know variously as intra-atomic, electronic, or subelectronic. No one would take this statement to mean that chemistry is *unimportant*—indeed the whole point is that the more superficial can mean the more important, in a definite operative sense. It may even be in the cards that there is no such thing as "Language" (with a capital *L*) at all! The statement that "thinking is a matter of *language*" is an incorrect generalization of the more nearly correct idea that "thinking is a matter of *different tongues.*" The different tongues are the real phenomena and may generalize down not to any such universal as "Language," but to something better—called "sublinguistic" or "superlinguistic"—and *not altogether* unlike, even if much unlike, what we now call "mental." This generalization would not diminish, but would rather increase, the importance of intertongue study for investigation of this realm of truth.

Botanists and zoologists, in order to understand the world of living species, found it necessary to describe the species in every part of the globe and to add a time perspective by including the fossils. Then they found it necessary to compare and contrast the species, to work out families and classes, evolutionary descent, morphology, and taxonomy. In linguistic science a similar attempt is under way. The far-off event toward which this attempt moves is a new technology of language and thought. Much progress has been made in classifying the languages of earth into genetic families, each having descent from a single precursor, and in tracing such developments through time. The result is called "comparative linguistics." Of even greater importance for the future technology of thought is what might be called "contrastive linguistics." This plots the outstanding differences between tongues— in grammar, logic, and general analysis of experience.

As I said in the April, 1940, *Review,* segmentation of nature is an aspect of grammar—one as yet little studied by grammarians. We cut up and organize the spread and flow of events as we do largely because, through our mother tongue, we are parties to an agreement to do so, not because nature itself is segmented in exactly that way for all to see. Languages differ not only in how they build their sentences but in how they break down nature to secure the elements to put in those sentences. This breakdown gives units of the lexicon. "Word" is not a very good "word" for them; "lexeme" has been suggested, and "term" will do for the present. By these more or less distinct terms we ascribe a semifictitious isolation to parts of experience. English terms, like "sky," "hill," "swamp," persuade us to regard some elusive aspect of nature's endless variety as a distinct *thing,* almost like a table or chair. Thus English and similar tongues lead us to think of the universe as a collection of rather distinct objects and events corresponding to words. Indeed this is the implicit picture of classical physics and astronomy—that the universe is essentially a collection of detached objects of different sizes.

The examples used by older logicians in dealing with this point are usually unfortunately chosen. They tend to pick out tables and chairs and apples on tables as test objects to demonstrate the objectlike nature of reality and its one-to-one correspondence with logic. Man's artifacts and the agricultural products he severs from living plants have a unique degree of isolation; we may expect that languages will have fairly isolated terms for them. The real question is: What do different languages do, not with these artificially isolated objects but with the flowing face of nature in its motion, color, and changing form; with clouds, beaches, and yonder flight of birds? For as goes our segmentation of the face of nature, so goes our physics of the cosmos.

Here we find differences in segmentation and selection of basic terms. We might isolate something in nature by saying, "It is a dripping spring." Apache erects the statement on a verb *ga:* "be white (including clear, uncolored, and so on)." With a prefix *nō-* the meaning of downward motion enters: "whiteness moves downward." Then *tó,* meaning both "water" and "spring," is prefixed. The result corresponds to our "dripping spring," but synthetically it is: "as water, or springs, whiteness moves downward." How utterly unlike our way of thinking! The same verb, *ga,* with a prefix that means "a place manifests the condition" becomes *gohlga:* "the place is white, clear: a clearing, a plain." These examples show that some languages have means of expression—chemical combination, as I called it—in which the separate terms are not as separate as in English but flow together into plastic synthetic creations. Hence such languages, which do not paint the separate-object picture of the universe to the same degree as do English and its sister tongues, point toward possible new types of logic and possible new cosmical pictures.

The Indo-European languages and many others give great prominence to a type of sentence having two parts, each part built around a class of word—substantives and verbs—which those languages treat differently in grammar. As I showed in the April, 1940, *Review,* this distinction is not drawn from nature; it is just a result of the fact that every tongue must have some kind of structure, and those tongues have made a go of exploiting this kind. The Greeks, especially Aristotle, built up this contrast and made it a law of reason. Since then, the contrast has been stated in logic in many different ways: subject and predicate, actor and action, things and relations between things, objects and their attributes, quantities and operations. And, pursuant again to grammar, the notion became ingrained that one of these classes of entities can exist in its own right but that the verb class cannot exist without an entity of the other class, the "thing" class, as a peg to hang on. "Embodiment is necessary," the watchword of this ideology, is seldom *strongly* questioned. Yet the whole trend of modern physics, with its emphasis on "the field," is an implicit questioning of the ideology. This contrast crops out in our mathematics as two kinds of symbols—the kind like $1, 2, 3, x, y, z$ and the kind like $+, -, \div,$ $\sqrt{}$, log—though in view of $0, \frac{1}{2}, \frac{3}{4}, \pi$, and others, perhaps no strict two-group classification holds. The two-group notion, however, is always present at the back of the thinking, although often not overtly expressed.

Our Indian languages show that with a suitable grammar we may have intelligent sentences that cannot be broken into subjects and predicates. Any attempted breakup is a breakup of some English translation or paraphrase of the sentence, not of the Indian sentence itself. We might as well try to decompose a certain synthetic resin into celluloid and whiting because the resin can be imitated with celluloid and whiting. The Algonquian language family, to which Shawnee belongs, does use a type of sentence like our subject and predicate but also gives prominence to the type shown by our examples in the text and in Fig. 1. To be sure, *ni-* is represented by a subject in the translation but means "my" as well as "I" and the sentence could be translated thus: "My hand is pulling the branch aside." Or *ni-* might be absent; if so, we should be apt to manufacture a subject, like "he," "it," "somebody," or we could pick out for our English subject an idea corresponding to any one of the Shawnee elements.

When we come to Nootka, the sentence without subject or predicate is the only type. The term "predication" is used, but it means "sentence." Nootka has no parts of speech; the simplest utterance is a sentence, treating of some event or event-complex. Long sentences are sentences of sentences (complex sentences), not just sentences of words. In Fig. 2 we have a simple, not a complex, Nootka sentence. The translation, "he invites people to a feast," splits into subject and predicate. Not so the native sentence. It begins with the event of boiling or cooking, *tl'imsh;* then comes *-ya* ("result") = cooked; then *-'is* ("eating") = eating cooked food; then *-ita* ("those who do") = eaters of cooked food; then *-'itl* ("going for"); then *-ma,* sign of third-person indicative, giving *tl'imshya'isita'itlma,* which answers to the crude paraphrase, "he, or somebody, goes for (invites) eaters of cooked food."

The English technique of talking depends on the contrast of two artificial classes, substantives and verbs, and on the bipartitioned ideology of nature already discussed. Our normal sentence, unless imperative, must have some substantive before its verb, a requirement which corresponds to the philosophical and also naïve notion of an actor who produces an action. This last might not have been so if English had had thousands of verbs like "hold," denoting positions. But most of our verbs follow a type of segmentation that isolates from nature what we call "actions," that is, moving outlines.

Following majority rule, we therefore read action into every sentence, even into "I hold it." A moment's reflection will show that "hold" is no action but a state of relative positions. Yet we think of it and even see it as an action because language formulates it in the same way as it formulates more numerous expressions, like "I strike it," which deal with movements and changes.

We are constantly reading into nature fictional acting-entities, simply because our verbs must have substantives in front of them. We have to say "It flashed" or "A light flashed," setting up an actor, *"it"* or "light," to perform what we call an action, "to flash." Yet the flashing and the light are one and the same! The Hopi language reports the flash with a simple verb, *rehpi:* "flash (occurred)." There is no division into subject and predicate, not even a suffix like *-t* of Latin *tona-t* ("it thunders"). Hopi can and does have verbs without subjects, a fact which may give that tongue potentialities, probably never to be developed, as a logical system for understanding some aspects of the universe. Undoubtedly modern science, strongly reflecting western Indo-European tongues, often does as we all do, sees actions and forces where it sometimes might be better to see states. In the other hand, "state" is a noun, and as such it enjoys the superior prestige traditionally attaching to the subject or thing class; therefore science is exceedingly ready to speak of states if permitted to manipulate the concept like a noun. Perhaps, in place of the "states" of an atom or a dividing cell, it would be better if we could manipulate as readily a more verblike concept but without the concealed premises of actor and action.

I can sympathize with those who say, "Put it into plain, simple English," especially when they protest against the empty formalism of loading discourse with pseudolearned words. But to restrict thinking to the patterns merely of English, and especially to those patterns which represent the acme of plainness in English, is to lose a power of thought which, once lost, can never be regained. It is the "plainest" English which contains the greatest number of unconscious assumptions about nature. This is the trouble with schemes like Basic English, in which an eviscerated British English, with its concealed premises working harder than ever, is to be fobbed off on an unsuspecting world as the substance of pure Reason itself. We handle even our plain English with much greater effect if we direct it from the vantage point of a multilingual awareness. For this reason I believe that those who envision a future world speaking only one tongue, whether English, German, Russian, or any other, hold a misguided ideal and would do the evolution of the human mind the greatest disservice. Western culture has made, through language, a provisional analysis of reality and, without correctives, holds resolutely to that analysis as final. The only correctives lie in all those other tongues which by aeons of independent evolution have arrived at different, but equally logical, provisional analyses.

In a valuable paper on "Modern Logic and the Task of the Natural Sciences," Harold N. Lee says: "Those sciences whose data are subject to quantitative measurement have been most successfully developed because we know so little about order systems other than those exemplified in mathematics. We can say with certainty, however, that there are other kinds, for the advance of logic in the last half century has clearly indicated it. We may look for advances in many lines in sciences at present well founded if the advance of logic furnishes adequate knowledge of other order types. We may also look for many subjects of inquiry whose methods are not strictly scientific at the present time to become so when new order systems are available." [1] To which may be added that an important field for the working out of new order systems, akin to, yet not identical with, present mathematics, lies in more penetrating investigation than has yet been made of languages remote in type from our own.

[1] *Sigma Xi Quarterly,* XXVIII (Autumn, 1940), 125.

PART IX

Escape from Verbalism

A shroud of talk to hide us from the sun
Of this familiar life.

SHELLEY

And what if all-avenging Providence,
Strong and retributive, should make us know
The meaning of our words, force us to feel
The desolation and the agony
Of our fierce doings?

COLERIDGE

Indeed, the first difficulty the man in the street encounters when he is taught to think mathematically is that he must learn to look things much more squarely in the face; his belief in words must be shattered; he must learn to think concretely.

HERMAN WEYL

But how is this freedom from the word to be obtained? What can be done if men are to avoid the follies of verbalism in their talk? The ways to wisdom are asserted by many. Maybe all the proposals are needed. Some seek simple distinctions only. Some begin with the speaker. Some focus on the hearer and reader. Some start with the relationship between language and behavior. Some attack the man-evaluating. Some call for far-reaching reorientations. In any event, we are not without things to do.

Sensation and Cerebration [1]

THOMAS HORNSBY FERRIL

The other day I was looking at a spread of 10,000 sheep in a Colorado mountain valley way up high. Sheep are the most idiotic beautiful things that ever lived. I can't believe my senses when I look at them and I half envy people who don't have to make the effort. It occurred to me that the best place to find people who don't have to believe their senses about sheep or anything else would be New York, and I'd throw in Washington also. Ten thousand sheep wandering down Wall Street would be put up with as a temporary inconvenience but it wouldn't be remembered any longer than a Sioux war dance in Times Square. It would go down as just another stunt of some kind in the minds of people who believe their senses very resentfully because they have so little use for them.

The trouble is that these people's senses don't get enough exercise. Sensation is becoming vestigial among them, like the flabby muscles we still have for wiggling our ears like mules. About all their senses are used for is setting up reflexes that come in handy for getting around in traffic, eating, and mating.

The rest of what used to be called sensation has been taken over by cerebration, because these writhing seaboard masses are jammed together so tightly that they have to live for the most part by symbols instead of things real to the senses. They have no choice in the matter. There's nowhere near enough room for the people themselves to shove their bodies around in, while they work all day with all the biggest and bulkiest things in the world in the way of commerce: the vast herds and flocks of mountain and prairie, the food and fibre of millions of acres, the enormous tonnages of mines and mills. To be manageable at all,

[1] From "Western Half-Acre," *Harper's Magazine*, No. 1154, July, 1946, pp. 79–82. Copyright, 1946, by Harper & Brothers. Reprinted by permission.

every bulky reality has to be pulled down into something it isn't—some tight little representation of itself, a symbol or cryptogram, such as converting 10,000 real sheep into a flicker of teletype. New York would be buried in half a day by the physical substance it handles symbolically in the same half day. (Be fun digging it up like Pompeii: way down deep, under the seventh layer of wheat or cotton, you'd find a mummified broker hugging a firkin of butter and his stenographer serenely clasping a pump handle.)

It follows that, in handling such volumes of physical material by spirit rather than sense, the mind feels a bit guilty. It feels that it ought to know more about the outside world, it ought to make some effort to connect up with the reality behind the symbol but, hang it all, there isn't time. You can't go high-tailing it off to Butte to learn about copper, or off to Kansas to learn about wheat. So you come to rely more and more on imagined concepts of what the outside world would be like if you could ever bring it into the field of sensation. These imagined concepts are fortified by no end of information services, respected because of their brevity. They presume to tell in one paragraph what Iowa is thinking or what California wants. But such summarization carries the mind, not closer to reality, but farther from it. The net effect has been to increase, rather than diminish, reliance on the symbol.

I never cease to marvel, and I shudder also, at what begins to happen when man, as a partially educated animal, becomes subject to mass congestion. Congestion and literacy, it seems to me, are heading seaboard people for the most skillful manipulation of unreality in history: they are well on their way to the mysticism of the lower Ganges Valley, but they lack the complacence that goes with the symbolic life. They are too well off, too healthy; they have been spared the fatalistic peace of mind that accompanies pestilence, famine, and high mortality. Thanks to literacy and prosperity, all they get out of this manipulation of unreality is the jitters. Their Karma is the sanitarium. Their capacity for fear thrives on having nothing real to be afraid of except each other.

The five senses in these congested areas are always at a loss to find anything to work on. The hardest-hitting seaboard realist, however close to Nature he may have started his life, owes his ultimate success to manipulating things he never sees or touches at all. His desk is clean save for one vacuum bottle of cold water. He no longer affects a telephone. He eschews all sensual pleasures: if he ever did any lusty helling around he has long since given it up. He is the top mystic, wearing his stomach ulcers like a hair-cloth shirt. In his air-conditioned retreat he is quietly attended by industrial nuns who whisper low rituals and occasionally give him some paper fetish to contemplate. This paper fetish is a ritualized art form—for example, the annual report of some corporation, representing symbolically the expenditures of life and energy of some whole countryside. The paper will show assets, say, of $26,109,612.04 and liabilities of precisely the same amount, $26,109,612.04. This has been got up by the accounting priesthood—artists highly trained in selection, emphasis, and understatement—assets and liabilities have to rhyme and chime as inexorably as the final couplet of an Elizabethan sonnet.

Somewhere along the line, far back in his youth, this top mystic qualified for this cloistered unreality by getting his hands into things that pushed back when he pushed them. He knew sensation: he worked in a steel mill or slaughter house. And he still has a Faust-like hankering for it. This protects his judgment; he still has some carry-over reference to Nature and, as long as he can keep it going, his wisdom is useful in mercantile abstraction. It isn't easy, for he is surrounded by small-fry mystics who have long since broken with Nature if they were ever integral to it at all. They flounder in the limbo of statistical cryptograms: the small virtues of interpolation become the fantastic vices of extrapolation. The statistical curve is so plausible to them that they think that all you have to do is push it just one mite farther to know all about tomorrow. These curves are as distinct a contribution to the history of mystical art as the Gothic arch was to substantial art.

Reliance on abstraction increases directly with density of population. Denver differs from New York only in degree. Our Seventeenth Street neophytes make devout pilgrimages to receive the blessings of the lamas of Wall Street. We are all on the road to congestion-abstraction but don't know what it is doing to us.

In small towns, with plenty of land around them, people are closer to original materials and farther apart from each other; consequently, they require fewer symbolic abstractions. Robinson Crusoe didn't need any. Go back to when nearly everybody lived in the country, a century or so ago, and note how slowly and begrudgingly people added new symbols to their traditional stock. Agricultural superstitions showed little variation from one generation to another. Established religions were constant and repetitive. Outrageous excursions such as Unitarianism or Mormonism shocked the whole country by their novelty; but symbolic innovations, for the most part, were quickly absorbed by cross-roads politics where such abstractions as "the tariff" or "nullification" could carry the venturing mind as far as it wanted to go. But nowadays less, I suppose, than one fourth of our people are farmers in the old-fashioned sense and our capacity for making new symbols is nourished by city congestion.

Everybody is hell-bent to live in the city and thinks that the biggest city is the best city. This means a wider chasm between men and original materials, more dependence on representation as a substitute for fact, and less dependence on sense for confirming truth. It's an odd contradiction that industrialization itself, which we think of as putting men very close to physical materials, carries with it, the farther it goes, the obligation to increase the number of representations of what the material once was and the kind of life it stood for. The extractions of the earth have to be pretty well fabricated into simpler forms before the city can tolerate them at all. The man who makes shoes out of leather has no sense of cattle. There's nothing about the garment worker's cloth to remind him of blue flax in bloom, fields of cotton, or sheep being clipped. Even a lamb chop—to go back to my 10,000 sheep again—gets all snarled up in symbolism blurring its original actuality. To the Easterner who munches it down there's no hint of the ranges, grass, or water, because the lamb chop comes, if it comes at all, from the corner store: it stands for something wrong or right about the store, something wrong or right about the bureaucrats, wrong or right about the world food economy. The poor little lamb chop carries such a mystical burden that there's almost no fun eating it.

Being jammed into the symbolic life a good deal ahead of the rest of us, it is natural that seaboarders should be more adept at pure theory. Obviously, they have had more practice. It is easy to explain why they are more disposed to superstition, witchcraft, devil worship, and appeasement. This is characteristic of anybody who lives preponderantly in the world of the spirit. Their plant equipment for the vicarious life is superb. Nowhere else on earth does anybody have such access to all the representations of what life elsewhere *must* be like: here are the greatest libraries, the greatest museums of art and natural history, the greatest foundations to explore economic symbolism, and the greatest concentration of universities to make fullest use of every representation. Like anybody breaking new ground, these pioneers on the frontiers of abstraction naturally romanticize their activities. They are as blameless for parading their mental garments as the cowman for wearing a ten-gallon hat. It is inevitable that they should feel that they have superior intelligence, superior humanity, superior insight into world affairs.

What they actually have is, obviously, more mental activity with proportionate sacrifice of sense reference as to its accuracy. What they mistake for superior intelligence is no more than accelerated cerebration—quicker turnover of very volatile and interchangeable symbols. They work the mental squirrel cage harder simply because there are so many more squirrels queued up to get into it. Their claims to superior humanity and global love for their fellow man have a curious relationship to mass fear. With fear as a catalyst the seaboard masses churn themselves up to a crusading hysteria, but, in the absence of fear, these humanitarian impulses degenerate quickly, to the sad disillusionment of the intellectuals.

All these mental traits belong to the general phenomena of excess population that we don't understand very well and ought to try harder to understand because all our problems of war and peace are more concerned with them than anything else. What these masses want, but don't know how to say it, is some sort of integration with the land. They are bewildered when anybody tries to encroach on what little they have—witness the hue and cry about fundamental rights when the UN wanted to stake off a little acreage in Westchester County.

Clearly, seaboarders are doomed to a far greater variety of heavens and hells than we inlanders who have made slower progress on the road to abstraction. Quite apart from fear, which always thrives on congestion, emotional intensity of all kinds is part and parcel of the symbolic life. This is characteristic of all artists and prophets. A symbolist like Dorothy Thompson has as vivid a conviction of reality as the mad poet, William Blake. The eye surveys the whole world with stereopticon clairvoyance; international problems take on a four-cocktail clarity.

An Iowa farmer would have to get all hopped up on hard cider to have the faintest inkling of those burning awarenesses, even at their most sluggish Monday-morning level of intensity. As I look back on it, the only sin of the Corn Belt farmer in recent years was that he didn't stay plastered all day. It was metaphysical inagility rather than lack of patriotism that made him the arch-enemy of world peace. He was clumsy about swapping the abstractions of peace for the abstractions of war, for the simple reason that he'd never had much truck with abstraction of any kind in the first place. He couldn't transfer hysteria he didn't have to something somebody else was afraid of, nor did he have the stimulating disadvantage of being elbowed around by people who were afraid of each other. He was stigmatized for wanting to hide behind the haystack but, in my opinion, he was so well integrated with the land, and required so few abstractions to make what sense there was out of his life, that he had little feeling of either security or insecurity until people started calling him names.

I'd conclude these remarks by suggesting that people who live by symbols are forever fugitive from them. Somewhere behind the flicker of teletype that stands for 10,000 sheep there must be real sheep; somewhere behind the greatest library in the world there must be the kind of life that caused all those little black vowels and consonants to be put into all those millions of books. The real thing is worth going after. The horizon beckons. It becomes a consuming drive. But the first sally is merely the flight from the city itself, and the first destination is the pastoral illusion. Actually, it isn't a flight from the city: the city is more convenient than the country, more comfortable, healthier, the food is better. The real flight is from the symbolic life. You've got to make your senses go back to work, get your hands into materials that push when you push; you've got to get your nose into the smells of Nature and your eyes into the kind of distance that keeps on going. You've got to remodel some upstate barn or race off to Connecticut to fondle a real lamb.

The pastoral illusion, however, trips you up, because you are too experienced a symbolist to break whole-hog with the city you love best. All you are asking for is another adventure in symbolism. Unfortunately, rustic innocence is not retroactive. The only people who really have it are the ones who grew up with it and never found it out.

By the time you get to wanting it at all, it's too late to do more than increase the draft on your already over-developed talent for making the unreal stand for the real, plus a lot of fatigue in shuttling back and forth a good many miles from one illusion to the other. What I'm saying is as true of the city poor as the city rich, but the poor are spared the embarrassing privilege of running away only to traipse back home with their tails between their legs. And they thank no one for their good fortune, nor should they: every man to his own adventure!

An Address on Words and Things[1]

T. CLIFFORD ALLBUTT, M.D.

In brief discourse—for an address may be brief and yet tedious—I desire to avoid those regions of metaphysical thought by which we are landed in remote and irreducible antinomies. It is not inconsistent, I hope, with a proper mistrust of common-sense to assume for current purposes an objective world and a subjective; that we are we and that things are things outside us. In this necessary assumption our concepts are models of the external world, and are useful in so far as they coincide with what we must venture to accept as "reality." Curiously enough, the human mind is not as the "mind" of animals seems to be, a mere print off of the outer world; it has an amazing liberty, or license, of speculation, largely independent of phenomena, a faculty at any rate of conceiving the world much other than it is; in part a dreaming faculty, in part an abstracting faculty; or in other words a compact of imagination and intellect. To make for himself an idea of the big world as it is must be the work of ages, meanwhile man has for working purposes this faculty of making little provisional images of it, on the lines of which he may make corresponding periodical progresses. But, as by enlargement of needs and experience mankind is prepared for larger and larger conceptions, the surviving images become idols, and these, like other idols, have from time to time to be smashed. Some men foresee more clearly the imperative iconoclasms; others see more clearly the converse side of progress—namely, that tradition, sincerely used and understood, is better than no provisional scheme of life at all. In the less mature periods of culture man is so proud of his mind, and of the little worlds it fashions, that he attaches himself most tenaciously to one or other of these images rather than to the objective world; and furiously resents any scrapping of his subjective worlds, however inadequately they may have come to represent the stage of contemporary experience. . . . By things, then, I mean what we sup-

[1] From *The Lancet*, October 27, 1906, pp. 1120–1125. Reprinted by permission.

pose to be an external world, after the manner of which we are or ought to be continually remodelling our ideas; by words, on the other hand, I mean signs, arbitrary and very variable signs, by which we endeavour to indicate these ideas and to converse with them. In a full view of symbolism these signs would appear in more than one kind; for instance, they must include drama, painting, and music: but at present we will confine ourselves to those signs only which we call language—to literary signs, and of these chiefly, of course, to scientific prose. . . .

Those of us who are trained in science, reverent as we are to the memory of Aristotle, cannot help seeing that, after a widely different fashion indeed, he occupies himself too much with words. This defect in him it was which endeared him to the spinners of verbal webs in the scholastic period of modern Europe. Like them their oracle too often when seeking for causes sought them among words. Aristotle would not be the august man he is had he not laid a masterly hand also on things, especially on zoological things; but in many spheres he failed to perceive how artificial are the logical bridges by which too often he carried himself over anything but solid ground. We are told to remember in excuse that Aristotle lay under the disadvantage of knowing but one language; that had he enjoyed the advantage of a classical education, had he been educated in the comparison of words, he would have become so far detached from them as to have discovered that words are but labels, that labels are very liable to get shifted, and in no case make the museums they interpret. That this defect, in the work of the greatest mind perhaps that the world has seen, was due to his confinement within the boundaries of one tongue I hesitate to admit. Many great men, comparable perhaps with Aristotle in native intellect, although like him confined to one language, have compassed ends if less vast yet more enduring. Such men have lived, it is true, in polyglot times, but personally not a few of them, had enjoyed either no linguistic culture or but a nominal degree of it. Nor in our own times, indeed, do I observe that those whose linguistic culture has been the most liberal have distinguished themselves chiefly by an emancipation from words and a devotion to things. I can conceive, indeed, that a contrary thesis might be maintained.

Now to dwell upon things rather than on words is the method of observation, which in its fulness contains the experimental method; and although it would not be fair to say that the Greeks never attained the use of this method, its practice by Aristotle, by his pupil Theophrastus the botanist, by Archimedes, or Hipparchus, never attained anything like the maturity to govern their conceptions. In so brief a bloom of culture such a consummation would scarcely be conceivable. Both before and after the Socratic period the pursuit of knowledge was mainly not by this method but by the method of public discussion. The perversions latent in this method we can see better than greater men than ourselves could perceive them at the time, and the method of public discussion and pursuit of truth by verbal controversy became almost more rampant and more perverted in the polyglot medieval universities than among the monoglot Greeks, and with less excuse. . . .

Locke said of logic that one cannot apply the syllogism until the truth is ascertained, and that then one does not want it. The answer may be, nevertheless, that having apprehended a truth we apply the syllogism to discover and formulate the deftest, most economical, and most effectual mode of expressing it. Yet there is no small danger lest we should not use logic thus clear-sightedly, but should be tempted to suppose its manipulation of words to be a manipulation of things; lest the constructor of syllogisms should suppose himself a creator of truth. In the Middle Ages men fell into this kind of aridity: they forgot that as we abstract we are departing from things, and passing into a land of symbols; out of the turmoil of natural events, colours and contingencies, into a land of artificial schemes, and may too readily leave observation for ingenuity, and things for formulas. Thus we are prone to suppose that truth is to be revealed by the conflict of argument, and, what is worse, to construct "thought cages" for ourselves and to hop contentedly about in them. . . .

Some of you who have heard my teaching before must forgive me if I repeat my insistence that the name of a disease is not, as it is continually regarded, a thing. There is no such *thing* as typhoid fever, as angina pectoris, as spleno-medullary leucæmia, and so forth; the things so called are Wilkinson, Johnson, and Thompson, who after their kinds are afflicted not alike, but within such limits of similarity as to lead us to class them together and to form a general conception of them. Yet still we overhear at learned societies physicians whose shoe latchets I am not worthy to unloose contending, even with heat, whether this name or that is a "morbid entity." Now "entity" is anyway a bad word, as words can be bad; it was born badly, and has kept bad company. It was born to signify that reality of substance which was once supposed to underlie abstract names, and in these ontological circles it has moved ever since. If we are to speak at all of "entities" in disease, these must be not the names, nor even our concepts, but the things—the thing Thompson and the thing Wilkinson in certain phases of their being. The moment we depart from these objects we desert the names of things for the names of abstractions in which no entity can lie, the name being but a label to denote a somewhat arbitrary and ideal group of characters, or type, never perhaps manifested in nature as a whole, but to which certain individuals are continually approximating. I do not pretend for a moment that we can do without abstractions; without them reasoning would be impossible: our safety lies not in avoiding reason but in being quick to recognise the tendency of ratiocination to carry us away from the only pregnant subjects of reason—namely, from things, with which reason should never cease habitually and steadily to concern itself.

It is only by examples that discussions such as this can be made clear. In epilepsy, for instance, we observe a vast number of persons attacked in modes not identical but similar, modes, however, the features of which shade off by insensible transitions into the features of other groups of symptoms; so that our concept is not of an absolute but only of a relative uniformity. This we should remember when we use the name; as we remember that when we call a certain group of stars Orion, or Charles's Wain, that there is no rigid division between these star groups and those of the neighbouring constellations. Now epilepsy is no more an entity nor an absolute idea than Orion; it is the name of an arbitrary group, so separated for the convenience of the thinking faculty of finite beings. So far as to the nonentity. But, as I have hinted, we proceed, having set up our entity, to treat it as savages treat their images, to shake and to harry it at our caprice. Surely, having accepted a name for a group, we ought to keep to it; and yet we find our friends daily calling widely different concepts by the same label of epilepsy; for instances, puerperal or uræmic convulsions, Jacksonian convulsions, certain insanities, and so on, events so very different both in nature and grouping that, if we give them also the same name of epilepsy, we shift our things without shifting our labels. Or, again, consider angina pectoris; if there be a uniformly recurrent group of clinical features it is that for which this name was invented; yet we shift the label about, now to spasms of neurotic women, now to vague and casual cardiac pains or discomforts consistent with almost any kind of heart disease. Most grotesque, perhaps, are the "pseudo" compounds, such as "pseudo-angina," "pseudo-leukæmia," and the like; think for a moment of calling scarlet fever "pseudo-measles"! yet it is not very long since these two maladies were distinguished. It were but too easy for me to prolong such a list of ambiguities due to shifting our labels, or to shifting our concepts under the labels; but these must suffice. Remember that when it is asked if such and such a group of systems be a "morbid entity" or not, that since the day of William Ockham we have given up entities, that the question is now one only of convenience of reason; but that when we have once agreed to give a certain name to a certain morbid series of events—arbitrarily agreed, that is—then we must stick to our label; for if the label is to be shifted about, or the things under it shifted, all accurate reason comes to an end. The best labels for diseases are such names as epilepsy, measles, leprosy, Graves's disease, and the like, which, having no attachment to hypotheses, are readily carried to new anchorages. One may walk dryshod from one disease to any other, yet on the other hand it is no less true that, because of the large differentiation of his parts and organs, in Man his morbid processes tend to a corresponding uniformity of recurrence; his symptoms recur in similar groups and orders—symptom-groups or syndromes as they are called by certain nosologists who are desirous of some name finer than the old term "disease," or are possessed with the tenacious notion that a disease is a real something in itself. But diseases are not even species, such as cats and toads, but abnormal, though not altogether irregular, behaviours of individuals.

Once more; not content with this ambiguity we entertain the converse notion also that, give it a name big enough, we can make a disease of a symptom. For example, bradycardia and tachycardia, symptoms, in their degrees, of many a morbid process, impose upon the unwary student as even themselves "morbid entities," a notion twice removed from the truth, a shadow of a shade. . . .

But I must hasten on to another direction in which logic is apt to generate a reliance on words to the neglect or misinterpretation of things. In logic we are able to separate qualities of things, and to place them in divers categories so distinct that we are seduced into regarding these factitious categories as things. For purposes of analysis we may, and indeed we must, often study divers aspects of a thing separately, but only as an artificial and temporary expedient; not, as we have seen, so as to conduce to a habit of endowing these several aspects or qualities with independent life, or so as to blind us to their essential and active unity and integrity. We have hampered ourselves, for example, not exactly by considering structure and function severally, as a temporary device of thought, which is not illegitimate, but by dwelling on either to the exclusion or neglect of the other. Thus absorbed in the discoveries of morbid anatomy pathologists for many years forgot the genetic processes in which their specimens had their origin. Both in pathology and in clinical medicine, moreover, logical definitions were formulated which tied up living medicine in bandages as stifling as those in which Andrea della Robbia swathed his babies on the Loggia of the Hospital of the Innocents: but in biology definitions can never be more than summary descriptions. In a higher sphere of speculation the Athanasian creed is a notable collection of the surds which logic can manufacture for those who take abstract qualities for things. It is not the life but the mechanism of thought. A bitter controversy raged for centuries over a purely logical distinction between faith and works; the one being of course a function of the other. So, again, in psychology analytical divisions are made between Intellect, Imagination, and Will, factitious divisions which find their way into practical matters, to the prejudice of the gravest interests of education, sound criticism, and the conduct of life. Even yet it is hard to convince people that these distinctions are purely logical, having no several function; and that every action consists in a fusion or rather in the integration of all three qualities. That these qualities exist in various proportions in different individuals does not prove the independence of each of them any more than of various noses; but the assumption of such an independence . . . has thwarted, vitiated, and even sterilised our theories of mental life and growth. In forgetfulness of the imagination, with which he himself was so largely endowed, Francis Bacon forgot likewise the part of this great faculty in scientific discovery, and fell into the narrow view of it as a mere intellectual stringing of fact to fact, as on a necklace; whereas imagination is the pioneer faculty, always beckoning intellect on; though too often, if the sisters do not walk hand in hand, feverishly and fancifully. An apple falls from a tree, everybody's fact; it was Newton's large imagination that saw in it a symbol of universal gravitation. Darwin may have collected no greater pile of facts than some other naturalists; at first, indeed, specialists for the most part fought against him; but Darwin saw the facts common to him and to them in the light of a vast imagination. Much of the work which is done in our laboratories and dignified, not improperly perhaps, with the title of research, much plotting of curves, much watching of levers and thermometers, nay not a little morphological dissection and cabinet-making, are really little more than clerk's work. To be no more than learned in facts and opinions, with whatsoever skill in methods, is not to make knowledge. Bundles or files of facts are not science until the man with the formative, let me say the creative, insight comes along, who by the fusion of intellect and imagination seizes upon the significant facts, those which give him the lines on which to build up aggregates of materials into a conceptual edifice. Emil Fischer waxes very bold, and speaks of the "intuition which is the essential gift of the organic chemist." It almost makes one's mind ache to try to conceive the mental detachment, the power and compass of the imagination which realised the heliocentric astronomy; a conception which, for the ordinary man, flouts all earthly experience. Yet we were warned from Olympus a few weeks ago that "it is the business of science to present the facts, and to let them alone"!

No less factitious and eviscerating is the verbal division between "pure" and "applied" science, as if we could have a science of nothing; such was the divorce between medicine and surgery with which I have already dealt elsewhere. The homily of all this is to insist that as we abstract we depart from things; and the wider the successive abstractions the farther we are leaving things behind, the more and more are we eliminating those conditions and contingencies in which processes, organic and inorganic, essentially consist. Science is not creation but analysis of creation; and the strange adoption of the word "synthesis" to signify not the fullest life in the fullest environment but the uttermost epicycles of abstraction is an instance of the confusion wrought by misuse of words. General principles then are not applicable to things until we have reconstructed all or much of those very complexities in real processes which we had been at the pains to abstract. In medieval times so fastidious were logic and abstraction that practice became a vulgarity, and he was the greatest teacher who carried his pupils farthest from things; a departure from reality which brought about a grievous revenge. Since Galileo we have been discovering that our abstractions must incessantly be fertilised, tested, braced, and articulated with facts; that is to say, with systematic but common experience. . . .

It may be protested that logic has surely been an engine of progress in reason in the past, and it may be asked what is to take its place! The answer is, first, that no one desires to banish logic but, while keeping it in a subordinate place, to remember always its artificial nature; secondly, that formal logic is now surpassed, if not superseded, by the interpretations of evolution, by a natural logic of affinities. But this is too large and perhaps too familiar a chapter for our thoughts to-night. . . .

For my part I think less harm is done by metaphor, which can be appreciated as such, than by equivocal words; and it is to such words, to misused or degenerated words, and to the impostures and tyrannies of words, that I would in my few remaining paragraphs, however briefly, engage your attention. Of equivocal words and of the harm they do, there is no end. Some of you may remember the words of Plato in the *Phædo* that false words are not only in themselves evil but infect the soul with evil. So in science they infect the understanding. I must run the risk of discursiveness, and point to a few of them as they come. Some words are by nature of elusive temper; thus the word "force" by its equivocations has caused infinite trouble to men of science; they have been hunting it down this hundred years, but it has not been quite cornered yet. "Law" has more mischief to account for, as by its double dealing it carries error in all directions. Day by day we see well-meaning men confusing themselves and others by ignoring that in science law is not a rule imposed from without but an expression of an intrinsic process. The laws of the lawgiver are impotent beside the laws of human nature, as to his disillusion many a lawgiver has discovered. The word "compensation" we find frequently used in Medicine as a *vis medicatrix ex machinâ;* whereas we ought to mean that when a system in equilibrium has found itself able to re-adapt itself to a certain incident disturbance it survives, otherwise it is upset; this re-adaptation, on which its stability depends, varies not with any benevolent purpose or guiding principle, but with the intimate limits and conditions of the system itself. Other words are question-begging; such, in my opinion, is the word "mechanical" in its modern application to the cosmical order. Surely a machine is a system of tangible parts arranged to compass certain effects when it is set agoing, directly or indirectly, by human agency; left to itself it is impotent. We note the old error of Paley and the watch restored to respectability by modern philosophers. The philosopher may say that he does not intend the word to be used in its vulgar sense, but his readers do; and not only so, he himself vitiates his argument by many an implication of this meaning and speaks scornfully of a mechanical conception of the universe. "Utility," again, and its adjective "utilitarian"—what wars have been waged over these words; some disputants using them, as in common parlance, in the sense of immediate profit; others in the sense of remote profit—the old quarrel, by the way, between the "pure" and the "applied" science champions. Nay, let me spy into the citadel—into truth itself! Pilate was no "jester" when he asked—What is truth? for we have not yet agreed what the name is to mean. Is truth an absolute transcendental existence; a transcendental whole, yet in relation with us so far as to govern our ideas with an authority, as it were external? Or is it natural, partial, and relative, and to be found in the gradual establishment of a harmony between man's normal desires, and his satisfactions in experience? Or again, does it lie simply in affirmative propositions? The word is used chaotically. No doubt, as we have seen, a word may have two or more orderly senses, to be severally determined by the context; and truth may be used by metaphysicians in the first sense, by naturalists in the second, and by logicians in the third; but if so let this discrimination be steadily observed. On the other hand, the word is unduly neglected when truths are called "facts." Few abuses of language are so perverse as the misuse of the words "fact." I have grown accustomed to anticipate, on hearing it, a more than usually hazardous opinion, and nearly always some general statement depending upon facts: rarely indeed the proper sense of the word—namely, something which *has happened*. The word has become indeed so ambiguous that it is no longer trusted alone but has to be guarded as in the phrase "actual fact." The common use seems to be that my opinion is a fact, your opinion is a theory. Theory, on the other hand—the highest range of scientific truth—is used almost as a term of contempt. A brilliant author and man of science wrote the other day —"this which was never more than a mere theory"—never, that is, more than conjecture; or shall we say fad, craze, or moonshine! We cannot defend ourselves by pleading that we have more care for the thing than for the word. We might as well shuffle about the names of our collections of butterflies and beetles and so qualify ourselves for the giddy supremacy of Toinette—"Moi, je suis l'inexactitude même." Thus dull Britons are encouraged to vilipend the systematic results of investigation and to content themselves with rule of thumb. . . .

Nihil in intellectu quod non prius in sensu: mind in its widest sense is, as we know, fed and built up by the senses, by the incessant streaming in upon us of outside impressions. Thus it is that animals, which within their narrow and immediate sphere live incessantly in sensation, are so extraordinarily successful in it. Their almost infallible perception and memory of experience is rather unconscious absorption than deliberate observation. We see the same high seriousness in children. Academic man, on the other hand, by abstraction is continually tending to arrest or ignore the inspiration of these centripetal nervous streams which should not antagonise but continually conspire with thought. Reflexion is imperative for us; thought is that attribute which is most divine in us; by its symbols we make the universe our own: yet if we permit divorce of thought from its materials—and it is by words that we think—if we let thoughts and words drift away from things, the mind itself, our minds individual and collective, must be surely impoverished. If we give no heed to our symbols—to our means of conceiving, recording, and formulating the conditions under which we have to design our world, our lives and our faiths, we shall be drawn almost as inevitably into error as if our observations were themselves erroneous. Watts, who with the creative faculty of an intellectual imagination, had in supreme degree the artist's power of penetrating, selective observation, and his mastery of expression, was ever counseling this incessant openness to the senses, with their burdens of things and experience. And, as our minds are thus enriched, as they become not less and less but more and more receptive of impressions, our words must be kept moving and continually re-tested for appositeness and values. They are winged things which grow, flourish, and decay, and are spiteful if we misuse them. Our most fundamental assumptions must be always under reconsideration, our rules of evidence made stricter and stricter, our appreciation of values more and more refined, and our principles of selection more and more severe.

And not our facts only, but also the *litera scripta*—documents, traditions, authorities—must lie always under question. Without the past the present cannot appear to us in its true perspective nor be fully interpreted. Without the history of medicine, and study of the words in which it is contained, modern medical ideas cannot be fully understood, nor the place and genius of our profession rightly known. Medicine is not a game to be played merely with science, coolness, and dexterity, but a calling to be pursued as humanly as the humanities must nowadays be pursued scientifically.

Finally, for this debating society our discourse on Words and Things has had little result unless I have led you to see more clearly that the purposes of it ought to be an unwearied contribution and verification of things; a vigilant criticism of insidious plausibilities, dislocations, ambiguities, unveracities, and insincerities of language; and not only a care for the choice of words lucid and exact, but also a training in the use of them in a significant context. As you grow in wisdom you will see more and more clearly that the gain of your debate is not to bowl each other out, but to translate the values of each of your minds into the permanent values of each other and of truth. The last counsel I leave with you is that you shall take me as an awful example of talking too much; and remember the saying of Izaak Walton that "words are men's daughters, but God's sons are things."

Life and the Symbols of Life [1]

J A M E S   S .   P L A N T

[We must] teach children the difference between life and what are but the symbols of life. This statement is not easily clarified. It is relatively easy to point out what are the symbols of life; to say what is life itself is to answer what no one has answered up to now. One can accept this impasse, and at the same time recognize that we peculiarly live in a period of inability to distinguish life from its symbols.

An immediate example presents itself from the school. Certainly there was an earlier time when grades and marks were simply easy symbols of the child's stage of achievement. Who would question today that these symbols have become to most children the realities? We parents, we teachers have done our task so well that it is the rule rather than the exception that the twelve-year-old child does what his report card demands rather than what his intellectual curiosity demands.

[1] From *Personality and the Cultural Pattern*. New York: The Commonwealth Fund, 1937, pp. 408–409. Copyright, 1937, by the Commonwealth Fund. Reprinted by permission.

Money presents another example. It is difficult for us to realize that but a hundred years ago money was only a symbol of goods. One of the disturbing trends of these intervening years has been this development of money into something which is sought for itself, which itself is endowed with reality. One might in this way travel the gamut of our pattern—citing automobile, street address, position, possessions thought of as happiness, achievement, or contentment, because they may symbolize happiness, achievement, or contentment. The outstanding example lies in our verbalization. Early in life generalization must, and does, replace multiplying experiences. And generalization requires verbalization. The artistry of life lies in the balance between symbol and that for which it stands which allows one to use the former freely without ever forgetting that it simply stands for something. But our culture refuses freedom to the individual in this matter. One of its most insistent queries is how soon in life words replace realities. Children are admitted to school on this basis, school progress is built about language ability, and preeminence is given to verbalization in testing intelligence. We have had much to say about the non-verbal modes of communication—those facile, universal modes of telling to others those things which defy words. These psycho-motor tensions are not adequate for our complex civilization. We cannot escape symbolization. Nor are we sure of those *real* values of life which might unfailingly serve everyone.

But we can go a considerable way. We can make persistent efforts to lessen the importance of marks and grades. We can make persistent efforts to exhibit in the other phases of life what are merely its symbols. We not only can, we must, do these things. The problems which our children will face will be poorly met by a group that cannot make these distinctions. We have those of our own generation to prove this. We do not know whether the time will come when we can point out what is real life. We suspect that this is a highly idiomatic affair — that perhaps generalization here is as artificial as it is in any other phase of our problems. Nor is this our only difficulty. Symbolization is for many an escape from that which it is impossible to face. As we build walls of armor about our bodies—painting and furbishing them to show what we would be—so there are many who cannot afford to look behind their marks, their street number, to what they really are. We can't escape symbols—often in sheer kindness they hide from us what we cannot afford to see. But we can know them for what they are and in a world that is built for the happiness and growth of personalities it is necessary that we teach children more clearly which are merely the symbols, and which are the things they really want and need.

Experience with Languages[1]

WARNER FITE

I have always avoided the word "concept": what it suggests to me is a poker-chip. I cherish the primitive notion that when a man talks to me, say about horses, and wishes me to see what he has in mind, he should bring along a horse, or a picture of a horse, or at least of a zebra if he happens to have one. This is all the more important when he is talking about an idealist or a realist. The Socratic method of definition, as I make it out, is an accommodation of things to words; and its aim—which the Socrates of the Platonic dialogues seems never quite to achieve— is apparently to find one word, and one alone, which will cover a variety of objects and then to reduce the whole world of things to a verbal classification; which is then represented as a system of concepts. Yet all the while it seems that the nearer we come to the one word the further we find ourselves from any imaginable reality; and when we have finally defined the concept what we have before us is not an object but a word and a definition which relates it to other words. I have then a similar suspicion about the Platonic dialectic. It seems to me that the whole of Plato's metaphysics is guided by an assumption of which he himself is unconscious: namely, that for every word in the language there must be a corresponding element in reality.

We can see the naturalness and even the necessity of such an assumption when we remember the probability that none of the founders of logic, Socrates, Plato, Aristotle, knew any language but his own. For

[1] From "The Philosopher and His Words," *The Philosophical Review*, Vol. XLIV, No. 2, March, 1935, pp. 127–128. Reprinted by permission.

the matter of that there was in their Hellenic view nothing else that could be called a language—just as there was for Aristotle at least no life but the Greek that could be called civilized. A barbarian language was then by definition "gibberish." I think that for an understanding of the beginnings of logic and metaphysics this item is vastly important. For one who knows no language but his own the correspondence of words and things is an assumption almost inevitable. For him then the words are not merely conventional symbols for things but real properties of the things; and a grasp of the relations of words is a grasp of the things themselves. It is then a disillusionment to discover, upon learning a foreign language, that what can be expressed in a word in one tongue requires a pair of words or a whole phrase in another, and that between no two languages is there more than a rather loose correspondence of word to word. This wrenches the word loose from the thing; it also introduces what is for me the most characteristic product of philosophical reflection: namely, a consciousness of the variety of human points of view. And the fact that this consciousness is slight in ancient philosophy, acute in all of the modern period, may be traced, I think, to the fact that the modern philosopher lives and works in a world of many tongues where the Greek philosophers knew only one. And I will go a step further and suggest that this experience of language which the ancients lacked is the most important item in any education for reflective thought. It has been almost an axiom in the past that the special instrument for a training of the mind is geometry. If the essence of mind is reflective thought, must we not say that the chiefly important item in its development is a study of foreign languages and literatures?

Two Kinds of Knowledge [1]

ELTON MAYO

================

A simple distinction made by William James in 1890 has all the significance now that it had then; one can only suppose that its very simplicity has led the universities to brush it aside as obvious, which is true, or as of small account, which is not true. James pointed out that almost every civilized language except English has two commonplace words for knowledge—*connaître* and *savoir*—γνῶναι and εἰδέναι, *knowledge-of-acquaintance* and *knowledge-about*.[2] This distinction, simple as it is, nevertheless is exceedingly important; *knowledge-of-acquaintance* comes from direct experience of fact and situation, *knowledge-about* is the product of reflective and abstract thinking. "Knowledge derived from experience is hard to transmit, except by example, imitation, and trial and error, whereas erudition (*knowledge-about*) is easily put into symbols—words, graphs, maps. Now this means that skills, although transmissible to other persons, are only slowly so and are never truly articulate. Erudition is highly articulate and can be not only readily transmitted but can be accumulated and preserved."[3] The very fact that erudition (logic and systematic knowledge) can be so easily transmitted to others tends to prejudice university instruction in the social sciences heavily in its favor. Physics, chemistry, physiology have learned that far more than this must be given to a student. They have therefore developed laboratories in which students may acquire manipulative skill and be judged competent in terms of actual performance. In such studies the student is required to relate his logical *knowledge-about* to his own direct acquaintance with the facts, his own

---

[1] From *The Social Problems of an Industrial Civilization,* Boston: Division of Research, Graduate School of Business Administration, Harvard University, 1945, pp. 16–17. Copyright, 1945, by the President and Fellows of Harvard College. Reprinted by permission.

[2] William James, *The Principles of Psychology* (London, Macmillan and Co., Limited, 1890), Vol. 1, p. 221.

[3] From a letter written by Dr. Alan Gregg (November 13, 1942).

capacity for skilled and manipulative performance. James's distinction between the two kinds of knowledge implies that a well-balanced person needs, within limits, technical dexterity in handling things, and social dexterity in handling people; these are both derived from knowledge-of-acquaintance. In addition to this, he must have developed clinical or practical knowledge which enables him to assess a whole situation at a glance. He also needs, if he is to be a scientist, logical knowledge which is analytical, abstract, systematic—in a word, the erudition of which Dr. Alan Gregg speaks; but it must be an erudition which derives from and relates itself to be the observed facts of the student's special studies.

Speaking historically, I think it can be asserted that a science has generally come into being as a product of well-developed technical skill in a given area of activity. Someone, some skilled worker, has in a reflective moment attempted to make explicit the assumptions that are implicit in the skill itself. This marks the beginning of logico-experimental method. The assumptions once made explicit can be logically developed; the development leads to experimental changes of practice and so to the beginning of a science. The point to be remarked is that scientific abstractions are not drawn from thin air or uncontrolled reflection: they are from the beginning rooted deeply in a pre-existent skill.

The Study of Man [1]

L. J. HENDERSON

The subject of this address is neither man nor the propriety or the appropriateness of the study of man; it is that study itself. It is not an examination of what chiefly interested Pope and Bolingbroke; it is a consideration of certain biological and social sciences. It is not even

[1] From *Science*, Vol. 94, No. 2427, July 4, 1941, pp. 1–4, 7, 8–10. Reprinted by permission.

primarily the study of man; it is the study of men as organisms, of their structures and functions, in sickness and in health, and of men as persons, in their activities and their interactions; for the characteristics of man are but the uniformities observable among men. Again, our subject is not the examination of what such studies ought to be; it is merely a fragment of a description and analysis of what they are, of how they have been, and of how they have not been, effectively prosecuted. Let us note at once that effective work involves both doing what is effective and not doing what is not effective.

The study of men—even the scientific study—is ancient and respectable. It goes back to Aristotle, to Hippocrates and beyond them to obscure beginnings. To-day it is one of the chief studies of the learned. Like our other activities, it may be divided into two parts, the successful part and the unsuccessful part. Speaking very generally and with due regard to numerous and important exceptions, it may be said that the successful part of the scientific study of men is related to medicine, the unsuccessful part to philosophy and to the social sciences. These relations are not only historical, they are also to be seen in methods, attitudes and traditions.

The successes of medicine and the medical sciences have not been lightly won; from a multitude of failures they are the survivals, the fortunate productions of the best or the most-favored men among an endless succession of skilful physicians. Though pedantry, incompetency and charlatanry have often hindered and in evil times, even for long periods, arrested the accumulations of medical science, since Hippocrates, at least, the tradition of skilful practice has never been quite lost—the tradition that combines theory and practice. And this tradition is, especially in three elements, indispensable.

Hippocrates teaches first, hard, persistent, intelligent, responsible, unremitting labor in the sick room, not in the library: the all-round adaptation of the doctor to his task, an adaptation that is far from being merely intellectual. This is adaptation chiefly through the establishment of conditioned reflexes. Something like it seems to be a necessary part of the mastery of any material or of effective work in any medium, for such adaptation is the mark of every master-workman in every field. Galileo refers to it among artisans, saying: [2] "Indeed, I myself, being curious by nature, frequently visit [the arsenal of Venice] for the mere pleasure of observing the work of those whom, on account of their superiority

[2] *Dialogues Concerning Two New Sciences*, Macmillan, New York, 1914, p. 1.

over other artisans, we call 'first rank men.' Conference with them has often helped me in the investigation of certain effects including not only those which are striking, but also those which are recondite and almost incredible." . . .

Hippocrates teaches, secondly, accurate observation of things and events, selection, guided by judgment born of familiarity and experience, of the salient and the recurrent phenomena, and their classification and methodical exploitation. This is descriptive science. It is not necessary for the craftsman, it is for the scientist. The more complex the things studied by a science, the greater—in general—the importance of descriptive knowledge. For example, taxonomy is more important to zoology than description to mechanics. In the scientific study of men much systematic descriptive knowledge is almost everywhere indispensable.

Hippocrates teaches, thirdly, the judicious construction of a theory— not a philosophical theory, nor a grand effort of the imagination, nor a quasi-religious dogma, but a modest pedestrian affair, or perhaps I had better say, a useful walking stick to help on the way—and the use thereof. Theoretical science is not necessary for the craftsman, or, perhaps, for the descriptive scientist, because both may think in terms of the world of common sense. But theory in the form of some kind of an abstract conceptual scheme seems to be necessary for the effective exploitation of even descriptive science.

All this may be summed up in a word: The physician must have, first, intimate, habitual, intuitive familiarity with things; secondly, systematic knowledge of things; and thirdly, an effective way of thinking about things.

Experience shows that this is the way to success. It has long been followed in studying sickness, but hardly at all in studying the other experiences of daily life. Let us, therefore, consider more carefully what Hippocrates did and what he did not do. He was in reaction chiefly against three things: first, against the ancient, traditional myths and superstitions which still prevailed among the physicians of his day; secondly, against the recent intrusion of philosophy into medical doctrine; thirdly, against the extravagant system of diagnosis of the Cnidian School, a body of contemporary physicians who seem to have suffered from a familiar form of professional pedantry. Here Hippocrates was opposing a pretentious systematization of knowledge that lacked solid objective foundation; the concealment of ignorance, probably more or less unconsciously, with a show of knowledge. Note well that such concealment is rarely altogether dishonest and that it may be practiced in thorough good faith.

The social sciences to-day suffer from defects that are not unlike the defects of medicine to which Hippocrates was opposed. First, social and political myths are everywhere current, and if they involve forms of superstition that are less apparent to us than the medical superstitions of long ago, that may well be because we recognize the latter class of superstitions for what they are while still accepting or half-accepting the former class. Secondly, there is at least as much philosophy mingled with our current social science as there was at any time in the medical doctrines of the Greeks. Thirdly, a great part of the social science of to-day consists of elaborate speculation on a very insufficient foundation of fact.

Hippocrates endeavored to avoid myths and traditional rules, the grand search for philosophical truth, the authority of philosophical beliefs, the concealment of ignorance with a show of systematic knowledge. He was concerned first of all not to conceal his own ignorance from himself. When he thought abstractly, or in general terms, his thought was limited and constrained because he had wide intuitive knowledge based on the habit of responsible action in concrete situations. There is a test for this kind of thinking: the question, "For example?" Those who generalize from experience almost always pass this test; others do not. Indeed, the test is frequently destructive of unfounded generalization and is apt to lead to painful embarrassment. For this reason its use is often inexpedient.

Experience shows that there are two kinds of human behavior which it is ordinarily convenient and often essential to distinguish:

The one is thinking, talking and writing, by those who are so familiar with relevant concrete experiences that they can not ordinarily forget the facts, about two kinds of subjects. These are: first, concrete observations, and observations and experiences which are representable by means of sharply defined or otherwise unambiguous words; and secondly, more general considerations, clearly and logically related to such concrete observations and experiences.

The other kind of behavior is thinking, talking and writing about vague or general ideas or "concepts" which do not clearly relate to concrete observations and experiences and which are not designated by sharply defined words. On the whole, the works of Plato belong to this second class, the Hippocratic writings to the first class.

The so-called genuine works of Hippocrates reveal a method in the exploitation of everyday experiences with the lives and deaths of men that can never be too carefully studied. In the beginning are the cases, the clinical records of the great physician. They consist of bare observations of bare facts, uncolored by theory or presupposition and condensed to the very limit of possible condensation. These are the practicing physician's data, freed so far as possible from everything that is not a datum. The data are of two kinds: the first kind, often contained in the first part of the record, are single observations; the second kind, commonly presented at the end, are observations of uniformities throughout a particular sickness of a particular person.

The next step, after the recognition of uniformities in a particular case, is the recognition of a wider kind of uniformity: the recurrence again and again in different cases, often otherwise very various, of single events or of the uniformity observed within a single case, for example: regularities in the duration of certain fevers, the frequent discharge of fluid through the nose in what we now call diphtheria, and in general the prognostic importance of a wide range of symptoms. The most famous of all the descriptions of such uniformities is that known as the "facies Hippocratica," the appearance of the face at the point of death in many acute diseases: "Nose sharp, eyes hollow, temples sunken, ears cold and contracted with their lobes turned outwards, the skin about the face hard and tense and parched, the colour of the face as a whole being yellow or black."

Throughout a great part of his work Hippocrates is thus moving step by step toward the widest generalizations within his reach. In great part he is seeking a natural history of acute disease, or at least of those acute diseases that were prevalent among his patients. His success was great, and the whole history of science goes far to support the view that such a methodical procedure is a necessary step in the development of a science that deals with similarly complex and various phenomena.

Beyond this stage there is one even wider generalization that plays an important part in the writings and thought of Hippocrates. This is the principle that came to be known, and is still remembered, as the *vis medicatrix naturae*. It may be stated in modern form as follows: Organisms exist in a state such that when a modification, not too great and different from what will otherwise occur, is impressed on them, a reaction appears tending toward the condition that would have existed if the modification had not been impressed. This is by no means only true for organisms, and indeed it has been more clearly recognized in recent years by certain economists in their theoretical studies than by physicians and physiologists.

In order to construct a useful conceptual scheme, Hippocrates proceeded to analyze this process, as he abstractly conceived it, into elements. His analysis and the resulting elaboration of the theory need not detain us. To them we owe the survival of such words as "crisis" and "coction." But the theory, having served its purpose, is obsolete, like Ptolemy's astronomy.

We must, however, note carefully that this obsolete theory, like so many others, once served its purpose well. In particular, it was the firm support of the Hippocratic principle of expectant treatment and of the precept "Do no harm," a principle and a precept which still preserve their utility in the practice of medicine and even in government and the affairs of everyday life, and which are too often disregarded by physicians, surgeons and politicians.

The Hippocratic conceptual scheme suffers from one particular defect that should be carefully noted: It presents a view of the physiological system in a state of equilibrium, without giving a satisfactory picture of the constituent parts of the system or of the forces that operate between these parts. We now know that it is convenient and reasonably satisfactory to think of the constituent parts as chemical substances, fluids, cells, tissues and organs; and of the forces as the forces with which theoretical physics and theoretical chemistry are concerned. Such a conception was not available to Hippocrates. Nevertheless, his conceptual scheme worked and for a long time worked well. This is, in fact, the test of a conceptual scheme and the only test: it must work well enough for the purpose of the moment. A conceptual scheme survives just so long and just in so far as it continues to be convenient to use it for the purpose of scientific work.

In a discussion of scientific hypotheses, Henri Poincaré once remarked:[3] "These two propositions, 'the external world exists,' or 'it is more convenient to suppose that it exists,' have one and the same meaning." The proof of Poincaré's assertion is that in scientific work no use can be made of the proposition "the external world exists" that can not just as well be made of the statement "we assume for the present purpose that the external world exists." Moreover, all our

[3] *La valeur de la science,* Paris (no date), p. 272.

conceptual schemes are in a state of flux. There is hardly one we now use that was used in precisely its present form fifty years ago. It is therefore dangerous to believe that a conceptual scheme is a description of some ultimate metaphysical reality. In other words, belief in the "truth" of a conceptual scheme is for scientific purposes not only irrelevant, it is often misleading.

Our modern theory and our modern practice of medicine are so different in so many ways from ancient theory and practice that only by an effort of thought and imagination can we clearly conceive what ancient medicine was. I have tried to suggest that its merits were great and to specify the nature of some of these merits. To specify its deficiencies is almost unnecessary. However, we may note that until long after the time of Hippocrates experiment was but a feeble aid to observation and that applications of physics and chemistry were altogether lacking because there was nothing to apply.

In our modern period all this is changed. The sciences of anatomy, physiology and pathology, with their many branches, have grown up. They have become experimental sciences and they are becoming more and more sciences of applied physics and applied chemistry. This development has been accompanied by the growth of a conceptual scheme in which the broader generalizations of the medical sciences are incorporated and synthesized.

But it is still true that the investigator must have intimate, habitual, intuitive familiarity with the things that he studies, systematic knowledge of them and an effective way of thinking about them. This is just as true in the anatomical laboratory or the physiological laboratory or the pathological laboratory as it is in the clinic. There is, I believe, no broader induction from our experience of scientific work than this, and few inductions are more important. . . .

The social sciences are very different from the medical sciences. Their development has been different; their present state is different. The habits, the attitudes, the procedures of social scientists are, in general, very different from those of medical scientists. And to-day the applications of medical science are innumerable, while it is hard to find effective applications of social science. . . .

In the social sciences special methods and special skills are few. It is hard to think of anything that corresponds to a mathematician's skill in performing mathematical operations or to a bacteriologist's skill in cultivating microorganisms or to a clinician's skill in making physical examinations. Even in conducting an interview, skill is to be sought among physicians, or certain lawyers, rather than among the generality of social scientists.

Classificatory descriptive knowledge, which is so conspicuous in the medical sciences and in natural history and which has proved so essential to the development of such sciences, is relatively lacking in the social sciences. The most serious effort in this direction with which I am acquainted is Pareto's taxonomic study of the residues, that is, of the manifestations of sentiments. Successful and important as this is, it is but the beginning of a vast and difficult undertaking. Moreover, there is no common accord among social scientists concerning the classes and subclasses of the things they study, and there is even much disagreement about nomenclature.

The theories of the social sciences seem to be in a curious state. One body of theory, that of economics, is highly developed, has been cast in mathematical form and has reached a stage that is thought to be in some respects definitive. This theory, like those of the natural sciences, is the result of the concerted efforts of a great number of investigators and has evolved in a manner altogether similar to the evolution of certain theories in the natural sciences. But it is hardly applicable to concrete reality. As Marshall has said:[4] "There is . . . no scope in economics for long chains of deductive reasoning; that is for chains in which each link is supported, wholly or mainly, by that which went before, and without obtaining further support and guidance from observation and the direct study of real life." Pareto goes quite as far in condemning the applications of economic theory.

The reasons why economic theory is so difficultly applicable to concrete events are that it is an abstraction from an immensely complex reality and that reasoning from theory to practice is here nearly always vitiated by "the fallacy of misplaced concreteness."[5] Such application suggests the analogy of applying Galileo's law of falling bodies to the motion of a falling leaf in a stiff breeze. Experience teaches that under such circumstances it is altogether unsafe to take more than a single step in deductive reasoning without verifying the conclusions by observation or experiment. Nevertheless, many economists, some cautiously and others less cautiously, are in the habit of expressing opinions

[4] *Elements of Economics of Industry,* Macmillan, London, 1905, p. 397.
[5] When men reason deductively about the complex affairs of everyday life they nearly always leave out something, or rather many things, both things they forget and things they don't know. More often than not their conclusions are therefore unsound.

deduced from theoretical considerations concerning economic practice. There is here a striking contrast with medicine, where it is almost unknown for a theorist inexperienced in practice to prescribe the treatment of a patient, and where it is well understood that apprenticeship in a hospital is the only effective preparation for practice.

In other fields of social science theories are generally not held in common by all investigators, but, like philosophical systems, tend to be sectarian beliefs. This is true even in psychology, where the conflicts of physiological psychologists, behaviorists, Gestaltists, psychoanalysts and others sometimes almost suggest theological controversy.

Further, it should be noted that social scientists often seek something else rather than convenience in the construction of their theories. Consider, for example, the following remarks of Durkheim: [6]

A concept is an essentially impersonal representation; it is through it that human intelligences communicate.

The nature of the concept, thus defined, bespeaks its origin. If it is common to all, it is the work of the community. Since it bears the mark of no particular mind, it is clear that it was elaborated by a unique intelligence, where all others meet each other, and after a fashion, come to nourish themselves. . . .

The collective consciousness is the highest form of the psychic life, since it is the consciousness of the consciousnesses. Being placed outside of and above individual and local contingencies, it sees things only in their permanent and essential aspects, which it crystallizes into communicable ideas.

And now note that we are well acquainted with a great number of essentially impersonal representations, such as acceleration in dynamics, entropy in thermodynamics or natural selection in biology, that we well know to have originated with a particular person or persons. Whatever his motive, Durkheim is endeavoring to set up a hypothetical entity that can only cause inconvenience in work because, so far as we know, consciousness is a function of, or is associated with, individual nervous systems. Long ago the biologist Le Dantec said of the Ehrlich school of immunity that when they discovered a new phenomenon they invented a *phenominine* to explain it. And very much longer ago William of Occam stated the precept known as Occam's razor: "Entia non sunt multiplicanda praeter necessitatem," which is to say that our con-

---

[6] Selections adapted from *The Elementary Forms of Religious Life*, pp. 432–37, in R. E. Park and E. W. Burgess, *Introduction to the Science of Sociology*, University of Chicago Press, 1921, pp. 194–96.

ceptual schemes should contain no more than the necessary elements.

On the whole, it seems fair to say that the social sciences in general are not cultivated by persons possessing intuitive familiarity, highly developed, systematic, descriptive knowledge, and the kind of theories that are to be found in the natural sciences.

There is not a little system-building in the social sciences but, with the striking exception of economic theory, it is of the philosophical type rather than of the scientific type, being chiefly concerned in its structural elements with words rather than with things or, in old-fashioned parlance, with *noumena* rather than with *phenomena*. This involves what I have already described as thinking, talking and writing about vague or general ideas or "concepts" which do not clearly relate to concrete observations and experiences.

For scientific purposes, or for clear thinking of any kind, experience shows that such things will not serve. In support of this assertion I venture to appeal to the late Justice Oliver Wendell Holmes, who once remarked:[7] "I have said to my brethren many times that I hate justice, which means that I know if a man begins to talk about that, for one reason or another he is shirking thinking in legal terms." I shall presume to make a single exegetical remark on Holmes's text: the phrase "shirking thinking in legal terms" may be generalized to read "shirking thinking in terms that can be used for even rough and ready logical purposes or for any sort of clear thinking."

I believe it not unfair to take as an illustration of what is here in question Reinach's definition of religion:[8] "An ensemble of scruples which impede the free exercise of our faculties." After stating this definition, Reinach at once goes on to remark: "This minimum definition is big with consequences, for it eliminates from the fundamental concept of religion, God, spiritual beings, the infinite, in a word, all we are accustomed to consider the true objects of religious sentiment." He has previously pointed out that definitions of religion are many and diverse and that they have not been found convenient in scientific work. The general confusion that has ensued from their use might well suggest the inference that to set up definitions of such a word, at all events without taking very unusual precautions, is inexpedient. Reinach's definition, like most definitions of religion, is a more or less precise

[7] *Justice Oliver Wendell Holmes: His Book Notices and Uncollected Letters and Papers.* Edited by Harry C. Shriver, New York, 1936, p. 201.

[8] *Orpheus, A History of Religions,* Horace Liveright, New York, 1930, Introduction, p. 2.

designation of attributes of some religions; in other words, the statement of what the author believes or wishes to believe a satisfactory *differentia*. Reinach's remark about the consequences of his definition is almost comic. What are the possible consequences of adopting a definition? Assuredly, no definition can modify the phenomena or the relations between the phenomena. On the other hand, it can and ordinarily does modify the behavior of the person who accepts it, and Reinach naïvely admits as much by noting that certain things are eliminated from the fundamental *concept* of religion. Now, what he eliminates in the beginning will, unless he blunders, not be found in his final conclusion.

Why does Reinach speak of "scruples which impede," and not of needs which further "the free exercise of our faculties"? He is evidently referring to phenomena which arise, at least in part, from systems of conditioned reflexes, and his restriction is pejorative. We know that hostility to contemporary religions was common in Parisians of his class at the time when he wrote "Orpheus." It is therefore not unlikely that such hostility partly explains the defects, from the scientific point of view, of his definition.

A further difference between most system-building in the social sciences and systems of thought and classification of the natural sciences is to be seen in their evolution. In the natural sciences both theories and descriptive systems grow by adaptation to the increasing knowledge and experience of the scientists. In the social sciences systems often issue fully formed from the mind of one man. Then they may be much discussed if they attract attention, but progressive adaptive modification as a result of the concerted efforts of great numbers of men is rare. Such systems are in no proper sense *working* hypotheses, they are "rationalizations." Or at best they are mixtures of working hypotheses and "rationalizations."

Thinking in the social sciences suffers, I believe, chiefly from two defects: one is the fallacy of misplaced concreteness, the other the intrusion of sentiments—of Bacon's Idols—into the thinking, which may be fairly regarded as an occupational hazard of the social scientists. There can be little doubt that this intrusion is one of the factors that make the quotations just cited from Durkheim and Reinach unacceptable as science. Let us consider one more example.

Macaulay says: [9] "[The errors in the works of Machiavelli] arise, for

[9] Essay on "Machiavelli."

the most part, from a single defect which appears to us to pervade his whole system. . . . The great principle, that societies and laws exist only for the purpose of increasing the sum of private happiness, is not recognized with sufficient clearness." What is the source of this great principle? Evidently it is not an induction from experience. What is the meaning of purpose as applied to the existence of societies? From a scientific point of view, purpose must be somebody's purpose. Like consciousness, it is associated with individual nervous systems. How can the sum of private happiness be measured? Assuredly not with any instruments or by any procedures that were at the disposal of Macaulay. Is it not evident that Macaulay's "great principle" and his "purpose" of the existence of societies are both expressions of his sentiments, and that "the sum of private happiness" is, in the sense of the logic of modern science, a meaningless phrase? Finally, what is the probability that if Macaulay were writing his essay on Machiavelli in September, 1940, he would feel disposed to make similar assertions? The sentiments, like most other things, vary with time.

Sentiments have no place in clear thinking, but the manifestations of sentiments are among the most important things with which the social sciences are concerned. For example, the word "justice" is out of place in pleading before the Supreme Court of the United States, but the sentiments associated with that word and often expressed by it are probably quite as important as the laws of our country, not to mention the procedure of the Supreme Court. Indeed, such sentiments seem to be in many ways and at many times the most important of all social forces. The still dominant European intellectual tradition treats such things as if they had their origin in the logical thinking of those who manifest them. Yet the sentiments arise and manifest themselves in a manner that is hardly more appropriate for such treatment than is the manner in which the instincts and the passions manifest themselves.

The attribute "justice" is by men variously ascribed to various actions. This ascription varies with time, with place, with age, with sex, with social status, with purpose, with economic interests, with emotional excitement and with innumerable other factors. For the word "justice" is the expression of an attitude. In general, it is irrelevant to inquire whether an assertion which is the expression of an attitude is logically and objectively true or false.

Such attitudes and sentiments are closely related to conditioned reflexes and in part arise from the process of conditioning. This may be illustrated by considering the contrast between the meanings of such pairs of words as house and home, woman and mother, man and comrade, acquaintance and friend or enemy.

The acquired characters of men may be divided into two classes. One kind involves much use of reason, logic, the intellect; for example, the ordinary studies of school and university. The other kind involves little intellectual activity and arises chiefly from conditioning, from rituals and from routines; for example, skills, attitudes and acquired sentiments. In modified form, men share such acquired characters with dogs and other animals. When not misinterpreted, they have been almost completely neglected by intellectuals and are frequently overlooked by social scientists. In their study a great opportunity seems to present itself for the application of physiology.

The conclusions of this comparative study are as follows: First, a combination of intimate, habitual, intuitive familiarity with things; systematic knowledge of things; and an effective way of thinking about things is common among medical scientists, rare among social scientists. Secondly, systems in the medical sciences and systems in the social sciences are commonly different. The former resemble systems in the other natural sciences, the latter resemble philosophical systems. Thirdly, many of the terms employed currently in the social sciences are of a kind that is excluded, except by inadvertence, from the medical sciences. Fourthly, sentiments do not ordinarily intrude in the thinking of medical scientists; they do ordinarily intrude in the thinking of social scientists. Fifthly, the medical sciences have made some progress in the objective study of the manifestations of sentiments; the social sciences, where these things are particularly important, have neglected them. This is probably due to the influence of the intellectual tradition. Sixthly, in the medical sciences special methods and special skills are many; in the social sciences, few. Finally, in the medical sciences testing of thought by observation and experiment is continuous. Thus theories and generalizations of all kinds are constantly being corrected, modified and adapted to the phenomena, and fallacies of misplaced concreteness eliminated. In the social sciences there is little of this adaptation and correction through continuous observation and experiment.

These are very general conclusions to which, as I have already said, there are numerous and important exceptions. Perhaps the most important exceptions may be observed in the work of many historians, of purely descriptive writers, and of those theoretical economists who scrupulously abstain from the application of theory to practice.

When we reflect upon these differences between the two kinds of studies of men, shall we not do well to think also of the fruitfulness of the medical sciences and of the unfruitfulness of the social sciences? But let us not try to say what is here cause, what effect. Human interactions are intricate and obscure, and the art of studying them is difficult. That is, we can but feel, a part of the cause of the habits of thought and procedure of social scientists, and of the unfruitfulness of their science as well. Yet, assuredly, there is no simple cause of the present condition. What we can say with some confidence, for it is the lesson of experience, is this: The social sciences will become more fruitful when in certain ways the thought and procedures of social scientists conform more closely to those of medical scientists.

Preparation of the Child for Science[1]

M. E. BOOLE

In the old days a certain ideal of nursery discipline evolved itself, suited to prepare the child for entering into relations with the classico-theological schoolmaster under whom he would presently be placed. That ideal was summed up in the old rime:

> Speak when you're spoken to
> Do what you're bid,
> Shut the door after you,
> And you'll never be chid.

"Speak when you're spoken to," in this old summary of the whole duty of the child, did not merely mean respond when you *are* spoken to; it distinctly was understood as an injunction not to speak till

[1] From *The Preparation of the Child for Science*. Oxford: at the Clarendon Press, 1904, pp. 131–157. Reprinted by permission of the Clarendon Press, Oxford.

spoken to; never to start questions; never to ask for anything till it was offered you. It was in line with nursery proverbs, such as: "Children should be seen and not heard," "Ask no questions and you'll be told no lies," and so on. About that ideal nothing need be said now, except that it is inadequate to prepare children for entering into right relations with science teachers.

Science teachers found that the old sort of nursery discipline, what I may call the speak-when-you're-spoken-to training, sent up children to their classes unable to enter thoroughly into the relation which they wished to establish, which is found to afford the best condition for imparting and imbibing a conception of scientific method. . . .

If Science is making children too wide-awake to think there is any merit in believing what they are told and doing as they are bid, as it most assuredly is doing, Science is bound to set about helping parents to organize such discipline as shall prepare children to judge what is worth believing, and to obey their own higher selves: two things which the undisciplined and careless never can do. I feel that we science teachers will be guilty of grave neglect if we allow any slipping between two stools to take sanction from our supposed example. It may be well to give parents a picture of the kind of ethical code which some science teachers are trying to introduce into the nurseries in which they have influence. Perhaps I may be allowed to sum up that code in a new nursery rime. (It is doggerel; but so was the old one.)

> Know what you mean to say; think what was said;
> Fence round your fairyland; then you'll have a clear head.

What I may call the know-what-you-mean code of nursery ethics includes these elements:

(1) A training in the sense of personal responsibility for detail.

(2) A training in giving clear reports of what has been done.

(3) A training in knowing when an incident is closed, when a cycle is completed.

(4) A training in answering the exact question that was asked.

(5) A training in distinguishing apart different sources of knowledge.

(6) A training in keeping the world of imagination and of hypothesis distinct from the world of ascertained fact.

(7) A little, though very little, elementary training in judging what is most relevant to the matter in hand.

All this can be done, and is being done, before the school age, without intellectual strain to the child, and without the aid of special educational books or apparatus, by means of the water-tap and the wash-hand towel, of pinafores and spoons.

There comes a stage in every child's life when he is anxious to be sent messages; and this phase can be taken advantage of to train him in one or two habits which it is difficult to acquire at a later age, and the lack of which hampers the development of the scientific faculty. When a child is two or three years old, you ask him: "Would baby like to go a message for mother?" When you find him willing, you say: "Put down that toy (or whatever he may have in his hand) and come and stand in front of me: put your hands straight down, head up, look me straight in the face, say: 'Please, Anne, a spoon.' Say it again. I am going to send you to Anne to fetch a spoon. What are you going to say to Anne? Now you will say nothing else, don't talk, don't play on the way for fear you should forget. Now tell me once more, what are you going to say to Anne?" When the child comes back with the spoon, you say to him: "Now go back and say: 'Thank you, Anne.' What are you going to say to Anne? Well, now go and say it." When he comes back the second time, you ask him what he said to Anne. If he cannot remember, or is not clear whether he said it properly, you send him back to try again. As soon as he brings a clear and crisp report of having given his message properly, you at once restore whatever he may have had in his hands before you began. This habit of withdrawing all possible sources of distraction before business begins, and restoring whatever you deprived him of directly the business is completed, is of importance; it answers the same purpose as is fulfilled later by making a child put a big A opposite the final answer to a sum. All these precautions help to induce the habit of knowing when a cycle is completed, a duty fulfilled, an incident closed.

Next day the message may be, "Please, Father, a pencil," or "Please, nurse, a clean pinafore," but it is well, while varying the material of the lesson, to keep the routine exactly until it becomes quite easy and mechanical; until the mere fact of being called to a lesson at once throws the child bodily and mentally into the attitude of "stand at attention." After that you tell the child that whenever you send him to fetch anything he may say "thank you" to the person who gives it to him before bringing it to you; but he is still not to talk of anything else when on his way. Just at first you will have to explain to the household that they are not to tempt the child to dawdle or talk when sent on a message; but as soon as he is old enough you may tell him that if any one speaks to him when he is on his way, he should say: "I am on a message for Mother, I will come back to you when I have done what she told me."

As early as possible you choose some little function, which the child has learnt to perform (such as washing his own hands), as a means of training him further into the sense of responsibility in carrying out orders. For instance, when you see that he is able to wash his hands properly you explain to him that it is not safe for him to touch the hot-water tap, as the water is sometimes hot enough to scald him. You tell him that he is not to touch the hot tap unless you are there to give him leave. If you intend that any other person shall have authority to give leave, mention that person formally at once; say: "Unless nurse or I give you leave," or "Unless Father or I give leave"; and, having said so, let it be understood that any grown-up person whom you have not formally mentioned may draw hot water for the child if she wishes, but may not give leave for him to touch the hot tap. At this point there will probably come little difficulties with servants and relatives. "As if I didn't know as well as his mother when the water is too hot!" You must explain to the complainer that, if the business in hand were *only* preventing Jacky from scalding himself, you would have perfect confidence in her care; but that Jacky is just now getting a lesson about what he is responsible for, and to whom, and that no confusion should be introduced into his mind. A little tact and a little firmness are needed to soothe affectionate jealousies; but the results of the method are so satisfactory to the whole household that people soon begin to say that, after all, the mother seems to have known what she was about. Well, you send Master Jacky up to wash his hands, giving him minute directions as to his order of procedure, which you make him repeat each day until you find that he no longer needs to be reminded of them. Every day he comes back with his report, which may be as follows: "Cook was upstairs; I asked her to draw me some hot water; I washed my hands; I used soap; I rinsed the soap off; I used my own towel; I think I wiped my hands quite dry; I did not touch any one else's towel; I put my own towel back on the proper rung"; varied occasionally by: "There was no one upstairs to draw hot water, so I used cold and gave my hands an extra scrubbing; I think they are quite clean," etc. The report must include the details as to which you cautioned him. Amongst its other advantages this has a tendency to check a child's natural inclination to occupy the conversation with details of his own affairs and performances. He understands that reporting the details of what he has been about is a piece of business to be done at a certain hour of the day, and heard no more of.

Jacky may come down brimming over with information about something he has seen while upstairs, some effect of light from the falling water, or a big bubble that the soapy water made "with all sorts of colour in it." We must be very careful not to discourage this eager and glowing interest in natural phenomena; but if we can, without discouraging him, introduce the conception of graduated relevance, it will be so much the better for his future clearness. This may be done by asking him whether he thinks he could manage to tell you all that over again in a different order, to tell you the business part first and about the soap bubble afterwards.

Care must be taken that all this accuracy does not degenerate into superstition about particular actions, that the child attaches chief importance, not to this or that action, but to accuracy in carrying out whatever are the orders for the time being. We need to induce the algebraic, as against the superstitious, conscience. In algebra, a must stand for exactly the same value throughout the one problem, but may stand for something quite different in the next problem. Great use may be made in this respect of a visit to a strange house. You may say to a child, for instance: "I am going to send you upstairs (to fetch me a handkerchief, etc.). This house is not arranged for children; it is different from our house. The wall-paper is white, you might easily stain it; the stairs are slippery; the windows have no bars in front of them. In this house you must hold tight by the banisters, come downstairs very slowly, never touch the wall-paper, and never go near a window that is open at the bottom. Now tell me what are the things you are not to do in this house?" (Touch the wall-paper and go near windows which are open at the bottom.) "And what are the things which you are to be careful to do in this house?" (Hold by the banisters and come downstairs slowly.) When he comes back he brings his report formally: "I fetched your handkerchief; I held tight by the banisters; I came downstairs slowly; I did not touch the wall-paper; there was a window open at the bottom, I didn't go near it"; varied by "there were no windows open at the bottom to-day."

It must be particularly noticed that a child can be trusted about amongst dangers, such as hot-water taps and open windows, *immediately* after such a catechism and while he has it on his mind that he will have a report to give, at a much earlier age than it would be possible to trust him vaguely and promiscuously. Once, or at most twice, in the day is as often as a child under six ought to have the strain of responsibility thrown on him; for the rest of the time he should be allowed to be his natural, careless, impish self; and other people, not himself, should guard him from mischief and danger.

If a child is sent a lesson-message, and is asked on returning whether he gave it, he will sometimes answer, "I could not find cook," or "She was not in the kitchen." For the mother's own immediate practical purpose that is sufficient; but logically speaking it is not a categorical answer. This elliptical mode of speech is allowable in ordinary conversation, but I am now describing specific lessons intended to evoke the algebraic super-consciousness. They are intended to serve the same purpose as is served later by occasionally making a child write out in full every step in the working of a sum, including many steps which, on ordinary occasions, he leaves out.

With a view to preparing for scientific training it is well to accustom children early to answer the exact question asked before entering on any side issue. The question "Did you do so-and-so?" must be answered either as "yes" or "no." "She was not in the kitchen" is the answer to a further question; and if said at all must come after the answer to the one actually asked. This habit of logical distinction is of great use in preventing friction with the future science teacher and confusion to the pupil. At an early age, when no lessons are on hand, when learning to make the distinction is itself the lesson, it can be made non-worrying and even interesting to the child. One does not wish children made to speak, habitually, in a formal or priggish way; but it does seem desirable that, before a child goes to school, he should be in such training that the request, "Please answer the question I asked" shall meet with intelligent response, shall not produce in his mind a sense of mere bewildered pain. . . .

The power to distinguish apart different sources of knowledge may be evoked by an occasional very gentle, playful sort of "how do you know?" jesting. The lesson might well take place when a child has poured out a heterogeneous mass of scraps of information gathered during his walk. "Oh! Father! there was a red butterfly with black spots on his wings. And he had a trunk just like an elephant's. And he drinks honey with it. And that butterfly and the bees were *so* hungry; there were a lot of bees. And there's a butterfly with a *'normous* trunk —so long—and he ran a race with a great white flower," etc. "How do you know there's a red butterfly?" "I *saw* him; he flew across the road in front of me." "Could you see the black spots as he flew?" "No; but he went and sat on a flower in the hedge; and then I went close to him and saw the spots." "So he had a trunk just like an elephant's, had he?" "Yes; just like an elephant's." "Are you sure it was quite as big?" Then, "So the bees were very hungry? Did they say so?" "No, they couldn't speak." "How do you know a person is hungry when he does not say so?" "Well, they were all in such a bustle; they went so quick from one flower to another." "Well, I'm in a bustle sometimes just after breakfast; but I'm not hungry then." "You are going off to your office; bees haven't an office to go to. They were getting honey." "How do you know it was honey?" "I sucked one of the flowers myself; and it was sweet; and Mother said the bees were getting honey." "Do you put things in your mouth when you are out walking?" "No; not unless Mother is there and gives me leave; but she said I might suck one of those flowers." "That's all right. Well, the bees were getting stuff that tastes sweet, and Mother told you it was honey. And you think they were hungry because they worked hard; I work hard often when I am not hungry." "But Mother says you work to get money; bees don't get money." "No; they don't get our sort of money; but are you sure there is no one at home they want to get something else for?" And so on. About the butterfly with the eleven-inch trunk you elicit the avowal that no one told the child about it, and he did not see it; he heard Mother telling Auntie about it; she had read about it in a book. By asking whether the big white flower in Mother's book had legs to run with, you make it evident that the child does not understand what is meant by an evolution-race; and if he answers as a puzzled child sometimes will, "Well, I heard Mother telling Auntie about it, so it must be true," you can explain that Auntie knew what Mother meant, but he apparently does not; so he may as well leave that part of the tale out till he is older, and for the present only tell people about things he really understands. Of course one must keep a discreet limit on the extent to which one stirs up a child by this kind of "how do you know" questioning; specially one must be careful that it does not degenerate into becoming a worry and a check on his flow of talk. But a little of it, occasionally, is of great value in preparing the way for science teachers by getting the child into the right attitude to receive their instruction.

It should be noticed that a child accustomed to ever so little of it is likely to ask his elders how they know so-and-so. Parents should be prepared for this. If the child says: "How do you know?" in a saucy or ill-tempered tone, it is rebuke enough to say: "If you really want to know, you will ask me nicely." If the question is put politely and seriously by a child, the parent should be prepared to answer honestly either "I saw it," or "I read it in a book which I believe to be true," or else "I cannot explain yet how I know; I know in a way which you cannot understand till you are older." Parents who object to the "how do you know" line of inquiry being started at all in their nurseries ought to reflect that the passively receptive attitude towards elders, though a satisfactory preliminary for a merely classico-theological education, puts needless and unfair obstacles in the way of science teachers.

It is a good thing to afford a child the opportunity for perceiving that there are three ways in which he might become aware of the connexion between cause and effect, e.g., in which he might learn which handle sets a certain bell ringing. In one case Mother might have told him; in another he may have heard that particular bell ring when that handle is pulled so often as to feel compelled to connect the two; in the third case he may have followed, once and for all, a series of wires or cranks all the way from handle to bell.[2] All these ways of learning are equally legitimate, and all are useful; but he should be clear which he is relying on in any given case.

A child is very prone to mistake the intensity of his own conviction that a statement is true for proof of its truth, or even for comprehension of the statement itself. It is astonishing to see with what simple conviction a lad or girl will sometimes assure one that he or she *quite understands* a certain process in Science, say the process for finding G. C. Measure, or for solving Quadratic Equations, or for doing something with chemicals, as to which one finds that in reality he only knows empirically the steps which he ought to take and the order in which to take them; he has been shown what to do; and repeated trials have proved that he can do it aright. This confusion points to something unscientific in the nursery training. A child who was scientifically

[2] The three methods of acquiring instruction about the bell illustrate respectively (1) learning from authority, by inheriting the stored-up knowledge of the race, (2) ordinary scientific induction, such as that by which a law of nature is inferred, (3) the specifically mathematical induction. Boole, *Laws of Thought*, p. 4.

trained in infancy will sometimes say, "I know how to do these sums; I do them easily, and I always get them right; but I don't understand *why* they come right." Now that kind of pupil is the delight of a good science teacher, and a perplexity to a bad one. The more logically we treat our children in infancy, the more likely they are to make the neighbourhood uncomfortable for unscientific teachers of science.

True, it is often necessary to know what to do and how to do it, when we have no means of knowing why it answers. But it is very unscientific not to be clear in one's own mind when one only knows that a process does answer, and when one can see beforehand that it must answer. Nothing can be thoroughly done in mathematics till the child quite understands the difference between these two things; and it is unfair that a mathematical teacher should be interrupted by the necessity for insisting on the difference. Very many ordinary teachers are themselves so unscientific that they do not know how to explain it; all the more is it desirable that their pupils should be clear about it before entering their classes. Indeed, it is not a thing that can be made clear by mere explanation; it is a matter of mental habit, and must be begun early.

The same kind of reason holds good for accustoming children occasionally to that kind of mental action which is involved in answering such apparently foolish questions as: "Are you sure the butterfly's trunk was exactly like the elephant's? Was it quite as big?" A very great deal of the difficulty of teaching mathematics would be non-existent if the parents would accustom children very early, by means of jokes, to realize that a thing may be like another thing in one respect and quite unlike in another.

There is nothing more important in teaching Algebra than to make the pupil understand clearly the difference between an equation of identity (a dozen is twelve), an equation of real values (e.g., the circumference of a circle is three and a fraction times the length of the diameter), and an equation of hypothesis or arbitrary equation (such as: Let a red counter be supposed to stand for ten white ones). It is impossible to teach Algebra properly unless this distinction is quite clear; and it is almost impossible to make it so during the Algebra lesson itself, where the material in which we work is abstract. I cannot say that I ever found a child to whom I failed to make the distinction clear in Arithmetic, where the values are concrete, if I took trouble enough; but I have met many girls of sixteen to whom it seemed a new and puzzling conception; and I do think it is disrespectful to the teacher, and unfair to the better prepared pupils, to have to stop the work of a class in order to teach to the others something which ought to have become an easy and automatic action of the mind long before.

Again, such words as *same* are very misleading if used without care to distinguish their various meanings apart. If you say, "This blue aster is of the same species as the pink one I had last year," or "My dog is of the same breed as my neighbour's," that connotes that the two asters or dogs are (in spite of superficial difference of colour, etc.) so nearly alike as to need similar food and care; experience gained in treating the one will be of use in guiding us how to treat the other. But if you say, "This gnat is the same which was swimming as a wiggler in my aquarium this morning," that does not imply anything of the sort. The wiggler of the morning would have died if kept out of water: the gnat of the afternoon will die if kept in it. You can infer nothing about the one from what you know of the other.

All this may sound very childish, and so indeed it is. This is the very reason why I venture to think it is well when this part of the work of training for Science is done, and well done, at a childish age, pleasantly and as mere fun, instead of throwing upon the teacher of science classes the burden of introducing such elementary conceptions for the first time to young persons whom he is preparing for stiff examinations in Science.

The effect on a science class is as distracting as it would be if a literature teacher had to interrupt a lecture on Shakespeare to help some of the pupils to spell out ordinary English words.

We now come to the fencing round of the imaginative faculty. As we can never be sure how far a child's statement is consciously and voluntarily false with intent to deceive, many people prefer never to accuse a child of lying. Children often have no clear notion of the boundary line between fact and imagination. And indeed the modern child is far too logical to accept from grown-ups who tell fairy tales any such dictum as that it is wicked to say what is not true. But because we no longer talk to small children about the wickedness of lying, that is no reason why we should not try to help them to learn the art of telling truth. For it is an art; at least as difficult as playing the piano; as little to be done at any given moment by mere effort of will; as necessary to begin learning young. Most children have access to some sort of fairyland in which they spend a good portion of their existence. There is nothing unscientific in that; indeed, every scientific man worthy of the name, every one who is not a mere mechanical adapter of other people's discoveries, spends a good part of his time in that grown-up sort of fairyland, the world of scientific hypothesis. It is from this fairyland of his that he draws the inspirations which guide his researches. We have each a private domain of our own in that Unseen World; and no mortal has the right to deny the truth of what another says he sees there.

I received a good lesson once from a little friend of mine whom I found on the sea shore, earnestly imploring some fishermen to bring her home a mermaid. I told her that there are no real mermaids. "Oh yes, there are," said the little maiden imperturbably. As I persisted, she became troubled; but presently recovered herself and said cheerfully, "Oh well, if they are not in this world they must be in fairyland, for I *know* there are mermaids somewhere." I had received a well-merited rebuke. What right had I to say there are no real mermaids? what do I know about it? There may be some in Mars for all that I can tell to the contrary; and the child may have had some *Ahnung* of something which I do not understand. What I did know, and what I ought to have said, was that there are no mermaids living under such conditions that fishermen in this world can bring them in boats to little girls.

Many children have imaginary friends, and give names to those friends; besides having a name of their own for the imaginary world in which these friends are supposed to live. This simplifies the work of teaching the child to be truthful. One can listen gravely to any sort of statement he pleases to make, and then ask quietly, "Did all that happen in this world or in mermaid world?" (or fairyland, or dream world, or Charley's world, or whatever name he gives to his bit of the Unseen). He may be puzzled at first; he really does not know which world he has been looking into. But he gradually learns how to distinguish between the visible and the invisible worlds; to know an impression, however vivid, on the mental retina from the image projected from the outside on the physical retina. Sometimes he will confess that part of the story happened in the outer world and part in fairyland. This mixing up of things should be discouraged, in the same spirit in which we discourage writing down tens in the units column of his little sums; we do not assume any intention to mislead; we assume that he would have preferred to locate the things in their proper categories, but was not expert enough, or was too careless, to do so properly, and must try again.

If we suspect that the child is giving a garbled version of some transaction to screen himself from blame, it is well, before asking any other person concerned what were the facts, to ask the child himself what version *he thinks* that other person would give, e.g., when he says, "I didn't break the plate; I fell up against the table and the plate fell and broke itself," if you ask, "What do you think nurse will tell me about it?" the child will perhaps answer, "I think nurse will tell you that she had told me not to go near that table at all while the crockery was on it." A child who has thus corrected his own one-sided statement has had a very good lesson, and been much helped to become clear-headed and truthful. Nearly all the scientific truth known to man has been arrived at by successive processes of correcting error; the condition for telling truth is not the mere negative fact of abstaining from inventing falsehoods, but the acquiring of positive skill in distinguishing our own inventions from fact before we speak to men. Now the child's parents should be to him a sort of outer conscience; he should not be reproved for giving to them fact mixed with fiction, but helped to distinguish which is which, before either he or they take action in consequence of his statements or mention them to other people.

Suppose one suspects that a child is inclined to be really untruthful, one might sometimes take the opportunity, when he says he is hungry or complains of a little pain or hurt, to explain to him that there is no use in trying to bathe, or bandage, or otherwise minister to pains and aches and hungers in fairyland; and that one cannot be sure which world the statements he makes refer to.

Few things that we do are more unscientific and more confusing to a child's logical faculty than telling him, about some of his pains, that they are not real. Many so-called imaginary pains are due to inspiration, or the effect on the sensory nerves of over-rapid illumination from within. They are so real that they have been known to re-act on the fleshy tissues, producing actual swellings or haemorrhage from the skin. Imaginary pains are as real as anything in a child's experience. But the true remedy for them consists in a habit of exerting the will in turning the mind to external objects. The habit of seeking what we may broadly call medical remedies for pains which come to the flesh from the imagination is a dangerous one; it is largely responsible for the alcohol and morphia manias; it should be checked at its source in childhood. The way to check it is not to say, what is false (and, I venture to add, profane), that these pains projected from fairyland are not real, but to accustom the child to acquire the power of controlling them from within instead of seeking help from without. The importance of this habit to health and morals is obvious enough; my present purpose, however, is to call attention to its importance with regard to the child's future science teachers. The pupil who limply and helplessly flings himself on his teacher for help in difficulties which he ought to grapple with in his own mind and conquer for himself is very difficult to teach properly; while, on the other hand, many a mind possessed of really scientific insight has been wrecked by the bad habit of pondering for weeks or months, trying to set to rights, by sheer thinking, what should have been cleared up at once by appealing to a teacher or a book. And I am convinced that every step gained by a young child in the direction of clearly distinguishing the within from the without helps to lay a good foundation for all his future relations to Science. . . .

The physical attitudes, habits, and modes of handling things necessary in the chemical laboratory differ in some respects from those acquired in ordinary domestic and social life; so also do the moral and spiritual habits and modes of handling facts necessary in an intellectual laboratory differ a little from those ordinarily considered amiable and agreeable. Those who wish to give their children a scientific training had better count the cost.

One word, however, I would venture to say to the objectors. Whether they like it or not, Science is sweeping on, and swallowing whatever stands in its way. Now no ordinary teaching of ethics constitutes a safe basis of conduct for the young person immersed in a scientific life, for that life is one of actual communion with the Unseen, the Eternal Organizer, who is also the Eternal Destroyer. It is a reflection of creative activity, an incessant process of reorganization of thought-material. Only those who have the orderly habit of organizing thought-chaos, of correcting the disorderly first impressions by reference to laws of organic thinking, can be morally or spiritually safe in that glorious whirlwind which we call scientific progress.

Significs [1]

V. WELBY

The term "Significs" may be defined as the science of meaning or the study of significance, provided sufficient recognition is given to its practical aspect as a method of mind, one which is involved in all forms of mental activity, including that of logic. . . .

In the *Dictionary of Philosophy and Psychology* Semantics is defined as "the doctrine of historical word-meanings; the systematic discussion of the history and development of changes in the meanings of words." It may thus be regarded as a reform and extension of the etymological method, which applies to contemporary as well as to traditional or historical derivation. As human interests grow in constantly specialized directions, the vocabulary thus enriched is unthinkingly borrowed and reborrowed on many sides, at first in defining quotation, but soon in unconscious or deliberate adoption. Semantics may thus, for present purposes, be described as the application of Significs within strictly philological limits; but it does not include the study and classification of the "Meaning" terms themselves, nor the attainment of a clear recognition of their radical importance as rendering, well or ill, the expressive value not only of sound and script but also of all fact or occurrence which demands and may arouse profitable attention.

The first duty of the Significian is, therefore, to deprecate the demand for mere linguistic reform, which is indispensable on its own proper ground, but cannot be considered as the satisfaction of a radical need such as that now suggested. To be content with mere reform of articulate expression would be fatal to the prospect of a significantly adequate language; one characterized by a development only to be compared to that of the life and mind of which it is or should be natu-

---

[1] From *The Encyclopædia Britannica*, 11th Edition, 1910–1911, Vol. XXV. Copyright, 1911, by Encyclopædia Britannica, Inc. Reprinted by permission. The argument is developed in some detail in Lady Welby's *Significs and Language* (1911), *What Is Meaning?* (1903), and *Grains of Sense* (1897).

rally the delicate, flexible, fitting, creative, as also controlling and ordering, Expression.

The classified use of the terms of expression-value suggests three main levels or classes of that value—those of Sense, Meaning and Significance.

(a) The first of these at the outset would naturally be associated with Sense in its most primitive reference; that is, with the organic response to environment, and with the essentially expressive element in all experience. We ostracize the senseless in speech, and also ask "in what sense" a word is used or a statement may be justified.

(b) But "Sense" is not in itself purposive; whereas that is the main character of the word "Meaning," which is properly reserved for the specific sense which it is *intended to convey*.

(c) As including sense and meaning but transcending them in range, and covering the far-reaching consequence, implication, ultimate result or outcome of some event or experience, the term "Significance" is usefully applied.

These are not, of course, the only significal terms in common use, though perhaps sense and significance are on the whole the most consistently employed. We have also signification, purport, import, bearing, reference, indication, application, implication, denotation and connotation, the weight, the drift, the tenour, the lie, the trend, the range, the tendency, of given statements. We say that this fact suggests, that one portends, another carries, involves or entails certain consequences, or justifies given inferences. And finally we have the *value* of all forms of expression; that which makes worth while any assertion or proposition, concept, doctrine or theory; the definition of scientific fact, the use of symbolic method, the construction of mathematical formulae, the playing of an actor's part, or even art itself, like literature, in all its forms.

The distinctive instead of haphazard use, then, of these and like terms would soon, both as clearing and enriching it, tell for good on our thinking. If we considered that any one of them were senseless, unmeaning, insignificant, we should at once in ordinary usage and in education disavow and disallow it. As it is, accepted idiom may unconsciously either illuminate or contradict experience. We speak, for instance, of *going through* trouble or trial; we never speak of *going through* well-being. That illuminates. But also we speak of the Inner or Internal as *alternative* to the spatial—reducing the spatial to the External. The very note of the value to the philosopher of the "Inner" as opposed to the "Outer" experience is that a certain example or analogue of enclosed space—a specified inside—is thus not measurable. That obscures. Such a usage, in fact, implies that, within enclosing limits, space sometimes ceases to exist. Comment is surely needless. . . .

We speak of beginning and end as complementary, and then of "both ends"; but never of both beginnings. We talk of truth when we mean accuracy: of the literal ("it is written") when we mean the actual ("it is done"). Some of us talk of the mystic and his mysticism, meaning by this, enlightenment, dawn heralding a day; others (more justly) mean by it the mystifying twilight, darkening into night. We talk of the unknowable when what that is or whether it exists is precisely what we cannot know—the idea presupposes what it denies; we affirm or deny immortality, ignoring its correlative innatality; we talk of solid foundations for life, for mind, for thought, when we mean the starting-points, foci. We speak of an eternal sleep when the very *raison d'être* of sleep is to end in awaking—it is not sleep unless it does; we appeal to a root as to an origin, and also figuratively give roots to the locomotive animal. We speak of natural "law" taking no count of the sub-attentive working in the civilized mind of the associations of the legal system (and the law court) with its decreed and enforced, but also revocable or modifiable enactments. Nature, again, is indifferently spoken of as the norm of all order and fitness, the desecration of which is reprobated as the worst form of vice and is even motherly in bountiful provision; but also as a monster of reckless cruelty and tyrannous mockery. Again, we use the word "passion" for the highest activity of desire or craving, while we keep "passive" for its very negation.

These instances might be indefinitely multiplied. But it must of course be borne in mind that we are throughout dealing only with the idioms and habits of the English language. Each civilized language must obviously be dealt with on its own merits.

The very fact that the significating and interpretative function is the actual, though as yet little recognized and quite unstudied condition of mental advance and human achievement, accounts for such a function being taken for granted and left to take care of itself. This indeed, in pre-civilized ages (since it was then the very condition of safety and practically of survival), it was well able to do. But the innumerable forms of protection, precaution, artificial aid and special facilities which modern civilization implies and provides and to which it is always adding, have entirely and dangerously changed the situation. It has become imperative to realize the fact that through disuse we have partly lost the greatest as the most universal of human prerogatives. Hence arises the special difficulty of clearly showing at this stage that man has now of set purpose to recover and develop on a higher than the primitive plane the sovereign power of unerring and productive interpretation of a world which even to a living, much more to an intelligent, being, is essentially significant. These conditions apply not only to the linguistic but to all forms of human energy and expression, which before all else must be significant in the most active, as the highest, sense and degree. Man has from the outset been organizing his experience; and he is bound correspondingly to organize the expression of that experience in all phases of his purposive activity, but more especially in that of articulate speech and linguistic symbol. This at once introduces the volitional element; one which has been strangely eliminated from the very function which most of all needs and would repay it.

One point must here, however, be emphasized. In attempting to inaugurate any new departure from habitual thinking, history witnesses that the demand at its initial stage for unmistakably clear exposition must be not only unreasonable but futile. This of course must be typically so in the case of an appeal for the vital regeneration of all modes of Expression and especially of Language, by the practical recognition of an ignored but governing factor working at its very inception and source. In fact, for many centuries at least, the leading civilizations of the world have been content to perpetuate modes of speech once entirely fitting but now often grotesquely inappropriate, while also remaining content with casual changes often for the worse and always liable to inconsistency with context. This inevitably makes for the creation of a false standard both of lucidity and style in linguistic expression.

Still, though we must be prepared to make an effort in assuming what is virtually a new mental attitude, the effort will assuredly be found fully worth making. For there is here from the very first a special compensation. If, to those whose education has followed the customary lines, nowhere is the initial difficulty of moving in a new direction greater than in the one termed Significs, nowhere, correspondingly, is the harvest of advantage more immediate, greater, or of wider range and effort.

It ought surely to be evident that the hope of such a language; of a speech which shall worthily express human need and gain in its every possible development in the most efficient possible way, depends on the awakening and stimulation of a sense which it is our common and foremost interest to cultivate to the utmost on true and healthy lines. This may be described as the immediate and insistent sense of the pregnancy of things, of the actual bearings of experience, of the pressing and cardinal importance, as warning or guide, of that experience considered as indicative; a Sense realized as belonging to a world of what for us must always be the Sign of somewhat to be inferred, acted upon, used as a mine of pertinent and productive symbol, and as the normal incitant to profitable action. When this germinal or primal sense—as also the practical starting-point, of language—has become a reality for us, reforms and acquisitions really needed will naturally follow as the expression of such a recovered command of fitness, of boundless capacity and of perfect coherence in all modes of expression.

One objection, however, which before this will have suggested itself to the critical reader, is that if we are here really dealing with a function which must claim an importance of the very first rank and affect our whole view of life, practical and theoretical, the need could not have failed long ago to be recognised and acted upon. And indeed it is not easy in a few words to dispose of such an objection and to justify so venturesome an apparent paradox as that with which we are now concerned. But it may be pointed out that the special development of one faculty always entails at least the partial atrophy of another. In a case like this the principle typically applies. For the main human acquirement has been almost entirely one of logical power, subtle analysis, and co-ordination of artificial means. In modern civilization the application of these functions to an enormous growth of invention of every kind has contributed not a little to the loss of the swift and direct sense of *point:* the sensitiveness as it were of the compass-needle to the direction in which experience was moving. Attention has been forcibly drawn elsewhere; and moreover, as already pointed out, the natural insight of children, which might have saved the situation, has been methodically silenced by a discipline called educative, but mainly suppressive and distortive. . . .

Students, who are prepared seriously to take up this urgent question of the application of Significs in education and throughout all human spheres of interest, will soon better any instruction that could be given by the few who so far have tentatively striven to call attention to and bring to bear a practically ignored and unused method. But by the nature of the case they must be prepared to find that accepted language, at least in modern European forms, is far more needlessly defeating than they have supposed possible: that they themselves in fact are continually drawn back, or compelled so to write as to draw back their readers, into what is practically a hotbed of confusion, a prison of senseless formalism and therefore barren controversy.

It can hardly be denied that this state of things is intolerable and demands effectual remedy. The study and systematic and practical adoption of the natural method of Significs can alone lead to and supply this. Significs is in fact the natural response to a general sense of need which daily becomes more undeniably evident. It founds no school of thought and advocates no technical specialism. Its immediate and most pressing application is, as already urged, to elementary, secondary and specialised education. In recent generations the healthy sense of discontent and the natural ideals of interpretation and expression have been discouraged instead of fostered by a training which has not only tolerated but perpetuated the existing chaos. Signs, however, are daily increasing that Significs, as implying the practical recognition of, and emphasizing the true line of advance in, a recovered and enhanced power to interpret experience and adequately to express and apply that power, is destined in the right hands, to become a socially operative factor of the first importance.

Fate and Freedom[1]

ALFRED KORZYBSKI

In this lecture I propose to analyze the principles on which the foundation of the Science and Art of Human Engineering must rest, if we are ever to have such a Science and Art.

As my aim is merely to offer a somewhat rude outline, I shall, as

[1] From *The Mathematics Teacher*, Vol. XVI, No. 5, May, 1923, pp. 274–290. Reprinted by permission.

much as possible, avoid the use of such technical terms as would be essential to the precision demanded by a detailed presentation.

By Human Engineering I mean the Science and Art of directing the energies and capacities of Human Beings to the advancement of Human Weal.[2]

All human achievements are cumulative; no one of us can claim any achievement exclusively as his own; we all must use consciously or unconsciously the achievements of others, some of them living but most of them dead.

Much of what I will say has been said before by many others.

It will be impossible to give a full list of authors but the names of a few stand prominent; two Englishmen, Alfred Whitehead and Bertrand Russell; one Frenchman, Henri Poincaré; one American, Professor Cassius J. Keyser; one German, Albert Einstein. I will largely use here their ideas, methods and language, as my main concern is the practical application of some of their great ideas. It would be very difficult to acknowledge fully all I owe to these authors; yet anyone acquainted with the literature of the subject will recognize my obligations, which are heavy.

The term Engineering, in its generally accepted meaning, I take as derived from the Latin ingenium, cleverness, that is, designing, constructing, building works of public utility. As a matter of fact, there does not as yet exist a science of human engineering. The semi-sciences such as sociology, economics, politics and government, ethics, etc., are supposed to deal with the affairs of man, but they are too hopelessly divided and have not as yet emerged from the mythological prescientific era.

If there is to be a science of human engineering, it must be mathematical in spirit and in method and if we do not possess methods to apply mathematical thinking to human affairs, such methods must be discovered. Can this be done?

Let us say a word about what has already been accomplished in this direction. The latest researches in the foundations of mathematics, chiefly accomplished by Whitehead, Russell, Poincaré and Keyser, have disclosed the insufficiency and fallacies of the traditional logic and have produced an internal revolution in logic and mathematics. Mathematics and logic have been proved to be one; a fact from which it seems to

---

[2] *Manhood of Humanity, The Science and Art of Human Engineering,* by Alfred Korzybski. E. P. Dutton, New York City, 1921.

follow that mathematics may successfully deal with non-quantitative problems in a much broader sense than was suspected to be possible.

Let me recall a delightful mathematical joke. A distinguished mathematician, I do not recall his name, produced some very pretty but very abstract mathematical work. He being intensely disgusted by the commercialization of science, wrote to a friend: "Thank God, I have finally produced something which will have no practical application." The irony of life is that a few years later, his discovery was applied to some branch of physics with great results.

That is what is happening now in another field. Engineers are getting hold of some of the latest, very general and very abstract, discoveries of mathematics and are trying, with increasing success, to apply them to the ordering and direction of human affairs.

Somewhere I read in a review of a book written by one of the scientists I have just named that, not all in the book is "real mathematics." I am not convinced that the writer of this review meant what he said. Every growth of mathematics, be it in the superstructure or in the deepening of the foundations, is "real mathematics," if those words are to have any significant meaning.

It is true that such familiar concepts as "sine," "cosine," "derivative," "integral," "graph," and the like, have, for the time being, a subordinate importance in human engineering; but, as I conceive it, mathematics is not limited to such concepts; it embraces many others, such as existence, class, type, dimension, order, limit, infinity (Cantor), non-existence of metaphysical infinitesimal (Weierstrass), invariant, variable, propositional function (Russell), doctrinal function (Keyser), the physico-mathematical theory of events and of objects (Whitehead) and the relativity of space and time (Lorentz, Minkowski, Einstein, Whitehead), etc. These concepts are of immeasurable import, for without them the foundations of human engineering could not be laid.

When I speak about the relativity of space and time, I do not refer to Einstein Theory alone. I use the term here in its broadest meaning as generally accepted in science, namely that absolute space and absolute time do not exist. The work of Einstein is very important, yet it seems to me that the theory of the relativity of space, time and *matter* as elaborated by Whitehead is more comprehensive and is more directly applicable for our immediate purpose.

Before proceeding further we will have to establish a vocabulary for our mutual understanding. Human engineering, if such a branch of science is to exist, must be democratic—dealing with all mankind, and its outline must be clear. I will sacrifice minute precision to general clarity.

No matter where we start, we must start with some undefined words which represent some assumptions or postulates. We see that knowledge at every stage presupposes knowledge of those undefined words. Let us call this fundamental fact the "circularity of knowledge." Words written or spoken and mathematical symbols are like signs, labels, which we attach to ideas, concepts corresponding to our experience.

The concrete facts of nature are events exhibiting a certain structure in their mutual relations and certain characters of their own. The aim of science is to express the relations between their characters in terms of the mutual structural relations between the events thus characterized. The mutual structural relations between events are both spatial and temporal. If you think of them as merely spatial you are omitting the temporal element, and if you think of them as merely temporal you are omitting the spatial element. Thus when you think of space alone, or of time alone, you are dealing in abstractions, namely, you are leaving out an essential element in the life of nature as known to you in the experience of your senses. . . . What I mean is that there are no spatial facts or temporal facts apart from physical nature, namely, that space and time are merely ways of expressing certain truths about the relations between events. . . . To be an abstraction does not mean that an entity is nothing. It merely means that its existence is only one factor of a more concrete element of nature.[3]

The dynamic theory of "matter" alone (I omit other considerations) makes it obvious that we can not *recognize* an event because when it is gone, it is gone. Yet our daily experience tells us that amidst events there is something which is fairly durable, which we can recognize from day to day. Things which we can recognize are called objects. A label attached to an object is called a word. The meaning of a word is a complex notion; for our purpose we may say that the meaning of a word is actually or potentially given by a definition.

Here we must take into consideration a grave fact. The above mentioned mathematicians have introduced a new concept which they stress very justly. Not only do they distinguish between true and false propositions but also recognize the existence of statements which have the form of propositions, but which are neither true nor false, but are mean-

[3] A. N. Whitehead, *The Concept of Nature*, pp. 167, 168, 171.

ingless. These meaningless verbal forms should be of great practical concern because our daily language and even some would-be theoretical disciplines are interwoven with meaningless statements. It often happens that such a meaningless statement is designated by a special "noise" which can be reduced to a combination of letters giving it the semblance of a word. Obviously this noise is equally meaningless, even though volumes be written about it.

And now we are approaching the central problem of all human knowledge. A sign or a label, if attached to nothing is a pseudo-symbol which symbolizes nothing; that is, it is not a symbol at all but is merely a noise if spoken, or blotch of black on white if written. Before a sign may acquire meaning and therefore become a symbol there must *exist* something for this sign to symbolize. The problem of existence has several aspects and is extremely important though not all of these aspects concern us at this state. Poincaré defines *logical* existence as one free from contradiction. Russell derives existence from his theory of propositional function. "If $\phi(x)$ is sometimes true, we may say there are x's for which it is true, or we may say 'arguments satisfying $\phi(x)$ exist.'" Russell's conception is much more fundamental, but for the time being, Poincaré's definition will be sufficient.

As we observed before, events, in the Whitehead sense, cannot be recognized, but the things we can recognize are called objects. An event is a very complex fact, and the relations between two events form an almost impenetrable maze. Events are recognized and labeled by the objects situated in them. Obviously an object is not the whole of the event, nor does the label which symbolizes the object cover the whole of the object. It is evident that everytime we mistake the object for the event we are making a serious error, and if we further mistake the label for the object, and therefore for the event, our errors become more serious, so serious indeed that they too often lead us to disaster. As a matter of fact, we all of us have from time immemorial indulged in this kind of mental stultification, and here we find the source of most of the metaphysical difficulties that still befog the life of man.

In his last book, *Mathematical Philosophy,* Professor Keyser stresses the importance of recognizing that mankind is under the rule of logical fate. The concept of Logical Fate seems to be self evident when stated; it essentially means that from premises consequences follow. But the moment this is analysed with a full awareness of the circularity of all human knowledge those few words gain the significance of a discovery and formulation of a neglected law of immeasurable importance. By laws I mean propositions asserting relations which have been or can be established by experiment or observation.

The few first words with which mankind started its vocabulary were labels for prescientific ideas, naive generalizations full of silent assumptions, objectifications of non-existents, and our ignorant ancestors began to impose upon nature their naive fancies, which were mostly arbitrary. Sad to say, we continue to do the same in a great many fields.

Our daily speech and in very large measure our scientific language is one enormous system of such assumptions. The moment assumptions are introduced, and it is impossible to avoid them, logical destiny begins its work; and if we do not go back all the time, uncover and discover our conscious or unconscious fundamental assumptions and revise them, mental impasses permanently obstruct the way. The history of human thought gives us many examples. One single concept, one generalization, be it meaningless (dealing with non-existents) or loaded with significance, gives rise to whole systems of thought—absurd or wise. Most of the false theories in the world are not so deficient in their reasoning as in the assumptions and concepts about which they reason—concepts that are vague, false to facts and often deal with non-existents.

Allow me to give an example in the wording of Whitehead. This example alone is enough to emphasize the exceeding importance of mathematics in the clarification of our mental processes.

Aristotle asked the fundamental question, What do we mean by "substance"? Here the reaction between his philosophy and his logic worked very unfortunately. In his logic, the fundamental type of affirmative proposition is the attribution of a predicate to a subject. Accordingly, amid the many current uses of the term "substance" which he analyzes, he emphasizes its meaning as "the ultimate substratum which is no longer predicated of anything else."

The unquestioned acceptance of the Aristotelian logic has led to an ingrained tendency to postulate a substratum for whatever is disclosed in sense-awareness, namely, to look below what we are aware of for the substance in the sense of the concrete thing. This is the origin of the modern scientific concept of matter and of ether, namely they are the outcome of this insistent habit of postulation . . . what is a mere procedure of mind in the translation of sense-awareness into discursive knowledge has been transmuted into a fundamental character of nature. In this way matter has emerged as being the metaphysical substratum of its properties. . . . Thus the origin of the doctrine of matter is the outcome of uncritical ac-

ceptance of space and time as external conditions for natural existence . . .
What I do mean is "the unconscious presupposition of space and time as
being that within which nature is set." [4]

Otherwise absolute space and absolute time.

It becomes clear now, that "logical destiny" is a law which works
within us consciously or unconsciously. Our language as a whole may
be regarded as a vast system of assumptions and potential doctrines with
fixed logical boundaries. It was built with the metaphysical background
of metaphysical infinitesimals, metaphysical infinity, absolute space
and absolute time. A great many of the most important terms like
change, continuity, cause and effect, moment, duration, etc., present a
not only perplexing but insoluble problem because of the silent assumption of the existence of those non-existents. With the mathematical
clarification of a very few of such fundamental concepts we may con-
fidently expect that many of our difficulties will vanish, that the universe will become correspondingly intelligible, and man correspondingly intelligent.

Professor Keyser's "doctrinal function" reveals the inherent structure of doctrines and, therefore, in a large measure, of language and
teaches us the methods by which to judge and to revise them. The circularity of knowledge shows us the absolute necessity of constant revision of our assumptions.

Most of what I have said is hardly so much as a sketchy outline of a
vast coherent system, due, in the main, to the recent work of the few
mathematicians before mentioned. The sharp formulation by these
thinkers of the conditions of knowledge and progress promise that the
coming epoch will be more fruitful for man than any other recorded by
history. When the mathematicians themselves digest this new material,
they cannot fail to see their rôle clearly as the leaders of pure thought
and consequently of human progress.

Thought, taken in its broad meaning, is a process. Man thinks with
his *whole* being; this process is not clearly delineated; it starts somehow with hazy "instincts," "feelings," "emotions," and crystallizes itself
in a concept. We cannot but see that any divisions that we make in the
process called thinking, are *arbitrary* and often misleading, or even
meaningless.

There are, however, two aspects of this great process with which we

[4] A. N. Whitehead, *The Concept of Nature*, pp. 16, 18ff.

can deal in a rigorous fashion. I refer on the one hand to that great invariant called the laws of thought, and, on the other hand, to those crystallized products of thinking which we are wont to call concepts. We should not fail to note that, at the various stages of this process, there is a striking difference in respect to what may be called its velocity. The velocities of so-called instincts, intuitions, emotions, etc., are swift, like a flash, while the analysis of the raw material thus presented and the building out of it of concepts and speech is slow. In this difference of velocity lies, I suspect, the secret of "emotions," etc. Unexpressed, amorphous thought is somehow very closely connected with, if not identical with, emotions. We all know, if we will but stop to reflect upon it, how very slow is the crystallization and development of ideas.

It is useless to argue which comes "first," "human nature" or "logic." Such argument has no meaning. "Human nature" and "logic" have their common starting point in the physico-chemical changes occurring in man, and as such, start simultaneously. We are thus enabled to see the supreme importance of concepts, which, as before suggested, are crystals of thought. Such crystals once produced, are permanent and they serve to precipitate their kind from out the supersaturated solutions of the emotions.

It is now evident that intellectual life is one long process of abstractions, generalizations, and assumptions; the three things are so many aspects of one *whole* activity. These processes materialize in symbols which we call words. We see also that all intellectual life is one vast (probably infinite) system of doctrines and doctrinal functions in the making, inherently governed by logical fate. As Professor Keyser has said: "Choices differ but some choice of principles we must make . . . and when we have made it, we are at once bound by a destiny of consequences beyond the power of passion or will to control or modify; another choice of principles is but the election of another destiny." The disturbing and dangerous side of the question is that the great majority of mankind are unaware of the silent doctrines which govern them. They take labels, creations of their own rational will for objects, and objects for events as true constituents of nature, and they fight and die for them.

We have come to the point where mathematics and our daily language meet. They both of them operate with concepts which, in the last analysis, are disguised definitions, generalizations, assumptions. In this respect the concepts "a cosine" and "a man" are identical, neither "a cosine" nor "a man" physically exists (John Smith, or Bill Brown exists, but not "a man"). A cosine and a man are both conceptual constructions. The "a cosine" is defined consciously and precisely; the other term "a man" has *no* scientific definition; we are still in the caveman stage of confusion about this most important of all terms. Mathematicians are conscious of what they do; others are less so. That is why mathematical achievements stand better than any others.

Let me point to a fact which seems to me to be extremely important, and which I shall call the "Physiological point of view of mathematics." We have seen that man has a great freedom in building up his abstractions. It happens that in mathematics the external universe has imposed the generalizations upon man, whereas, in the other disciplines, man has imposed his fancy upon external nature.

Let me explain a little. Modern mathematics deals formally with what can be said about anything or any property. Here it may be explained why mathematics has this exclusive position among the sciences. It must be emphasized that it was not some special genius of the mathematician as such, that was responsible for it. With the coming into existence of the rational being—man—rational activity began spontaneously (no matter how slowly) and this rational activity manifested itself in every line of human endeavor—no matter how slight such activity was. Today we know that we humans can know nothing but abstractions. The process of constructing abstractions is quite arbitrary. Since man began he plunged into this process of constructing arbitrary abstractions—it was the very nature of his being to do so.

Obviously, in the beginning, he did not know anything about the universe or himself; he went ahead spontaneously. It is no wonder that some of his abstractions were false to facts, that some of them were devoid of meaning, and hence neither true nor false but strictly meaningless, and that some of them were correct. In this endless spontaneous process of constructing abstractions he started from that which was the nearest to him—namely his own feelings—and ignorantly attributed his human faculties to all the universe around him. He did not realize that he—man—was the latest product in the universe; he reversed the order and anthropomorphized all around him. He objectified his labels, mistook them for events, and became an "absolutist." He did not realize, and this is true even today in most cases, that by doing so he was building up a logic and a language ill fitted to deal with the actual universe, with life, including man; and that by doing so he was building for himself mental impasses. In a few instances good luck was with him; he made a few abstractions which were at once the easiest to handle and were correct; that is, abstractions corresponding to the actual facts in this actual universe.

These were numbers.

Let us see what was and is the significance of numbers. Any one may see that there are actual differences between such groups as * or as *, *, or as *, *, *, whatever the group was composed of, be it stones, figs, or snakes. And man could not miss for long the peculiar similarity between such a class * * of stones or such a class * * of snakes, etc., and here happened a fact of crucial significance for the future of man. He named those different classes by definite names; good luck saved mankind from his ignorant speculations; he called the class of all such classes as * "one," the class of all such classes as * * "two," * * * "three," etc., and a number was born.

Here as everywhere else "le premier pas quite coûte"; number being created the rest followed as a comparatively easy task. Man could not long fail to see that if such a class * is joined to such a class *, he gets such a class * *, but the other day he had called such classes "one" and "two," and so he concluded that "one and one makes two"—mathematics was born—exact knowledge had begun.

Good luck combined with his human faculties thus helped him to discover one of the eternal truths.

The creation of number was the most reasonable, the first truly scientific act done by man; in mathematics this reasonable being produced a perfect abstraction, the first perfect instrument for training his brain, his nerve currents, in the ideal way befitting the actual universe (not a fiction) and himself as a part of the whole. Now it is easy to understand, from this physiological point of view, why mathematics has developed so soundly. The opposite can be said about the other disciplines. In the main they started with fictions, and even today the fictions persist, and bring havoc in the life of man.

Mathematics alone started aright!

To professional mathematicians all that I have said here may appear as platitudes hardly worth mentioning. I have taken the liberty of repeating them to show that this system of doctrinal functions, of pure thought, which we call pure mathematics (Keyser) has a direct and most vital application to all the other problems of man.

In order to deal rationally with any object, no matter what, though it is not always possible, it is always desirable, to have an analytical definition of the object. In this case where the object is man, the importance of such a definition is absolutely indispensable for the obvious reason that the results of all our thinking about man depend upon what we humans think man is.

Without an analytical, sharp, and precise definition, no demonstration is possible. How can we hope to establish anything whatever about a term if we do not take into account its meaning, its conceptual content? Now the content is given by the definition and by it alone. No definition, no demonstration.

At the very outset of our journey we find a fact so astonishing—so shocking—that it takes some effort to admit the shameful truth. Man deals with man without a scientific definition of man. Some day treatises will be written on this subject alone and in such treatises the responsibility will be traced for this calamitous omission in the intellectual life of humanity.

A definition of man is, of course, the first concern of human engineering. How shall we define our object, man? We are told by the naturalists that an organism must be treated as a whole—that sounds impressive—but they have not told us how to do it. It seems that the traditional subject-predicate logic leads automatically toward elementalism, and that this organism-as-a-whole theory will forever remain *pia desideria* as long as we use the old logic. Yet this concept of the "organism-as-a-whole" is extremely important for us, particularly in the dealing with man (see *Manhood of Humanity*), and all experimental evidence seems to prove that it is correct. We are told on the other hand, that the organism is too complicated to be treated mathematically. It seems to me that these two statements are incompatible. Of course, it is true that, if we pursue the elementalist's point of view, then the organism is too complicated; but, if it is a "whole," then, if a proper generalization is found, the "organism-as-a-whole" *could* be treated mathematically because we could deal with this one generalization.

By definition I do not mean a nominal definition which is merely the fixing of a name, a label to an object, but that analytical definition which will enable us to make the greatest number of general and significant assertions. Let us see how we could define man. Man, among all living beings, is the only one which has a chin; this characteristic is unique. Also he is the only mammal having no tail.[5] We could, if we chose, define man as a "chinful" or "tailless" mammal; these definitions would comply with the minor conditions for a real definition but they would not comply with the major condition, without which a definition is not a real definition, namely, it would not give important logical results. These examples alone show that we could define man in a great many ways, yet the definitions would be practically worthless or fruitless. It is simpler by far to find out by reflection, what are the terms in which an ideal definition of man should be made, and a definition which would, if possible, give us the "organism as a whole."

To find such definitions is not difficult, but what is extremely difficult is to have the moral courage to admit the sad fact, that, in spite of all advancement of science, man—the creator of science—deals with man on the old mythological base.

If we go back to our schoolbooks, we will find in an old edition of the *Elements of Logic* by Jevons-Hill, published by the American Book Co., in 1883, just 40 years ago, that: "It is necessary to distinguish carefully the purely logical use of the terms genus and species from their *peculiar* use in natural history. . . . If we accept Darwin's theory of the origin of species, this definition of species becomes entirely illusory, since different genera and species must have, according to this theory, descended from common parents. The species then denotes a *merely arbitrary* amount of resemblance which naturalists choose to fix upon, and which it is not possible to define more exactly. This use of the term, then, *has no connection whatever with the logical use . . ."* (pages 230–231, italics are mine). Surely blind prejudices are still active, and they are doing their work thoroughly, because, as yet, the need for a scientific definition of man is still ignored.

To perform our task we will have to observe, and think, and this little old book of logic at once gives us the valuable advice that: "Nothing is more important in observation and experiment than to be *uninfluenced* by any prejudice or theory" (page 207, italics are mine).

Just that is the first great obstacle in our path, for since our birth, we have been fed with mythological, fundamentally false ideas about the distinctive nature of man. The struggle to overcome this will be hard, as all possible odds are against us and a free independent logical issue. Once this clearing of the way is accomplished, and I know

[5] Since the delivery of this lecture the author has seen pictures of a savage tribe with tails. This fact, be it a fact, does not alter the argument.

too well how difficult it is to free oneself from prejudices, nothing of importance stands in the way.

The ideal definition for man would be a definition in the same terms in which, in the exact sciences, we have attempted the formulation of the universe around us. The benefit of such a definition would be, that it would be in familiar terms and would keep man logically inside of the universe, as an actual part of it.

Observing living beings, we find that the plants bind solar energy into chemical energy, and so we may define plants as the energy or chemistry-binding class of life. The animals have an added mobility in space—they are the space-binding class of life. Humans differ from animals in that each generation does not begin where their respective ancestors began; they have the faculty to begin where their ancestors left off; they benefit by and accumulate the experiences of all the past, add to it and transmit it to the future. Man and man alone is active in a peculiar way in what we call time—so we must define man as a time-binding class of life.

The above definitions are self evident when stated. Here we must at once make clear that we have to use a static language to cover the dynamic march of events. The classes of life overlap but so do the physical, "matter," "space," "time" overlap. So in our definition we are true to facts. Matter, space and time which do not overlap are abstractions and abstractions only, and I use them *as such.*

It is easy to see that this definition of man is unique. Beyond doubt animals did not produce civilization—man did, and he was able to do so because, and only because, of his capacity to bind time. Here we get for the first time, the logic of the "organism as a whole" as applied to man and the affairs of man. To produce this long desired logic, a new concept, a new generalization was needed.

Heat is measured not by heat but by the effect of heat; in the same way, by this new generalization, a mathematical treatment of man becomes possible, by the analysis of man's activities. This leads to the exponential function of time, "PR^T" as given in the *Manhood of Humanity.*

Now what of the logical fertility of this definition? The consequences of it far surpass our most sanguine dreams, the details of which are to be found in my book I mentioned before. I will mention here only a few.

The law of the survival of the fittest remains true, but true in the proper type or dimension; survival of the fittest in space is a natural law for space-binders. Physics tells us that two bodies cannot occupy the same space at the same time, and, therefore, the survival of the fittest in space—the obvious law of animals—means brutal fight where the strongest, most ruthless, survives. With the time-binder the same law takes on an entirely different aspect. To be a natural law for time-binders it must be the survival of the fittest in time. Who indeed "survives in time"? The strongest or the best? Here at once we come to a foundation on which scientific ethics can be built.

A short inquiry will easily reveal that most of our civilization hitherto has been built upon the generalizations taken from animal life. This man-made civilization was an "animal" civilization because of the fundamentally wrong ideas man had of himself.

This definition also complies with the mathematical theory of logical types or, as I prefer to call it, the theory of dimensionality. It is obvious that animal and man are different types, they are of different dimensionality, as different factors enter which make them distinct. The realization of this makes it obvious that no rule, no generalization taken from animal life, will apply to man any more than rules of surfaces will apply to volumes. If we confuse our types or mix our dimensions in reasoning about man, his structures (called civilization, in this case) must collapse every little while; just as a bridge built on false formulas, would collapse. All the tragic history of mankind proves that this conclusion is true. Man is not a mixture of beast and angel, but man is man, and must learn to think of himself as such.

Professor Keyser in his *Mathematical Philosophy* has done me the honor to devote a chapter to the new concept of man. I am frank to say that it is the best analysis of the concept in existence. He made here an important addition, namely, that for animals it matters what animal is; for man it matters not only what man is, but even more what man thinks man is. *One* factor for animals, *two* factors for man.

These simple but undeniable observations at once prove that the fashionable school of behaviorists is perfectly scientific in respect to all creatures below man. In respect to man, their doctrine appears fallacious. Their doctrine deals only and exclusively with what something *is,* how it behaves in the animal dimension; but it cannot deal in the same fashion, without grave error, with something in which two factors enter, namely, what this something is and what it thinks it is. It is the same as applying the rules of surfaces to volumes; this would be poor mathematics; all our bridges would collapse in the same way our social structures recurrently collapsed, because built upon a false conception of human nature.

It does not really matter much if the definitions as given here will survive for long, what matters and matters much, is the fact that we see clearly our neglect and the new and fertile fields now open for inquiry. The theory of time-binding is the study of the "behavior" of man, and man alone, but in its proper dimension, true to facts and free from logical confusion.

The old civilization is crumbling. The new will require a complete revision of old fallacies and prejudices, and most probably mathematicians, who are today the best logically trained men, will be very active and productive in this coming reconstruction of science and life. A thoroughgoing scientific revision will lead to a complete reversal of many traditional beliefs. It will be found that the belief in the existence of non-existents such as, metaphysical "infinitesimals," metaphysical "infinite," "absolute space," "absolute time," is very widespread; indeed it embraces practically the whole of humanity. This has been taught to us since our birth; it is even taught in some schools and universities today by such expressions as "matter is that which occupies space," and similar fallacies which fatalistically lead by the law of logical fate, which applies to all, educated or non-educated, civilized or non-civilized, to a world-conception, contrary to human nature. Such conceptions are deadly, they lead to mental impasses, making man feel hopeless and helpless in a hostile and strange universe; he rebels and this leads him to mystical and mythological delusion, which also fail him. This feeling of hostility all around him transforms him into a hostile being, and the antique proverb: *"Homo homini lupus"* is too often a bitter, yet entirely logical consequence of the silent or conscious assumptions of the truth of fundamental fallacies.

Yet the actual universe is *not* hostile; it is at most, indifferent. The vicious fictions, the abuse of his power to assume, to abstract, to generalize and invent non-existents has vitiated the whole outlook of man, in all fields. Man saw that animals fight and he imposed upon himself "fighting" as the "manly" art, and blinded by his prejudices and vicious logic he did not stop to think that cooperation—which has been and is now artificially hampered—is the basic law of a *human, time-binding,* rational class of life.

Any inquiry into the above mentioned problems and their mathematical solutions will disclose that no branch of human knowledge has ever contributed more to humanity than the mathematical inquiry into mathematical foundations. The psychological transformation will be complete. Man will understand himself. Needless to say that the semi-sciences will be transformed into sciences.

A new school of history will arise which will show to mankind what disasters the wrong conception of man by man has wrought to mankind. Philosophers will compile charts of "logical destiny," showing what consequences one concept, one abstraction, one generalization have brought to us. This probably will bring mankind to its senses, and this will probably start the true reconstruction of science and life.

Allow me to summarize my lecture and try to justify its title. Mathematical discoveries of the last few decades, culminating lately in the works of Whitehead, Russell, Keyser and Einstein, have made us conscious of the power of rigorous thought and have also disclosed the inner structure and working of this subtle instrument called human thought. They have proved and it has been ultimately formulated by Keyser, that human freedom is not absolute; that we are governed by logical fate. We are free to select our assumptions; if we select false assumptions, disaster follows. But to exercise this freedom, man must first know that he is thus free; otherwise he will continue to accept false assumptions, the old language, etc., as final "innate ideas," etc., without realizing that the moment he does so, he renounces the freedom he has, and becomes the slave of logical fate of his creeds.

This also explains why mankind is divided into so many fighting factions. We are not conscious of the silent, often false assumptions which underlie our language and actions, how do we expect to prove anything to the satisfaction of all if we do not possess a scientific definition of man? As was said before: No definition, no demonstration, no demonstration, no agreement possible.

A diagram may help the visualization of these few ideas.

If we start with *A,* as most of us do, we can *not* reach *D* and *convince* all, because inconsistencies *E* arise which prevent the universal acceptance of some high-sounding but logically unsound doctrines. If we want to reach *D,* the new and truer theory, we *must* start with new and more fundamental, truer premises. In order to know which are truer we *must first investigate them,* without being shy about it.

No doubt mathematicians, and those who have mathematical training are the best fitted for this work. There are signs that this work has already been started, and indeed, nothing could be more important for the future of man.

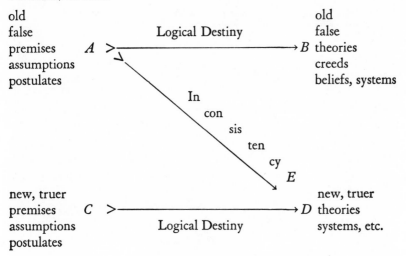

old
false
premises A
assumptions
postulates

Logical Destiny

old
false
B theories
creeds
beliefs, systems

In
con
sis
ten
cy
E

new, truer
premises C
assumptions
postulates

Logical Destiny

new, truer
D theories
systems, etc.

Index